Advent Term

(or- Snowmen don't wear thermals)

Nicholas Barrett

To Dolores: for constant love, support and inspiration.

In loving memory of Mum and Auntie, for love, light and laughter.

And in Loving Memory of Mollie O'Farrell, an Irish Rose who made me smile every day…And always will.

To my wonderful Family - Mike, (my very own Hero!) Pat, Jacquie, Ann, David and Jenny.

To Jean Clark – for just being Jean.

also, Alan and Tracy Clark, for their constant support.

I also dedicate this book to Sir Terence David John Pratchett OBE.

"The comedy is enhanced by the well-crafted and larger-than-life characters who bring Saint Onan's Academy to life, and that they are so vivid is down to Nick's mastery of the writing craft, a skill that many people profess to possess but in fact is the preserve of a select few. Comedy fiction is one of the hardest genres to master - but Michaelmas Term, and now Advent Term prove that Nicholas Barrett has entered the first division of writers in this field, and should be ranked alongside Frances Hardinge, Michael Logan and Douglas Adams."

Peter Darman, acclaimed author of the Parthian and Crusader Chronicles, Blood Sweat and Steel, The Ice March, Heroic voices of the Spanish Civil War, One Hundred events that shaped World War II, and SAS – the world's Best.

Acknowledgements:

I wish to acknowledge the constant support of some of the wonderful individuals who have either inspired me, or urged me on during the writing of this book.

For my dear friend, Bill Peake:
(he will tell you that he doesn't deserve it)
Yes you do Bill...for so much more than you realise.

And to a Brilliant writer of things Historical:
Mr Peter Darman.
A real inspiration.
It is an honour to count you as friends...

Mr Rocky Newton, Rock-God Bass player, and all-round fine fellow.

Mr Robert Rankin; for taking the time to help a fellow author.

To my Family and friends – I love you all dearly.

To Jo Harrison; for all of her expert help with "Format's last Theorem" – thank you!!

And not least, to all of you lovely people who have bought and read, or have yet to read, or intend to read, my growing list of bizarre writings. I thank each and every one of you for your kind comments, and would remind you that cash is always an acceptable alternative...

NB

About the Author:

Nicholas Barrett was born in rural Lincolnshire. He grew up in a house which was shared by a ghost known as "Mr Goodman" who was polite and very tidy. Educated in Grantham, and then at Lincoln College of Art, Nick went on to do a variety of jobs including session musician, rock drummer, stand-up comedian, roadie and manager in a large company. He now lives in rural Essex. Having always had the urge to write, he did just that.

His first book "Michaelmas Term (or- why is that boy naked?)" was published in August 2016. Embarrassingly, most of the incidents which happen in his books did occur! He has drawn on many of his varied life experiences for the books - but has used washable crayon, so it will probably wipe off... He misses his drum kit - but the laptop takes less time to set up! He guarantees that reading his books will be the best fun that you have had whilst fully dressed...

ADVENT TERM: (or- Snowmen don't wear thermals) a novel by Nicholas Barrett.

Welcome to a world painted in muted images and ghostly half-tones. The thick cloying fog covered the town with its all-encompassing blanket of secrecy. The moist air blended away all sharp edges from buildings, and traffic lights gave out a muted glow: more of a serving suggestion than a warning to drivers. Beneath the stone which was perhaps his most favoured daytime place of rest, our learned friend Bufo dozed away the dripping morning. Here and there, the taller buildings and most energetic of the trees poked up out of the grey haze, and the tall church spire stood arrogant and proud, higher than them all.

But all this was above. Below the cloisters and crypt of the church, and under the hallowed foundations of St Onans Academy, seven boys were standing back to back, and terrified...

(Perhaps before we set off, we need to take a small step back...)

The circle of faces illuminated by the meagre glow of the candles began to close in on the boys. None of the friends uttered a word- it was too late for speeches. There were no screams, no desperate prayers, no hysterical pleading. The mass of bodies drew nearer, and raised their arms...

The boys were enveloped by the crowd; all attempting to give them a welcoming hug. Nicky and his fellow pupils were stunned as hands were thrust out to shake their own. Only then did the laughter and cheering begin. Davis looked down, and noticed that one of the smallest children had pushed his way through the throng of people to the front of the throng- and was wearing a 'Ramones' tee-shirt. With his hair having been thoroughly ruffled several times, Merry turned to Nicky and whispered, 'Is this for the pies? - just 'Thank you' would have done!'.

Just then, the tallest of the group raised his ear to the roof of the cavern, as if some sound from overhead demanded his attention. He raised a hand, pointing a finger as he did so. Without any instruction, the crowd stepped back from the boys, all of them placing their hands at their sides. The tall man Gideon raised both arms, and the whole gathering began to enthusiastically sing the hymn 'Jerusalem', which the congregation in the church above them were singing, and which the boys had been too confused to notice. Not quite knowing how best to respond, the friends joined in with the joyous song of the crowd around them, with Weatherill respectfully removing the fez which he was wearing...

'We give all praise and thanks to HoBi...' said Gideon.

Now; if you are ready, settle down, and we will take a step forward...

Chapter One:

The beginning of the Advent Term was always a busy time at St Onans. There seemed to be some unspoken sense of urgency in the lead up to Christmas, and the joys of the Festive holiday. The overall impression atmosphere generated was that there was something around the corner- even for people who wore their normal clothes when they did their impressions. The everyday routines of classes had grudgingly settled into habit. The boys were older now, and knew how things worked, and had discovered to a degree the limits of what they might possibly get away with.

Binding themselves as a tight-knit social unit, Nicky and his friends had stuck to their pact which they had made on their first days at the Academy- they had survived thus far: and fear had slowly given way to measured caution. There were still moments when the intimidation which they felt would come rushing back like a tidal bore, but these were now infrequent, as they had more or less learned how to "play the game". More often than not, the game in question at St Onans would be "Silly Buggers".

This morning, the game had begun in the staff room, where in accordance with multiple-player games everywhere, the dice had been rolled, and one of them had shot off the table and under the furniture. This had led to the chance discovery of a nearly-used biro, a two pence piece, and an unsucked but fluff-covered Worthers Original sweetie. Treasure indeed.

Dr Goodwill the Head Master was addressing the assembled ranks of the staff of St Onans; concerning a matter which was close to his heart - and even closer to the secret safe in his study.

'In short, Ladies and Gentlemen, we find ourselves in a state of pecuniary embarrassment, the like of which I cannot ever remember before. Though I have endeavoured to ensure stringent financial control within all departments, and made severe, nay somewhat savage cuts in the budgets of all departments - we find ourselves hazardously indigent and necessitous.'

A sea of blank looks confronted the man.

'To put it in simple, if rather crude terms, Esteemed Colleagues: we do not have a pot in which to piss'.

'But how can this possibly have come to piss- er, pass, Head Master...?' asked Gideon Rundell, Latin Tutor and social climber.

'Well, you know how it is Gideon.. .' the Head replied nonchalantly, 'An Old Boy's lunch here, a Silver-Service high tea with local dignitaries there, the odd trip to Aintree and Newmarket, plus the "twinning" beano over to Greece, indoor hang-gliding lessons for the fifth-formers, not to mention the exorbitant fee demanded by that pompous sweaty actor with the big nose from that *ghastly* television Soap Opera, just to cut the ribbon on the new cricket pavilion- well, it sort of all adds up: or in our case, takes away..'

The staff looked from one to the other, each silently making a decision as to which of the departments the Academy could well do without (obviously not their own...) The tension became unbearable, and the atmosphere crackled with the unspoken professional jealousies of a group of Academics all absolutely determined to save their own arse at any cost. The headmaster appeared about to burst into tears, and hurriedly sat down in a convenient chair whist he dabbed at his eyes with a handkerchief. Dr Chambers leapt to his feet and took over the discussion.

'Instead of wallowing in self-pity, we need to take drastic and immediate steps to increase our Profile' he said, banging his hand down on the coffee table- destroying several innocent biscuits which were simply minding their own business.

'Nasal implants?' said Thwaite, helpfully, 'that would raise our profile, I mean -'

'We need to get the Academy into the local Press' growled Chambers.

'I imagine the fact that we usually do everything that we can to keep the Academy out of the press has added to the considerable costs which we seem to have incurred' added Captain Brayfield. Bell-Enderby the Art Master was much affronted by this remark, and rounded on the Captain 'I say- that remark was rather unfair: I mean to say, I borrowed that rubber dinghy in all good faith, and I made every attempt to clean all of the marmalade off it before I returned it. As for the so-called 'expose' as reported in the paper- well, I had no idea that a sheep was capable of such behaviour...' The Staff stared at him in disbelief.

'We need to make ourselves more visible'

'Got it- we paint the entire Academy bright yellow.'

'Why on earth would we do that?'

'I like bright yellow.'

Chambers continued...'We need a BIG media event, to attract attention Chaps'

'Kipper racing?' suggested Mr Newhouse.

Bell-Enderby raised his hand, with a strange and distant look in his eye 'We could have a parade of local beauties dressed in mini-skirts, with stockings and thigh boots - all in Academy blazers, which would barely conceal their fulsome bedroom bumpers...'

The staff sat aghast. The Head spoke first - 'I think that perhaps something a touch more cerebral might be more appropriate?'

'They could carry a book?'

Madame Dreadfell waved her arms in anger: 'I have never been so insulted, and I feel personally affronted' she snarled.

'Madam- I would certainly include you in the parade...' said Bell-Enderby

'I would never stoop so low as to flaunt myself in such an unseemly manner...'

'You certainly flaunted plenty at the Christmas do that we had at Kiddley Manor though...' said Hyde-Jones, in a louder voice than was possibly necessary. He and Newhouse exchanged the customary high-five.

'Why don't we hold some sort of special event- like a Mediaeval Banquet?' asked Bannister.

'Cracking idea that Man!' shrieked Bell-Enderby, 'We could have serving gels dressed as Wenches, in those tight bodices- with guaranteed glimpses of their bounteous kn -'

'I will add the idea to my list...' interrupted Chambers, swiftly.

'What about a Parisian fashion show in the dining hall?' queried Madame Dreadfell - 'we could get the girls to parade along the big tables'

'Yes! Yes!' Shouted Bell-Enderby - 'They could parade in swimwear - and as they passed, you would be able to look up th -'

'-Not a practical idea I fancy...' said Chambers 'For one thing, Mrs Bradley will never wear it'.

'Thank Christ for small mercies...' said Mr Newhouse.

Captain Brayfield stood up and addressed the staff: 'What about a recreation of a Jousting Tournament? I can supply horses?'

'Good Lord Yes!' said Bell-Enderby, eagerly rubbing his hands 'Gels in swimwear on horseback: and as they gallop toward each other, we can admire the bounce of their full and pert Br -'

'-Why not simply hold a ball?' interrupted Madame

'Buy me a couple of pints and I'll let you hold both of mine...' laughed Newhouse. Madame scowled him an admonishing scowl.

Hyde-Jones chipped in 'Actually, we could sell tickets for an Old Boy's Ball'

'But not everyone likes to dance' said Chambers

'Personally, what I had in mind was a raffle...' giggled the English Master.

'What about a good old (hic) Cheese and Wine evening' asked Matthews - 'providing we don't ruin it with all of that unnecessary cheese rubbish'.

Matron had now joined the throng of contributors - all eager to suggest an event which might curry favour with the Head, and so aid an elevation in pay. The ideas came thick and fast, but unfortunately, there were very few fast entrants...

'Why don't we recreate a Victorian School Experience' asked Bannister

'Just turn up on any normal day then...' said Newhouse

'No really - with all of the old desks, and old uniform, and really strict discipline...'

'I could help with that, if you wish' offered the Matron.

Professor Strangler suggested 'Why not charge visitors to be the first to break the earth and help us with the new Science Block extension- we could even rent them a spade each?'

'No, I think not, the ground is far too wet' said Chambers. Bell-Enderby's eyes were aflame- 'Mud Wrestling!! Gels could wrestle for the honour of the first spadeful- and if their tops were to accidentally come open, we could see their heaving ch -'

'Are you on any Medication?' queried Chambers

'No - why?'

'Should you be?'

Mr Newhouse had his hand raised. 'Can we go to a vote on the Swimwear idea now?' he asked.

The Reverend stroked his carefully sculpted beard, and said 'I suggest that we hold a Psychic Evening. We can have crystal balls and Tarot cards, and the Laying-on of Hands...'

'I can assist with that, if you like?' said Matron.

Goodwill considered this latest offering. 'Well yes: might be popular, might be popular - but where could we accommodate a large crowd?'

'The Assembly Hall?'

'God No! - Mrs Finucane was quite specific as to what she would do with her mop handle, should I allow her highly-polished floors to become badly scuffed again (he shuddered at the thought)'.

'We could hire Ffouke Hall?'

'What did you say?' asked Chambers

'I said "Ffouke Hall", Deputy Head' said Bannister.

'No - you distinctly said something, I heard you Man...' Chambers insisted.

'I meant the Old Annexe - Ffouke Hall chamber would be ideal for a function' said Bannister.

'Ah yes, point taken, but what about catering? I can hardly expect our Mrs Bradley to be put to even more work. I suppose that we could always rope someone in?'

'I could help with that, if you wish?' added Matron.

Hyde-Jones had a sudden flash of inspiration – 'Hey- what about Speed Dating? it's all the rage?' His comrade Mr Newhouse gave him a look and said 'Bloody Hell Roy- dating is hard enough after three or four pints: can you imagine Matron on Amphetamines?'. A look of realisation, visualisation, and abject horror passed between them.

Goodwill looked somewhat defeated, 'Look, couldn't we just have a good whip-round?' he asked.

'I can help with that...' stated Matron, confidently.

The Head said to the group 'We should contact my old friend Montague - who is still I believe, a big noise in Events Management circles. If we have some possible dates in mind for some events, then I will try to find out if he can assist us - always assuming of course, that he is not too busy. He may well be completely tied up...'

(Matron immediately offered her services - should the need arise).

Bannister seemed to be having a conversation with himself. When the look of confusion had left his face, he brightened, and turned to the Staff exclaiming 'Why don't we try a jolly old film show? I know where the projector has been stored- although the old screen might need a bit of attention. The last time I attempted to use it, I was fiddling around for ages, before I finally managed to get it to stand upright'

'I can *definitely* be of help in that department...' said Matron.

Moving on swiftly, Madame Dreadfell hurriedly suggested 'A French-Style Market' to be held in the quad. 'It would be very chic' she insisted 'we could sell wine, cheeses, French bread, and all manner of

Gallic delicacies. I will telephone my good friend Jean-Claude Derriere, who is the town Mayor of Saint Gussette in Normandy. He could come over with a few of his friends and open the event for us'.

'And where exactly do you propose that these visiting Dignitaries should be stabled, fed and watered?' asked Captain Brayfield (whose personal belief was that 'foreigners' began at the Nottinghamshire borders).

Madame swept an angry gaze over the Staff members, like a moody lighthouse...

'I will take personal responsibility for ensuring that they are given succour - STOP THAT SNIGGERING...' said a now annoyed Madame.

'May I raise a point of order?' said Mr Newhouse, having been prompted to speak up by his giggling friend Hyde-Jones.

'Certainly you may.' answered Chambers.

'Can Roy and I volunteer for the Succour if the Froggy Lads can't make it?'

Bell-Enderby rose to his feet, assuming a haughty demeanour. 'I think that we should consider something which has an altogether more Artistic content' he stated.

'Such as?' queried Dr Chambers

'Well, you may remember the wide press coverage that we received when we held the Winter open day Ice Sculpture competition last year - it was extremely popular, and certainly got the Academy noticed' said the Art Master.

'Yes, indeed I do remember it; none of us are ever likely to be able to forget it' answered Dr Chambers.

'Yes indeed! Only this time we could award a special prize to the entrant who creates the best sculpture of a gel with the bigges -'

'-is just the sort of publicity that I am hoping never to be repeated...' Chambers stated. 'Look: the quality of the sculpture which you submitted for judging was not in question. It was by anyone's standards a thing of beauty, and extremely accurate on a technical level. The point of contention was the fact that it was considered by many to have been ill-considered and rather insensitive to have produced an ice sculpture of the *Titanic*.'

'Before matters get quite out of hand, let us recap and list our possible suggestions for fundraising events.' said the Head. Scrabbling for a piece of paper, he produced, dropped, and recovered his pen and began to make hurried notes. 'So far, we have -

A Mediaeval Banquet (please do be quiet Mr Bell-Enderby)

A Fashion show of some description (I shall not tell you again...)

A Jousting Tournament

An Old Boy's Ball

Cheese and Wine evening (yes Matthews- actual *cheese* to be kept to a minimum)

Victorian School Days

A Psychic Evening

Cinematographic Night

A French Market (do take something for that cough Captain Brayfield...)

Anything else?'

'What about "Ghost Walks?"...' said Bannister.

'Explain please?'

'Well Head, there is a great interest in ghosts and "hauntings" at the moment, and I believe that several of the more historic castles and stately houses are taking visitors on what they are calling "Ghost Walks" around their premises. The general public seem to like it, and apparently, the people who stage these events are making a small fortune from ticket sales. We have no shortage of ancient buildings- and with Halloween coming up, we could get 'in on the action' and make ourselves some serious cash.'

'Damn good plan that Man, good thinking - but how do we provide the 'Ghosts' for this enterprise?'

'We issue all purchasers of tickets with a pamphlet telling them all about the dozens of ghosts that haunt the Academy. All we have to do is to get a couple of Staff members and perhaps some of the boys, to dress up as spectres, and scare the pants off the visitors.'

'I may be ab -'

'No Matron - I think not; I really do think not...' said Goodwill. 'Righto then! Ladies and Gentlemen: we will undertake all of the suggestions on our list of cash-raising ideas. Since the costs will be minimal, may I suggest that we begin with the 'Ghost Walks' as soon as possible?

Dear Colleagues - It is time for St Onans to give the general public the Willies...'

Chapter Two:

Nicky was now thirteen, officially a Teenager, and occasionally still just as confused and confounded by the world at large. Whatever magical or mystic event he had been expecting to occur on the day of his Birthday, had failed to materialise in quite spectacular fashion. He was not entirely sure as to what he had expected to happen, but it was a dreadful shock to find that things had remained exactly the same. Yes, he was taller, but he still felt dwarfed by the Academy and life in general. As with his first School blazer - he supposed that life was something which you just had to grow into. Sometimes it fitted, and sometimes it came apart at one or two seams. The main thing seemed to be to ensure that your name tag was very securely sewn into everything- that way, there was no chance of forgetting who you are...He was now at the age where he still enjoyed setting up and playing with his 'Hot Wheels' cars, but would be mortified beyond words if anyone saw him doing it. This was the time that a boy would remember removing the trousers of his Action Man figure - only now he could categorically state that the figure was obviously not built to enjoy any sort of 'action'. He was 'on the cusp' as it were, like his friend Kenny - who was born on the cusp of Leo and Capricorn, thus making him a Leprechaun...

As it turns out (and if it does, I am sorry - corrective surgery is now cheaply available) Nicky was not the only Village Kid on the threshold of change.

The formerly prim, proper and haughty elder daughter of that doyenne of the would-be Haut Monde Mrs Hislop, had recently emerged from her own childhood chrysalis. Mrs H had allowed her daughter Jocelyna to go and stay for the weekend with her best friend from school. The fact that they were a "Titled" family had absolutely no bearing upon her decision, and had not influenced her in any way to cancel her subscription to "Knitting Monthly" in favour of "Harpers and Queens" magazine. Mrs Hislop had required immediate sedation when her daughter had returned home after the visit sporting a jet-black Mohican hairstyle, short leather mini-skirt, fishnet tights, and dark eye shadow. She now insisted on being called 'Jozza', and her 'Marylin Manson' tee-shirt had caused panic in the village post office. It is an accepted fact that Girls do mature far quicker than Boys, but this was a case of pre-pubescence delivered at warp speed. Granny had dropped several stitches in the antimacassar which she was attempting to crochet, and Benjy the dog had to have therapy.

At school, she now had new and bizarre friends. Gone were Bunty and Jemima, along with poor Felicity. Her new 'hip' crew were Wilhelmina- "Wazza", Rosemary- "Rozza", Belinda- "Bezza", Geraldine - "Gezza", and Lesley - (who for some reason didn't want a nickname).

When she had asked to borrow various Heavy Metal CD's from Nicky, his old dislike of the girl had been replaced by a curious kind of admiration. Well I never...

There was another most alarming development in the boy's life. It would appear that he was destined to become what his Mother would term 'an early developer' (which he presumed was a photographic enthusiast who began his day at five a.m.). There was no doubt about it- and no chance of avoiding it: little Nicholas was showing all of the alarming traits of a beard, which was hinting at its arrival chinwards. More alarming were, shall we say 'other areas' that were determined not to be left out of the race toward Manhood. More in panic than curiosity, Nicky had cautiously raised the matter with Auntie (he had certainly 'bottled' any enquiry via Mum), and had been told 'Well- nothing to worry about there, you are just becoming a Man- and I like hairy men...' Nicky replied that he was very fond of roast chicken- but he had no desire to find one in his underwear. It was all very well and good that he was "becoming a man", but what terrified him was the outside chance that he was becoming a carpet.

Cataclysmic news had also arrived in letter form, concerning the very fabric of the family's idyllic rural existence. It would appear that the Council had decided that the big field at the bottom of their garden was going to be subject to a large housing development- consisting of a range of bungalows for elderly and disabled residents. From the look of the plans which had been included with the letter, it seemed as if the greater part of the field would be built upon- including the removal of the huge elm trees. To Nicky, this was like a family bereavement. Those trees had been spaceships, river boats, tree houses, observation posts, and had afforded him sanctuary when urgently needed all through his early years. He was angry- why would they tear down perfectly good trees? Did they not know that those trees were his "friends"? and after all, they were living things - not to be disposed of at the whim of some property developer. He felt like a part of his life was being erased. They were his trees - he hadn't finished with them yet. Those Elms were just as old as the Village, so why should some bastard with a chainsaw tear them down when they had never had the chance to speak about all of the history which they had witnessed? He would fight this plan. He would throw himself in front of the diggers as they attempted to tear up his childhood. Surely, he would be able to rally support from the Villagers in order to prevent the desecration of the landscape? As far as he knew, Squiddy still had a kite stuck up in one of the trees, which they had never managed to retrieve: surely he would help to stop the building?

Mum read the letter, and merely said 'Well I suppose that's progress...'

Auntie read the letter, and said 'Well...that's bollocks'.

Nicky knew who, in his personal opinion, had made the more valid point.

His dark and sombre mood was interrupted by a knock at the back door. It was Uncle Joe, with a broad grin on his face as per usual. 'Hello Joe - fancy a cup of tea?' asked Mum. Uncle was in a high state of anxiety, and over tea and biscuits (taking his favourites from the bottom layer of the tin, Nicky noted) began to enlighten them as to the details of his most recent "Money-spinning invention". It would appear that Joe had taken note of the increased number of television advertisements aimed at people who were suffering from constipation. Just why Joe had taken such an interest in the problem was unclear, but he had taken it upon himself to come up with a product to assist the blocked-up millions. As Joe dunked and slurped, he explained that he had invented a brand-new product which would change the lives of the sufferers of constipation forever. His brainchild went under the name of "GVB". After much probing in order to prise out of Uncle the exact nature of the product on offer, it was discovered that his "Miracle Scientific Cure" consisted of five pints of Guinness, a Vindaloo Curry, and a bucket. Nicky was certain that this would be an absolutely unmissable episode of "Dragon's Den".

There had also been one or two social developments within the cloistered world of the Academy. As with any school, business, or club, sooner or later there tends to occur a coming-together of individuals who gravitate towards each other for a very varied set of reasons. Such was certainly the case at St Onans. Over the course of two years, students from varying walks of life (including staggers, sidles and lurches) had formed up into gangs. These units comprised a motley collection of individuals who a) thought that their chances of survival were significantly greater if they allied themselves to a gang, and b) pupils who wanted to be seen as "Hip and Trendy", and generally "Cool". So, various little trainee hordes had collected together in the pursuit of attaining some sort of elevated status within the Academy. Their formation owed as much to the need to avoid inter-pupil bullying, as to cementing the bonds of friendship. Currently, any potential applicant could choose from the following selection:

"The Fury"

"The Furry" (very similar- but catering for the Dyslexic student)

"The Killer Seven"

"Sucker punch Five"

"Dubious Trouserboys" (best not to ask eh?)

"Sausage Floggers" (just possibly not a euphemism - as Kevin's Dad was a Butcher, but then again, there were rumours)

"The Unpleasant Six plus Brian"

"Moist Cloth Assassins"

"Jolly Fine Fellows One and All" (the gang that taunted their opponents' supporters at rugby matches by chanting 'You're going Home in a nice warm Mini-bus'...)

"Razor Twins" (Ironically, there were four of them in the gang. They had originally been called "Eraser Twins" - but Tarquin Fanleigh had an allergy to rubber. This was hereditary - as could be confirmed by his five Brothers and three Sisters...)

Stand-offs between gangs occurred on a daily basis, and each group would face each other in the quad at break times, and make over-polite noises at each other. Lordsley had been rejected as a member of every gang, on health grounds (everyone was sick of him), and so had formed his own gang. He regularly instigated a "beef" with other gang members, who he felt had disrespected him. This gave him the whole Academy from which to choose - although he did not include any vegetarians in his "beefs" out of respect for their individual choices. They in return, chose to continue to regard him as a complete twat.

Moving up into the Third Form at the Academy had both advantages, and some other points which were not quite as beneficial to the aspiring student. The boys had been mixed into different Forms due to the "Streaming" process (Merry had said that on some mornings, that water was bloody freezing). This meant that the lads were graded by the Masters, and placed in groups which more accurately reflected their academic prowess: or even more accurately, enabled the Establishment to separate what they termed as "the Wheat" from "the Chaff". Nicky chose to ignore this fact, as he, Merry, Calderman, Trevill, and the irascible Weatherill had all managed to stay together. Jackson, Kendy, Davis and DeVere were in the "High Flyers" Form - but their bond of friendship was still holding as strong as ever. The other great advantage was that the boys were given the choice to drop (or retain) Latin and Greek. It should come as no shock whatsoever that Nicky chose to drop Latin - and Davis chose to pick up a kebab.

Some members of the Academy, however, were seemingly stuck fast by an invisible and immovable adhesive to one particular set of goals- which more often than not, would turn out to be classic Own Goals. Such a man of misguided purpose, who frequently hit the bar (not as frequently as dear old Matthews) or the post, was the Reverend. After a particularly rigorous bout of research, he had come to the unswerving conclusion that the thing that he most needed in order to enhance his standing within the circles of the Black Acolytes - was a familiar. Now the Rev had done his research, and had formulated the conclusion that no practitioner of the 'Black Arts' could really be considered as dedicated to his or her particular following without the companionship of a Familiar. To this end, he had scoured the pages of the local free newspaper, and decided on visiting the local Cat Recue Centre, wherein he would select a suitable animal accomplice.

He toured the various cages which housed the pets which were waiting to be re-homed, and after staring intently into the eyes of one particular feline individual, decided that he would make an ideal partner in his search for the link to the Dark Realms. He stared at the cat: and the cat stared back at him. Would this poor dumb creature be a suitable and committed companion? Did it have any trace of intelligence or personality behind those beady eyes? The cat would have to wait to find out...

Armed with a stout box in which to transport his chosen confederate, he had returned to the darkened rooms of his cottage in triumph. All that he had to do now, was give the cat a name which encapsulated all of the terror and dark energy which he hoped that it would manifest. He thought of various names for the animal, such as

"Graymalkin", "Night Hunter", "Soul Devourer", "Stalking Demon" and the like. He really should have paid a little more attention to the blue velvet collar which the animal was wearing, and the few possessions with which the cat had arrived. Having checked out his new abode most thoroughly, the cat had taken a great delight in relieving itself mightily in the Rev's slippers. The cat didn't scratch at the furniture: it didn't moult and deposit lumps of fur throughout the house, and it didn't yowl at the door for freedom. What a well-behaved little cat was he.

Despite the Rev's wishes to confer the title of a member of the hierarchy of Hell upon the poor beast, it seemed that he was destined to live up to the name engraved upon the collar tag which had come with his bed and his favourite toys. In no time at all, the Rev discovered that the title bestowed upon the animal by his previous owner was absolutely accurate in every respect – namely, that of "Mr Piddles".

Undaunted, the Rev decided to ignore the moistened copies of the Sunday newspapers, and opt to get a dog. The cat had got wind of this plan- and had taken up station under the Rev's wardrobe, and was furiously resisting all attempts to remove him by means of claw and fang. The man thought that a dog would be more like it - he saw in his mind's eye a fiend from Hell which would proudly march on a chain at his side, and strike fear into the heart of all who laid eyes on him. This plan did not go quite as he had imagined, after weeks of attempting to feed the poor creature on rare meat, and repeating the phrase 'Who's a good Boy who wants to tear the soul out of the unbeliever then?', the dog had come to its own conclusion concerning the sanity of the man attempting to train it...It had run off to the local Pub - where it sat at the end of the bar and whined pitifully until it was given a bowl of beer (or five). At the weekends, it was joined by the cat, and the two sat at the end of the bar and drowned their sorrows, sharing their contemptuous opinions of their new "Owner" in very descriptive terms to all and sundry.

Now then- why not a Goat? Oh yes! That was altogether more like it... Never mind the droppings- just think about the inherent symbolism of owning such a creature. After choosing a suitable candidate from a local farm, the Rev settled down to acclimatize his newest conscript to his plans. It may have benefitted the Rev to have done just a tad more research into the habits of goatkind before taking his decision however, because rather than embody all that the man had come to hope would symbolise his link with the Legions of Hell, it merely ate his pants, and took up residence in his shed- from where it steadfastly refused to be moved. It ate (anything and everything), slept, farted hugely, and swore at him in goat. Of demonic influence was there none. It had cost him a small fortune to replace all of the pants too.

He then considered a familiar on a much smaller scale. Visiting a local pet shop, he finally settled upon a rat, which he thought embodied all of the characteristics which he hoped would possibly endear him to the Dark Lords. The rat had twitched its ratty nose at him, decided that he was a complete pillock, and set about devouring all of his ritual incense with a vengeance. It also set about on a programme of systematic chewy destruction of any books which it could come across. Particularly tasty had been the ancient, treasured and priceless copy of the *Malleus Malefecarum*, which not only had been comprehensively nibbled, but used as nesting material by Ratty. The Rev was ready to throw the book at him - but he was fast running out of intact items with which to do it. The rodent had a cousin who had been a laboratory rat, and who had explained to him all the wonders of electricity. Armed with this knowledge, Ratty had taken a great delight in gnawing through cables at inopportune moments - plunging the Rev and any guests at the time into total darkness. He had also made contact with distant rat relatives on the outside, who he introduced to the house, and showed them the vast array of things which were available for chewing (not to mention widdling on). When Ratty had got bored with gnawing, chewing, nibbling and piddling, he had left the Rev to his own devices (in the dark again, just for the fun of it) and had headed off across the road to a large white building. Popping his head around the swing door, he had spied a cat and a dog sitting together at the end of a long wooden structure, where they were apparently enjoying a drink of some sort. He immediately joined them and struck up a friendship, all three declaring a profound dislike and utter contempt for the Rev, and all vowing retribution against the man. As soon as they were sober, they would get a plan together. They all drunk a toast to future endeavours - and quite forgot what it was that they were supposed to be planning...

Say what you will about Felchingham, he had the tenacity of a limpet at low tide. He had set his mind on a course of action, and was not about to be put off by missing dogs, wet footwear, chewed literature, or a blacked-out house. What about something which could actually articulate his allegiance to the Dark Side? Why had he not thought of this before? He sped back to the pet shop and chose a sadistic-looking parrot, with a look of pure malice in its eye. Now Dear Readers - there are parrots: and then there are Parrots. Some individuals of this loquacious species had sat upon the shoulders of their Pirate owners, and said things like 'Pieces of Eight'. Some birds were the best friend of fearless Sea Captains, who had the creature by their side as they fought with the wheel of their ship as it tossed and lurched its way around Cape Horn. This particular parrot had been banned from casual contact with its own kind, and was kept securely locked in a stout cage - because it had The Horn. This serial avian rapist had made a nuisance of itself with everything from a shy Cockatiel to a very surprised Toucan (having infiltrated a local aviary). It was constantly on the lookout for any victim upon which it might force its unwanted attentions, and thus was a particularly pervy parrot in perpetuity. Even the Budgerigars were constantly gossiping about it, with one eye always keeping a look out in case of a "sneak attack" ...

The Rev had set about his task of teaching the bird to speak. Again and again, he would repeat the phrase 'Satan is our Master...'He would bribe it with treats, and repeat the words that he wanted to hear over and over again. The parrot remained resolutely mute. He even went to the length of recording the speech onto a tape recorder- and played it whilst he was out, so that the parrot might learn what he was expected to say without distraction. Nothing. The pet shop said that they could not explain it, as the breed was well known for its ability to talk, and no- they would certainly not be giving a refund. Felchingham had returned to his dwelling with a sense of utter defeat, and had hurled the tape recorder at the living-room wall. He poured himself a stiff drink, and flopped into his leather armchair to drown his sorrows- or so he thought.

It would appear that there was another Teacher whose power of instruction was vastly superior to his own. This was a teacher who had taught the bird a short phrase with much patience. The Rev's drink leapt up into the air, and he kicked over the coffee-table, as he recognised the accent which the clever bird had so brilliantly mimicked. He knew instantly who had been talking to the parrot, when it broadcast loud and very clear.....

'OOOOOO's A KNOB THEN...?'

Chapter Three:

Uncle Joe was in a bit of a state again. Urged and goaded by his Wife (who had become sick of his constant complaining) he had at last decided to bite the bullet and book an appointment with the village doctor. He had sat impatiently in the waiting room (he hated these places- they were always full of sick people) until his name was called. In fact, it was called three times, until he finally answered, 'Who wants to know?'. Grudgingly, he made his way into Dr Gibbley's consulting room.

'And what appears to be the problem Mr Prentiss?' the doctor had enquired.

'There's something wrong with my foot- it's bloody painful' said Joe 'What do you suggest that I should do?'

'You could try limping...' said the doctor.

The doctor gave Uncle a thorough examination. After a rather protracted silence, he announced 'Well, I can find nothing basically wrong with you Mr Prentiss- unless it's the drink?'

'Then I will come back when you're sober...' answered Uncle.

Exit one J Prentiss- who was going to go private in future. At least when a *private* doctor asked you for a urine sample, they wouldn't take the piss...

With the approach of Bonfire night, there came two more dreaded occasions on the Term Calendar at St Onans. One was Parents' Evening; which Nicky could neither avoid nor prevent. This was a regular event designed to publically humiliate Students in front of their Family. If you had done appallingly (and knew it), then the Masters in whose subjects you had 'under-achieved' would 'take the fortunate opportunity' to have 'a discreet word' with the parents of the lacklustre boy. This involved declaring the poor progress of the individual in a very loud voice. At the sound of such a discussion taking place, the other parents would automatically fall silent, and tune in to hear the disgraceful results being broadcast. The accepted drill was then to nod to each other smugly, all the while hoping to God that their own progeny had at least managed to spell their own name correctly.

To be deemed to have "done well" was really no better, as the brilliance of the student was loudly declared across the room, and was warmly greeted with looks of envy and hate from other adults. Boys would be seen to physically cringe in fear, just in case they had not achieved the same high academic standard as their classmates - honestly, sometimes you just couldn't win. Nicky had always aimed high, and hoped that his marks would fall in the "middle ground" where they were not that awful that they attracted rebuke - but not that high that they gained undue praise and attention. In truth, he was still not comfortable with either end of the spectrum. His friends didn't seem to find these occasions such a trial. Calderman breezed through everything that was put in front of him (as did Davis, providing it was concluded by a full cheese board). Merry was a well-above-average student in all subjects, and Trevill - well Trevill was himself. His broad smile and Dorset charm had won over even the sternest of Masters. He had an innate ability to reduce a room full of boys to hysterics, just by saying 'Mornin' Y'Buggerrs'. His Parents were really friendly, and immaculately dressed. The one point of interest was the fact that Trevill's Father had chosen to wear a ludicrously expensive Saville Row suit- but kept his wellingtons on underneath. As for Weatherill, there was nothing that you could do or say that would affect him. Time and time again, he had proven himself to be "lecture proof", and utterly impervious to all forms of punishment. Jackson and DeVere (wherever he was currently located) were top class pupils, and Kendy was an absolute genius, whose thirst for knowledge and factual retention were out of this world...Nicky fitted in well with his friends, but felt that he often needed to run in order simply catch up with them. Maybe -just maybe, those old roller-skates were still somewhere in the shed? Anyway, he had got glowing reports from his Music, Art and English Masters, so for the moment, life was sweet.

Life was also sweet for Dr Matthews, who had hit upon a brilliant idea for staving off the threat of dehydration during classes. He had spent a long time after lessons, preparing the wall at the side of the old blackboard. He had checked it for structural integrity, and had made determined use of an old spirit level from his shed (he wondered what the spirit contained within actually was, and if it were still drinkable?). Finally, he had screwed battens to the wall, and affixed various pub optics to the wood. Oh Happy Day! Now he could consume the drink most appropriate to the period in History which he was teaching.

For the Scottish Rebellion- it would of course be Whisky.

The French Revolution demanded a fine Cognac

Victorian Social Depravity would be accompanied by Gin.

Tales of Pirates and Privateers in the South Seas- well, it had to be Rum.

Early American History seemed to suggest Bourbon.

Ancient Greece? Then Ouzo was the obvious choice.

Russian Revolution = Vodka.

Mediaeval English History...He would try Mead or Wine (he was not too sure about the wine - he may have to mull that one over)

And just in case (well in a small cask in the stationary cupboard...) was a good supply of Beer, so that he could 'Quaff like a Viking', or 'Hurl down a cold one' like Ned Kelly.

Yes - that appeared to have covered all of the bases, not to mention a greater percentage of the wall. Now: time to test his handiwork...where did he put the glass?

'But I don't want to go Mum...' Nicky had moaned. 'What sort of bunch of idiots would possibly wish to send thirteen-year-old boys out into the wilds of the Derbyshire Peak District, under canvas for four days, and at the end of October? It won't be fun- it's torture I tell you...'

The boy was referring to the annual 'Four-Day Self Reliance' exercise, which the Academy forced upon all students who were about to join the Cadet Corps. The boys would be taken to a spot up in the Derbyshire Dales, and would be expected to march across the moors to a pre-determined pick-up point four days later. Days would be spent walking the National Park terrain, and nights would be spent under canvas in "Army" tents. The boys would be given maps, compasses and first aid kits - but only one day's rations. They were expected to forage or collect anything else they could along the route, in order to supplement their meagre complement of food. Mum had said 'Just think of the fun you will have, camping out with all of your friends...' Nicky had answered 'Just think of the newspaper headline saying, "Among the boys missing are...".

'It's character building' said Mum

'In October? - it's Mental!' said Auntie

The discussion had already taken place at the Academy. Most of Nicky's friends were really enthusiastic about the trip, apart from Trevill, who was a little confused it would seem.

"Ere, woi is they'm sendin' us out inter the arse end of the back of beyond then?'

'It is part of our Duke of Edinburgh award'

'Well- that's bloody pointless is that, for a start'

'Why do you say that, young Trevill?'

'Well loike - see 'ere...even if we'em don't die, and we'em passes the award- there ain't no point'.

'How come?'

'Because there's already a Duke of Edinburgh - so they'm ain't goin' to make us one too...'

Despite this brilliantly logical argument, it appeared that the gang were all signed up for the excursion into the great unknown, and so would have to try and survive it. (One boy who had heard all about the 'Four-Day-Camp' and was desperate to take part, was a rather strange chap known by the title of "Limp Maurice", who it seemed had misunderstood the purpose of the exercise...) The trip was to be supervised by two Masters, who would camp out with the boys - what could possibly go wrong?

According to the solid, immovable and xenophobic world of Captain Hercules Brayfield, things had already gone very wrong indeed. He had listened with interest during the Staff discussion at which various suggestions for raising revenue had been mooted. He had raised an eyebrow of disapproval at the suggestion that OUTSIDERS should be ADMITTED willy-nilly to his hallowed turf for the purposes of so-called 'entertainment' in the form of 'Ghost Walks'. He had dismissed as ridiculous the idea of any so-called 'Fashion Show' or frippery of that ilk. What he was incandescent with rage about was the fact that someone (that damnable Froggy-woman, by Jove) had put forward the suggestion that they take part in something which celebrated the culture of THE FRENCH (devil take them all...). Never in all his years at the Academy had he heard something so utterly offensive to the ear. There would be something done about this. He had stormed into the Head Master's office, causing Miss Piggott to drop the tea-tray and consign three hot buttered crumpets to the carpet. Placing both his hands on the front of the Head's desk, he had insisted- nay, demanded that the absurd idea be stricken from the record, and replaced immediately by an event which celebrated all that was good, pure and Holy about ENGLAND, dammit! There must be roast beef and mustard (good wholesome English mustard), and Staff dressed as Yeomen of the Guard. Costumes will include Hereward the Wake and Boudicca in all of her bloody fury, standing proud on a huge block of good old English Cheddar Cheese. There must be appearances by Churchill and Isaac Newton. The great English Sausage must be purveyed, and waved in the faces of Johnny Foreigner (Miss Piggott fainted clean away at this point). Bulldogs must stand proud amongst the tables - which will be decked out in the Union Jack flag. We shall proudly stand and sing 'GOD SAVE THE QUEEN' (May She live for a thousand years - like her Mum did). We shall NOT sing the bloody 'Mayonnaise' or whatever that heathen Gallic anthem is called. Spitfires shall over-fly the Academy, and a Lancaster bomber full of English Humbugs shall rain down sweeties to the children who play and frolic in the streets now once again made safe by the Heroic and Noble Royal Air Force. And that Bloody Volkswagen in the quad can sodding well go for a start......

'I'll add it to the list, shall I?' whimpered the Head Master.

With his eyes still blazing, and saliva flecking the corners of his grimacing mouth, the Captain made his way back to his classroom. It would be an unwise student who chose to upset him until his fury had subsided. He began instructing his pupils on the methods for determining "Hard" and "Soft" water, still growling curses under his breath. Suddenly the door was flung open. The whole class turned to see who had invaded their lesson - and moreover, who had committed the cardinal sin of failing to knock first. The figure scanned the room, and took in the sight of a scowling Brayfield at the front of the class. 'Where's Bloody Duggan?' the man asked. 'I beg your pardon, who the Strap of Hades are You?' demanded Brayfield, emerging from behind his desk. 'Never mind 'Oo I am' said the man, 'I asked you, where's Duggan?'

'I imagine that he is in his workshop...' said Brayfield

'No he ain't - just been there' answered the man, who then left as quickly as he had appeared. Those boys who were members of the Archaeology Society recognised the intruder as none other than Norman Figg- a 'helper' on the digs which the boys went out on. He seemed in a particular hurry to locate Mr Duggan the Metalwork Tutor, perhaps a file had been put back in the wrong place?

Standing adjacent to the fume cupboard, clenching and unclenching his hands: The Captain fumed.

Down in the mysterious recesses of the Physics preparation room, the wormhole had played another trick. Now well known as unstable (as could be said of 98% of the Staff), it had developed a tendency to default for short periods to the Cretaceous Period. This was not a proven fact, but was a reasonable guess. Professor Strangler had been forced to put up a notice which declared that under NO CIRCUMSTANCES was food to be left or consumed in the area of the prep' room. This hasty move had been made following an incident where Strangler had witnessed the head of a Tyrannosaur emerge out of the wormhole vortex, and snatch his lunch from off the bench.

Stranger still was an occurrence which came sometime later. The lab assistant (good scientist, bad complexion) had left his wrapped peanut butter and banana sandwiches on the bench. When he had returned to enjoy his tasty snack- he had found it gone. On the bench where the sandwiches had been, was a sandwich-shaped gap, where they most certainly should have been- but weren't. In their place, a note had been left on the table. The assistant had no idea who would have been interested in his peanut butter and banana sarnies, and all that the note said was '*Thankyouverramuch...Uh Huh Huh...*' Search as he might, the assistant could find no trace of even a stray crumb. His lunch had definitely left the building.

Stig of the Damp had made a brief foray through the vortex- or so it would seem. From some time and space, he had brought back another cave dwelling friend. The two were now often seen performing handy-man's duties around the Academy. They had also sneaked into some of Mr Bannister's Mathematics classes- and their apparent Stone-Age familiarity with all forms of pebbles gave them a surprising skill at calculus.

The time of the Camping Trip of Doom was now upon them.

Twenty-four hours from now, Nicky and his friends would be cast out into the wilds, to be preyed upon by bears, wolves, eagles, and probably a squirrel with a flick-knife. Calderman had expressed his view that they were very lucky to be given the chance to get out into the wilds, and experience Nature in all its unfettered glory. Trevill had said that he was looking forward to getting away from the claustrophobic confines of the Academy (well, at least that was a summary of what he had said). Nicky was wondering which section of the museum their bleached skeletons would be placed in- assuming that they were ever found, that is.

The day before their trip out into the great unknown, there had been the fun of another Academy photograph. The ever-enthusiastic Mr Heath had turned up with his archaic equipment, in order to capture the current inmates of St Onans. Surprisingly, the session had taken place on a warm, clear morning- and without incident. Well, nearly without incident. Having captured the happy smiling faces of the Staff and Students on his panoramic camera, the renowned Mr Heath had made full use of all of the new technology which was now at his disposal. What would have taken several days to produce, could now be printed in a matter of minutes- thanks to his high-tec state-of-the-art studio. The very technology which the Academy spurned had turned a laborious process into the work of a few minutes. With consummate pride, Heath examined the print which he had made of the assembled throng. Ah...Anyone who subsequently viewed his handiwork was bound to ask the same question as he now asked himself. Who was the mysterious naked student? And why was he grinning out at the camera wearing only a huge sombrero hat and a pair of sunglasses? Unable to "mask" the nude apparition on the negative, Heath was forced to present the photograph to the Head Master and make some sort of apology. Goodwill had studied the image for some considerable time. He pressed the intercom buzzer, and when Miss Piggott answered, asked that a student by the name of Mr Weatherill be sent immediately to his office. Although taken in for a bout of very severe questioning - no charges could be proven against the boy.

There was also the matter of the strange new "Master" that the boys had first seen at the Parents' Evening. He seemed to have arrived as if by magic with absolutely no warning or introduction. All through the evening, he seemed to have been busy ingratiating himself with the various groups of Parents who had come to the Academy, and asked some rather strange questions concerning the boys' involvement with their Metalwork Tutor - and any other people with which he seemed to have a casual contact. All that anyone seemed to be able to find out about the man was that his name was "Mr Posta", and that his first name was possibly "Mike". Everything else was shrouded in mystery. No-one was certain what he was supposed to be teaching: where he had suddenly appeared from, or why they had not been told about his arrival. Perhaps he had some connection to the list of extra-curricular activities which each student had been notified of by letter (all costing extra, of course). These "extras" all seemed to be sports-based, and included:

Fencing: In Nicky's opinion, a cross between Judo and Extreme Bee-keeping (with a sword). The origins of this "sport" came from the Elizabethan era. Each combatant would attempt to dislodge the wig of his opponent by means of prodding him with a thin sword - and if successful in removing the hairpiece, would shout 'Toupee'.

Kendo: This involved men in dressing gowns, who were involved in a violent neighbourhood dispute, with curtain poles.

Judo: "The Gentle Way". This was fighting in your pyjamas with your elder Brother, until told off by your Mum. (There was also available the sport of 'Non-Jewish Judo'- or "The Gentile Way")

Combat Macramé: 'Listen Pal – get knotted...'

Wet Towel Flikko: (optional)

Chinese Burns Club: This was an after-school group aimed at Asian students, who were diehard fans of the Scots Poet.

It was to be hoped that the Tutors of these potentially deadly Martial Arts were fully trained and qualified. So far, the only member of the Staff who had offered to assist was the Matron, who had offered to demonstrate her Marital Arts proficiency. Little did she realise, that being flung onto the floor by Matron was already becoming one of the favourite fantasies among certain boys within the Academy...

The Headmaster had summoned the Art Master Mr Bell-Enderby to his chambers (to his study that is - not to Dr Chambers, who was totally unaware of the clandestine meeting...) Still firmly on his quest to secure extra funding for the Academy, the Head had come up with a somewhat dubious scheme in order to achieve a pecuniary advantage. He regarded the Art Master over the top of his half-moon spectacles.

'I have been thinking, Bell-Enderby'

'Oh very well done indeed, Head Master!!'

'Please hear me out. We have a fully equipped and state-of-the - art printing press within the environs of the Art Department - do we not?'

'Why yes indeed, Head Master'

'Well a thought has occurred to me that we might approach the Royal Mint, and offer to produce and print banknotes for them: this would greatly reduce the pressure of work upon their staff, and provide us with the opportunity to vastly overcharge them for the work which we undertake on their behalf...'

'And if they agreed to this suggestion...?'

'Well obviously, we would be required to obtain the relevant Royal Permissions for the work, but when all is said and done, - it could be a license to print money...'

After school that evening, Auntie could see that Nicky was disturbed at the prospect of the camping trip. She decided on a little 'diversion' with which to take his mind off the worry of the Self-Reliance exercise. When they had finished dinner, and before it got too dark for what she had in mind, she asked Nicky if he would come with her - whilst she explained a little of the Village history to him.

They walked and chatted as they made their way to the yard of Nicky's Primary School. The boy felt a particular sense of loss and unease as they opened the iron gate and stepped into the school yard. He remembered games and friends that he had been forced to leave behind when he had moved on to St Onans. He remembered the kindly Teachers and comforting classrooms, and stories told by Mrs Pacey as the children all sat together in front of her chair. 'Now then...' said Auntie 'Have you ever wondered why we Villagers are always referred to as "Clockpelters"?'

'Well, I did wonder Auntie, now you mention it...' said the boy.

'The name comes from the test of Manhood that took place on this very spot' she said. 'Now go and fetch me six apples from the churchyard tree, and we shall see what we may see...'

Nicky did as Auntie had instructed. He climbed over into the church grounds, and collected six rather hard apples from the ancient tree which stood before the first and oldest of the dark slate gravestones. He returned as quickly as he could. Auntie had produced a cigarette from the pocket of her cardigan, and lit it with all the assurance of an Oxford Don.

'Okay My Lad...' she said, 'The test of Manhood was to stand on this spot, and hit the face of the church clock with a snowball'.

'Why do we need apples, Auntie?' asked Nicky

'Because the chances of a foot of snow falling in the next ten minutes is remote, to say the least, you silly arse. Right - stand on that spot, and try to get the apple to hit the face of the clock. Aim high: just past the gargoyle that has a face like Cousin Sheila - and see if you can hit the clock'.

The boy felt the weight of the apple in his hand, and felt the weight of history urging him to propel his missile toward the centre of the old church clock face. He concentrated, and let fly...The apple fell about eight feet short of its intended target, bouncing off the weathered ear of the gargoyle, who showed its contempt for the poor effort by not responding at all.

Auntie was very kind. 'Not bad for a first effort, but you won't get into the Team if you throw like you've got rubber arms...' she said. Choosing an apple for herself, Auntie stood back and threw the projectile up into the air a couple of times - assessing the weight. She then turned to an angle of ninety degrees, checked the wind factor by means of a raised wet finger, then let fly with terrific force towards the clock. The apple described a quite beautiful parabolic trajectory, and time seemed frozen as it flew. There was the almost gentle sound of a "Squdd" (a sort of blend of 'squish' and 'thud') as the apple hit the clock face almost dead centre. 'Oh Yeah! - I've still got it...' said Auntie.

Nicky knew what was expected of him. He carefully chose the most perfectly circular apple. He carefully and methodically went through the same pre-flight checks that Auntie had performed, and turned his body to give him the best possible angle for the throw. With two trial moves of his arm in order to get the height right, he let fly on the third. They both stood still as the apple rose higher and higher in front of the church. At last it reached its zenith, and began its hurried descent. There was a "pop" as it exploded on the large gold-painted hand of the church clock, and a "clang" as something metallic gave up the struggle for grip and came loose. The two watched in horror as the large clock hand gently and gracefully fell away from its central mounting, and turned elegant circles as it fell to the base of the spire. 'Mission accomplished- nice shot Kid! - now you're official!' said Auntie, slapping him firmly on the back. 'Oh bugger, now I will really be in trouble...' said Nicky. Auntie gave him a knowing smile 'No proof, no fingerprints, no witnesses, no problem' she told him 'Anyway- at least it will give the Verger something to do on his days off'. She then asked Nicky to give her one of the remaining missiles, and took up station for another throw. Without any hesitation this time, she flung the apple skywards with tremendous force, and it sailed upwards and past the clock face- which was now deficient to the tune of one big hand. 'Oh bad luck Auntie, you missed...' said Nicky. Auntie regarded the boy with a sympathetic look, and replied 'Depends on what you think I was aiming at..' Their destructive work done, the pair walked out of the school yard and back toward their house via the narrow side path of the church. As they turned the corner, they came upon the sprawled figure of Mr Seaton, who was laid out on the church path, surrounded by dropped pens and Neighbourhood Watch leaflets. Adjacent to the unconscious figure was a battered apple. His briefcase had landed in a conveniently-placed holly bush, and a curious magpie was investigating his hat. 'Shouldn't we do something, Auntie?' said the concerned boy. 'Of course we should...' said Auntie. She walked back to the recumbent neighbour, and helped herself to a few of the scattered pens which he had dropped. 'Better take a leaflet while I'm at it' she said, 'We need to be aware of anything awful which might be likely to occur in the street'.

As they walked off, Nicky turned to his giggling Auntie, and asked 'So what happened to Mr Seaton then?'

'Act of God...' replied the fruit marksman.

The headline in the local paper on the following Friday had declared;

'LOCAL COUNCILLOR FELLED BY MYSTERY ASSAILANT IN CHURCHYARD'

'Do you know anything about this, by any chance?' Mum had asked Auntie.

'Yes indeed- it's the local newspaper: we get one every Friday...' Auntie replied.

(Under her breath, Auntie muttered 'How d'you like them apples, Seaton...)

It was a racing certainty that the local Constabulary would haul in Granny Smith for questioning...

Chapter Four:

Today was the day that would see Mother's youngest Son sacrificed upon the green and pleasant altar of a National Park- and worse, had actually paid £15 for the privilege. Nicky had reluctantly put on his own clothing for the trip, but had felt a strange yearning to be back in his Academy uniform, hidden away from the danger of a rural demise at the hands of homicidal sheep. He had been supplied with a waterproof jacket (just in case...), waterproof over-trousers which crackled like the wrapper on a loaf of bread (just in case...), two packed lunches containing geriatric cheese and pickle donated by a neighbour (wasn't that kind.) and a mysterious 'waistcoat' which Uncle Joe had insisted that he take with him. This was a padded and multi-pocketed item; which Uncle had assured the boy 'Had seen him through many sticky situations in the past'. Nicky hoped that none of the "sticky" items had been left to hibernate in any of the multitude of pockets which the garment had. He bundled the various items into his rucksack, kissed Mum and Auntie goodbye, informed them where he had left a copy of his Last Will and Testament (just in case), patted Dave the Chicken - and set off for his appointment with destiny...

As the boys assembled in the quad, all decked out in their arctic survival gear (Weatherill sported a rather fetching Russian Tank Commander's fur hat), there was much talk of which Masters would be leading the Route March into doom. General consensus was that it was unlikely to be Mr Thwaite: he would not want to risk chipping his nail varnish, and would possibly be the very worst person to lead any kind of expedition. Although an exceptional Geography Teacher - he had the uncanny ability to become "Locationally Challenged" at the drop of a hat. In fact, wherever you dropped the hat - Thwaite would never be able to locate it. This was a man that thought *Addis Abeba* were the Swedish pop group that sang "*Mama Mia*".

Meanwhile, back up in the Village, the disabled church clock showed the time as either something to, or something past nine...

In the quad, two hired coaches stood awaiting their fill of victims. Predictably, the Academy had chosen to procure the services of the local village bus company. Nicky's spirits lifted slightly - because not only was there little likelihood that the aged buses would actually make the trip out into Derbyshire without mechanical catastrophe: it was doubtful, to say the least, that any of the appointed drivers would have the faintest clue which way to point the coach. His small hint of glee soon evaporated. Striding up to the transport came Chambers and Rundell... As the gang met up in the quad, they were all agreed that there could not have been a worse combination of Masters to accompany the boys. 'Oh Crap!...' said Calderman with considerable feeling, 'It's Dickheadicus Rex and Dr Happy'. Nicky had a swift vision of an earthquake on the moors - with the two Masters standing laughing hysterically as pupils plunged into an open chasm...

'Right You Boys- stop larking about. Stand in line and answer your name when called' barked out Rundell. He ran through the roll-call and counted the boys as they were loaded onto their coach. There was a minor fracas as Merry decided that he had an urgent appointment with the lavatory, and had to navigate and force his way off the coach at a crouch. When he eventually reappeared, there was a chorus of cat-calls and light-hearted abuse from the rest of the impatient passengers. With a hacking cough, a quick look at an aged map, and a word which the boys would never ever use in the presence of Nuns, the driver set off.

'I bet you a quid that the bus will stop in the lay-by outside the Academy...' said Merry

'How can you be sure of that?' asked Nicky

'Because we've just driven off without old Rundell...' he replied.

In the third-floor corridor, just outside the Metalwork and Craft rooms, Mrs Finucane the Cleaning Supremo and all-England mop champion, was fiddling with her large bunch of keys- attempting to find the one which would allow Mr Posta access to the domain of Duggan. The correct key was at last located, and handed over to Posta with a look of suspicion. 'Thank you, Mrs Finucane, - that will be all for now, I shall ensure that I lock up when I leave' he had assured her. She watched as he turned the key in the lock and slipped soundlessly into the room. What did he want? What was all the urgency to see inside the workshops? Why had no-one seen Duggan for a couple of days? She didn't know the answers to any of these questions, but she would bloody well find out...

'How do you fancy a night out at The Golden Lion, Roy?' asked Mr Newhouse, as he casually flicked through a copy of *Classic Rock* magazine 'My treat- and there's a good band on so I hear...'

'I may well take you up on that, my Heavy Metal Guru: who's playing then?' said Hyde-Jones.

'It's a tribute band, an all-girl Heavy Rock group called "Judith Priest"- not bad, so they say'

'Sounds like a plan, my fine fellow...but please let's not have a repeat of the performance that we had last time we sallied forth together to a gig'

'Whatever can you be alluding to Sir?'

'The incident where you took it upon yourself to practice "Stage Diving" is the occurrence to which I refer...'

'And what was wrong with that? Lots of punters do it'

'Not when you land on top of a crowd of punters who are standing at the bar, they don't...'

'Well, I managed to get us a pint, didn't I?'

'Your point is well made Sir; I salute your technique and style. We shall indeed attend. Let us Rock - and should space permit it, possibly Roll.'

Mr Posta had started to examine the Metalwork rooms with forensic precision. He knew what it was that he was looking for, but the room seemed to offer an endless supply of potential hiding places. He checked cupboards, he checked shelves, he rummaged carefully in bins. He removed the thicker and larger tools from their roost on the walls, and hefted them in one hand- assessing the weight of each item. The devious bugger must have hidden it somewhere in here, but with so much metal around, it was going to be the devil's own work to find it. The trouble was, there were so many items which the boys had made as "projects", not to mention various things produced by Duggan himself as part of his little "side-lines". Would there possibly be a hollow storage space beneath the window cill? He lifted one of the heavy cast-iron garden urns from in front of the window, placed it carefully on the floor, and tapped the wood beneath - no, it felt and sounded quite solid...damn. He replaced the urn on the cill. Duggan was probably making a tidy little profit from selling these to local garden centres, as he had six of them sitting in the window space. He checked inside each one just in case, but found nothing. I know, he thought, I just bloody well know that he has put it where he can keep an eye on it. If I were him, where would I hide it?...

After an hour's worth of looking out at unchanging scenery, the boys were getting rather restless on their coach. They had long since run out of variations of head-locks and arm holds to try out on Lordsley, and when Merry had said 'I spy with my little eye, something beginning with "W"'- well, Trevill had got it straight away (Lordsley again). However, they were getting ever nearer to their destination, and behind them, dark and mischievous storm clouds were sneaking up behind them. Trevill had noticed, and gave an impromptu weather report: 'Now if Ee looks over yonder, that be them Stormin' clouds. They'm actually called "*Curious Nimble*" clouds- an' I tell Ee, they bring some roight 'orrid weather with 'em. They'm different from yer other clouds what is very much higher- what is known as "*Cyril Curious*" or "*Cyril Stratford*" if they'm even higher up...'

'And the Long-Range Forecast, Professor?' asked Nicky

'Well See: if they stays at long range, that will mean that we'em not gonna get piss wet through...'

'How do you know so much about the weather?' asked Kendy

'Oi gets it from moi Granddad see' said Trevill, 'E'em always 'ad a piece of seaweed 'angin' on his shed door, and it would predict the weather with great accuracy...' he answered proudly.

'How did it work?' asked Kendy

'Well now, Pops said that if that there seaweed was dry - then you knew that it were goin' to rain...'

'What if the seaweed was wet? 'asked Nicky

'Ah well, then you see. If it were wet, then you'm knew that it were rainin'...'

The cup of tea which had arrived upon his immaculately tidy desk, and which had been so lovingly prepared by his not-so-secret admirer Miss Emelia Piggott, sat stone cold and untouched. The carefully buttered crumpets on their tea plate (willow pattern- not too gaudy or presumptuous) lay untouched and neglected as a cheap can of supermarket lager would be spurned by a choosy wino.

In his hand, Doctor Gerald Goodwill held the letter which he had been staring glassy-eyed at for the past seventeen minutes. His ordered and fastidious mind refused to comprehend that which his now tear-filled eyes reported to his soul. Had it finally come to this then? Had he not striven long and hard, and given over so much of himself to his beloved Academy that he had little left for, well, for anything else? He stroked the noble head of his dog, who sat by his side in sympathetic proximity. He had told himself that this letter was a very, very long way off as yet- but today, this morning, here it was. Well, he would do nothing at this moment. No rash moves were called for. There would be no panic, and no alarm. Life would continue in the warm rosy glow of everyday comfort until - 'Miss Piggott...Ask Dr Chambers to come to my office if you please...'

'Sorry Head, you will recall that he is away with the boys on the Camping trip...'

'Ah yes indeed...Who is the next most senior Staff Member?'

'That would be Dr Matthews, Head Master...'

'Oh F – Dear...'

Mr Posta was now out of breath, sweating profusely, and fast running out of places to search. He had begun to talk aloud to himself: 'Now come on- you have had more training than the Pope has preached about, and you've had fifteen years' experience in the field - you can't let this little toe-rag of an amateur get the better of you. What would you do with it if you had it? You wouldn't want to leave it lying around, especially if there was the chance of it getting seen by these nosey schoolboys - so think man, think, where would you hide it?' He sat down heavily on one of the wooden workshop stools, wiping the sweat from his brow with his handkerchief. He was now going to have to face one of those embarrassing telephone grilling from the Boss, especially when he had the pleasure of informing him that he had made absolutely no progress as yet. There would be the usual lecture about how much specialist manpower is costing the Department. There would be the not-so-veiled threat of replacing him with a younger operative "should circumstance dictate", and the shame of having to return empty-handed.

Well, he was not going to get any hint, clue or result whilst he was in this frame of mind, so he might as well pack it in for the day. He looked down at his loose and trailing shoelace. If he could only tie up a loose end himself, then he mi - hang on...there was a tiny but significant glint of light from the sole of his shoe. He carefully and slowly turned the sole upwards, and there! There it was again. He quickly removed his shoe, and strained his eyes to see what it was that had reflected the light. On the sole of his brogue, was the smallest spot of a very reflective yellow-white metal, which had escaped the cleaners' broom. He put down the shoe on the bench, and opened the nearest desk drawer that held tools and sundry items. His breathing became more rapid as he fumbled around in the drawer, until his fingers closed over the item which he was looking for. He picked up the shoe again, and focussed the small magnifying glass over the spot....

'Got you - you bastard...'

Agent J-Cloth gave the secret knock and crept inside the building (actually, the knock could not have been all that secret- or the recipient of the knock would not have known that it was the secret knock: I mean, it could have merely been a casual visitor who suffered from Knock Tourette's, who had happened upon the secret knock by pure chance. How do I know this? I can't tell you - it's a secret...). Technically, she was Mrs Finucane until she entered the premises, and had been recognised by the Leader of the ODD. Albert Brooks was recognised by everyone within the Academy - and treated with a healthy respect, not to mention a certain wariness, by those not accepted by him as a friend.

'Greetin's, Agent J-Cloth...' said Brooks

'Feck all that - get the kettle on, me throat is fair seizin' up for the lack of tay...' she answered. 'And don't be hoidin' dem posh choccy biscuits neither, cos' I know's you've got 'em stuffed away somewhere...'

Proceeding with orders duly received, and having given up all hope of being given the agreed secret password, Brooks did as he was told and hurriedly made the tea. He carried two steaming mugs over to a small rickety table in the corner of his "office", and sat down. He watched fascinated as the lady spooned several sugars into the mug, fearing greatly for the safety of her teeth. When she had torn open the packet of chocolate biscuits, and dunked the first of several of them into her tea, he spoke.

'Did yer find out what yer man was up to with all his pokin' around then?'

'I'm still keepin' an eye on the little fecker - but I reckon that he smells like the Law if you ask me...'

'What's he after then?'

'He seems in some sort of mighty hurry to find out what yer man Duggan is up to, and them eejits who help out with the diggin' up of old bones (she crossed herself) seem to have got the wind up something cruel. I tell yer - dere's sometin' very fishy goin' on, and I mean to get to the bottom of it. Are dere any more of dem biscuits?...'

'Did you find out what the important letter that Goodwill got was all about?'

'I only managed to get a look at the heading on the letter, and the first line - and then I had to seal it back up sharpish, because that potty wumman with the blue hair was comin' down the corridor'

'And did you sort out the equipment for our next little mission?' he asked.

'Indeed Oi did. The stuck-up fecker has gone off to the country with the lads - but I can't wait to see the face of him when he sees what has become of his latest posh trophy...'

'Well done Agent J-Cloth. Now, was there anything else to report?' said Brooks

'Yes dere is - dis tay needs a little drop of something in it to put a bit of life into it...'

'Such as?..'

'Such as a good drop of the stuff that ye have in that bottle in the cupboard, and don't pretend that ye haven't - 'cos I seen it when you got the mugs out, you devious little fecker...'

Brooks sometimes wondered just who was running the ODD. However, he treasured the company of this intelligent, observant and extremely efficient lady, who swore more expressively than he did. They shared a hefty measure of spirits, and the conversation loosened a little, as the whisky began to take effect.

'Did ye hear the latest shite that yer man Goodwill is after suggestin'? She asked Brooks

'No, what's all that?'

'Feckin' 'Ghostie Walkin'- I ask ye: is dere any more proof needed to show that the man has his arse where his head should be?'

'Well if it's a fright that they're after, I'm sure that we can oblige?' said a smiling Brooks.

'Aaah, now - would ye look at dat...' said Mrs Finucane, in a sad voice.

'What's the problem?' asked Brooks

'Me feckin' mug is empty....'

Chapter Five:

It was just about lunchtime when the coaches containing the unwilling cargo of boys pulled off the winding Derbyshire road, and up a muddy farm track. Strangely, there had been no breakdowns on the way up here (apart that is, from the driver-who had several each time he had to drive any further than the local villages). As they stepped cautiously off the bus, the boys looked around them at the bleak and foreboding moorland onto which they had been deposited. Most were looking very unhappy at the prospect of nights under canvas- especially if the weather was going to take out its revenge upon them. Kendy however, was ecstatic: 'Wow! - look at all of the moorland, and heathland, and wind-blown landscape, it really is like something out of a book!' he reported to the rest of the assembled group.

'Oh yes indeed...' said a morose Nicky, 'I expect that somewhere out there, Heathcliff and Cathy are at it like knives...'

'Do they live here then?' asked Kendy.

'No Jon- they're not real people, they're characters in a book' Nicky replied

'Sorry, I was just wondering'

'Surely you mean "Wuthering"?'

'Please shut up, Trevill...'

Out of the belly of the coaches came two enormous green rolled bundles, which resembled Army-issue whales tied up with straps. These were unceremoniously dumped onto the wet ground in front of the boys, and Rundell stepped forward - stepping first into something which is best described as "rather rural". He looked down at his besmirched footwear with disdain, and then began his speech.

'Right, you boys. The tents are to be taken up to the top of the field. You will unroll each tent carefully and lay it out on the grass. Inside are the poles and the ground sheets. You will assemble the tents according to these instructions (at this point he produced a printed sheet, which the wind took hold of and snatched out of his grip - lifting it skyward, and away across the moor). Well, you will just have to work it out. I shall attempt to assist if required, but I am sure that so-called 'educated boys' such as yourselves will have no trouble with the erection...'

"Haven't so far!...' said an unidentified voice at the back.

Rundell gave a look of contempt in the general direction of the heckler. Just then, there was the sound of a car horn, and Rundell's

Volvo came lurching up the farm track- driven by none other than Dr Chambers. Rather than take the coach with the other boys, Chambers had been persuaded to drive up the Latin Master's car to the camp site. The two men had a short, urgent conversation, with Rundell indicating something off in the far distance. Chambers had glanced at the boys, shrugged, and handed the car keys to its owner. He walked over to the group of boys and said 'Good afternoon Chaps- gosh! This takes me back; I used to do a lot of camping when I was a lad. Right, now where are we? Ah yes - soon have this tent up, and then we can eat...' With that, he sped around the tent arranging poles, sheets, ropes and other rather lethal- looking pieces of equipment. In no time at all, he had single-handedly erected the tent, and began putting together the small stove for cooking.

'Thanks for your help Sir...' said Calderman

'My pleasure - don't mention it!' replied Chambers 'We will get some hot food on the go for you all before it gets too dark'

'May Oi arsk a question Surr?' said Trevill, hesitantly

'Of course, Trevill: what is your query?'

'Wearin' them thur shorts in October Surr - takin' a bit of a chance aren't Ee?'

Rundell had returned. Lecture two was about to commence:

'Now Gentlemen. As you can see in the distance, there is a farmhouse. We are allowed to camp on this land by kind permission of the farmer and his Lady Wife. You will consider the farm absolutely out of bounds. There will be no horseplay or harassment of the owners. Should any boy choose to disobey my order, the penalties will be severe: Is that understood?'

There was a general murmur along the lines of 'Yes Sir'.

'You will study your maps provided tonight, in readiness for your first walk across the moors tomorrow. Dr Chambers will ensure that all lights are out by 10:00 pm - and there will be no tomfoolery whatsoever. You will not disturb Dr Chambers - who will be sleeping in the tent adjacent to the stone wall over there'.

'So where are you sleeping Sir?' asked Merry.

'I have made my own arrangements, and will be very close by' answered Rundell.

The boys ate what was technically called their evening meal, as the light began to dim around them, bringing the high limestone edge in the distance into a dark and foreboding shadow. The wind had risen in the last hour, and now howled around the two tents, flapping the fabric like a trapped bird. It was considering changing its name to Gale, just as soon as it had finished tormenting these silly humans who had ventured out onto the moor. From inside the tent, the boys listened to the rising howl of the wind. A head emerged from a sleeping bag and said:

'We're going to die, aren't we...'?

'No Merry, we are not going to die' said Calderman.

'The storm is getting worse, that wind might pick us right off the moor...'

'No Gerry- that's a tornado that does that' answered Nicky.

'Do we get tornadoes in England?' asked a nervous Merry.

'Actually, that's a really interesting point,' said Jackson 'Do you know that we actually get more tornadoes in England than they get in America?'.

'Thanks for that Jacko' said Nicky, 'I'm sure that has set Merry's mind completely at ease' .

'Sorry- I was just saying...' replied Jackson.

DeVere had somehow been able to shut out all sounds of the storm, and was currently working his way through his repertoire of motorbike impressions, as he snored his way through the night. He was taking it easy. He could rest soundly and not worry.

Because he had plans.

Back at the Academy, Dr Goodwill had called an emergency Staff Meeting. The Masters were all clustered expectantly at the far end of the Head Master's office. The door was flung open, and a highly-agitated Goodwill crashed into the room waving a copy of the local newspaper. 'I have it!! By Jove - at last! I have an idea which will make us a ton of money, and ensure that our name is writ large in the annals of history!' he cried.

The confused Staff looked at each other. Hyde-Jones was the first to speak: 'What is it that you have discovered Head Master?'

'Here Man- here...look will you - this is just what we need!' They looked.

'What - incontinence pants?' said Mr Newhouse. Goodwill looked at the paper...

'No, Not there - here, just here for Goodness sake!'

He turned to the correct page of the newspaper, and tapped urgently with his finger on the article which took up one entire page.

'Foreign Statues?' said Bannister, rather confused

'No, not just the statue- read the article: this is a must for us and the Academy' said Goodwill.

The article in question was a story about a statue in a foreign church, which had miraculously begun to 'cry' tears. The incident was being hailed as a modern miracle, and was being widely covered in the press all over Europe. The phenomena had been going on for some time, and was generating huge amounts of cash for the church, as public and pilgrims alike flocked to see the weeping statue. They came and bought photographs, and tee-shirts, and tea-towels, and coasters, and badges, and posters, and books, and pens, and writing paper, and tissues, and Goodwill wanted some of the action...

'This is what we need!' he insisted, 'We have a load of statues in and around the Academy, and it cannot be beyond the wit of man to rig up some sort of pump and piping to get it to 'weep'? Just think of the profit that we could generate! I will get Mr Brooks to salvage the pump out of the old fountain, select a statue, and rich! I tell you: I shall - I mean, *We* shall all be rich!!'

The Staff looked at each other again, and then into the mad eyes of their Head Master. Had the old boy overdone the dry sherry? Had Miss Piggott added some forbidden herb into his mid-morning almond slice? Had the tight old git finally torn open his wallet and purchased a newspaper? Had Matron left those buttons undone on purpose? Whatever the truth of the matter- the Head was serious.

Or Mad.

Or seriously Mad.

Professor Strangler was himself suffering from a certain level of mental torment. The Vortex had been acting up again, and had seemingly allowed admission to yet more "visitors" from wherever it was that the other door opened into. His lab assistant (brilliant scientist - complexion still somewhat problematical) had run up to him in the quad, and informed him of a small matter which required his immediate attention. They had both sprinted back to the Physics laboratory, where the Professor had gingerly opened the door to the prep room - expecting to witness mayhem and destruction. What confronted him was the sight of around a dozen Chimpanzee-type primates, who were all lounging in the lab chairs and having a rather heated discussion about the authenticity of the Shakespeare sonnets. There were some very forceful theories being expressed- and a large amount of fruit had obviously become airborne in the heat of the argument. One particular large Male had felt that his own theory had not been considered with sufficient credibility, and was showing his distaste by displaying his bottom to his debating opponent.

Give 'em a decent shave- and it's just like break time in the Staff lounge, thought Strangler.

Across from the quad from the somewhat confused environs of the Physics Department, there was a similar Large Male who was outwardly displaying his anger and opposition to one particular idea which had been put forward by the Academy. Captain Brayfield was holding court up in the Chemistry block, where he was tutoring a terrified group of Second-Year students. He had just finished berating one hapless individual for the improper use of a Bunsen burner, and stood gripping the desk edge in muted fury. Such was his state of agitation, that his yellowed teeth were gritted - and they were not even particularly slippy...

"French Market" indeed - this insult to his Grim and Peasant land would not be tolerated. Why, the very idea was like a wart on the nose of Civilisation, and a curse upon the so-called "colleagues" who had gone along with the suggestion: because he would mount his own strategic offensive, and liberate the Academy from the plague of the Foreign Invader. As with his Ancestor who had taken part in the Crusades (helping to liberate Yorkshire from the Moors...), he would ride out and take back what was rightfully his - ensuring that children may once again safely graze upon English perfectly-manicured lawns.

Further across the map still, there was another pocket of unrest. Up in the Village, Uncle Joe had decided to visit the local Pub at dinner time. He went in and ate a Ploughman's lunch.

A fight had ensued, when the Ploughman had come back from the toilet...

Out on the Derbyshire Moor, the thunder was crashing around like a climatic version of very foul language. Partridge and Pheasant whirled away into the gorse and heather for shelter, rabbits hid under the wind-swept hedges, and sheep stood impassive and wet - discussing amongst themselves the impact of Tourism on the ecosystem of the National Park.

The boys huddled in their tent, as each paparazzi flash of lightning lit up the tent side like a huge television screen on the blink.

'We are going to die, aren't we...' said Merry, staring up at the tent roof.

'No my friend, there is no reason at all why we should consider ourselves to be in any particular danger. What we are witnessing is merely the random electrical discharge of static generated by rising air currents within a localised storm cloud system. Since we are not at the highest point on the Moor - it is highly unlikely that we would present a point at which the electrical discharge would be likely to earth itself. So you see, there is little chance of a strike which could result in serious injury or death...' declared Kendy.

'Could you explain that to my underwear...?' replied Merry, timidly.

'There is water coming in under the tent.' stated Weatherill, 'I shall summon help from our Venerable Leaders. I am just going outside - I may be gone for a while...'

With that, the boy adjusted the strap on his Fisherman's hat, and dived out of the tent and into the deluge. He was indeed gone for some time. Eventually, the tent flap was flung back, and a dripping Weatherill stumbled into the tent. As he removed his hat, the water cascaded off the brim, and poured onto the cheese and pickle sandwich which Nicky was attempting to eat. The water soaked the bread- but failed to soften the armour-like cheese within.

'What news from the Colonies, oh Great Venturer?' asked Calderman.

'The Bastards have abandoned us...' said Weatherill 'There's no sign of Rundell or Chambers - their tents are empty...'

'What, you mean they've left us out here on the Moors in this storm?' said Nicky

'We're all going to die, aren't we...' wailed Merry.

'Right - sod this for a game of Soldiers....' Weatherill angrily declared.

He rummaged in the pockets of his jacket, and produced a mobile phone. The other boys stared at their friend as he tapped at the screen with a look of determination. No-one spoke for a minute or two, and then Weatherill broke the silence...

'Ah-Ha! I bloody thought so. The devious pair of Arses - I knew that they were up to something.' he said.

'What do you mean?' asked Nicky

'Well look here - (he showed the boys the detail on the screen of the phone) When I found their tents empty, I thought to myself "now where would the old scroats have chosen to hide themselves”? You can see here that just over the hill, there is a small Pub and Hotel. Let’s have a wild guess at where The Brothers Grim have toddled off to...’

‘So what are we going to do?’ chorused Kendy, Jackson and DeVere together.

‘Get your waterproofs on my Lads! we’re going to pay our respects to our neighbours, Farmer Giles and his Wife...’ answered a determined-looking Weatherill.

And so it came to pass, that through tempest, storm and assorted droppings of assorted wildlife, the gang splashed and squelched their way up over the brow of the hill, and on toward the farmhouse. Arriving at the door, as the lightning played out its evening performance all around them; they crowded around the small window near the front door- and peered in. Asleep in an armchair was who they took to be the farmer, boots off, and with a big toe which had made a break for freedom poking through a large hole in his sock. Nicky was voted as “Window knocker”, and so he tapped as politely as he could on the glass. There was no response. He rapped a little louder this time, but still the slumbering man did not stir. Trevill then pushed his way to the window, and clattered on the glass with so much force, that the boys feared that the window might fall into the living-room. Still, the sweetly dozing farmer did not wake.

‘Just our bloody luck...’ said Weatherill ‘dozens of farms around the moors, and we choose the one with a deaf owner...’.

DeVere was standing a little way off, regarding with some interest the tractor and trailer which was standing haphazardly in the farmyard.

‘Right Lads...’ he said, ‘There’s our limousine right there- we all get on that, and take a little trip down to the local Hostelry, and see what our so-called ‘Leaders’ are up to’.

‘We can’t just steal it- the farmer will report us to the Police’ said Nicky.

‘If he didn’t hear Trevill attempting to remove the window frame with his knocking - I don’t think that he is likely to hear us “borrow” his tractor’ replied Calderman ‘Anyway, we are so far out in the wilds, that even if he rings the local ‘Fuzz’, it will take them hours to get here’.

The general consensus was that Calderman was probably correct. There was however, one hurdle to overcome in the Great Plan...

‘Hold it!..’ said Weatherill ‘Call me “Mr Picky” if you wish - but can anyone tell me one vital piece of equipment which we might just possibly need at this point?’

The boys looked at each other, then back at their friend. ‘For goodness sake - we won’t get far without a driver, will we?’ said the boy.

The gang parted as a slight but proud figure stepped forward; with a chest so far puffed out that he was in danger of exploding.

‘Oi believe that Oi may be of service ‘ere... stand back, and let the Maaster take the controls...’ stated Captain Trevill the Superhero. ‘Oi was born droivin’ these ‘ere devices..’

‘I bet that must have been very painful for your Mother...’ said Nicky.

Like a troop of clowns in an Agricultural Circus, the group of boys loaded themselves onto the tractor - and when space ran out, the trailer. Weatherill placed an overlarge cloth cap upon the head of Trevill, who turned the peak backwards, and began to fiddle with the wires beneath the steering wheel. ‘Won’t be a minute, oi just needs to ‘ot wire this little beauty.’ said Trevill, rural expert and tractor thief.

With the rain still cascading off them, Trevill expertly brought the engine to life with the throaty chugging of tractors everywhere. He reversed the unit and trailer out of the farmyard, and a little way back up the trail. ‘That was brilliant Mate!’ said Nicky ‘How come you are so good at driving farm equipment?’

‘Been doin’it since Oi were Seven years old - when Oi took me Dad’s Land Rover down to the local shops’ said Trevill.

Calderman was genuinely shocked: ‘Why on earth did you drive a Land Rover down to the shops at the age of Seven?’ he asked

‘Well now see, oi ‘ad run out of Jelly Babies, adn’t Oi...’ came the reply.

After a period of ‘Off-Roading’ which had tossed the boys around like a Sunday salad, the Pub and hotel (“enjoy the Peak of Dining in the Peaks”) came into view through the rain. Trevill parked the tractor some way away from the building, and the boys crept up to the lighted windows which were facing them. They all clustered around a window and looked in at the warm glow of a welcoming, and above all, very dry restaurant. Sitting at the candle-lit table, enjoying what looked like rump steak and chips with peas and a side-salad, were Rundell and Chambers. The boys saw Rundell lift an expensive-looking bottle of wine, and pour his dining companion a generous measure. The men smiled at each other, and clinked their glasses together. Rundell waived at a waiter, who disappeared, returning to the table with another bottle of wine. There seemed to be much laughter and jollity, not to mention enjoyment of the roaring log fire which was in the corner.

Nicky and Calderman turned away from the window, sharing a look that said "Revenge".

'How many sheep did we pass before we got to this field?' Calderman asked.

'About twenty or so I think - why?' asked Jackson.

'Okay...Trevill, DeVere, Jackson, Merry- go and round up those sheep. Herd them up here, and keep them moving right up to these doors. I see that Mutton is on the menu for the diners tonight.'

The lads did as they were asked. The unprotesting sheep were driven up to the rear doors of the restaurant, where Nicky and Calderman were holding open the doors. As the flock swept forward, Nicky darted inside and opened the connecting door to the dining area. Both boys then let the doors go- and returned to their friends, in order to watch the entertainment begin. There were tourists, there were casual diners, there were romantic couples out for a lovely evening, there were two Public School Masters enjoying a lavish steak meal - and suddenly there were twenty-six wet, confused and panicking sheep stampeding around the dining room. The restaurant exploded in a cacophony of noise, as sheep, waiters and diners fought to get out of each other's way. In a tight space, this was never going to be a realistic proposition. Tables, chairs, glasses, and expensively-printed menus flew into the air, plus a set of false teeth, which were picked up and tried by a sheep. Friendly woolly faces nibbled at the salad whilst terrified diners looked on. That carpet was never likely to recover. Waiters attempted to push through the livestock, waving their arms - and a Scottish Couple at the back wondered if the Management would waive the bill? The boys looked on as the pandemonium continued, and laughed hysterically as Rundell tried to wave away a particularly curious sheep with the wine bottle, only to hit Chambers squarely in the face with it. Calderman took a step back from the window.

'That'll do Lads...That'll do' he said.

With tears of laughter mingling with the rain, they loaded themselves back onto the tractor, and chugged their way back to the farmhouse, and its sleeping occupant. They parked the tractor and trailer just as they had left it in the yard. As they dismounted, DeVere looked around the yard, and informed the group 'Thanks for that Chaps - now Cohones to the lot of it...I'm going to get me some transport out of here...'

'You're not going to steal the tractor are you?' asked Merry, nervously

'Oh no - don't worry..' answered DeVere- 'what I have in mind is something with slightly less horsepower...'

The group of boys followed their friend over to the big barn. De Vere opened the small door and went inside. From within came the sounds of horses. Ah- this is what he had planned then: the boys waited with baited breath, expecting to see DeVere emerge from the barn on the back of some wild stallion- silhouetted like the Lone Ranger as lightning lit up the yard.

Inside the barn, there was the sound of a deep bellowing. Slowly, ever so slowly, the huge barn door swung outwards, and the boys saw DeVere sitting proudly astride Geoffrey - the prize Hereford bull. Now Geoffrey did not rear up theatrically, but evacuated in rather a spectacular fashion onto the cobbled yard. Weatherill stepped forward, stroked Geoffrey's enormous woolly head, and placed a Stetson upon the bonce of the Lone DeVere. The boy looked over at his fellows, tipped his hat to them, and trotted off down the farm track on his muscular mount. 'Good luck – Kemo Sabe...' Merry called after him.

Nicky's thoughts returned to the two Masters who had forsaken their charges in lieu of their own comfort. He noted what Geoffrey the bull had deposited on the farmyard. He noted that there was an awful lot of it. He knew exactly to what purpose he would put it.

The boys acquired shovels and spades from out of the barn. They loaded up the trailer with what they needed. They decided to pull the trailer back to their tent area by hand, just in case the Farmer had been miraculously cured of his catalepsy. Arriving eventually at the required spot, Kendy was sent to check that Rundell's Volvo was unlocked - it was. With all of the doors opened (including the sun roof) it did not take the gang too long to transfer all of the manure from the trailer, to the inside of the Master's car, which they filled from floor to ceiling in record time. When they had finished their task, it looked as if Rundell had tinted every window on the car - dark brown.

'I thank each and every one of you for your assistance' said Nicky to the group. 'I think that I speak for everyone, when I say that this is not the first time that this car has been filled with bullshit...'

Chapter Six:

'I won't bloody well have any part of this...' declared an irate Mr Brooks, as he banged his fist down onto the desk of the Head Master. 'What you're suggestin' is immoral, illegal, and just a way of conning money out of the gullible Public - I'm havin' nowt to do with it, and you can't bloody well force me.'.

'I rather think that I can - if, that is, you have any desire to retain your current employment status and levels of remuneration...' purred Goodwill. He looked down at his dog, and just for a moment thought of purchasing a long-haired white Persian cat, which he could stroke in an unnerving manner. 'I feel that you may take a completely different view, once you have viewed and cogitated upon the content of this missive' he said.

Brooks looked nonplussed: 'What the buggery are thee goin' on about?' he asked.

Goodwill thought that the vital moment had arrived. The message that would allow him control over some of the more free-minded and resistant members of the Academy had already been written by other hands. All that was required of him was to deliver that message. He passed the letter over the desk to Brooks. He took the piece of paper and sat down, never once taking his eyes away from the print. When he did speak, he did so with a calm yet unconcerned voice. 'So the Buggers are putting thee out to grass eh? I take it that you are after goin' out with a bang - is that it? Or do yer think that if I agrees to 'elp ye pull this little stunt off, that they might change their minds?'

'If you care to turn over the page Dear Albert, you will see that my own small financial consideration is not the only expenditure which the Board of Governors are seeking to cut back on...'

Brooks swiftly turned over the letter, and scanned the rest of its contents like a man possessed. What he discovered amounted to a case of a man being dispossessed. He raised his head and stared at Goodwill, then re-read the salient paragraphs of the letter. When eventually he felt he could speak, his voice was croaky and charged with emotion. 'What, I mean - bloody 'ell...What? not Mrs F and her Girls as well? Have they all gone stark ravin' bloody mad?'

'The suggestion from the Venerable Board of Trustees is that immediate action is taken to reduce expenditure within the Academy, and this will include putting out certain currently "in-house" performed duties to outside contract. Contracts such as Grounds keeping and Cleaning will be put out to tender to the highest bidder, in order to cut out unnecessary financial pressure - I am most terribly sorry to be the bearer of bad tidings Albert...'

'Balls!' shouted Brooks. 'Let's cut to the chase, shall we? What you're sayin' is that if I go along with your mad scheme to build a statue that will produce water at the flick of a switch- then we can raise enough cash to make sure that Me and Mrs F and the Girls keep our Jobs?'

'Oh well done Albert! I just knew that you would soon come around to my way of thinking, it really would appear to be the sensible thing to do in the circumstances...' said Goodwill. He pressed the intercom button. 'Be so kind as to bring in the tea now if you please, Miss Piggott...'

As Goodwill sat back and let his Secretary pour out the tea, Brooks gently reached down into his jacket pocket and flicked the switch on his miniature radio from "transmit" to the "off" position. He knew that Agent J-Cloth had heard every word of the conversation...

As the boys were replacing the trailer unit in the farmyard, there was a sudden scraping sound behind them. They spun around, and were confronted by a worried-looking farmer with only one boot on, but more urgently, a twelve-bore shotgun in his hands.

'What the 'ell do ye think ye are playin' at?' he shouted. Weatherill stepped forward:

'Sorry to disturb you Sir- my friends and I have been sent out to camp in the field just over the way. We heard a noise in the night and rushed up the track, just as a gang of men were attempting to tow away your trailer. We thought that we had better do the decent thing and return it to you- sorry to have caused you such inconvenience...'

In the face of such guilt-free innocence, and obviously taking pity on the poor sodden boys, the farmer lowered his gun. 'Well...I see...Do you know that you're all piss wet through?' he asked.

'We did sort of notice that it is raining a little bit.' answered Weatherill, smiling at his new-found friend. The farmer turned as his Wife called from the open doorway 'What's goin' on there Jack? Is everything alright?' 'Yus Dear, just some out-of-town lads wot 'ave done me a bit of a favour as it 'appens...' he answered.

'Well for 'eavens sake bring them in out of the rain, and I'll put the kettle on. Poor little mites must be soaked through' she demanded.

The boys sat around the farmer's huge kitchen, while his Wife attempted to dry most of their wet clothing over the Aga, several chairs, an antique clothes horse, and a large lurcher dog (who had stood still for a couple of seconds too long). Mrs farmer produced mugs of steaming hot, sweet cocoa for the boys, and Nicky explained just how they came to be out in the storm on such a bad night. He told them that they had been deserted by the Masters, and that vandals had done something to their car. He also explained that the plan was to complete the four-day walk in as shorter time as possible - marching at night if the terrain was safe enough to allow it. Both the farmer and his wife gave them a look of abject horror, and the woman hurriedly checked the farmyard through the curtain, before closing and bolting the kitchen door. The farmer pulled his chair up to the table:

'I tell Ee, it would be a careless and irresponsible man that will walk the Moors on such a dark and menacing night at this time of year...' he began 'There's rabbit holes that will snap an ankle, and sinkholes which can swaller a man up - never to be seen again' he told them. The boys began to feel uneasy.

'I forbid 'ee to walk the Moors during the hours of darkness, lest ye should happen across Black Mort...'

'Who is he Sir?' asked Nicky

"Tis not a 'He' my boy - 'tis a 'What'...

'What's this 'What' that isn't a 'He' or a 'Tis' exactly?' asked Merry

'He be Black Mort… an' he's a Fiend from the very bowels of Hell...'

'Oh... a bit like a Prefect then?'

'Ye would do well not to mock young Sir. There's many that have - and are not 'ere now to hear themselves laughing.' said the farmer.

'But if they were not here, then how c-'

'Please be quiet Kendy - carry on Sir...' said Calderman

'Black Mort takes the earthly form of an enormous Hound, black as the pit of the Devil himself'.

'His armpit?' asked Kendy (a quick smack on the head from Trevill silenced him)

'Ye should not treat the legend lightly young Sir. There's plenty that 'ave mocked the tales of Black Mort and have lived to regret that mockery - because they 'ave not lived...'

'But how -...' (smack!)

'Were they found with their throats torn out, and a look of frozen terror on their face?' asked Jackson.

'No...' said the farmer. 'They was not found like that - on account of the fact that they was never found...'

'Ah- you mean that they were found missing?' said Nicky

'Exactly young Sir. Black Mort will hunt ye down on the Moors like a sacrificial lamb - or else lead ye astray until ye falls into one of the caves.'

Kendy was rubbing his head where Trevill had made contact. He drew in a breath, and asked 'Why is it that all of these local legends seem to feature an enormous Hound - I mean, surely there must be the provision for the ghastly duties to be undertaken by some other canine breed?'

'I just can't feel the terror in an attack by 'Dennis the Deadly Dachshund of Dewsbury' can you?' said Merry

'It's the whole racist element that is beginning to give me cause for concern...' said Calderman.

'What do you mean, Ian?' asked Kendy.

'Well, you must have noticed that in all of these myths and local legends, it always seems that the major protagonist is a Canine of Colour. Here we have "Black Mort". On the cliffs of Sherringham and Cromer we meet a "Black Shuck" et cetera, et cetera. There surely must be equal job opportunities for an enormous White dog somewhere in the mix?' he said. 'I just think that it is unfair that the Black Hounds get all of the bad publicity when it comes to the luring and tearing out of throats in general...'

Throughout this exchange, the Farmer and his Wife swivelled their heads from side to side as if watching a particularly energetic rally at Wimbledon. The Farmer's Rich Tea biscuit had fallen into his cocoa, and floundered there like a soggy island.

"Trevor the Terrible Terrier of Treorchy" ...' said Merry.

'Was he an evil Messenger from Hell?' asked the farmer.

'Not as such..' said Merry, 'but he didn't half bite my Dad's ankle when we were on holiday'.

Conscious that they had already enjoyed a considerable amount of free hospitality from their hosts, the boys decided to thank them graciously, and return to their canvas hotel. The farmer's wife packed them off with an enormous bag of home-baked goodies, which would have to be kept away from Davis at all costs - just in case he had his "jam tart radar" turned on. His skills in pastry detection were legendary. This was a boy who could actually hear chicken pie...

They strode off down the lonely farm track under a half moon. The rain had finally stopped, or perhaps popped home to get more water. The boys continued their discussion about the merits of various canine breeds, and their inherent homicidal tendencies. 'I mean - what about The Hound of the Baskervilles'? asked Jackson, 'he was a big white dog wasn't he?'

'I think you will find that his colouration was due to painted-on phosphorescence...' said Calderman.

'What about Lassie then?' asked Merry

'How do you mean?' said Nicky

'Well Lassie could have turned nasty if unduly provoked, and perhaps it was him who actually pushed them children down the old mine shaft?'

'Yeah - but we are talking about Lassie here...He would have at least phoned for a Paramedic' said Merry.

Weatherill spun around, directing his torch over the moor and the gorse bushes, which threw up odd and disturbing shadows across the field. Just before he turned the beam of the torch back to the front, Nicky and a couple of the boys were sure that they had seen the torchlight reflect back from a pair of large red eyes...

Walking a little faster than they were willing to admit, and with an ear cocked in case of Hell Hound attack, they finally came to their tent. After checking the inside, Calderman had declared it fit for human habitation. Tired and a little fed up, the boys readied themselves for sleep. There were the usual comings-and-goings for those boys who really needed to go. Finally, Weatherill had turned off his torch. Kendy was the last one into the tent, and eased himself into the last space available on the edge of the groundsheet. There were various murmurs of 'G'night...' from the friends. Nicky turned over to massage some comfort into his ad-lib 'pillow', and saw in the dim light his friend Kendy. The boy was already asleep- with his arm lying over an enormous black hound. It opened one glowing red eye at Nicky, then lay down again with his new friend, and began to snore.

As unbelievable as it may sound, back in Nicky's village, Uncle Joe was in trouble again. He had been hard at work in the shed at the bottom of the garden, when a group of the village children had come to his house. They were having a "water fight", and pleaded for Uncle Joe to join them.

They had proved to be no match for Uncle Joe - and his kettle...

Goodwill was sitting back in his office chair and sipping his morning tea. He had just enjoyed a forbidden Bakewell Tart (hmmm...since there were no eye witnesses, we may have to draw our own rather sordid conclusions...). So: they planned to retire him, did they? Well when he was able to show them that he personally had masterminded the schemes for filling the Academy bank accounts to bursting point- they would be forced to conclude that they could not do without him. His Grand Plan was coming together nicely. There would soon be a series of events which would draw in the crowds. He would welcome each and every member of The Great Unwashed into his school with open arms- providing that they turned up with an open wallet. Just the thought of the merchandising alone made him salivate. He had faced down the aggressive and argumentative Brooks, and had bent him to his iron will. The rest of the Staff would be easy prey. He chuckled to himself as he thought of his recent triumph, when he had successfully argued the case for a high-tec security camera and monitoring system to be installed throughout the Academy. The Board of Trustees had wilted under the pressure of his diatribe on Safety and Security. He had obtained the release of twenty thousand pounds from Academy funds, for the purpose of installing the systems. In order to maximise the amount of money that he could "siphon off" into his own account, and minimise the actual cost of doing a barely adequate job- he had called in that pinnacle of local electrical skill, namely, Biggley's Electricals.

Mr Biggley had rushed round to the Academy in his two-tone van (white and rust). He was attired with all the sartorial elegance of a landfill site. Having had the job described to him by Goodwill, he had hooked his greasy thumbs into the pockets of his equally greasy overalls, and executed the slow intake of breath which translated as 'This is gonna cost you Pal...'. His Apprentice "Big Norman" looked up at his Boss. Actually, he had little choice in the matter - as Norm was a mere three feet and three inches tall. Goodwill stared at the small man, and knew that he could save a great deal of money by getting

Norm to crawl through the ducting in order to lay the electrical cable. Yes, the Head Master certainly knew a nice little earner when he saw one.

The job had been agreed, with many a corner cut, and much financial slight of the handage department. In nearly every room within the Academy, there was now a wall-mounted security camera box fitted. Some of the cameras even worked. The main monitor screens and control box were located in the office of Miss Piggott, who studied the screens like some evil James Bond Villain - with blue hair and a plate of Dundee cake.

Across the road from the safety and imagined security of the Academy, a rather urgent and animated conversation was taking place between Dr Matthews and the Landlord of the "Five Crowns". Matthews currently had a grip on the poor man's tie, and had pulled him over the bar until he was nose-to-nose with him. The Landlord was desperately trying to plead his case: 'No Sir- I never suggested for one moment that you were mentally unstable...'

'You damn well did, you Bounder - when I explained about how the state of the front of my garden was causing me problems...'

'But if you remember, it was you yourself that said that the problem was so bad, that what you really needed was to get Counselling...'

'I said that I NEEDED TO GET THE COUNCIL IN... You insolent Pup!' said Matthews.

Much offended by this completely understandable mistake, Matthews decided to steady his nerve with another pint of Scruttocks Old Despicable, with a large whisky chaser. Since he could not rely on the athletic prowess of that chaser, he ordered a large cognac - which he thought would beat it to the finishing line. In the dugout, sat a large gin and tonic- in case an emergency substitution had to be made. Just as he was settling down to the business of pleasant anaesthesia, the pub door came open, and in came a face which Matthews nearly recognised through his alcoholic fog.

'Hello Gus! Said the possible non-stranger...Can I buy you a pint?'

'I should say so! Capital idea - well done that Chap!' exclaimed Matthews. 'I say Dear Boy- you're the new fellow aren't you? How are you (hic) fun-fan-finding things at the Arct-Arse-Accid- School then?'

'You have all made me very welcome, thank you' said Mr Posta 'But if I can ask you a question, has anyone seen Mr Duggan recently?'

Matthews pondered, floundered, focussed and finally remembered: 'Ah yes- big lad...plays about with metal and the like upstairs somewhere - talks a bit Scottish (never seen him in a kilt, mind you) and swears at you if you borrow a screwdriver?'

'That's the chap...' said Posta.

'No- not a sign since he went off with that Figg character - don't like him at all - bad egg don't cher know-dodgy type if you ask me - eyes too close together (burp)...and his matey boys - criminal sort if you ask me (you didn't did you?), can't stand that sort - something (hic) not (fart) quite right with 'em - did you say a Pint?' answered Matthews.

Posta downed his half, placed another foaming glass in front of Matthews, and left by the same door he came in.

'Was that fella from the Council?' Matthews asked the Landlord.

'No Sir- he said he is one of your colleagues at the Academy.' the barman replied.

'Do the Council know that he is doing two jobs - by Gad?' said Matthews.

'Nice of him to buy you a drink though Sir...?'

'Oh Yes Please...Mine's a Pint.' said a happy Dr Matthews.

'And that's about the size of it...' said Brooks to Mrs Finucane. The two had arranged a clandestine meeting at one of the small cafes in the town. They sat in the back corner of the little establishment, plotting their response to the apparent blackmail being meted out to them by the Headmaster.

'Well Oi think he's some sort of cheeky old bastard...' said Agent J-Cloth 'And this is after me cleanin' and moppin' and toidyin' up after himself and the rest of them eejits for years: well Oi tell ye - there's a big boot needs to be applied to the arse of Himself, and no mistake...'

'I think that we should do what the bugger wants.' said Brooks

'Jaysus! - are ye after gettin' a bang on the head or what?' said a horrified Mrs F.

'No- hear me out...I said that we should do exactly what he wants, and I mean exactly. He wants a statue that produces water - well I shall see to it that he gets it. He wants to "go out with a bang" does he? Well I 'ope that the old Miser has got good earplugs - because I intend to give him a bang that he will never forget. When the bloody dust settles, we'll see just who is left standing. He thinks that with all these fancy schemes and daft ideas that he is going to make a bomb - well two can play at that bloody game...'

Mrs Finucane did not answer Brooks. The look on his face was enough to force her into silence. She had seen that expression once before, when his beloved cricket pitch had been vandalised as an end-of-term prank. He had found out the name of the individual who had perpetrated the crime, and strode into the Academy armed with a cricket stump, with which to exact his dastardly revenge. Waiting until the stump had at least been removed; Brooks had telephoned the hospital, and asked in a loud voice- 'Owizzee...?'.

The sun had risen on a quite beautiful autumn morn: moorland birds were singing, larks were larking about, and corncrakes were looking for more corn with which to crake. The early mist had evaporated, leaving a diamond-glistening dew across the fields.

In this particular field stood two middle-aged men in cagoules. Next to them were two vehicles. One was a bright yellow AA response van, and the other was a Volvo estate car. The vehicles were easy to tell apart from each other, as only one of them was completely filled with cow shit. The driver of the AA van was leaning against the side of his cab, crying with laughter and banging on the side of the van.

'I think it's flooded!!' he announced - before collapsing into more hysterical fits of laughter.

Rundell and Chambers had instructed the boys to get up, get packed, and get on their way as soon as possible. The boys were now striding their way across the limestone edge, on their way to the first stopping point, some twenty miles away. They would reach this with ease if they kept the pace up - and if the weather held. Kendy had set off ahead of the main party, and was busy enjoying hands-on study of the countryside. He called over to Nicky 'Look! I have found my first grass snake - how wonderful!' Nicky had replied that what the boy had found was in fact his first Adder, and he should carefully put it back where he had found it. "Mortimer", the huge stray dog which seemed to have adopted Kendy, was busy frolicking in the gorse, chasing rabbits, and generally bounding around - having a hell of a good time. As the gang crossed a junction which had last seen a motor vehicle in 1974, they noticed a car drive up to the "give way" sign. The window was wound down, and a head poked out, scanning the road in all directions. It then drove off at high speed, leaving the unmistakable odour of an expired MOT certificate hanging in the air. 'Did you see that car?' asked Merry- 'I'm sure that was Swall and Fletcher who help out with the Archaeology Society: it looked like they were searching for something, or somebody?' 'Probably just lost.' said Calderman. 'It's a long way to come, just to get lost...' said Davis

'Yeah - but they wouldn't have come this far if they hadn't got lost in the first place' Jackson answered. As the boy spoke, a bus came up the long road and rattled past the boys. As it passed, the gang saw the other camping party of boys waving to them from the back seats.

'Well - the cheatin' bastards...' said Merry- with feeling.

Mr Brooks had stripped and cleaned the water pump from the old fountain. He had taken his time, because if a job is worth doing, then it is worth doing well. For what he had in mind, the mechanism had to be in perfect working order. On a long bench in his "workshop" was an old life-size statue reputed to resemble good old St Onan himself - with a hollow space cut out of the back, to enable the pumping mechanism to be fitted. He would fit the pump, test the works, and then refit the stone at the back leaving no trace of a crack or seam. He would then use all of his skills to "age" the stone, so that it would show no trace of ever being tampered with. He was whistling a little tune as he worked. Why, he hadn't felt this happy in ages.

'I am telling you Loopy - never again...never EVER again...' said Hyde-Jones.

'I don't see what you are so angry about, Roy.' answered Mr Newhouse..

'You promised me that we were going to have a good night out, with a couple of beers, and watch a decent Rock band.'

'And so we did - that's exactly what happened.'

'Oh yeah - plus or minus a couple little incidents which I notice you seemed to have forgotten to mention?'

'Like what, exactly?'

'Like the "couple of beers" turned out to be what I believe are referred to as "Depth Charges". And the Tequila shots which seemed to appear out of thin air? And the six "Black Russians" which you said we had to have, to celebrate Peter's Birthday'.

'That's right- it was his Birthday...'

'Okay, okay...and, refresh my memory if you will: who is "Peter" may I ask?'

'My Hamster.'

'So, we gave ourselves liquid brain damage and the risk of kidney failure all for the sake of a Hamster's Birthday?'

'Well be fair Roy - the poor things don't live all that long.'

'Neither will I if I let you throw booze down my neck like that again.' said Hyde-Jones.

Newhouse gave his friend the smile normally witnessed before a major hangover.

'And then, just to put the icing on the cake - there was the other little matter' said Roy, with just a hint of major disapproval in his voice. 'I refer to the small matter of your impromptu appearance with the featured Artists at the gig.'

'I got chatting to them - they were really nice girls...' said Newhouse.

'That may well have been the case, but you took it upon yourself to get up onto the stage with them'.

'They asked me to...'

'They were in the middle of a song, Loopy...'

'Yeah - but I told them that I knew all of the words...'

'That is not the point- and well you know it'

'They were playing *The Green Manalishi with the Two-Pronged Crown*, and they told me to come on stage with them.'

'Yes - and you were, not to put too fine a point on it - stark bollock naked...'

'Ah...'

'From where I was standing, I could only see one "Prong" my friend - and so could the audience, and that Policewoman who arrested you.'

'Yeah, but she let us off, didn't she?'

'Yes, what an absolute stroke of luck that you used to go out with her many years ago, or we would still be in the back of that van. I can still hear the sniggering...'

'She gave you her phone number.'

'That is as may be...When next we sally forth; it will be to the theatre. You will behave. You will at all times remain fully clothed. You will refrain from heckling, and you will not get me to drink myself unconscious during the interval - do I make myself clear?'

'Yes Dad...'

The two looked at each other. Hyde-Jones grinned at his friend:
'Bloody great night though, wasn't it Loopy!'
'Groovy Royster - groovy...'

Chapter Seven:

The rain held off.

Splashing through small lakes and peaty puddles were a group of young men who found that they were actually quite enjoying themselves, out in the expanse of the Wild Country. Every so often, they paused on their trek, and the heavy tent was swapped over to each boy in turn. Mortimer, the "adopted" mascot of Kendy even took a turn, before bounding off with the load into the distance - returning with a boot which he had found (luckily there was no foot inside it.). The conversations now reverted to the bizarre exchanges which were a regular feature of the group's daily contact.

'I'll tell you something which I can never understand.' said Calderman

'What's that?' asked Nicky.

'Japanese.' answered his friend.

'I've got a wasp up my nose...' wailed Merry.

'D'you know Lads: - Oi keep gettin' this feelin' that Oi 'ave 'ad Déjà-vu before...' said Trevill.

'When's dinner?' asked Davis.

'My Dad bought me the DVD of the film 'Pirates of the Caribbean' for my birthday.' said Jackson. 'I played the extra disc which said, 'Deleted Scenes'- and there was nothing on it...'

'What were the 'X'-Files, after they were files?' asked Nicky.

Mortimer the mascot came bouncing up to the group, and Merry noticed a problem. 'Oh Hell, Guys - he has lost the tent! Now we are really in trouble.' Suddenly, and without due warning, "Mortimer" became Kendy right in front of them. 'Jesus Kendy...!' said Calderman - 'don't do that again, you scared the living daylights out of us!' Kendy just laughed and ran off to locate his new-found best canine pal.

At the halfway point of the walk, a Volvo estate car sat in a lay-by with all of its doors wide open. The driver and passenger stood some way away from the vehicle, and scowled in opposite directions.

Outside the Jewellers shop of Ingle and Son on the high street, a battered Nissan car sat with its rear doors open, and its engine running. The driver was scanning the road in a highly-agitated manner.

'You really do have to do something about that "vortex" of yours, you know.' said Darwin to Professor Strangler, 'it's all starting to get a bit out of hand.' 'It's not "my vortex" Dear Boy.' answered the Professor, 'it sort of just "occurred". His colleague regarded him with a quizzical eye: 'Well you need to do something to stop anything that feels like it just popping through for a wander around. I mean, people are beginning to notice'. Darwin picked up the tennis ball which had been dropped at his feet. He picked the ball up again, and said 'Good Boy- fetch the nice ball for the Teacher...', before throwing it away down the lawn outside the Physics lab. The small dinosaur wagged its tail, and sped off after the ball, enjoying the game. Strangler regarded the creature as it caught up with the bouncing ball and caught it delicately. 'You might be correct- it does look a bit like a Velociraptor...'

The box had arrived this morning. In truth, the Reverend had been up since the crack of dawn, like an excited child on Christmas morning. He couldn't wait for it to get here. It had been a case of 'see it-want it-order it' for the Rev. There was just something about the look of the thing which had spoken directly to the Rev's tarnished soul, and the voice had said "Buy Me Now". Just the vision of the object in the catalogue had sent his trembling hand straight to his credit card. It was elegant, it was black, and it was everything that he could possibly wish for. This would draw gasps of admiration (and he hoped, no small amount of jealousy) from his friends when they saw it. No matter if the Headmaster had banned them from the Academy - the old fool could look on in wonder at its futuristic splendour, and weep.

The doorbell tried its best to ring out with its death-march melody. The Rev leapt up out of his armchair, and attempted to walk to his front door in the manner of James Bond. On the whole, a smoking jacket would have much better suited the chosen image - as his black towelling dressing-gown was now extremely battle-scarred, where the goat had opted to feast on most of the left sleeve. He opened the door in anticipation:

'Parcel for the name of Belchinharm...' said the Postman.

'I think you will find that is "Felchingham"..' said the Rev.

'It don't say that on the label' replied the Postman, 'It says "Riverbend Belchinharm".'

'What address does it say on the label?' asked the Rev, impatiently.

'Says 'number 13, Harms Way' replied Postie 'Is that you Mate?'

'Yes, yes...that's me- can I have my parcel please?'

'You said that it wasn't you a minute ago.' said Postie, taking the parcel back out of the Rev's reach.

'It's a mis-print, then, obviously.' said Felchingham.

'It don't mention a 'Miss Print' Mate- it says 'Riverbend Belchinharm...'

'Look here...' said the Rev- now exasperated 'The sender of the parcel is a firm called "CallFirstDirectSameday" of Brighton- alright? The serial number of the item is 066356561/27, and I am the planned recipient of said item, the Reverend Felchingham of number 13 Harms Way, Granchester. Here is my photographic identification. This is me - I am still me, and I have no plans to be anyone else -understand?'

'Well when will this "Miss Print" be back then?' asked Postie.

'I will see that she gets it - now can I have the parcel please?' said the Rev.

'No - 'fraid not...' said Postie.

'WHY THE HELL NOT???' shouted the Rev.

'You 'ave to sign for it...' answered Postie. The Rev hastily scribbled a signature on the grubby pad that was offered to him.

'Thank you, Mr Riverbend, - and pass on my best wishes to Miss Print when you see her...' said Postie.

The Rev grabbed the parcel and slammed the front door. He rushed off down the hall, and found himself sprawled upon the carpet, as an intact remnant of the dressing-gown was trapped in the front door. Houdini-like, our man tore himself out of the garment, and sped into the living room. He sat in his chair and placed the parcel on the coffee-table in front of him. He opened the box like a sacred relic. He removed the mobile phone from its box, hardly daring to take it out of its plastic wrapping. Oh yes - this was top-of-the-range this was. Just wait until those other mere mortals saw this little beauty in action. Smart Move, Smart Man- and now a Smart Phone.

He plugged in the charging unit and began to ready the phone for use. So many people to call - so many frie-...well none as yet, but he soon would have when they saw that he was now a master of new technology. He checked the number of the phone. Oh yes indeed - it was 07666 666666 as ordered. All was well. The Rev thought that a cup of tea (black of course) was just the thing to celebrate with, so he skipped off into the kitchen, whilst the new phone prepared itself... Having finished chuckling at the misfortunes of people who had called in to the local radio station phone-in, he extracted his mystic runic toast from his special mystic runic toaster (£59.99 from "Enchantments", 22-24 High Street, Wittering), and took his tea into the living room. Even as he sat down, he could see the steady blink of the ice-blue light in the corner of the phone. Wow!!! He had only just received the new phone - and already he had received his very first message!

He peeled the protective plastic film from the screen. He turned on the phone, and hummed along with the cheery "welcome" jingle. He touched the icon for "messages", and the screen appeared - one message. He pressed the tab to hear the details of his first contact, and a pleasant female voice informed him that 'You have one new Voicemail message: to hear your message- please press 1 on your phone.'. Wonderful! As he pressed the number as instructed, he thought of what the message might be? Had he won some sort of competition? Had he qualified for a special offer of some description? The possibilities were endless...

The pleasant female voice informed him 'Message begins...'

There was silence for a few seconds, and then what he thought was a throaty chuckle.

A familiar voice said 'Ha Ha Ha Ha HA!!! – YOU'RE STILL A KNOB...'

The Staff lounge suffering from its usual atmosphere of "Entente Corblimey", as the various Heads of Department proffered their suggestions for the first of the "Ghost Walks" which was soon to take place.

'I mean to say, I don't think that I would be a suitable "ghost" at all..' said Professor Strangler, 'I cannot say that I am happy leaping out on the General Public'.

'Especially since the Magistrate gave you that Restraining order...!' said Mr Newhouse.

The Physics Tutor scowled at him, and Loopy gave him a cheery wave in return. Hyde-Jones took charge of the room: 'Now look - it will only take about five of us to slap on a bit of zombie-style makeup and loiter around corners, looking a bit scary'

'Sorry- what was that about makeup?' said Mr Thwaite, looking up from his copy of *Today's Woman* magazine...

'I said that what we need to do is get a few of us done up in raggy old clothes, with a bit of white makeup, and a good covering of white powder to look like dust. All we really need to do is to be seen, or glimpsed, lurching around the old school, and the punters will think that they have got a bargain. We have some decent Period clothing in the drama props store, so it shouldn't be too hard to create the right look'.

'But do think that I for instance, would be able to pull it off?' asked Madame.

'Buy me a drink - and we'll talk...' answered Mr Newhouse.

At this ad-lib, the meeting (such as it was) descended into the fracas that all Staff meetings were prone to become, sooner or later. Hyde-Jones banged on the table for quiet, and having more or less achieved it, carried on: 'Look- all I am saying is that if we are going to do it at all, then we might as well take it seriously and at least try to do the best job that we can. We will have to sort out the locations for each "ghost", but off the top of my head, I would probably suggest one outside the Library, one walking through the Dining Hall cloister, one or two kids just inside the Boarding House lobby, one at the top of the Old School staircase, and we could take one more up the back corridor - STOP LAUGHING, LOOPY...'

Hyde-Jones was forced to admit defeat at this point, and called the meeting to a temporary close. He himself now had a fit of the giggles, and his friend Newhouse was lying on the floor, crying with laughter. What was he to do about the Boy...? Eventually, Newhouse recovered from his hysterics, and said 'Sorry about that...Actually, I'll have a word with my mate Dennis - he works in the Special Effects department for a film company. I'm sure that he'll be able to help us out with a few bits and pieces that will help us frighten the sh - the life out of our "guests". I'll give him a call tonight'.

Even Madame was impressed by Mr Newhouse's suggestion, right up until he passed her on the way out of the Staff room that is: as his impish sense of humour had once again kicked in.

'Nice to see that The Twins are okay...' he said to her, as he ducked out of the door.

Well- that's another coffee cup which she would have to replace...

The boys had set up camp and bedded down for the night. This time, they had pitched their tent in the lee of a dry-stone wall and a thick cluster of trees. They lay in the tent discussing the Academy and the Staff in general. 'There's something going on...' said Calderman, 'Goodwill was in one heck of a foul mood in the Assembly just before we left'. 'Yeah - and I saw old Albert Brooks storming up the path to his office' said Merry. Nicky added 'Well I suppose we'll find out all about it when we get back. Has Kendy come back yet?' Jackson answered him: 'No, he's still out sniffing trees with Mortimer'. Davis, munching on a late-night packet of something particularly noisy, said 'I don't mind Kendy letting the dog sleep in here with us, but you must admit that there is quite a smell. Do you think that we should say something?' Trevill thought for a second, then answered 'Well as far as Oi'm concerned, that there 'ound will just 'ave to get used to it...' The conversation veered...

'What did Matron do before she came to the Academy?' asked Merry

'Mr Newhouse told me that she worked in S&M...'

'My Nan buys all of her pants from them.' said Davis.

Kendy returned. Mortimer climbed over the recumbent boys and chose a spot which he liked. The rest of the gang were soon fast asleep. The now domesticated Hound of Hell decided to spend the night giving flatulence lessons free of charge.

Although it was almost midnight, in the Academy cleaners' store, a light burned in the corner. A meeting was taking place. Amidst the toilet rolls, hand towels and spare mop heads, a plan was coming together.

'Do we have everything for "Operation Anti-Gravity"?' said Brooks

'Oi have all me bits and pieces ready an' waitin' Surr...' answered Agent J-Cloth.

'Good work Mrs F - we will put the plan into operation tomorrow night, just in time for the return of that stuck-up pillock. I can't wait to see the look on his face. I have the big steps ready, and I'll confirm by radio when we are ready to move'.

'Did ye finish the statue, Albert?' said Mrs Finucane

'Oh yes indeed - and a grand job it is too, even if I say so myself. I tested it this mornin' and it works a treat. When this plan takes off we'll have old misery guts out on his arse before he knows what has hit him...'

Poor Uncle Joe just couldn't understand it. It seemed that whichever way he turned, trouble seemed to follow him like a high-street charity "Chugger". He began to wonder if that woman in the supermarket really had placed a Voodoo curse on him, after he innocently asked her if he might help her with her melons. Once again, he found himself in front of the Magistrate, with whom he was now on first-name terms; he had even received a Birthday card from the man, enclosing a ten-pound note. He stood shame-faced in front of the bench, whilst the Magistrate considered what penalty he could possibly impose upon him. It all ended rather well as far as Uncle was concerned. Rather than impose some harsh and draconian punishment upon Joe, the Magistrate had declared that Joe should perform a service which would be of benefit to the Community at large (even though Uncle had pointed out that he was only a "medium"). Joe was to give lessons in English to newly -arrived Foreign Immigrants, and make sure that they had a solid grounding in our language and customs. This would greatly assist the new arrivals to integrate into the wider Society, and would enable Joe to perform work of value. Joe listened patiently to the speech which the Magistrate gave, and readily agreed to the plan (although he was not sure what a "paragon" actually was - maybe some sort of spice?). And thus, it had begun...

Perhaps the Official had failed to notice Uncle's somewhat eclectic sense of humour, or spot that he tended to approach life from a different angle than most - but either way, he had singularly failed to allow for the fact that Joe's weird and wonderful sense of humour would manifest itself sooner or later. The "lessons" had begun quite normally, and the students became more and more proficient at the language and its usage. It was when Uncle came to give the definitions of some particular words that the "fun factor" switch had tripped - and Joe had decided to re-write certain sections of the Dictionary in his own inimitable style. Much to the confusion of his "pupils", Joe gave several alternative definitions for everyday words:

'Impending' (according to Uncle) – 'The death of a Pixie...'
'Tadpole' – 'Slightly Polish...'
'Transistor' – 'A Nun with large, hairy hands'
'Midwifery' – 'Half way through a fart'
'Jocular' – 'A Scottish Vampire'

(Some were words that Joe had decided to invent for the fun of it, such as):

'Chafe' – 'A wealthy Chav'

'A La Carte' – 'A Muslim wheelbarrow'

'Shambolic' – 'A fake testicle'

'Cloisterophobia' – 'A fear of Monks'

'Crèche' – 'A motor accident in Knightsbridge'

'Diversity' – 'A Welsh College'

What was slightly more worrying was his explanation about what course of action that should be taken if the individual ever witnessed a threatening situation or a fight. Joe explained that all English people had a tremendous respect for their ancient Monarch Richard the Lionheart. He told them that it was the wish of all true Englishmen to be regarded as brave and valiant as he. He also explained about the abbreviated use of the name "Richard". Uncle had told the various groups that the best way to stop any threat of violence, was to approach the biggest and most threatening protagonist, and inform him that he was displaying all of the heroic and stout-hearted characteristics of the former ruler of the land. He should be shaken by the hand, and told 'My word- you certainly are a Real Dick...' This was guaranteed to instantly calm the situation.

It would probably not be until the poor individuals sat some sort of written or oral examination, that Uncle's linguistic terrorism would come to light, by which time he would have paid his debt to Society, and would have fitted a new lock on the shed...

Jedekiah sat with his head in his hands. This was most unlike the man, who was normally untroubled by any of life's problems, and always had a ready answer to any given situation. 'What ails Thee, Husband?' asked his Wife Jedekylie (she had chosen the name after something which she had heard, and now couldn't get it out of her head...) 'I think that there should be a summoning of the Elders, Wife of mine...we have much to consider. It may even be the time to once again raise our heads, and think of walking aloft...I fear that I may no longer have the strength or courage to prevent my people from wanting to take their place in the Uplands...'

'Art Thou certain of this, Husband?' said the woman.

'No - I am not certain at all...and that is why there must be a Summoning' he replied.

Left-Right-Left-Right...the boys marched onward (apart from Merry, who was going Left-Left-Left, because he was hopping at the moment). They were making good time and covering good distance. With Calderman's informal leadership, and the expert map reading skills of Kendy (minus the one map that Mortimer had eaten), the trek was turning into quite an enjoyable experience. Their walking had been interrupted when out of nowhere, a hang-glider had swooped down on them, the flyer laughing as the group of boys flung themselves to the wet ground. The laughter was cut short when Mortimer had leapt into the air and brought down the reckless pilot - pinning him to the wet earth and mercilessly slobbering over his face. As the Hound returned to the company of the boys, the downed airman shook a fist at them and shouted out a variety of threats, until Mortimer turned a glowing red eye upon him, at which point he hid himself under the twisted remnants of his expensive kite.

'Nearly there Chaps!! One more night and we're home and dry' said Calderman.

'I would settle for dry...' said Nicky.

'Do Ee think that fish ever get thirsty?' asked Trevill.

'What happens if you get scared half to death - twice?' said Merry.

'Was it Divorced, Beheaded, Survived, Died- or Divorced, Died, Beheaded, Survived?' said Nicky.

'Are you trying to remember the Six Wives of Henry VIII' asked Calderman?'

'No - sorry...' said Nicky, 'I was just thinking about Cousin Shelia's Boyfriends...'

As the miles piled up behind them (whoever he is...) the boys reached the site for their final night of wilderness exposure. As with most teenagers, the conversation had come around to the subject of Girlfriends. Most of the gang had not yet embarked upon that unnerving and perilous journey into the world of "relationships". They had friends who just happened to be Girls - so what of it? However, it was a well-known fact that the tousled good looks and irresistible personality of the boy Weatherill had already turned him into some sort of "Babe Magnet". He took the attention which he received from the Female of the Species with his customary ease. Even at the age of thirteen (and a half -almost) he had acquired several ardent admirers. Informally within the gang of friends, he was often referred to as "The

Weather Man". This title came due to the fact that although the day might well begin with Raine - it would be Claudia later tonight...

'Do you think that your Sister Angela would go out with me if I asked her?' said Jackson to his friend Davis.

'Not if you were the last man on earth, Mate!' he replied.

'Yeah- knowing my luck, I would probably be killed in the crush...' said a crestfallen Jackson.

Ponder as he might, Nicky was not at all sure just why his feelings toward the "recently -Gothed" Jozza, were a little confused. When he got the chance to speak to Wetherill privately, he would get his friend's advice. Whether he would possibly dare to take that advice was a completely different matter.

The boys got tented, fed and settled own before their "Custodians" turned up at the arranged meeting point. As the car pulled into the camping area, all of the lads couldn't help but notice that the vehicle resembled a mobile estate Christmas tree. From the rear view mirror, from rear door handles, and any possible appendage that would support them, hung a veritable forest of air fresheners. These hanging devices swung alarmingly as the car came to a halt, and gave the impression that it was being driven by a travelling earring salesman...The two occupants got out of the car and exchanged angry glances, before Rundell barked at the boys: 'You all know what to do - now get on with it. I want no tomfoolery on our last night out. I have no idea who vandalised my car - but rest assured Gentlemen: I shall find out. When I do… no amount of bleating from you or your parents will save you from the punishment which I intend to meet out'.

'I think that it has hit the fan.' said Merry, quietly.

'Oh yes, indeedy..' said Nicky 'and the air conditioner, the mirror, the floor mats, and the radio...'

Without further ado, the boys pitched camp and disappeared inside their tent. With Rundell in this frame of mind, it was best to leave him alone. Chambers was none too happy either, and when he had collected the route maps from the boys, had snatched them out of their hands with undue force. When darkness descended, the lads had sneaked out of the tent, and spent a while gazing up at the stars, whilst Nicky (feeling rather embarrassed about Kendy's significantly greater knowledge of all things celestial) had shown them all the Constellations and some of the notable features which were just visible to the naked eye. Kendy himself was very sad. His new friend Mortimer had jumped up at him, placed a huge paw on each of his shoulders, licked his face, and bounded back off onto the Moors. The normally unemotional Kendy had found that his face was wet with tears: but vowed to return and meet up with his buddy as soon as he possibly could. Merry saw the look on the face of his friend...

'I know how you feel Mate...' he told him 'I felt just as upset when my pet mouse "Elvis" died.'

'I am so sorry -What happened to him?' asked Kendy

'He got caught in a trap...' said Merry.

Chapter Eight:

The coaches arrived bright and early to pick up the boys. The drivers were complaining about the early morning start which they had been forced to make. As far as they were concerned, there were two "six-thirties" in a working day, and they had no desire to be seeing both of them. With scarcely a word spoken, the Masters had supervised the loading of the transport, and had then loaded themselves into Rundell's car with indecent haste. The Volvo had set off from the site with a screech of tyres, and would not slow down again, until Chambers noticed the badger which had stowed away in the back of the vehicle. The Police car had been following them out of the Peak District National Park, and was most intrigued by the swerving progress of the car. They had pulled the vehicle onto the hard shoulder of the road, and had been shocked when a sleepy badger had made a break for freedom once the car door had been opened. The small matter as to why the occupants had thirty-four air fresheners in the car was never fully discussed.

The buses had deposited each boy back in his village on the way home. Nicky was glad that he did not have to endure a day's schooling after the events of the last four days, and settled for a long hot bath and a chat with Mum and Auntie. It emerged that Uncle Joe was currently engaged in something that he had called "Black Ops". Upon further questioning, this had turned out not to be undercover secret operations - but a little job which Joe had on the side, where he swept chimneys for those people with a solid fuel fire. Nicky had enjoyed a celebratory meal of egg and chips (with tea out of an enamel mug - don't ask me why it tasted better, it just did...) and then gone to bed ridiculously early and pretty much flaked out for a good eight hours. In the morning, Mum and Auntie had expected a full and detailed account of the boy's encounters with nature, but to be honest, Nicky was just grateful to be back in the bosom of civilisation, and couldn't yet muster up the enthusiasm with which to recount the trip in full. He would certainly have to manufacture a version of events which didn't include rampaging sheep, tractor theft, manure delivery, or demonic hell-hounds who chased sticks and farted all night...

Meeting up at the Academy, the "Survivors Club" of friends collected together as always in their corner of the quad. 'Any news?' asked Nicky, as Davis fought with the wrapper on a particularly troublesome Mars Bar. 'Only bad I'm afraid...' said Calderman. 'DeVere got caught at Bakewell train station. Silly sod rode the bull into the station car park and tied it up. He might have got away with it- but they noticed that he hadn't paid for parking.'

Apart from the various chat about Bonfire Night (who was going to be invited to attend what bonfire party, and where - plus what firework was the one which should be inserted into Lordsley), the main excitement was the forthcoming "Ghost Walk". Nicky and the gang had all made a bee-line for Mr Hyde-Jones, and immediately offered their combined scaring services. The plan had been explained to them by the Master, and the boys were allocated various sites at which they would "haunt" the Public. There was one rather disconcerting problem, as far as the boys were concerned. The plan for the Ghost Walk involved opening up and using some of the tunnels beneath the Academy (at least the ones of which the Staff were aware). Nicky and the boys knew that the honest and correct course of action must be to contact the "Groundlings", not only making them aware of the plan to use some of the tunnels, but preserving their privacy at all costs. They had great respect for the people who they had discovered were living beneath their seat of learning, and would seek to help preserve their community by any means at their disposal.

It had begun two years earlier, when the boys had stumbled around the passages in the pitch darkness, and stumbled across the grand meeting room that the Groundlings used for their communal gatherings. Rather than attacking the boys, the people below had welcomed them warmly: their only insistence being that none of the gang would disclose their secret to the world above. It was a secret that had endured for hundreds of years....

The Academy had been founded by a group of scholarly Monks in around the year 1556. They were soon to feel the winds of Religious persecution blowing across the land. With this in mind, the wise Monks began to construct a labyrinthine network of hide-aways and tunnels beneath what was then, just a collection of small buildings surrounding the church. The Dissolution of the Monasteries was in full swing, and the Monks began to disappear below ground more and more frequently as danger threatened. They were joined in the tunnels by a small band of families who also wished to escape persecution. With all of the chaos taking place above, their periods below ground became longer and longer, as did the tunnels which they constantly extended by the light of crude candles. Weeks of hiding had become months, and almost without a conscious effort, underground life became to be accepted as normal for the group.

They had originally planned to leave the restriction of their tunnels in the 1640s, a plan which was hastily abandoned, as 'scouts' to the upper world had returned with news of the Civil War which was raging on the surface. The group continued to live their lives beneath the now expanding Academy, adapting their system of passages to permit them access to the kitchens of the buildings above their heads. Meetings were held, and although there were pockets of dissent from the fast-growing community of underground dwellers, it was decided that for the time being- they should remain below and 'ride out' the conflicts which were taking place above (at what point the vows of celibacy were permitted to "lapse" was never determined, but obviously, the Monks must have played some part in the enlargement of the community beneath the School).

In any case, they had heard about the great plague of 1665, and received news of the Great Fire of London in 1666, and decided that underground was the safest place to be for the time being (admittedly, Granchester was nowhere near the great City of London - but you know how news travels). So, the Groundling Community seemed to have flourished, prospered and grown for many years. They remained a deeply religious unit, and one visitor to the upper world was to return with a large leather and iron bound copy of the Bible. This book had been tossed aside when the old monastery above had been ransacked, and was badly fire damaged: nevertheless, it became the object of veneration for the Groundlings - being given its own hand-carved lectern on which to stand in the centre of their great meeting hall. Couples wishing to be married would meet across the lectern, and would have their union solemnised by placing their hands upon the Holy Book. As with any community, there were births, marriages, and of course deaths. It was a strange quirk of the living conditions that having located the graveyard above them, their dearly departed were buried above their heads – "Six Feet Over", as the Groundlings would say.

In the following years, there had been carious times where the community had decided to forsake their underground living - and return to the surface. Each time a decision to do this was taken (and the required number of votes cast in favour) there was seemingly yet another conflict taking place above their heads. The world above did not seem to be a safe place to visit, let alone live. Maybe they would give it a few more weeks, and see if things calmed down "upstairs", before they made a decision.

If you cast time forward three hundred years (well, they were busy extending tunnels and building - you know how long some little DIY jobs can end up taking), there came the Spring of 1914. They had heard about the outbreak of War in Europe.

Just at the point that they thought that now might be the time to emerge into the sunlight, it seemed to them that the world above them had gone mad yet again. They stayed put, and anyway, there were the new showers to be plumbed in and tiled. So now, crude tunnels became panelled avenues and walkways, although their personal "houses" still opted for the practical and functional furnishings - certainly nothing that leaned toward anything vain or ostentatious. They focussed on education and building a strong moral social unit, with care and regard for all Mankind. With so much war and destruction taking place above their heads, they saw it as their duty to HoBi to create and maintain a world below that acknowledged every individual, and cherished human life. From time to time, there were renewed calls to leave the safety of their hollows, and try for a life above ground. A big meeting had taken place where the majority had voted to establish themselves on the surface, and this time, the vote was categorically in favour. At that point, they had heard the banshee wail of the air-raid siren for the first time, and the men had tutted and dusted off their tool boxes again. 1939 might have to wait for a while...

The small deputation of Calderman, Merry, Trevill and Nicky made their way around the wall of the Dark Tower. When they were satisfied that they were in no danger of being observed, they climbed the old stone wall and dropped onto the overgrown grass behind. A few feet away, they located the second of two heavy cast-iron drain covers. Merry picked up a small rock from the grass, and gave a coded rap on the metal. Shortly, there was an answering signal from below, and the sound of heavy bolts being drawn back. The cover slowly lifted, and the tousle-haired face with huge eyes smiled at them. It was their friend Thomas- who beckoned them over to the opening into his domain. They climbed down the ladder inside the void, and secured the cover above them. Although Thomas led the way through the various twists and turns of the passages, the boys had visited their underground village often enough to have learned the routes quite well. They soon emerged into the great hall in which the Groundlings regularly met. Already sitting on the front row of the tiered benches were the Elders Jedekiah, Solomon, Thaddeus, Ruth, Naomi, Martha, Bethany, and Ezekielvis (he was the Elder with a quiff of jet black hair, a raised collar, and long sideburns). Jedekiah rose from his seat. He was a very tall man- even taller than Gideon, and living within the confines of the tunnels seemed to have had no effect upon his vertical progress. 'We greet thee, Friends!' he said 'You are most welcome among us. How may we help thee?'

'I am hoping that we may be able to help Thee- I mean you, Jedekiah.' Nicky said. He began to explain that the Academy was going to hold "Ghost Walks", and that they planned to include some of the Groundlings' tunnels on their routes. The Elders took a little convincing that the event was not at all "Satanic", and that there would not be any actual ghosts walking around the place - it was purely for entertainment purposes only. Martha in particular was far from pleased at the news: 'They wish to entertain themselves by making mockery of the spirits of the Departed? - this is an outrage!!' she said. Nicky assured them that the idea was not to mock the dead, just to take members of the Public on a tour around the older parts of the Academy, where members of the Staff and boys would put on period costume in order to create the required atmosphere for the event. All that the Groundlings had to do, was make sure that their tunnels to the living quarters and suchlike were sealed off - and perhaps keep any noise down to the very minimum. 'So Thee expect us to hide away like criminals, is that so?' asked Thaddeus. 'Oh no- certainly not' answered Merry, 'we just came to warn you that there might be a few people plodding around the entrance tunnel on the North Side. We are not suggesting that you have to hide - but just don't rush out at the people without warning, we are not trying to scare them..' 'But I thought that Thou said that "scaring the people" was the very idea?' answered Ruth. 'Well yes it is, but we don't want, I mean - Shep' - help me out here please!!' said Merry.

Nicky smiled at the Elders, and said 'We just want to make sure that you have your privacy. We don't want strangers poking around and frightening your children, and we don't want you to be seen unless it is your choice to be seen...' 'We shall act with discretion, and wisely.' said Solomon. 'I thank thee Friends for thy counsel; it shall always fill our heart with gladness to see thee'. Nicky remembered something: 'Can you please give this tee-shirt to Thomas? He could do with a bigger size, now that he is growing!' he said. The boy handed over a "Rush" tee-shirt to the Elder, who rolled his eyes as if he knew that the boy Thomas would wear the shirt constantly until it fell apart... ...(he had thought of getting the boy a shirt printed with the logo of "The Jam"- and the legend "Going Underground", but wasn't sure how the Elders might react...)

Reacting extremely badly at this very moment, was Mr Gideon Rundell, the Latin Master. He was suffering from having what he thought was going to be an easy trip out of school utterly ruined by some damned fool filling his car full of...well, full of something which four separate car valletings had failed to remove the smell of. He had been looking forward to settling himself into the antique leather captain's chair which he had bought at auction. The chair was an original, and much more suited to his upper-class standing within the Academy. The rest of the Staff would be so very jealous of his latest acquisition, and would automatically give him greater respect (he thought). He smiled to himself as he opened the door to his classroom. The smile instantly vanished as he saw that there was no chair, antique or otherwise, behind his desk. Had that idiot Brooks forgotten to install the chair as instructed? Where the bloody hell had the - oh no... Good grief...Surely not...

The chair, in all its antique glory and lustrous sheen, was indeed in his classroom. Admittedly, not exactly in the place which he had instructed it to be sited. The chair was fixed upside-down to the ceiling above his desk. Immediately behind the desk, lying on the polished floor, in the space that was noticeably devoid of chair, was a small white business card. He approached the raised dais and stepped up. He bent down and read the wording on the card. It said:

This has been an ODD job.

The rain had begun to fall again. It had considered all of the benefits and notoriety that falling upwards might possibly present - and then decided to follow traditional thinking. On the corner of the street, a man was standing in the rain, whilst doing his best to look inconspicuous. His collar was turned up against the elements, but only served to funnel the rain efficiently down the back of his neck. He leaned further back against the wall, trying to gain a little shelter. He took out a packet of cigarettes, and fumbled for his lighter - more to provide camouflage for his real actions than to actually smoke.

Fumbling into his inside pocket, he produced a radio, into which he whispered a commentary:

'Three targets located. Current location Auntie Dora's Cafe on Rope Street. No movement yet - Will wait for any further developments. Do you want me to approach targets?'

'No - do not approach. We will advise...' came the terse reply.

'Roger that - Tango Whisky out..'

'What was that about Whisky?' asked Matthews, who had soundlessly approached the man and overheard his conversation.

'Oh er...Hello Gus' said Posta, 'I was just on the phone to my friend - She has a dog called Whisky. It has just gone out'.

'Hair of the Dog eh? Heh Heh!' said Matthews 'Damn fine idea. My word yes - they're still open - care to join me for a "snifter" Old Chap?'.

'I might as well' said Posta "I think I am wasting my time standing here. Come on Mate - My Shout...'

The two strode off to the adjacent watering-hole known as the Five Crowns (well, Posta actually walked, whereas Matthews' locomotion seemed to be a little more random). The pair entered the disreputable watering-hole, and were greeted by the motley crew of early drinkers who had come in out of the rain, or perhaps not got around to actually leaving the premises. The atmosphere within the pub was a fug of beer fumes and cigarette smoke, and the clientele sat at the bar and around the room smoking, steaming, and in the case of one particular patron, slightly effervescing.

'Right then Gussie- what's it to be?' asked Posta, 'We've got Beer, Scotch, Brandy, Gin and Tonic or Vodka?'

'Yes Please.' answered Matthews, grinning hugely.

The early liquid lunch was served. Glasses filled with the various liver - threatening contents were lined up on the bar in front of the History Professor. Posta lifted his own pint, and stared smiling in disbelief at a Master Artist at work. Matthews chose a glass from the identity parade of Cirrhosis, and downed it in one gulp. 'I think mayhap; it is in need of a small chaser to prevent loneliness...' exclaimed the man 'Barkeep - a pint of "Old Thatcher's Gusset" if you will be so kind...' As the strong ale was poured by the incredulous barman, Matthews' eyes drank in the sight of the glass as it slowly filled from the tap. As the tankard was passed over the bar, he took the vessel with all the reverence of a skilled craftsman, and after turning the tankard this way and that, raised it in salute to the entire Company

- then downed it with supreme satisfaction. 'Ahh...Liquid History!' he said.

Posta took out his wallet in readiness to pay for his friend's imbibement, but fumbled it and dropped it on the floor of the bar. It had fallen open, openly displaying to the world his CID identification, and Police badge. He swiftly scooped up the fallen article, snatched a note out of it, and returned it to the safety of his jacket pocket. The unplanned exposure of his true identity had not gone unnoticed by Matthews, who drained his brandy with relish, and whispered 'It would appear that the game is afoot, Mr Holmes...'

Chapter Nine:

'WILL YOU ALL KEEP STILL- FOR GOD'S SAKE...!' said an exasperated Hyde-Jones. He rubbed his forehead, and regarded the assembled "cast" of the Ghost walk who stood before him. 'We will get nowhere if you all keep buggering around. We need to take this seriously if we are going to pull it off - STOP SNIGGERING LOOPY...Now I will have a look at all of your costumes to make sure that you have got the look right'.

Nicky, Calderman, Davis, Trevill, Merry, Weatherill and Kendy had been joined by Hyde-Jones, Mr Newhouse, Mr Bannister, and the Matron (of whom we shall speak later) in their quest to provide horror-based entertainment for the unsuspecting members of the General Public who had elected to buy tickets to attend the "Ghost Walk" around the Academy. The English Master lined up his troops, and subjected them to closer inspection. Joining the group were Ursula and Thomas from the Groundlings. Also joining in enthusiastically with the spirit of the event was Jedekiah - who was sporting a hooded black robe, and had put a considerable amount of work into what was a very convincing and eerie makeup job. Mr Newhouse was elegantly attired as a rock and roll zombie fresh from the crypt, and was busy giggling as he gripped the throat of Miles Bannister with hands the colour of the not-so-recently departed. Matron had insisted on volunteering her services as a "tour guide" for the evening. She had been told to dress herself in "something spooky" as befitted the occasion. The costume in which she had appeared was (one would assume) based on the "Vampira" character, but had incorporated some of her own more personal preferences in the line of Recreational Attire. She presented herself in a flowing crimson-lined cape, leather micro-skirt, fishnet stockings (complete with bat motif), a plunging leather basque, black thigh boots, evening gloves and a stout riding crop. Also about her person were more leather straps than had been enjoyed by the Prisoner of Zenda. Hyde-Jones had been forced to have a quiet word with the lady, and insisted that she go and tone down the outfit so as not to give the wrong impression to the visitors. He also had to have a discreet word with Mr Newhouse, who seemed to be dribbling and twitching disconcertingly.

She strode off in a huff, declaring 'But I thought that this evening was all about Ghosties and Ghoulies...?' Newhouse had laid a zombie hand on his friend's shoulder and whispered, 'Trust me Roy - there is nothing that you could possibly teach *her* about Ghoulies...'

Awaiting the return of the modified Matron, Hyde-Jones made sure that the crew all knew their roles, running over where the "extras" should be seen, and hopefully captured on film by the eager Ghost Hunting public. He gave the boys a final once-over before ShowTime.

'Davis- why the hell are you covered in spikes?'

'You said that I should dress like an Urchin Sir...'

'Take them off Davis, you look like an angry conker.' said the Master. 'Okay then- Trevill, what have you got?'

'An all-consuming sense of 'opelessness and futility caused by social depravity an' being downtrodden as one of the forlorn starving masses, who is beneath the contempt of the Upper Echelons Surr...' the boy answered.

'Very Good- and what else?'.

'Oi 'ave a dead rat Surr'.

'Very good- well done Lad. Now, ah yes- Merry...what have you got?'

'Rickets, Sir...'

'Good answer - see me afterwards. You should have a begging bowl - have you got it?'

'Yes Sir.'

He turned to his friend Mr Newhouse, and noticed that he was attired in a pair of "Air -Wear" boots. 'Those boots are not in keeping with the times Loopy' he said. Newhouse grinned 'They are indeed ancient boots my fine fellow: they are in fact "Apothecary Marten" boots, purchased in 1850 - or ten to seven if you prefer...' Hyde-Jones decided to let this small fact go, and also to ignore the six-pack of lager, half bottle of Jack Daniels, and large hip flask that his colleague had about his zombie-esque person. The Matron returned, having put away the whip and a small quantity of the leather straps. She stood before the group, flung back the cloak, and stood in wild-haired defiance, causing localised rigor mortis in at least two of the Masters...

Realising that he was staring, Hyde-Jones shook himself out of his hormone-driven trance and rallied the troops. 'Okay Gang...Here we go then - it's curtain up and at 'Em!!!'

The assembly of Ghost-hunting punters were grouped together just outside the huge heavy doors to the old school. As the evening was quite chilly, they were all wrapped up in various layers of mismatched knitted materials. There were quite a few expensive cameras in evidence, and one or two bobble hats which should have been labelled as evidence. The group were being given an introductory "potted history" talk by Hyde-Jones, who was himself dressed as a Victorian Gentleman complete with silver-tipped walking cane. Using all of his consummate skill as an actor, he delivered the speech in sepulchral tone, with the object of creating an atmosphere of fear amongst the tour group. He warned the people that they were very likely to encounter wandering spirits throughout the Academy buildings - and not to be unduly alarmed if they should happen to witness any "apparitions". 'That's what we have paid our money for, isn't it?' joked a rather severe man in a trilby hat. Unseen by the crowd, Newhouse swiftly lifted the hat from the man's head, and flung it into the air in front of him. 'It would appear that our spectral guests have already joined us...' said Hyde-Jones, handing the hat back to the now startled owner. 'Ladies and Gentlemen- we shall now proceed. The tour will take place in darkness, so as not to offend our departed friends. Please feel free to ask questions at any time. Please ensure that your mobile telephones are switched off, and should we encounter an apparition - then please do not interact with them unless they wish you to do so. 'Sounds like the Wife...' said a man at the back of the group.

The tour set off into the Old School corridor. Hyde-Jones let the great oak doors close behind them with a bang - causing the first fright of the evening. As the group walked slowly down the corridor, it soon became apparent that all of the ladies in the party seemed to be at the front of the tour. For some inexplicable reason, the male members of the group were walking very close to Matron. This caused various domestic rows between partners, and the errant men folk were quickly reclaimed by their wives and girlfriends, with many a scowl at the black-clad temptress into the bargain. The plan was that none of the "extras" would be seen until at least half way through the tour. Hyde-Jones was explaining about the history of the Academy, and what foul deeds were perpetrated behind the doors of each classroom which the group passed. One member of the public could not resist knocking at one of the classroom doors, and increased the size of his laundry bill when there came an answering knock from within...The English Master told the group that ghostly music had been reported by many people in this corridor, which had come from the spirits of long-dead musicians who would ply their trade for money in times gone by. He told the crowd that this was in fact a good spot in which to record

"EVP" phenomena. At this point, Mr Thwaite should have switched on the tape recorder in order to supply the ghostly melodies - but found himself tangled up in tape, with his torch batteries both flat, and in the wrong room completely. The effect of the story was somewhat spoiled, as Mr Newhouse could simply not resist stating 'Who you gonna call? - Ghost Buskers!!'. As the party progressed down the dimly-lit corridor, one member of the group encountered something strange. Edgar Blatt had arrived armed with audio recording equipment, night vision goggles, and infra-red camera attachments (well - there's always one, isn't there...). He would capture a ghost on film if it was the last thing which he ever did (but hoped it wasn't, as did his Mum). He was fiddling with a night vision filter on the lens of his hideously expensive digital camera. Whatever he tried, all he could see was a black view through the lens. As he raised his eyes away from the camera, he slowly looked up, and up again. He found himself looking into the skeletal face of a very tall figure in a black robe. The terrifying figure smiled at him and extended an arm, pointing out that he should catch up with the rest of the group down the corridor. Jedekiah the Groundling Elder was taking his role extremely seriously...

The Dining Hall Cloister was the next point on the tour. Here, the group were joined by Miles Bannister the Mathematics Master, who would lead them down the passages and around the Dining Hall. 'And legends have it that a local Highwayman was hung near this part of the Academy grounds - and this headless horseman has been witnessed by many reliable sources over the years...' Bannister told the group. He carried on telling them of the history around the Cloister and Hall, whilst hopeful ghost hunters snapped away with their cameras in the dark. Without any warning, there came another unexpected shock for the party. Unable to resist "a jolly good night out", Mrs Elsie Noakes (Bannister's resident spirit guide and permanent life coach) had come along to see what all of the fuss was about. It was at this point that her deep love of stage musicals overcame her in the dark passages, and she was forced to express her joy at being out for the evening. What the tour group witnessed was the "tour guide" Bannister suddenly burst into song with a high soprano voice - treating them all to an impromptu rendition of *The Phantom of the Opera* as they walked. When the verse was ended, Elsie was happy, Bannister was acutely embarrassed, and several of the punters actually threw coins at his feet.

Back down the passage, there was a rather tense discussion taking place between two ghostly individuals...

'Well I don't see what your problem is - I mean; you are always mentioned in the legend aren't you?'

'Yes, yes, but that's not the point. The story is misleading - it always refers to "The Headless Horseman" as if it's always all about you - whereas I don't get a look in'

'Well you can't really look can you - let's be honest here...'

'That remark was completely uncalled for. I am striving for factuality here. You are "The Man", and yes, I am a Headless Horse. All I am asking for is for the title of the legend to reflect the accuracy of my particular state'.

'Look...we keep on having the same old argument - if it means that much to you, then I'll get you a head'.

'And how, may I ask, will you achieve that, my fully-headed friend?'

'I will borrow the head from the wall of Rundell's study for you'

'Well thank you very much: that is a deer's head, as well you know. I would look like a ghostly transplant patient who went to a cut-price surgeon...'

'Sorry old friend - I was just trying to help. I shall have to ask someone for advice about how we can solve your predicament...'

'Like whom, may I ask?'

'I thought perhaps, the *Head*master...?'

'You really are asking for a good kick in the spectral codpiece, aren't you...'

The two wandered off down the passage in the opposite direction to the group, still locked in conversation. Another figure had joined the party, and he chuckled as he watched the two amble off into the distance.

Nicky and Calderman held their breath at the bend of the Boarding House Lobby corridor. They would wait until the group were just under halfway down the passage, and then slowly walk out across the stone flagged floor, and disappear through the connecting door at the end of the passage. With any luck, some of the people would see them glide past looking like ghostly street urchins. Mr Newhouse was providing the commentary for the group in this particular area, and had decided to liven up the proceedings by telling a story of his own making (with just a little help from the hip flask). The story detailed the plight of a former German Master who had been bitten by a bat prior to his taking up a post at the Academy. Newhouse sadly recounted that the poor man had been allegedly turned into a vampire by the bite, and could not trust his instincts not to be foisted upon the boys of the boarding house at night. He had left the Academy, and set up a small shop, from where he would dispense advice as to how placing furniture in a certain way in line with "lines of natural force" could enhance your health and well-being. It was a kind of Fang-Shui...

The boys walked slowly across the end of the corridor, and there was a shout of 'Bloody hell- look down there!!' from one of the tour group. They heard the clicking of various camera shutters as eager ghost hunters attempted to get a shot of their prey. As planned, they hastily opened the connecting door and disappeared from view. All was going to plan so far, and the punters were now getting quite excited. Also getting quite excited was one Dr Matthews, who had heard that the famous wine cellar vaults had been unlocked and opened for the occasion, and was on a hunt of his own - in search of vintage imbibement. He was happily walking along with the rest of the group, and flirting with the Lady Chair of the local Round Table. The Groundling helpers were really getting into the swing of things. From behind, below, above and beside the group, there came a variety of sounds such as whisperings, rattling of chains, and strange moanings (such as "ave I really shelled out twenty-five quid for this load of crap?'). Jedekiah was following at the rear of the group, causing Mrs Elsie Noakes to enquire of Bannister: 'Who is that nice tall chap at the back in the black robe?'

'He is playing the part of the Grim Reaper, Madam.'

'Oooh! I know who you mean - he lived in the town opposite the baker, his Sister was an assistant librarian until they saw her tattoos: he used to collect stamps - no, tell a lie - it was kettles, now I come to think of it...'

'Who on earth are you talking about...?'

'Graham Roper - nice young lad, such a shame about his rash...'

'No Madam- I said, "The Grim Reaper", harvester of souls, the Great Leveller - he's Death...'

'Oh, that's such a shame...but I'm sure that no one would notice if he wears a hearing aid under that robe?'

Also mingling with the crowd was the nemesis of the Reverend Felchingham, known as Stan. He had decided to attend the gathering in order to further torment the Rev - but had been disappointed to find that his intended target had failed to attend. He had contented himself by mingling with the party and recounting the interesting tale of how he came to be arrested for loitering in the church graveyard at midnight by the local Constabulary...

'How awful- you were arrested in the church yard?' asked a fascinated woman.

'Ho yurs indeed- but I mean, what was a body supposed to do' said Stan.

'What were you doing in the cemetery Stan?' she enquired.

'Well now, I was sittin' with me hammer and chisel, alterin' the name on the headstone, when I gets me collar felt by the Boys in Blue...' he told her.

'Why were you chiselling the headstone at that time of night Stan?' she asked.

"Coz like I told the Policeman at the time - I spent a small bloody fortune, and the ruddy stonemason only went and spelled me name wrong...' Stan answered.

With the crowd seemingly well pleased with the tour so far, and with the planned "sightings" of ghostly figures which the team had rehearsed to perfection having chilled the spines of the public, the party paused for refreshments at the halfway point on the tour. A small buffet had been provided and set out in the cellars on tables by the Groundling helpers. The vault was lit by a forest of candles, and looked like a book signing venue for Count Vlad himself. Away from the group, Matthews was lost in his search for the legendary wine cellars of the Academy, accompanied by Mr Thwaite, tottering along beside him in unsuitably high heels - who was just plain lost. Matthews lit a cigarette and regarded the ancient brickwork of the cellar vaults. Ancient, dusty, smelling of damp and looking in complete need of immediate restoration, he was nevertheless a brilliant History Master...

Whilst the visitors were busily nibbling their sausage rolls, assorted pastries and biscuits, several of the men were still contemplating how best to secure a quick nibble of Matron. Just to add an extra "spooky dimension" to the tour, Jackson had been instructed to dress in black, and walk heavily past the buffet area whilst tapping a metal-tipped stick on the stone floor. At this precise moment, Hyde-Jones was recounting the sad tale of a former History Master by the name of Bailey - who had a wooden leg and a silver-tipped walking stick. He had lost his life heroically during the First World War, but could still be heard on stormy days walking around the Academy and keeping a watchful eye on the boys. The thump and metallic tapping echoed down the passageway, and the crowd fell silent as the strange noise passed. Hyde-Jones and Mr Newhouse were extremely impressed with Jackson's timing and technique, which supplied just the required unnerving sounds.

Jackson bent down in the passage, and hoped that he would not get into terrible trouble - he had done his best after all. He had caught and ripped his trousers on a stray nail which had been protruding out of the wall, and had lost the metal tip of the stick somewhere within the dark passage. Tripping on the trouser remnants, he had fallen face-first into the wall, lost a shoe, and managed to swallow one of his fillings. Almost in tears, he had given up and decided to set off back the way he had come.

The group set off on the second half of the tour, after another ghostly legend recounted by Miles Bannister, with cameras at the ready. As they turned the corner and headed off into the dark, a proud and elegant figure dusted himself down and limped out of the gloom. Winston Alfred Bailey thought how rude it was of the group not to have waited for him, but merely shrugged his shoulders and set off to check on the rest of the Academy as usual. None of the tour party heard the thump and click of his silver-tipped cane, the sound gradually fading as he rounded the corner and melted into the darkness.

Thomas and Ursula from the Groundlings had played their master stroke. When members of the party were distracted, or listening to the guide, they would emerge from secret doors in the passage wall and hold the hand of an unsuspecting visitor. The ensuing panic and commotion would provide them with sufficient opportunity in which to escape back through the handy hidden doors and away. This trick had worked to spectacular effect, but had almost been spoiled when Elsie Noakes had tried to offer them both a mint humbug.

With much meandering through the dark tunnels and passageways, and with many a glimpsed vision of what might have been a ghostly visitor, the tour finally wound up back at the Old School Corridor where it had begun. Hyde-Jones and Newhouse thanked the public for attending, and asked them to be sure and let the Academy see any evidence of apparitions which they may have caught on film. There was a burst of sincere applause, and the sound of the tin for donations being filled up with coins. 'If you have not been scared enough- then please come back for our next spine-tingling tour, when I am sure that the ghosts of St Onans will be happy to meet you all again!!' declared Hyde-Jones. Matron informed the group that tee-shirts, leaflets and other souvenirs were available from her private quarters - and there was a sudden stampede as a crowd of men raced across the quad in the direction of the Boarding House treatment room. Those who did not currently require medical treatment would certainly be in urgent need of it when their Wives got hold of them...

Despite the Masters having reservations about the whole idea of the Ghost Walk, the event was very well received by the crowd who had attended. They all went away happy, apart from Edgar Blatt, who went home happy and damp in the trouser department. Mr and Mrs Critchings were extremely impressed. 'I loved the way that old feller seemed to walk off right through that wall at the end of the passage' said Mrs Critching 'they must have used one of them hollering-grammy thingies with sound'. Mr Critchings was slightly less complimentary, stating 'Well even for a hologram, I thought that old bloke was a right miserable old sod.' Stan heard this rather rude comment, and vowed to make their bedroom telephone ring at 03:40 in the morning, as well as hiding the television remote control. When they next watched "The Amityville Horror" on television, Stan would be only too happy to supply 3-D effects in their living room...

Hyde-Jones waited until the crowd had dispersed, and the "extras" had come out of hiding and assembled in front of him in the quad. 'Well done all of you - that was bloody superb! I am very proud of all of you. Thanks very much for all of your hard work, and I'll see you all tomorrow - you really have done the Academy proud tonight, thank you'.

If anyone had still been standing in the stygian gloom of the Dining Hall Cloister, and had strained their hearing to best advantage, they may well have heard drunken singing issuing forth from the large and dusty wine cellars beneath. Matthews and Stan had discovered a particularly fine vintage, and were alternatively toasting themselves, and singing a rousing and quite filthy old ditty in a drunken two-part harmony.

Mr Thwaite had eventually been led out of the tunnels, clicking along nervously on his ridiculously high heels, by an old limping Gentleman in Elizabethan dress, and a Highwayman, who was earnestly questioning Thwaite as to how he could best make a life-size horses head out of papier mache.

The boys and Staff went their separate ways. Hyde-Jones and Mr Newhouse walked casually over to the donations tin on the small table which had been placed near the doors. He nodded almost imperceptibly at his friend, who upended the tin onto the table. 'Say a big thanks to your mate for me Loopy' said Hyde-Jones 'Those hologram projectors worked a treat - I really like the old geezer who walked through the walls, and that ancient dude in Elizabethan gear with the limp was an absolute master stroke'. 'Yeah, sorry about that Roy...' said Newhouse, 'Dennis was really sorry that he couldn't get us the projectors and stuff, but his car broke down, and one of his kids has come down with chicken pox - but he said that we can have all the gear next time if we still want it...' Hyde-Jones looked at his friend as the facts dawned upon him. The two looked down. The two looked up. Newhouse was first to grin.

'Twenty-nine quid and seventy-two pence Roy...' he said.

'Enough?' said Hyde-Jones.

'Enough indeed, Dear Boy' answered Newhouse.

'Right - the Five Crowns it is...Lead on, and let's get acquainted with a few Spirits...'.

Chapter Ten:

Bonfire Night was the next most important event on the calendar of any young boy. Despite teenage protestations that they were too old now for sparklers, once the magic sticks were lit, no child (or adult, whether or not they would admit it) was able to resist writing their name in the air with the fizzing rod - leaving a glowing trail of wonder in front of their eyes. You might well try to convince yourself and others that you were actually playing the part of Luke Skywalker or Darth Vader (or "Daft Ada" as Auntie called him), but in actual fact, you were suddenly six years old again, eyes open wide in childish wonder. Bonfires once lit seemed to resurrect the comfort of safety from the monsters of the dark, or stir up some odd primeval memory within the soul of the observer. However one might chose to define the feelings engendered by the spectacle - one thing could be absolutely relied upon. It would piddle down with rain on November the fifth.

For someone on the very first rungs of the ladder of adulthood, Nicky was having some very grown-up and dark thoughts about what was about to happen to the fields at the bottom of his garden. It seemed that the Council were pushing ahead with their plans to bulldoze the field and build a new estate which would cater for the needs of elderly and disabled residents. Whilst Nicky was all in favour of helping the older people, and those with any form of disability, he was not at all in favour of the Council tearing up part of his own personal history. Those trees across the field were old friends - very old friends indeed. The rings deep within the bark of those trees mirrored the circle of friends who had climbed those trees every day, and hugged their rough bark for security. These trees had been dens, rocket ships to Mars, masts of Pirate ships, icy wind-ravaged rock faces, and a place where a boy could hide out from prying eyes or tormentors. They were family. They were part of each Village kids' history. More to the point - they were living things, who did not deserve to suffer and fall at the push of the mechanical digger's vicious bucket. Sooner or later, someone had to stand up for those without a voice, and it was morally wrong that one elderly species was being sacrificed to provide space for another...The older people needed bungalows it was true, but it was doubtful if they would let the local kids climb them (well, one or two of them might, but best draw a veil over that whole issue...)

In his mind, Nicky was beginning to formulate a plan.

Already as excited as an Elf at Christmas, the Reverend Felchingham was eagerly awaiting the arrival of Halloween. He could not wait to celebrate the Witches' Sabbath and its attendant rituals. He regularly put a chocolate bat under his pillow on All Souls Eve, and had Devils on Horseback for any guests that might happen upon his humble dwelling. He spent each day softly singing "Tis the Season to be Ghastly- Fa La La La La - La La La Laaah!' Oh what a happy little Satanist Reverend was He.

The only dark cloud on his personal horizon was the ever-present threat of intervention by Stan, who loved to rain on his dark Parade in one word comprising four letters...

Things at home seemed to have calmed down a bit in recent days, as Uncle Joe seemed nervous to extend himself into the realms of business and commerce any further after some of his more recent "adventures". He had enjoyed a quiet pint in the village pub with a new friend with whom he had struck up a conversation. Over a drink or five, (all funded by his acquaintance), Joe had suggested that he help out with the job of securing work for the individual, who was a contract sign writer. This was one Declan Seamus Murphy O'Shaughnessy by name, who was very good indeed at his chosen profession, and who had the capacity to absorb a pint of stout like a pallet of blotting paper. He was in constant demand throughout the county, and his name was known far and wide - not least for those companies and individuals for whom he had undertaken his craft. A gregarious and pleasant man, he had taken to Uncle Joe like an old school friend. Joe had instantly set about contacting everyone that he knew who could possibly make use of Declan's talents, and secured his new friend two very prestigious contracts.

All had gone well to begin with, as the man had turned up on time for the jobs, and had been the very paragon of efficiency whilst at work. It was only when the proprietors had viewed the finished work that the tiniest inkling of a problem had begun to raise its head. The problem was, that Declan had failed to mention that he had for many years suffered from a small stumbling block, only a trifling matter really, but which did present the smallest of hitches, given the nature of his work. Mr O'Shaughnessy suffered from a mild form of dyslexia which presented itself in the unfortunate ability to be unable to distinguish the letter "P" from the letter "B".

The first angry telephone call had come from the furniture shop in the town, known as "Pollocks". Mr Pollock was very unhappy with the foot-high name above the shop doorway, gold italic lettering or not. In its current form, it sent out a very different message to the sofa-buying public than the one which he had wanted.

The other local firm who were incandescent with fury at their new sign were the company who supplied materials to the local building trade. The sign above their ornate metal entrance gates should have read "Standing Bricks Limited". It did not...

To be candid, the owners were sick of chasing away members of the public who congregated outside their gates in order to point and laugh, not to mention take photographs. Joe had hurriedly dragged Declan back to the premises of both businesses, and under strict supervision forced him to make emergency alterations to the signs.

Joe was annoyed that so far, despite having been repeatedly invoiced, neither firm seemed to be in any great hurry to bay their pill...

Nicky had been in deep conversation with Mum and Auntie. It was the time in the academic year when students choosing to join the Combined Cadet Force were to choose which "Branch of the Service" they wished to sign up for. Nicky had ruled out the Army Cadets, as they tended to attract the more psychopathically - inclined pupils, who relished the idea of being given uniform which was camouflaged. Although his Brother Mikey had joined the Paratroops, Nicky felt that he did not have the required disposition which might steer him toward an unnatural relationship with a rifle. The Navy Cadets were not an option, as there was little chance of ever seeing a battleship or cruiser sailing up the river. The problem turned out to be a complete no-brainer. He would join the RAF Cadets and strap himself into a jet fighter in order to save Europe from the threat of invasion, or at least perform a very low-level fly past of his friend Squiddy's house - and serve him right too, after breaking Nicky's Action Man a couple of years ago. He would impress his sort-of-maybe-friend Jozza with a gracefully-executed barrel-roll, whilst he flung Iron Maiden CDs out of his open cockpit canopy, which she would catch and clutch to her breast in admiration. The Red Arrows would join him in a magnificent display above the village, and Mum and Auntie would gaze skywards in pride as the red smoke trailed from the rear of his aircraft, with the village girls all hoping that he would land and put his hand in -

'You've dripped tomato sauce down your shirt...' said Mum.

Yes, RAF Cadets it would be then.

Within the echoing cloisters and passageways of the Academy, a lone figure was proudly striding along whilst clutching an aged stepladder under one arm. This was a man on a mission. This was a man who had now been pushed to the edge of reason one time too many by a Head Master who treated him with utter contempt. This was the man who was not going to take any more threats or nonsense from the so-called "Upper Classes". This was Albert Brooks at his most focussed and determined. His mind was absolutely clear, and his objective firmly fixed. The Head had informed him that he was going to be made redundant, so that the Academy could go from Bust to Boom. His personal mission was to see that the man got his wish granted - in no uncertain terms.

He paused in the corridor of the Academy offices, just beneath the new CCTV camera box which had been fitted high up on the wall. The stepladder was opened up very carefully (it had long since developed a taste for human fingers, not to mention its tendency to randomly distribute vicious splinters to the unwary user). He climbed the steps and unscrewed the front cover from the box, leaving it to dangle loosely like the virtue of a "Reality TV" star. It took just the merest of moments for him to make the necessary addition to the camera box, and he replaced the casing with a wry smile playing at the corners of his mouth. He climbed down the steps, folded them, and set off for the next box to be "modified". He would not rush the job: he would take as much time as he needed in order to ensure that his workmanship was of the very highest quality. It was after all, several days before November the Fifth.

As he walked on down the empty corridor, Brooks did not notice the figure dart back out of sight behind the end wall. When Brooks had gone, the figure approached the CCTV box and stared up at it for some time. What was the Groundsman up to now? Why was he tinkering with the camera system when no faults had been reported? And why did the man insist on eating marzipan whilst he was working?

At a discreet distance, ensuring that he would not be seen, the figure followed Albert Brooks as he went about his mysterious task...

Goodwill was addressing the Staff: 'And so after deducting a small amount which paid for extras and sundries, I- sorry, We, made a total profit on the Ghost Walk Evening of four hundred and fifty-six pounds, seventy-five pence. The event was a resounding success, and we have already sold sixty advance tickets for our next tour - which I think should be held on the Halloween eve. The tee-shirts and souvenirs also seemed to sell very well - is that so Matron?'

'Yes, Headmaster, I did take a little in hand...' she purred.

There was a choking sound from the back of the room, where Hyde-Jones was vigorously thumping his colleague Mr Newhouse on the back.

'I am sure that the Halloween 'Special' will be even bigger and better' said the Head 'and we can also make a bucketload of cash by holding our own ticket-only fireworks fiesta up on the games field. I shall speak to Brooks about that urgently'

'He won't take kindly to hundreds of feet trampling all over his beloved turf, Head...' said Bannister, timidly.

'He will take kindly to exactly what he is instructed to take kindly to - without complaint or comment' stated the Head, 'I shall instruct our Mr Brooks to make doubly sure that the event goes with a bang...'

Outside the slightly-open window, the hand of Agent J-Cloth held up a radio with the button set to "transmit"...

'I cannot 'elp but notice that no-one has yet mentioned the French Market which we are going to 'old in the quad' said Madame Dreadfell, hands on hips.

The staff all turned around at the sound of a low and menacing growl from over near the coffee table. Captain Brayfield's sandy moustache was bristling with fury - his grip on his tea cup having tightened to the point of shattering the china.

The Head continued, with worried glances over at the red-faced Captain: 'there is however, one small "fly in the ointment" as regards the recent tour. It has come to my attention that several bottles of old and expensive wine seem to have been removed from the cellars by person or persons unknown. Can anyone shed any light on their disappearance at all?' He scanned the room, his eyes casually alighting on the smiling figure of Dr Matthews, who was leaning against the wall, glass in hand. 'Did you wish to comment at all, Matthews?' said the Head. Matthews raised himself up, and raised his glass as if to toast the assembled Faculty.

‘I am not willing to admit Lafite....’ answered the smiling man, drawing a spontaneous round of applause from his colleagues.

It was agreed that the “Halloween Bash” should incorporate the suggested “Psychic Evening”. There followed a serious discussion about where they might obtain the services of a reputable Medium, or any Psychic from the local area. Mr Newhouse had been the cause of more hilarity - when he had stated ‘well no need to advertise mates- ‘cos if they’re any good as a Psychic, then they will know when and where to turn up!!’.

The Rev was not happy with all of this ridicule of what he saw as “His night”. He vowed to make contact with someone who could be relied upon to provide them with a link to “the other side”. He had tried this once before - when the idea had first been put forward. He knew that certain members of his “circle” were in fact what could be termed “Radio Hams” (apart from Manny Goldstein, obviously), and so had used his own somewhat antiquated radio setup to make contact. He had dusted off the radio set, raised the retractable aerial at the rear of his house, eagerly put on the headphones, and sent out his message via the ionosphere.

He had passed on his request to anyone and everyone who he could contact. He had informed them of the upcoming event, and if truth be known, done quite a commendable job of publicising the Halloween evening. However, it was not long before the Rev became aware that it was not only his friends who were tuned in to his broadcast. Whilst speaking to the aptly-named Reverend Grimm, there had been a sudden burst of static interference in his headphones. Across the airwaves came a far-off sounding voice, almost a throaty chuckling, which was transmitting thus:

‘KILO NOVEMBER OSCAR BRAVO - Please come in...’

‘KILO NOVEMBER OSCAR BRAVO - Are you receiving me?’

The Rev hastily packed away the radio equipment in disgust.

Gideon Rundell was still attempting to hold court in the staffroom, and was trying to put over his own particular point of view to what colleagues still remained in the room. He was violently opposed to any member of the public being admitted to the Academy premises on any grounds whatsoever, and made no secret of the fact that he viewed the people outside the walls to be completely unworthy of setting foot on his hallowed ground. He stirred a cup of Earl Grey tea with unnecessary violence, and declared his displeasure in a loud voice – 'It is a well-known fact, and has been widely publicised by the Daily Mail, that persons of the lower classes all carry a particularly virulent strain of the Botulism virus - which can lower house prices...'

'You really do sound most concerned...' said Bannister.

'I think that your opinion is somewhat harsh...' said Darwin.

'I think you're a pompous little tit.' said Mr Newhouse.

Captain Brayfield made no comment: he merely continued to polish his cavalry sword in the corner of the room. Newhouse continued to make certain unmistakable gestures at the Latin Master, and Hyde-Jones did his best not to wet himself laughing.

Outside the staffroom window, Albert Brooks was on the telephone to his friend Bob Catesby, informing him that he had completed his "little task", and thanking him for his help and advice.

Professor Strangler had another strange problem with which to deal. The "Wormhole" had been acting up recently, and he was fast losing track of the various comings and goings of the plethora of life forms which seemed to be using the Vortex as an interdimensional airport lounge. These days he was not at all surprised when something (or someone) previously thought to be extinct decided to casually saunter past the window. Arnold the Dodo was now a permanent fixture, and was excellent company - if a little heavy on the custard cream biscuits. Stig of the Damp regularly made forays back to whatever time period he had emerged from originally, and more often than not, brought back guests (the Stone Age chaps had actually formed a very competent and tuneful barbershop harmony quintet). What troubled the Professor was the result of a failed experiment conducted by an over-enthusiastic laboratory assistant. The boy had attempted to modulate the size of the Vortex by means of some of the most complicated odds and ends that Strangler had ever come across. He had attempted to ascertain just exactly what the boy was trying to achieve, but most of what the student had relayed to him had gone far above even his own head. A lot of words like 'synchronous' 'oscillation' 'modulatory variance' 'vocal materialisation' and 'splat' had been used. There was a lot of use of the word 'Flux', but the Professor still had not managed to keep up with his student's explanation, for flux sake. Aha!! Perhaps a demonstration? The phrase that hammered inside the Professor's head was 'Famous last Words'. He would soon see that it was in fact words that would cause the problem...

Tossing aside his copy of *Electro Geek Weekly*, the student eagerly ran over to the side of the large frame, inside which the actinic blue vortex pulsed weakly. 'Right Sir- just you watch this!!' said the boy. The student hurriedly threw switches and turned dials on his "additions" to the machinery, rearranging a wire coat hanger which was stuck into the top of one of the new boxes of tricks. He cleared his throat theatrically, and stood to one side of the Vortex frame. He leaned in slightly, and in a loud voice said 'EGG...' The Vortex seemed to pulse and change colour at the sound, shimmering in a variety of electric rainbow hues. The light show finished, the wormhole settled down again.

'Is that it then?' asked Strangler.

'Just hang on a moment Sir - it's thinking...' said the enthusiastic boy.

With no prior warning, the Vortex suddenly pulsed brightly, and flying out of the bright circle came an artificial leg, which clattered to the floor. Strangler regarded the false limb. The student was beside himself with glee - saying 'see Sir...it works!!!'

'How are we defining the word "Works" in this case?' said Strangler.

'Well Sir, I say it - and the Vortex delivers it!' said the excited boy.

'I hate to nit-pick, but didn't you actually say 'Egg' to the machine?'

'Oh yes Sir - but the machine may require retro-recalibration to allow for disharmonic frequencies which I may have delivered across the Callisthenic interface at too indistinct a level....'

Strangler raised both eyebrows in quizzical manner:

'I have a cold, Sir...'

The Professor was not quite sure whether he should be stunned, amazed, angry or proud of his student and the thing that he had created. He decided to tread cautiously, and asked 'Do you have a name at all for this err...Thingy?'

'Why yes indeed Sir - me and the boys call it the 'Idiom formulation and Constructor unit' he said.

'And it does what - exactly?' enquired the Master.

'Well Sir, we stand at the side of the machine, and it provides an interface with your thought and spoken command, to produce out of the Vortex the item which you have requested. You do have to be careful not to get too close to the machine, otherwise you may get drawn through the Vortex - but if you stand on the footprints which we have painted on the floor you should be perfectly safe, and it will be even better when we have modified it a bit more' said the boy.

'So, at the moment...is it erm, I mean can it be trusted to err… is it dangerous?' asked Strangler.

'Oh no Sir. You just have to be very careful when you stand in position not to call for anything which you don't want, because at the moment the interface is very sensitive. If you said 'Sausage', yet thought 'Blue Whale'- then until we've adjusted the sensitivity you are quite likely to get a meat product for breakfast which is sixty feet long...'

'And will it produce anything you ask it for?'

'Anything it recognises Sir. If your request is unclear or confusing, then it will supply you with what it thinks you want...'

'So basically - it's a small version of Tesco then?' asked Strangler.

'Much better Sir, and no wasteful packaging either!!' said the boy. 'You just have to be really careful as to what you say when you are standing next to the machine, as we haven't actually managed to be able to turn it off as yet...'

Strangler stood on the painted footmarks, peering at the Vortex. He wasn't really paying attention to the boy, until he half heard 'turn it off yet'.

'Sorry - what did you say about not being able to turn it off?' he asked.

'We're working on it Sir- but please be careful until we have fixed it'.

'Oh... Bollocks...' said Strangler

Oh, how he would wish that he hadn't said that.

Chapter Eleven:

Miss Emelia Piggott was humming a little tune to herself as she prepared a pot of tea and a special selection of biscuits for herself and the object of her affections for many a year- the Head Master. She was increasingly happy and contented in her own little world of imagined romance and would-be elopement to a desert island in the South Seas, which would contain nothing but exotic flora, fauna, and Dr Goodwill and of course, herself. In her mind's eye she visioned herself in a grass skirt, engaged in an exotic dance before her Beau, as she served him with a cool drink from half a coconut shell. Her reverie saw her approach the Head Master, leaning over his reclining form as she placed a garland of fresh and fragrant island flowers around his neck. A vividly-hued parrot swooped down from the trees, and perched on a handy rock, where it called to them -

'Miss Piggott...you can bring the tea in now please'.

She walked to the Head's door with the tea tray - remembering not to shimmy, as she no longer had the grass skirt about her person. With the cash now rolling in (she knew that the Head's brilliant schemes could not possibly fail...) it would only be a matter of time before he informed her that he had booked first class tickets for the two of them on a South Seas cruise. They would sail off together in a snowstorm of confetti, leaving that ghastly Wife of his to sit in that ghastly bungalow, and wishing that she had paid him more attention. This must be what he had planned, because hadn't he given her the secret combination to the wall safe just last week? If this wasn't the Real Thing - then Julie Andrews had never made pants out of curtains for those German kids of the Von Krapp Family (how loud might they possibly have sung if she had not taken out the hooks first...).

Miss Piggott wished for the day that she might become the proper Mrs Goodwill, and gave herself an extra spray of "Captured by Night" perfume, before primping her hair in the mirror, and taking in the tea and biscuits to the object of her exotic desires.

'Ah thank you, Miss Piggott...' said the Headmaster, 'I feel that I can confide in you and divulge the fact that before much longer, I expect to be enjoying my tea in altogether much warmer surroundings'

She blushed ever so slightly, and knew that this was a hint at the fact that the man had the same dream in mind as she did (possibly excluding the bit where the barely-dressed and ridiculously muscled native boy helped her with her morning shower). 'I do hope so, Head Master...I really do' she whispered in reply.

She made a dignified exit from the Head's study, with only the slightest of glances back at his desk as she returned to her own office of dreams. 'You really are deluding yourself you know, Dear Lady...' said the voice. Emelia spun around in the corridor to see who had dared to speak such blasphemy - but only saw Baxter, Goodwill's faithful Labrador, stretched out on the carpet of the adjoining room. Confused, she shook herself, and returned to her duties, where she undertook some very violent filing, and typed one or two memos with the touch of a Samurai warrior. In a bad mood. With a migraine. And toothache.

Having long since overcome her terror at the daily intrusions into her kitchen, and having met and made firm friends of the Groundlings, Betty Bradley now gave classes in cookery and catering to the folk from the tunnels. One girl had proven to be so skilled at the craft that she had gone on to become Head Chef at a local hotel. It was considered rather strange however, that she seemed to produce her best recipes and culinary creations in semi-darkness, but alas, such were the idiosyncrasies of the truly talented...

Across the quad, in one of the smaller rooms devoid of character, boys were sitting at desks with parts of an old firearm in front of them. This was their introduction to the RAF Cadet Force, and some bright member of the Faculty had decided that none other than Mr Albert Brooks esquire was the very man to introduce the boys to the intimate workings of the Enfield .303 rifle. With his former military experience, Albert was in fact a very good arms instructor indeed. He could personally strip down, lay out, clean, oil, re-assemble and present a rifle in full working order in less than two and a half minutes. The boys stared at the collection of unfamiliar metal parts on their desks, and Merry wondered if he would be able to get his rifle put back together in under two and a half weeks.

'Best rifle ever made Lads...' said Brooks 'Treat it like a Lady, and it will perhaps one day save your life'

'What- you mean we should take it to the pictures, give it dinner, then stick it in a taxi home?' said Nicky, to a chorus of laughs.

'No, you daft bugger...' said Brooks 'You respect it. You caress it and polish it. You treat it as if it is your most delicate and valuable thing in your life. Then maybe someday...well if you are very lucky (he raised his rifle, and the boys ducked) then YOU MAY GET TO

BLOW THE BLOODY HEAD OFF SOME TOFFEE-NOSED BASTARDS WHO THINK THAT THEY ARE BETTER THAN EVERYONE ELSE ON THE PLANET! Sorry Lads - I think I went a bit over the top there (Heh heh!), but seriously, look after your rifle...'

Kendy sat looking extremely puzzled. 'Forgive my ignorance Sir, but am I correct in assuming that these weapons are primarily designed for the purpose of killing?' he asked.

'Killing, defending what's yours, and securing peace and harmony Son...' answered Brooks. 'When you are at war, and the chips are down- then we shoot them before they shoot us'.

'Why do I need to kill someone who I have never met?' asked the boy 'They might turn out to be a nice person'

'Well think of it as a deterrent then, if it helps.' said Brooks.

'We sticks it down the toilet then, do we?' said Trevill.

'The word was "deterrent", Son...' came the terse reply.

Trevill had reassembled his rifle in seconds flat, checked the gun sight, and laid the firearm on the desk for inspection. The rest of the boys were impressed beyond words.

'Where did you learn to 'andle a gun like that then Laddie?' asked Brooks.

'Oi dun a lot o' shootin' where Oi come from' answered Trevill. 'Oi done a lot of rabbit shootin Surr'.

'And where was it that you shot these rabbits then Son?' Brooks enquired.

'Well mostly, it were up the ar -'

'I mean, where abouts were you when you shot them...' said Brooks, quickly.

'On Moi Dad's farm Surr…' he replied proudly.

Having discovered a marksman among the boys, Brooks appointed Trevill to help him check the rifles once the lads had put them back together- which he did like a real professional. Albert made a mental note of the boys for possible future reference, especially young Trevill, who he thought may well come in handy for his "Master Plan".

School had finished for the day, and the Staff had ceased in their attempts to crow-bar knowledge into the resisting heads of their young charges. Nicky said his "see you laters" to his friends, and made his way to the bus stop, struggling against the strong wind that had sprung up without warning. Tiny tornadoes of leaves chased him along the footpath, and the odd chip paper flapped up into the air like a seagull on serious medication. The boy turned up his collar against the wind, and wished that he had the protection of his heavy school overcoat. This garment was temporarily out of service, as one sleeve needed repair - the satchel having caught him off guard, and ripping open a seam. High in the sky, a curious ovoid shape was drifting above the street, its surface reflecting the light in curious manner. Nicky studied its leisurely progress, wondering if it might be the ship of one of Kendy's relatives, come to pay a quick visit. He imagined being able to fly across the galaxy in such a vehicle, taking in the sights of objects that he had only peered at through his telescope. This small flight of fancy was instantly shattered as he realised that the object was in fact an airborne dustbin liner bag. So much for intergalactic voyages then. But wait a minute... what if the bin liner was in fact a kind of "seed", which was distributed across the planet by the wind? Didn't trees send out seeds like that? Perhaps the bin liner would drift across the country, reproducing as it went, until it found somewhere suitable for it to settle and grow? There may be hundreds of little swing-bins out there in towns and villages, who are constantly searching for their real Father...

A blast from a car horn gave him a start. Uncle Joe had screeched to a halt in front of Nicky, and the car door swung open. 'Ow do Lad! - jump in, and I'll drop you off...' said Joe. The boy was well used to the drill for accepting lifts from Uncle. The trick was to hurl your school stuff into the back of the car as swiftly as you could - as by this point, Joe's foot would be smashing down on the accelerator pedal. To delay would almost certainly result in being dragged up the road at speeds only normally achieved by Formula One cars, and with your legs flailing around in empty air until Joe hauled you inside. With the G-force fighting to pin him to the seat, Nicky scrambled for the seat belt. He was still fighting to get the belt clip to lock, when he heard a loud thump, a crash, and swearing fading into the distance.

'What was that Uncle?' he asked nervously.

'Probably a cyclist...' replied Joe, quite unmoved.

'Do you think he was injured?' Nicky asked.

'Well Lad, he seemed to be able to speed up pretty quickly didn't he?' Joe giggled.

'Will you get into trouble with the Police?' the boy asked.

‘I doubt it Son, I very much doubt it...’ said Uncle ‘I found out that he has been having a bit of a ‘liaison’ with the wife of my mate. I expect that she will be pretty pissed off though...’

‘Why’s that Uncle?

‘That’s her bike that he was riding’.

‘Should we help him do you think?’ said Nicky.

‘Certainly not- the bugger owes me twenty quid. He should consider that to be the cheapest flying lesson that anyone has ever got...It’s going to be interesting to think of him parading around the bedroom in his leopard skin pants - with a bike pump stuck up his jacksie!’.

The car lurched to a halt outside Nicky’s house. The boy grabbed his books, taking care to keep them between him and the homicidal satchel. ‘Must dash...’ said Uncle, ‘I’ve got to help out some bloke from Sotheby’s with some antique valuations before I have me dinner...’ With that, the legend that was Uncle Joe departed in a cloud of smoke, with just a hint of scorched rubber. Nicky was just about to open the front garden gate, when a Goth vision appeared in front of him. Jozza removed her I-Pod earphones, casually took off her dark glasses, and said to him ‘I’m probably having a bit of a party for Halloween, nothing lame or boring, so you can come if you want...’ She replaced the shades, put the earphones back in, and walked off up the pavement with Van Halen fading into the distance. Nicky stood open mouthed - he was not sure exactly what had just happened. Not long ago she was an annoying self-centred brat from further up the street. Just when had this transformation into Goth Goddess occurred? It was now a case of “Jekyll and Hide your Embarrassment” whenever he saw the girl. Had he actually heard her invite him to her party? For a moment, the earth seemed to spin backwards, and he remembered what his Grandfather had told him about the Fairer Sex - ‘If you mess around with Girls, then God will turn you to stone...’ Nicky was terrified that these words had come true, and the process seemed to have begun in the trouser department.

He reached his front door in a complete daze. As his shaking hand turned the handle, a cold tsunami of utter panic hit him...He had already committed himself to appearing as a “ghost” again at the Academy “Halloween Ghost Walk”. His hormones were already writing cheques that his brain would be unable to cash. How on earth could he tell the Goddess Jozza that he couldn’t come to the party, as he had already agreed to walk about in damp dusty tunnels, wearing torn clothing, sprinkled with talcum powder and wearing white makeup? Agreed - he would look like the rest of her new crowd of friends, but if he didn't attend the party, then she might never speak to him again. And come to think of it, she still had his Ozzy Osbourne CD...

Chapter Twelve:

The beam of the torch swept around the workshop like a tiny lighthouse searching for its front door keys. The holder of the torch was being very careful not to let the beam play up to the windows, and possibly alert a passer-by of his presence. The figure pulled out a high wooden stool and sat down. He pulled off his thin leather glove from his right hand, and lit a cigarette. Where was it? There must be something that was staring him in the face, and quite possibly making rude gestures to boot - but as yet, he just couldn't find a trace of what he was looking for. Not that he had a clue what he should be looking for. He had come across one microscopic piece of evidence which had confirmed what he had assumed about the "extra-curricular" activities of Mr Gregor Duggan, but that was it so far. He took another deep pull on the cigarette, letting the smoke spiral upward through the torch beam like a pantomime Genie. Urns - bloody Greek urns, the damned window cills were full of them. Duggan must be making a small fortune flogging them to the local Garden Centres. He didn't fancy shifting them all off from the window area, just to have to put them all back again, they were bloody heavy. He stood up and walked over to the furnace. He was just about to lean on its heavy metal cover, when he made a discovery. Now that was interesting: the furnace was still warm...Knowing Duggan's compulsive habits of keeping everything super clean and tidy, he didn't bother inspecting the furnace lid for any tell-tale residues (there would be no point as the man was obsessive about cleaning each and every piece of machinery), he merely lifted the lid and dropped his cigarette butt inside. Duggan was sure to notice this, and he hoped that this action might begin to make the man do something stupid, and leave further clues in panic at the thought that he was being watched. Either way - he needed to get a result pretty soon, as his superiors were getting rather fractious at his lack of progress to date. With winter coming on, he had no desire to end up back on traffic duty knee-deep in snow.

The next morning, the boys made a bee-line for Hyde-Jones and Mr Newhouse as soon as they saw them. As a group, they were hoping to "beef up" their role for the next Ghost Walk - especially as it was the "Halloween Special".

‘All we are asking for Sir, is that we get a bit more to do than just walking about at the end of passages, in the hope that someone might get a quick glimpse of us...’ said Calderman.

Nicky joined in: ‘Yes Sir- we know that you don’t want us to come rolling down the corridors on a unicycle whilst juggling with oranges, but couldn’t we perhaps work in something else?’

‘We could be flesh-eating Zombies if you like?’ said Merry.

‘Or preferably pie-eating...’ added Davis.

‘Please don’t think that we’re complaining Sir...’ said Kendy.

‘Ah Yes...The Ungrateful Dead!..’ said Mr Newhouse.

‘Okay, okay Chaps...’ said Hyde-Jones, waving his hands in mock submission, ‘I will see what I can come up with for you. I am sure that we can perhaps get away with a bit more theatrics - with it being Halloween. My colleague and I will throw a few ideas around: now be off to your lessons, my spooky little chums...’ The boys went off happy (but remained quite fond of the remaining six dwarves). Hyde-Jones asked Mr Newhouse ‘Have we got everything ready for the Halloween bash?’

‘Oh yes indeed, Great Learned One of the Tormented Trouser...’

‘Such as?..’

‘Twelve cases of beer, four bottles of Jack, two Vodka, two Brandy, various mix -’

‘I meant, vital equipment for the Night’.

‘Yup- so did I!!’ answered Newhouse, rubbing his hands with glee.

It transpired that all was ready to provide an entertaining and frightening evening for the participants, and with enough hard work, a possible threat to the underpants. Both Masters had a horrible feeling that they were both quite looking forward to the event.

Dr Goodwill had called in Dr Chambers, his second in command and self-appointed “hard man” of the Academy for an urgent meeting. Even the erstwhile Miss Piggott had been expressly forbidden to interrupt their conversation, and had been forced to sit in her lonely office whilst her tea became stone cold, and her once firm crumpets wilted over the edge of the plate.

‘Well Head, I cannot possibly see just how the Academy will be able to continue to function if we were to implement the drastic financial cuts which you are suggesting...’ said Chambers, his face pale with shock.

'My Dear Fellow...' smarmed Goodwill, 'I am merely stating the case set before me by the Venerable Board of Academy Trustees, who may I add were most forthright in their opinion, that each and every single item of unnecessary expenditure should be immediately and swiftly excised from the budget sheet.'

'But Head - I mean to say...how could we cope without the excellent cleaning staff? - the place would be a shambles within minutes! And Albert Brooks has an exemplary record of long and diligent service as Groundsman - just think of the awards which we have won for the state of our sports pitches...'

'None of which have provided us with a single penny in revenue My Friend. We can no longer afford to be so sentimental in these times of change, when all we have to our name is loose change' said the Head. 'There must be cuts. Sacrifices must be made for the Greater Good. We will lose some to ultimately save All. We must be leaner, greener...'

'And without a bloody cleaner...' chipped in Chambers, 'I cannot in all honesty support any notion which hacks away the ability of the Academy to be able to deliver the very highest of standards. I mean to say Headmaster - we would be taking the food out of the very mouths of those to whom we have a duty to provide sustenance...'

'Ah yes...now you remind me - that's another area which the Trustees have insisted must be cut. We shall terminate the employ of our quite considerable Kitchen Staff...'

Chambers was horrified. 'How on earth do you propose that we feed our Students without the excellent services of Mrs Bradley and her Girls?'.

The Head smiled a snake-like grin 'Within the environs of the town, there are a host of catering establishments which currently provide an over-the-counter service to the public, who would be only too willing to supply us with balanced meals on a daily basis, and at considerably less cost than we presently suffer...'

'You are talking about Take-aways, aren't you...' said Chambers.

'Cheaper and more economy-friendly sources yes - indeed I am. Why, the savings on washing-up liquid alone will pay dividends' retorted the Head.

'The boys will not stand for it...' Chambers said.

'They will if we sell off the antique benches and turn the dining hall into a walk-in buffet' stated the Head.

Chambers stared at the man. Neither of them wanted to be the first to blink, but eventually it was Chambers who spoke... 'Well I for one will have no part in this draconian scheme, Headmaster' he said firmly.

'That may in due course, prove to be the case Dr Chambers' said the Head.

Chambers rounded on his colleague - 'Your meaning Sir?'

The Head steepled his fingers over the desk, and adopted an almost pitying look toward his Deputy: 'I am rather afraid that certain long-standing Staff posts have been, shall we say, "earmarked for review" as part of the financial cutbacks. Just thinking aloud, you understand, it may well be that the Trustees decide to cut out certain levels of the Faculty in order to rationalise the Staffing structure, and achieve the required level of savings...'

'You mean that I may well be out on *my* arse, do you?' said Chambers.

'Dear Fellow - what you really must understand is that I have a duty in trust to safeguard every single penny for the Academy, and so it may be my unpleasant duty to suggest where the metaphorical axe must fall, in order to secure the best financial future for my- for our Noble Institution...'

The telephone rang, shattering the momentary silence. Miss Piggott's voice could clearly be heard on the end of the line 'I am so very sorry to interrupt you Head Master, but I have an urgent call for you' 'Well who the hell is it? Can they not wait?' said Goodwill. 'I'm afraid they will not wait Headmaster; they insist that the matter is most urgent...'

'Just find out what the blazes they want, will you?' snarled the Head.

There was a short pause, then the shrill voice of Miss Piggott was back - 'It is the Ridings Grange Golf Club, Headmaster...they are asking when you are sending the cheque to renew your membership...?'

Chambers stood up, the chair tumbling over as he stamped out of the room.

With the first event having gone so well, there was a real atmosphere of anticipation running throughout the Academy. The "Cast" for the Ghost walk tour had been well rehearsed (apart from Stan perhaps, who had already been "hearsed" so to speak), and re-costumed to provide that irresistible frisson of terror which the public would expect. Because the Academy premises would also be hosting a

"Psychic Evening", a lot more boys and Staff had been drafted in to help. Hyde-Jones had once again taken almost complete charge of staging the event, ably assisted and confused by his colleague Mr Newhouse. "Loopy" Newhouse had played a real masterstroke for the evening - by contacting his old friend Veronica, who just happened to be married to a local Undertaker. He had secured the services of a vintage hearse (complete with coffin in situ) which would be parked in the quad to give that extra spooky touch to the proceedings. Having been subtly warned by the Head master that there was to be no alcohol consumed on the premises, this was also the means of sneaking in the copious amounts of booze with which he planned to disobey the Head's orders. It was Halloween after all, and he saw no reason why he should be refused a bier...

The two Masters were discussing the Reverend Felchingham. 'What's up with old "Pisa Boy" then?' asked Mr Newhouse 'he seems weirder than usual. I asked him if he fancied a quick game of scrabble during the lunch break, and he ran off screaming 'The Letters!, The Letters!..' and hid in the lavatory'

'I know what you mean- he seems to be in an awful hurry to meet up with the psychic, for some reason...may I ask how come you keep referring to him as "Pisa Boy" all of a sudden?'

'I have christened him thus- because I am aware that he has "certain leanings", shall we say'

'Let us not say - let us merely spread malicious gossip pertaining to he...' said Hyde-Jones.

'Before our next classes, we must make fast our contract by means of liquid assent!' declared Newhouse, beaming.

'Ehh?' said Hyde-Jones.

'Eight cans of Stella with our names on 'em in the Music Room cupboard.' he answered.

'Lead on, oh Great Maestro...'

Dr Chambers sat alone in the room. Too angry to think of his own future, he pondered just how many other heads may be facing the "chopping block". He also thought about just how many years he had spent dealing with problems which Goodwill should have handled, how many times he had backed up the old fool even when his decisions were obviously doomed to fail, and how many times he had deflected the unwelcome attentions of the dreaded Auditors well away from the Academy's financial ledgers. If he was sacked, whatever would he do? Since leaving University, all he had ever done was teach at St Onans. Some of the other Staff members were guaranteed to float straight into another job, certainly the younger element of the Faculty. Masters like Strangler, Darwin, Bannister and Thwaite would perhaps go back into lecturing at a university. But what of say, Dr Matthews? Here was a man that had not visited sobriety since 1971, and who insisted that "transmogrification" was something to do with cats who liked to cross-dress. Madame Dreadfell would no doubt disappear back across the channel to France, and the Reverend would doubtless end up ministering to his long-term friends, when D-Wing held their next rooftop protest. He had always tried to uphold the highest standards of decency and decorum. Surely that should still count for something? If a man has lived a pure and honest life, then surely he was entitled to dignity and respect? Yes indeed - and he would make it so...

He called for Matron to untie him from the chair.

Early on in the evening, people had already begun to gather in loose groups inside the assembly hall. They were all eagerly awaiting their "brush with the unknown" at the Psychic Evening event. Mrs Finucane stood in the shadows, staring intently at a man who had dared to bring a cigarette into her clean hall. If he should drop the offending article onto her immaculate floor - then his jacksie would very soon receive the end of her new brush. Around the hall were various tables which were occupied by the purveyors of a wide range of "Mystic Arts". There were Tarot card readers, crystal ball gazers, I-Ching devotees, Psychic Healers, and a rather nervous-looking young girl named Claire Voyante. Betty Bradley had provided a magnificent buffet for the occasion, and boys dressed as Zombies, Ghouls, and for some reason, one member of the crew of the Starship "Enterprise".

Hyde-Jones took up a position in the centre of the hall, and on cue, a tremendous clap of thunder came from the hall's sound system - causing much droppage of vol-au-vents, and pockets of random swearing. He welcomed the people to the Academy, and informed them about all of the delights which were on offer (at very reasonable rates) within the room. From the back of the hall came a hissing sound, which may or may not have been the sound of a can of lager being opened (which may or may not have been Mr Newhouse's opening bid for the evening). Matthews was at the door in seconds, his alcoholic radar having picked up a signal. At the front of the crowd, and straining at the leash, were Mr Bell-Enderby and the Reverend. The art Master had his eyes locked on the very ample cleavage of the woman with the crystal ball, and the Rev seemed to be about to make a bolt for the table of a rather severe-looking lady Hypnotist. Standing so close together, the two looked like contestants in a three-legged race for Psycho patients. Another loud peal of thunder announced the end of his speech, and he said that he hoped to see all of the people on the "ghost tour" if they dare. He swept his opera cloak theatrically, and strode out of the hall. Mr Newhouse followed behind with a curious stooping, capering gait - like Igor to Dr Frankenstein. 'Great character walk there Loopy!!' said Hyde-Jones. Newhouse regarded his friend and answered, 'Great walk my arse Roy - I'm trying to get the bloody cork out of this bottle of Chateau Collapseau...' Matthews appeared before him, and offered to hold the wine whilst Newhouse fiddled with the bottle opener. After a couple of seconds, he had it fixed 'Right then Gus...will you join me?' he asked. Matthews smiled as he handed back the bottle.

It was empty.

Some of the Psychic crew seemed to be rather more genuine than others. One or two had all the trappings of their supposed "art", and had very well-rehearsed scripts. Some of them were obviously attempting to trick the public by employing the technique of "cold reading" - whereas others looked as if the act of reading was quite beyond them. Some were just plain bizarre: "Derek the Psychic Gerbil" was not doing what you would call spectacular trade, and "Mrs Dingley's Mystic Fortune-Telling Scones" were not shifting either.

The Rev had first visited the table of a cross-eyed young lady who boasted Romany heritage. She claimed to be able to see, explain, and cleanse the aura of a person. When the Rev had sat down at her table, she had given him a quizzical look, before declaring 'My word Sir- your aura is completely orange...This is what we in the psychic world refer to as a "Key Aura" ...' He had left the table as quickly as he had arrived. He had then spotted the booth of a rather charming looking young lady who advertised that she could perform "Regression Hypnosis". 'Find out who you were in your previous lives...' declared the banner above. The Rev saw his opportunity. This could be the answer to his perpetual craving for the Dark Side. He surely must have been a Pagan High Priest in a previous life, or better still a feared and all-powerful wizard from Iron Age times. Yes - now he would find out, and be one step closer to fulfilling his destiny. He sat down in the comfy leather chair and paid the woman her five pounds.

She introduced herself, then told him what was to happen. He paid scant attention to her introductory speech - he just wanted to get down to business. She produced a crystal on a silver chain, and asked him to follow it as it swung from left to right. With her soothing voice lulling him into a relaxed state, she was soon urging him to sink back in time and return to his previous life. As the "sitter" went back to their former existence, a rather spotty assistant named Denise scribbled notes furiously onto paper with a "Mr Men" biro.

It would appear that the Rev was not the dark weaver of spells that he had hoped for...As it happens; he was regressed back to the time of the French Revolution. It transpired that he was in fact a Peasant who made a living from selling garlic-based wart cures, and who resided in a dwelling which could best be described as a latrine with walls. The only name that everyone seemed to call him by was "Le Bouton".

When the lady brought him back to present day- he resolved to hunt down "Madame", who could translate his French name for him. Out of sight and earshot of the public, Stan was wiping tears of laughter from his spectral face. He didn't need a dictionary – he knew exactly what the word meant...

Nicky, Calderman and Merry were chatting whilst they got their costumes ready for their stint in the tunnels. Merry was complaining loudly: 'I'm really starving- I think I might have to run back up to the assembly hall and grab some sandwiches' he said. 'How come you didn't go home for tea first Gerry?' Calderman enquired. 'Because it's Thursday' he replied. Nicky looked at Calderman, then asked 'And what is the problem with Thursday then, Gerry?' Merry looked downcast... 'Thursdays are my Mum's Yoga nights' he said. The other two boys were still puzzled. 'How does your Mum going to a Yoga class stop you having your tea normally?' asked Nicky. Merry sighed, 'well, since Mum is still banned from driving, she came up with the bright idea of holding the yoga classes at the houses of each of the members in turn - so on a Thursday, the house gets invaded by the women who go to the class'. 'Could you not just keep out of their way?' asked Calderman. 'It's not that easy Mate- they take over the whole house; cover the kitchen with bowls of rice and something called "Toad Foo", and then they move all of the furniture in the front room out of the way, and put little rubber carpets everywhere. When they've done that - it's time for Psycho Delia to take command'.

'Who is she then?' enquired Nicky.

'Oh she is the worst of the lot; she's the sort of "boss" of the group - she tells Mum and the rest how to knot both their legs behind their heads, whilst they listen to sounds of the Rain Forest on my CD player- it's awful...' The boy looked both sad and angry at the same time. 'You can't imagine what it's like - they all suddenly appear in green shiny leotards. I looked into the living room through the serving hatch (he shuddered), and there were green twisted bodies everywhere: it looked like Kermit the Frog and some of his friends had been involved in a terrible road traffic accident...'

Nicky and Calderman were now laughing, not least at the tortured look on the face of their friend. 'But last time it got much worse...' said Merry, 'I was in my bedroom doing some homework, when I heard this awful scream - and Mum comes flying up the stairs, telling me to get on the phone and call an ambulance'.

'What had happened?' asked Nicky.

'Well Mum said that Mrs Halliday had been assuming the "Third position of the ever-vigilant Llama" and that was when she had dislocated her hip again...'

'So what did you do?' Calderman enquired.

'Well, I phoned for the ambulance, whilst Psycho Delia and the rest of the Kermits tried to un-knot Mrs Halliday, but the screaming got a bit loud by then. Mum said, 'Oh poor Mrs H- just look at her Gerald, what does the poor woman look like'- and that's when things went really bad...' The boys stared at Merry, who was looking dejectedly down at his feet.

'Why did things go bad Gerry?' Calderman tactfully asked.

'Because when Mum said, "what does the poor woman look like"- I don't think that 'Like five pounds of shit in a four-pound sack' was quite the answer which she was looking for. Now I have been banned from the house when she has the Kermits round for their bendy sessions'.

Nicky and Calderman gave their friend some very sympathetic pats on the back - well, about as sympathetic as it is possible to be when you are crying with laughter. By means of apology, they decided to revisit the assembly hall, and steal their friend a good selection of sandwiches and cakes.

In the assembly hall, unnoticed by the crowds, Arnold the Dodo strutted purposefully beneath the tables until he arrived at the tea and coffee section - where he happily helped himself to the last of the Custard Cream biscuits...

Having a quick look at the crowd in the hall before the Ghost Walk began, were Hyde-Jones and Newhouse, who was practising with his large hip flask. 'What a weird lot Loopy' said Hyde-Jones, 'Just a load of stupid fakers'.

'Nearly the right word.....' said Newhouse. He took another nip from the flask and said, 'That's why Psychics don't have many children Roy.'

'Why is that?' asked the English Master.

"Cos they've got crystal balls, and they can see what's coming...' giggled Newhouse. 'Enough of your banter and merry japing Sir...' said Hyde-Jones, 'let us take up our stations whereby we may frighten the very poo from our visitors.' The two set off to get ready to launch the evening's entertainment in the tunnels, sharing a few adult jokes, and attempting to trip each other up in a most non-adult fashion.

Already lurking in the dark torch-lit passages was Master Henry Albert Lordsley. Despite his frequent and earnest protestations to the Masters that he must be included in the cast of boys who would be helping to scare the public, it had been decided that for one very good reason, he should not be included. The reason being (as Mr Newhouse had stated) that the boy was a spiteful, malicious little turd. He had decided that having been wrongfully rejected, he would do everything within his power to disrupt the proceedings and ruin the event. He had in his possession several small fireworks, which he planned to toss down the corridors and interrupt the historical speeches that the Masters were giving at specific points on the tour. He also had larger rockets, and he chuckled merrily to himself as he pictured the crowd scattering as these missiles chased them out of the vaults. Currently, he was tucked away in one of the many shadowed alcoves in the passage walls, awaiting the best moment to commence his evil deeds. It would be many years before he would be able to grow a thick black moustache - but when he did, then he would twiddle the end of it and cackle. He had been slightly startled by the appearance of who he assumed to be the first of the "extras", clad in what he thought was a very shabby and thoroughly unconvincing Elizabethan costume. The man had asked him if he could have the cardboard box, when all of the fireworks were used - as he urgently needed to make a life-size horses head for a friend of his. Lordsley had petulantly replied 'No!'- and the man had vanished.

Back at the beginning of the passages, Hyde-Jones had begun his "Welcome Friends and Seekers of the Supernatural" speech. He let the tension build up, before setting off ahead of the group down the corridors. This time, there would be some of the Groundlings standing in alcoves, and at odd corners. They would stand perfectly still - and the crowd would assume that they were dummies. They would then turn to face them, or raise an arm, causing a quick fright to all concerned. Nicky, Calderman, Merry and the gang would alternate between gliding past the end of passages, and mingling unnoticed with the public. Mr Newhouse had his own plans - and apart from his "Rock and Roll Zombie" outfit, had a few more little treats in store for the crowd in general.

The tour had begun as usual with a walk down the long corridors of the Old School buildings. Hyde-Jones would pause in front of various portraits of Old Boys of the Academy, and tell of their prowess in battles of long ago (with lashings of gory detail for maximum effect). Notably missing from the historical oration was the tale of Sir Manley Smyth-Gilbert. This was the old boy of the school who had been present at the Charge of the Light Brigade. His actual achievement was to have been struck down with a particularly virulent bout of dysentery, which kept him firmly (if only) within the confines of the latrine tent. He emerged from the tent just in time to see the Brigade charge off to meet the foe - then had to dash back in, rather swiftly. Still, he was there. His portrait looked down on the corridor proudly, presumably hoping that he hadn't run out of toilet paper.

The crowd came to a sudden halt at the end of the corridor - as all of them could hear the ghostly rattling which echoed down the passage. Some of the braver members of the public approached the door to the cleaner's cupboard, and leapt back as the door handle began to slowly revolve. All was quiet for a few seconds, until again, there came a furious rattling of the door. Quite unnerved himself, Hyde-Jones stepped forward, and gingerly opened the door. The door creaked open revealing a dark, gaping void of blackness within. The silence was shattered when Mr Thwaite the Geography Master quickly emerged from the room declaring 'Well Blimey!! Sorry about that - I seem to have gotten into the wrong room and locked myself in - I didn't scare you, did I?' Hyde-Jones gave him a look of distaste. The man had supposed to have been in an adjoining classroom, where he was to flick the corridor lights on and off dramatically, at a given signal. What the crowd actually got was a confused, babbling man with a moustache, wearing a black off-the-shoulder evening gown and high heels - and a black wig which looked to have been styled by a free-fall parachutist. Luckily, the audience assumed that it was part of the Halloween spectacle, and merely edged their way past the happily grinning Thwaite, and on up the corridor.

In the cellar beneath the Dark Tower, Abolochyn the Demon brushed the lapels of his evening dress, and adjusted his bow tie in front of an ancient and cracked mirror. Although demons do not show up in mirrors, ancient or otherwise, he was nothing if not a stickler for tradition. When satisfied, he turned away from the mirror and adjusted his cuffs. Just for the hell of it, he spun back around to face the mirror once more, with both of his clawed hands miming an imaginary pistol. He raised a scarred eyebrow and declared 'The name 'sh Abolochyn - Demon Abolochyn...' before blowing imaginary smoke from the end of the imaginary gun. He had heard about the Halloween event, and was determined not to miss out on a good evening of supernatural fun. He had brought popcorn and toffee-apples in the shape of shrunken heads. He was going to have fun if it killed him. Or someone else. Which would be even more fun.

Chapter Thirteen:

The next port of call for the supernatural tourists was the Old School staircase, and the Boarding House Lobby corridor. Inside the History classroom on the first floor, Winston Alfred Bailey had heard the procession pass his door. This time, he paid them little attention, and merely settled down to continue teaching his spectral class all about Henry VIII. There were several pupils in the class who had passed over long before the reign of Henry, and so Bailey had to "bring them up to speed", so to speak. One poor little ghostly mite had sat patiently with his hand held in the air since 1602. Bailey thought that it might be finally time to let him go out to the toilet.

There had been a rowdy meeting which had taken place down the gloomy corridors of the Dining Hall cloisters. Some of the individuals had raised objections that the public were being allowed to trample through the Academy willy-nilly, destroying their painstaking handiwork without any regard whatsoever. Angry speeches had been made, and there were factions of the group that now wanted to take direct action against the intruders. A rather large female had attempted to put over the opinion that they should "live and let live", and that they should willingly share the space with any visitors who wished to come. She was silenced by a group of anarchic males, who surrounded her and cut short her pleadings. A large individual then addressed the assembled group. 'I say this to you Brothers and Sisters: have they not torn down our very homes? Have they not swept aside the webs which we lovingly created, and replaced them with fake ones sprayed out of some sort of cylinder? Have they not glued plastic images of us to the walls? Are we prepared to be stamped upon or beaten to death by rolled newspapers just because we have the temerity to call this place our home? I say - No More!! We will defy them. We must spin webs across the passages and block their progress. We shall dangle in a threatening manner from the ceilings. We shall run up trouser legs - and cause females to jump and scream in terror at the very sight of us. I say: Today the passage - tomorrow the cupboard at the back of the French classroom which is hardly ever used anyway because the female there saw one of us on the shelf and so dare not now open the door...'

There was a great reaction to this rousing call. There was much applause from the spiders (or whatever it is that spiders do that could possibly qualify as applause with six legs). Big Derek set off with his band of spider followers to cordon off the passages, and perhaps munch on a moth or two, should the opportunity present itself.

In the dark of the Head Master's unoccupied office, there was a strange squeaking sound from above the ornate fireplace. An observer would have noted that the top right-hand screw which held the polished mahogany shield was slowly and carefully unscrewing itself. When the screw had completed its revolutions, it fell to the carpet with a dull thud. Now the bottom screw began to wind itself free of the wood which surrounded it. It fell and joined its sibling on the carpet. Another fitting began to slowly unwind, and there was just the merest hint of a gentle humming - by way of accompaniment. All of the retaining screws but one were now lying in a heap in front of the fireplace. The stuffed head of the Zebra continued to look out at the world through its glass eyes with a look of surprised gratitude. As the last fixing came loose, the Zebra's head levitated without falling. It floated gently to the desk, where unseen hands laid it with great care. With due reverence, the head was removed from the shield by a gentle rocking back and forth. The animal's head moved this way and that, as if receiving inspection by an expert. A voice that sounded both very caring, and pleased with itself said 'Yes!! That will do nicely, soon have you sorted, my friend...'

Matron had assumed the role of "guide" for the next part of the tour, and Hyde-Jones was very pleased to see that she had chosen the costume of a Nun for the evening. At least now there would be no need to administer oxygen to the frailer male members of the party, and perhaps even Mr Newhouse would be able to persuade his eyes to return to his head. As it happened, she did a very able job of describing all of the spectral activity which could be expected in the area of the Dining Hall cloister. Hyde-Jones had sought out his friend Loopy, and the two were visiting the town of Hipflask- before resuming their roles as "frighteners-in-chief".

'One or two Yanks here tonight I see' said Hyde-Jones.

'Well yes indeed, and can I tell you a very strange but true fact?' said Newhouse.

'Amaze me Dear Boy...' said Hyde-Jones.

'Did you know that one in three Americans weighs the same as the other two...?' Hyde-Jones took the flask from his colleague, and took a large gulp. 'Sir...you are a genius!' he said.

'And that is why people claim to have seen the ghost of poor Neville Lympe on this very spot on the feast of the Turgid Weasel...'

said Matron. She felt so all-commanding in her role, that she opened the Velcro front of the Nun's habit, and stood dramatically, hands on hips- exposing fishnet stockings, leather studded garter, micro-skirt and a bra that the Church would have instantly excommunicated. Three men swiftly converted to Catholicism, and five men near the front of the crowd fainted...

The tour had now reached the dark open space which formed the junction between the Dining Hall Cloister and the Library passage proper. Lordsley had been waiting impatiently in his secluded alcove, and now prepared to light one of the explosive fireworks which he had brought into the tunnels. The trouble was, every time he tried to light the fuse, the wretched thing seemed to blow itself out. He could hear the muted chatter of the crowd as they made their way down the passage towards him, and the clicking of camera shutters as they attempted to get pictures of ghostly figures in the corridor. He tried again, this time using two matches held together. As soon as they flared, they were extinguished as if by some unseen breeze from behind. Using language that his Mother would surely blush at the sound of, he tried a third time. Still the same result. He was about to try the cigarette lighter which he had confiscated from a second-year boy, when a deep and menacing voice from behind him said 'Wot's up then Kid- 'as the cat pissed on yer matches?' He turned and looked up into the grinning face of Abolochyn the Demon, all fangs and evening dress, who dribbled and guffawed at him. He snatched up his bangers, screamed, and fled up the dark passage as rapidly as his legs would carry him.

Around the corner came the crowd, with Weatherill at the head, complete with flaming torch and Solar Topee placed proudly on his head.

To be quite candid, and factually more accurate, it was not really a "crowd"- more of a small group (+VAT) that were following our man Weatherill. The members of the public which had set off on the walk a little earlier had paused around the half-way point of the tour. During his own personal candle-lit walks, in pursuit of sustenance of the alcoholic variety, dear Dr Matthews had happened upon a large and comfortable chamber, which the Groundlings would normally use for Sunday School teaching. After he had introduced himself to the subterranean dwelling community, Matthews had been able to talk Jedekiah and the Elders into letting him "borrow" the chamber for an idea of his own. The Elders had found the History Master to be polite, erudite, extremely likeable and friendly - and as pissed as a fart...Matthews was not selling souvenirs or snacks: he was not handing out maps of the labyrinthine passages and tunnels - oh no... he had a much, much better idea.

The Doctor had set up an extremely well-stocked bar. He stood beaming in his white dinner jacket, with obligatory red carnation in the lapel, whilst handing out drinks to the happy public. The Groundlings had been happy to assist him in his little venture, providing that he did not take money for the drinks. This satisfied their specific moral code. This also satisfied Matthews, who was overjoyed at the prospect of an evening's serious drinking, where no money had to change hands! Yet no fool was he- at the side of the long "bar" table, was a biscuit tin. On the tin was written "Restoration Fund" in large letters. The free drink had certainly loosened the wallets and purses of the attendees - as the tin was steadily filling up with a substantial amount of cash. At this rate: Matthews would be able to pay off some of his considerable bar tab over at the "Five Crowns". He felt that he was entitled to the money - because let's face it; when all was said and done he was an expert on The Restoration. Although now happily five parts pickled, Matthews was giving a spirited lecture on the history of the tunnels and their original purpose (aided and abetted by stage whispers in his ear from Jedekiah, who by now was clutching a large glass of vintage red wine...). Things were going swimmingly, especially for Jedekiah, who was a complete novice at the sport of quaffing vintage booze.

Suddenly, the crowd fell silent. They edged back toward the far wall, as a figure appeared framed in the doorway. The candle light gave the vision an even more supernatural look, and there were a couple of screams as the vision lurched forward - blood dripping from the axe which was embedded in its head.

'Anyone got a couple of aspirins? - I've got a splitting headache...' said Mr Newhouse. A huge laugh erupted from the crowd as the nervous tension was released, and the Master received a quick round of applause for his performance. "Loopy" grinned at the crowd and removed the joke axe from his head, gladly receiving a triple brandy in his other hand from Matthews. Jedekiah put a brotherly arm around his shoulder, and he noticed both the fully-stocked bar, and the kid in the 'Rush' tee-shirt. This had all the hallmarks of a really fun night.

At the "official" snack bar and watering hole further up the dark cloister corridor, Miles Bannister was wondering just where the hell everyone had got to. Even Mrs Noakes had become tired of waiting, and had drifted off in her best Halloween hat to find out what was keeping the guests. The departure (albeit no doubt temporary) of his Spirit Guide had left Bannister feeling rather lost and alone in his alcove, where he twiddled absent-mindedly with a piece of cheese and pineapple on a cocktail stick. He had calculated the square root of four dozen cucumber sandwiches with the crusts cut off, as well as estimating the angular tangential of six dozen sausage rolls: but now he was bored stiff. The only thing which had provided a small window of entertainment was when Lordsley had run screaming down the passage a few minutes earlier, shedding fireworks as he fled.

In a side recess of the "bar", sat Mr and Mrs Quimm, enthusiastic members of the local Rotarians and staunch social climbers. Mr Quimm currently had his eyes glued to the vision which was the Matron, in all her alluring glory. She was set upon by an admiring horde of would-be suitors, all clamouring for both her attention, and her private telephone number. Mrs Quimm suddenly found herself beside a rather troubled-looking man in Elizabethan costume, who was attempting to engage her in a conversation about how one might best attach a stuffed head of a zebra onto a horse. She had tried unsuccessfully to get rid of the strange man by informing him that 'she didn't do her own sewing - they had a maid who took care of all of that sort of thing', but he was annoyingly insistent. Eventually, she had run out of what little patience which she might have had, and told the man to 'just go away...' The man gave her a contemptuous look, and declared 'So you think that you can scoop the workings out of a poor little fox, then wear it around your neck - but you are too posh to help a person who has a genuine problem and wants to help out a good friend do you? Well I wifh thee naught but ill fortune, and I hope that yon foxy haf a really good fhite down your coat, Miftress...' The man departed in a huff, and "foxy" duly obliged.

Hyde-Jones had to steer Matron out of the doorway and out along the passage, because that was obviously the only way that the male contingent could be persuaded to continue with the tour. Matthews was re-stocking the table with booze prior to the next group arriving, and Mr Newhouse and Jedekiah were playing air guitars - whilst singing a spirited version of *Run to the Hills* by Iron Maiden. Elsie Noakes had located Stan, and the two floated off with the crowd like a spirit version of Darby and Joan. Nicky and the boys now got the chance to do their "walk through", which both frightened and delighted the visitors in equal measure.

Not too far from the current tour route: The Rev had sneaked into the cellar of the Dark Tower by torchlight. He had drawn a rather hurried and wobbly-lined pentagram on the floor with chalk. Now was the perfect time to contact the Dark Legions, on Halloween eve. He unfolded the piece of paper upon which he had painstakingly written down the incantations for summoning the Lords of Darkness. As he began to chant the required words, he wished that he had remembered to bring his Satanic reading glasses (as some of those phrases were a real bugger to make out). At the end of the evocation - he raised both arms, and waited for the doors of hell to open. Slowly, so very slowly, a sulphurous red and yellow mist began to rise in the centre of the pentagram. The mist formed itself into a column taller than a man, almost becoming solid in front of his eyes. From all around him came the most ghastly, tinny music that he had ever heard - music that made his very skin crawl, and his teeth itch. He flinched, as the soul-scouring music was suddenly replaced by a guttural, yet high-pitched voice. The voice (which made his hair ache) stated:

'Thank you for trying to contact the Realm of the Damned. All of our Demons are currently busy tormenting lost souls, and cannot answer your incantations. Please select from the following options: For Curses (to place or remove) - please light candle one: To smite with disease or plague - please light candle two: To set up a Demonic Possession - please light candle three: For selling your mortal soul to Satan - please light candle four: To speak to a Demonic Entity - please light candle number five: To hear these options again - please sacrifice a chicken...'

'Oh- for Christ's Sake!!' said the Rev.

The light blinked out.

Now nearing the end of the tour, Hyde-Jones had gathered the party near the last bend of the passage near the Library. 'I must tell you Ladies and Gentlemen...' he intoned gravely 'That it is this very corridor that perhaps the most terrifying vision of all is often glimpsed. It is a sight that has sent many a strong man running for his life, and most to fall to their knees and pray for the help of God...'

'It's my pay cheque...' said Mr Newhouse, from the back.

He was "ssshhd" into silence by the audience. 'I refer of course to the ghastly severed head of Sir John Thomas deWinkel - martyred on this very spot in 1688. The disembodied head is seen floating along the corridor, grinning horribly - and to see the ghost is reputed to be a portent of doom...'

Goodwill had decided to attend the event tonight; after all, his Wife had gone out to her usual book club meeting, and besides - he wanted to see just how much mon- how much fun the public were having. With him, were three members of the Board of Trustees, and the ever-present Miss Piggott, in her twinset and pearls - with an expression like a badly constipated elk. The Trustees had enjoyed their tour so far. They had seen most of the ghosts (both real and created by special effects), and had been impressed by the boys' performance in costume. They had been somewhat confused when they had passed one of the rooms off the Dining Hall cloister, where a man seemed to be doing his best to fit the head of a zebra onto the body of a chestnut horse, which was protesting most vociferously. They assumed that this had been part of the "entertainment". They had altogether missed the spectacle of a man in Elizabethan costume as he came flying out of the room backwards, clutching at his nethers and moaning. They had also been extremely confused when they had come upon what appeared to be a very well-stocked bar in the vaults. They left the bar a great deal more confused - as Matthews was serving triple measures for "Happy Hour". Goodwill had another brainwave at this point. He could open up a permanent wine bar in the cloister, with an entrance up to the street above. Yes! He could call it "The Cellar" or "The Vaults" or something equally trendy - and rake in a small fortune for hi- for the Academy, of course. He would suggest it to the Trustees...

Down the corridor, Master Henry Albert Lordsley was busy retrieving the fireworks which he had dropped, in between bouts of terror in case that oaf in the Demon costume decided to come back. He dropped the pyrotechnics into the box, and made his way up the passages toward where he hoped the crowd would now be assembled.

The people had now reached the last few twists and turns of the cloisters. It was here that Big Derek and his group of Arachnoterrorists had spun their many webs across the passage, to bar the way of the intruders. He had taken up station on the wall, to observe the panic that his band of spider warriors would cause. 'None shall pass!! We shall be victorious!!' he shouted. 'Let this day be written as the first courageous act of' - **SPLATT!!!**

'Damn filthy things...' said Goodwill, replacing his shoe 'can't stand the wretched creatures- neither can my Wife. Here, let me brush these webs out of your way...' He led the Trustees past the remains of the spider leader, now embedded in the ancient mortar of the cloister wall. From the ceiling, just adjacent to the vaulted arch, one spider freedom fighter looked down, then spoke to his comrade:

'See that? That was a real shame that was. That was Big Derek if I'm not mistaken'.

'He was your flatmate, wasn't he?'

'He is now...'

Lordsley was panicking: he could hear the footsteps echoing up the passage in the gloom. If he didn't hurry, he would not be able to get clear and enjoy the panic as the fireworks caused mayhem amongst the visitors. With his hands trembling, he scratched the head of a match against the box - damn it - wrong side. Flipping the box over, he tried again. This time the match flared into life, but was blown out by Stan, who was standing at his side and sniggering. Quickly, he fumbled another match out of the box and struck it. Stan let it flame yellow for an instant, and then blew that one out too. The footfalls were nearing the corner- this was his last chance: he pulled the entire sleeve away from the match box and grabbed a cluster of matches. He then had to find where the box lid with the sandpaper had gone to. Kneeling like an Olympic sprinter, he ground the match heads against the rough surface, waited until they flared- then dropped them into the box which contained all of the fireworks- and fled up the passage. He caught up with the visitors, and did his best to blend in with the crowd, glancing back down the dark corridor and waiting for the fun to begin.

The fun began when a near-hysterical Mr Thwaite came sprinting out of the gloom carrying his high-heeled shoes 'My God!!!' he shouted 'It's the Head!!! I've just seen the Head - coming this way!!' There was panic amongst the visitors, who all attempted to get out of each other's way at the same time. The visual effect was that of a sudden outbreak of synchronised break dancing in a tin of sardines. Around the corner came the Dreaded Head, closely followed by the equally dreaded Trustees. The Head did not look at all happy. 'Hyde-Jones - I found these on the passage floor, damned dangerous things to leave lying about all over the place eh?' (He opened his hand - revealing a clutch of unspent matches and the box top). If I find out who it is that has been showing a complete disregard for the visitors' health and safety - then someone is going to get a rocket!' he fumed.

At the other end of the passage was the box of fireworks. In his haste to make himself look important, and in the gloom of the cloister, Goodwill had stormed straight past the box - from which now came an alarming and portentous fizzing. The crowd inched away from Goodwill as if he were handing out pinless hand grenades. The man looked down at his feet and spotted more matches on the dusty floor 'Great Gods!!!' he bellowed 'Here's some more of the damned things!!!' He bent down to scoop up the offending articles.

It is a fact that the Gods of Probability enjoy a bloody good laugh just the same as anyone else. The lengths which they go to in order to achieve their amusement can be rather odd, if not downright vindictive, on occasions. Lordsley had dropped the lighted matches into the box. This had been just enough to light several fuses of the fireworks. The largest of the rockets had the honour of being the nearest pyrotechnic to the flame. The fuse ceased to fizz- and now a shower of beautiful silver and yellow sparks gushed out of the end, as it strained to achieve take-off speed. The rocket shot out of the box and up at the wall, where it received a forty-five-degree deflection. It now shot up the dark passage at a cruising height of approximately two feet five inches. According to the laws of physical comedy, there are certain rules which must always be observed. What happened next had to be seen to be believed...

Goodwill was gathering up the fallen matches. Hurtling out of the darkness came a screaming, spark-spewing banshee. As the rocket shot toward him Goodwill turned his head to see what was causing the shriek - but kept his exposed backside at a height of, allowing for wind shear and current climatic conditions, oh, about two feet five inches. The rocket made a soft impact, and followed its mission instructions to the letter. Now it was the turn of the rest of the box of fireworks to join in with the mighty chorus. His pride as injured as his poor bum, Goodwill lay face down in the dust as the Blitz erupted above his head, with many a Bang! Pop! Whee! Fizzle! and Zing! There was little to do but call an ambulance, and try and make the poor man as comfortable as they could until it arrived. The Paramedics had dashed down the passage, and loaded the Head Master onto a stretcher face down. They had trouble carrying him out to the waiting vehicle, as they were almost collapsing with laughter. A large crowd had gathered in two long lines in front of the doors of the ambulance, and the Head was carried down between them, with the thick stick of the rocket very visibly protruding from his hind quarters.

'Well blow me down... it's a Toff- Apple!!' exclaimed Albert Brooks.

Hyde-Jones and Newhouse watched as the ambulance pulled away.

'Tell you what Loopy...' he said, taking a sip from the hip flask 'I don't think those trousers will be usable again'.

'Wrecked 'em'.

'Yep - and that too'...

Chapter Fourteen:

It was the day after Halloween - All Souls Day, but for some, the fog of weirdness had yet to evaporate. Uncle Joe had called at Nicky's house very early. He had come to drop off flyers for a new venture which he had just set up. He had become aware of how nervous the villagers seemed to be about becoming the victims of muggings and assault, as they went about their daily business. It was a real concern it would seem, and even Mrs Jenkins (who had her own permanent olfactory deterrent) had expressed her concern. Joe had also noted the current trend toward Vegetarianism, and the local Butcher had recently been heard to complain that several of the village ladies had refused his sausage.

Ever the opportunist, Joe had sat up all night, drinking copious amounts of tea until he had come up with his brainwave. It all made sense - he could combine self-defence and a vegetarian lifestyle in one sure-to-turn-a-profit scheme. He had dashed out early in the morning and secured a weekly booking for the village hall. His next port of call was his drinking buddy who worked in a small printing enterprise. Joe then set about designing a completely revolutionary system of unarmed combat. This would involve using just the feet for attack, with the hands providing defensive manoeuvres. He had studied Thai boxing and Karate moves, and had drawn up a comprehensive manual of deadly footwork. Combine this with a meat-free diet option, and he could sit back and wait for the cash to roll in...

He put up a large poster on the door of the village hall that very day. As he smoothed out the paper and pushed home the last drawing pin, he knew that he had finally come up with a winner. In large gaudy letters, the poster had shouted its message of "No Muggers - No Meat" to the world. He would be seen as one of the great beneficiaries of Mankind. People would stop him in the street, shake him firmly by the hand, and thank him for changing their lives.

He would be remembered in years to come as "The man who invented Toe-Fu..."

Nicky's own personal fog was one of early teenage depression. He had not been able to attend Jozza's Halloween party. She would probably never speak to him again. Apart from the fact that he would not get his CD back, he had blown the chance of ever getting to put his hand on h- 'Oy!!- Dreamer Boy- this is your stop!' called the bus driver. Nicky quickly gathered up his school equipment, with the satchel managing to wrap its strap around his arm and cutting off his circulation. Too fed up to really pay any attention, Nicky merely unwound it, and plodded off toward the Academy with his arm now tingling like nettle stings.

The daily 'meet and greet' session took place in the quad, with an agitated conversation already underway between Trevill on the one hand, and Jackson in the blue corner:

'Well Oi for one thinks that she'm gone barmy' stated Trevill.

'She's not barmy- it's what all girls do, so I'm told' said Jackson.

'Well Oi carrnt be seein' the sense of it: Oi mean...Pluckin' out her eyebrows- just to draw 'em back on with a pencil...' said the Dorset correspondent on Beauty Care.

'It's just what they all do, Trevill...' said Jackson.

'An' Oi still says that she'm barmy- Oi mean, Oi wouldn't shave off moi beard, an' then paint another one on, would Oi?'

'Tell her if she ever needs any assistance with shaving her legs - then she is welcome to take full advantage of my Personal Grooming services...' said Weatherill, hopefully.

A clip around the ear from Jackson put an end to the conversation...

Down in the Library cloisters, there was a moaning which was emanating from beneath the table which had served as a "bar" the previous night. Jedekiah was holding his head, suffering the after-effects of his introduction to the world of heavy drinking. 'Dear HoBi save me...' he groaned, as he rolled over and looked through bleary eyes to his left. The smiling figure of Matthews was lying on his back, still resplendent in white dinner jacket. He was a little creased, and his carnation had ever so slightly wilted, but the History Master appeared to be in a state of soporific bliss. He rolled over, and sat up, pushing the white table cloth from off his head.

'Ah- Jedders, my Old Fruit- how the devil are you?' asked Matthews.

Jedekiah peered at him through bloodshot eyes, and tried to respond: 'I tell thee my friend- someone has verily come in the night, removed mine eyes, relieved themselves into the holes, and then put them back...'

Matthews laughed, and told him 'What you need is the Hair of the Dog, Dear Boy...'

'I need to seek the services of an Apothecary, for within it I hear the mighty booming of thunder, and a lurching of the stomach as if I were borne upon the sea in a tempest' Jedekiah replied.

'I think you may have a hangover...' said Matthews.

'I think that I shall die- may HoBi strengthen my resolve never to touch the Demon Drink again, as long as I may live...' wailed Jedekiah. 'I need to get me to a hospital- and obtain such physic as will cure this fevered palsy, not this "Hairy Dog" of which you speak'.

'You don't drink, do you Jedders?' asked Matthews.

'Never! Strong liquor will mock the Soul' his friend answered.

'So when you get up in the morning, that's the best that you are going to feel all day!!' said Matthews. 'Anyway - what time is it?'

'Nine o'clock Mr Matthews'.

'Not opening time yet then?'

'No - I should not think so...'

'Good, then if that's the case - let's have a lie-in...'

On their way to their first lesson, the boys had been intercepted by Mrs Finucane the Cleaner, who was looking strangely worried- quite different from her normal amiable demeanour. She pulled the lads over to one side, and waited until they were alone. 'Oi think that we may need to convene a special meetin' of ODD agents...' she said, conspiratorially. 'Why's that, Mrs F?' asked Nicky. 'Is something the matter?' asked Calderman. Agent J-Cloth glanced this way and that...''Tis yer man Brooks: I'm thinkin' that he's after havin' some sort of breakdown. Himself has put on his full camouflage kit - and now the big eejit has locked himself in his shed, and he's playin' recordings of the speeches of dat fella Winston Churchill - never a good sign, I tell ye...' The boys could all see that the lady was concerned about the turn of events, and they promised to help as soon as they could. They would contact her at break time, and find out just why Albert was about to start fighting on the beaches...

On his way to the Academy was Mr Gregor Duggan. Now that the early morning fog had dissipated, he was enjoying the sunshine, and would take his time getting to his classes. There was time for a cup of tea and perhaps a wee slice of cake. He studied the menu of the cafe, and made his choice. Maybe a nice fresh cream slice would be just the thing to have w- 'Oy Duggan- we want a little word with you...' His arms were gripped by two very insistent hands, not yet causing him any pain- but hinting at the fact that pain was certainly an option should he choose not to comply. 'My word- you're a difficult man to get hold of' said the gruff voice of Adrian Swall.

'You're wrong there Mate, I got 'old of 'im quite easily...' said his accomplice, Bert 'Bendy' Fletcher. Swall gave him a disappointed look.

Fletcher spoke in an exaggerated manner, partly due to the roll-up cigarette which dangled permanently from one corner of his mouth. His crumpled suit had a most peculiar mottled black and grey colour, like marble with a heavy patina of dust. This was because it had formed its own peculiar colour from the combination of the original fabric, and the years' worth of accumulated cigarette ash which had fallen onto it. Fletcher was a habitual criminal, with a reputation of being able to get into a building very rapidly. The building in question was Prison. He had been in and out of jail so often over the years, that his cell had a revolving door fitted. He leered at Duggan, then leered through the window at the occupants of the cafe. He leered at the young waitress who was serving the teas: he was King Leer.... 'We are going to have a nice little chat with Mr Figg' announced Swall 'I'm sure that we shall find all sorts of interesting things to discuss. Mr Figg has been very worried about you. He will love to hear just where you have been, and what you have been up to- and possibly anyone interesting who you might have been having a chat with...' Duggan looked left and right- there didn't seem much chance of him being able to make an escape from the two thugs. 'Mr Swall...' said Fletcher, 'Do we 'ave to go right at this moment?' 'Yeah- we do' answered Swall. 'Well can we 'ang on a minute or two?' Fletcher pleaded. 'Why - what is it?' demanded Swall. 'It's just that them almond fancies look lovely - and I 'aven't ad any breakfast yet...'. Swall gave the man another look. He would charge him for any more of them. 'Stop buggering about, Bendy' he growled 'Go and get the car...'

Back in English class, one of the usual "debates" had ensued; when Davis had enquired if Mr Hyde-Jones intended to put on a special Christmas play (the boy had obvious aspirations toward becoming an actor). The Master had replied that he had been thinking about getting a small concert together, but that there may not be time to rehearse it before the epic Carol Concert in the church. It had all kicked off when Calderman had suggested that they put on a modern Nativity play - and Merry had hinted that Davis should play the part of Bethlehem...

Flying off at one of his normal tangents, Trevill had been most insistent to have a question answered. Hyde-Jones had listened patiently. 'Surr - Oi was just wonderin'...do Ee think that the Elephant Man was ever bullied at school?'

'What an odd question Mr Trevill- what makes you ask that?' said Hyde-Jones.

'Well Surr, Oi was up all noight worryin' about it. I thought that it would 'ave been 'orrible for the Elephant Man if 'ee 'ad been the victim of bullyin' - because Ee would never forget, would Ee?'

The car pulled up outside the rather tatty-looking house, and Swall drove up into the small parking space. The two men bundled Duggan out of the vehicle, and up to the front door. 'Don't forget to lock the car' said Fletcher, 'you know what theivin' bastards they are round 'ere'. Without looking at his accomplice, Swall pointed the remote device at the rusted car, and there was an arthritic "clunk" as the doors locked. Duggan was pushed up the stairs to a back room, where Mr Figg was standing behind a threadbare armchair - looking out of the window at the unkempt garden beyond. 'Ah hello at last Mr Duggan...' he said 'so nice of you to come and see me again. I really do love it when old friends call round unexpectedly for a nice cup of tea and a good old chin-wag. So- do sit down. Make yourself comfortable. Have a biscuit. Tell me what you have been up to, and where the bloody hell my sodding merchandise is - you devious little bastard...' Duggan flinched back in the chair, gripping the arms, and rather wishing that he hadn't, when his hands found something sticky on the fabric.

'I was coming to see you, Misterr Figg...' said the nervous Duggan. Figg rounded on him - 'You were, were you? Well you certainly took your bloody time getting here didn't you? I was going to swim the bloody channel naked, but I haven't done it yet...'

'You don't want to be doin' that Boss...' said Fletcher, 'that water is freezin', an' it will make your wi -'

'Shut up, Fletcher, shut up right now...' said Figg in tones of menace.

'You see, the trivial, niggling little problem which I have is this: I arranged for you to undertake a little bit of work for me, on behalf of my boss. We supplied all of the raw materials for you as arranged. We left you alone to get on with it. We arranged to come back and collect the merchandise, so that you were not put to any inconvenience. I was so very disappointed when my staff here informed me that when they came to see you in order to make a collection- there was no merchandise to collect: and no Mr Duggan to ask about it. My Boss has been asking me questions, Mr Duggan. They were very specific questions - and I think that it would be rude not to provide equally specific answers, don't you agree?' Duggan tried to sink lower in the chair, feeling the blood drain from his face.

'Let me tell you what is going to happen, Mr Duggan...' Figg said, 'You are suddenly going to think to yourself "Oh silly Me...Why here is Mr Figg's merchandise! I haven't lost it at all!! I must let him know straight away that I have found it, and he will be so happy". If my vision of the future does not come true, Mr Gregor Duggan - then the old bones that my colleagues and I help the Archaeology Society to dig up, may include some of yours...'

He leaned forward and gently patted the cheek of the terrified Duggan. Figg suddenly stood in front of the man, and growled 'You have got the rest of the week to remember where you have put the stuff, and then my friends and I will be calling on you and borrowing your pliers for a little job which I have in mind...Right you two- get this idiot out of here and back to that nuthouse where he plays with his tools'.

Fletcher had been looking out of the front window. 'Can't do that, Mr Figg' he said.

'Oh do shut up Fletcher- just throw him back in the car and drop him off' said Figg.

'Can't do that Mr Figg...'Fletcher repeated. Figg looked angrily at the ash-covered lackey. 'And why not?' he asked. "Cos someone's nicked the wheels -the car's on bricks Mr Figg.'

Agent J-Cloth and the boys who were card-carrying members of ODD had met up at the fortress shed of Mr Albert Brooks at morning break time. Mrs Finucane had already bruised her knuckles trying the secret knock, well before the boys had joined her. The small windows of the shed were set high up, and the heavy blinds were pulled within. Mrs F stood fiddling nervously with her rosary, and declared 'I think that Himself has gone mad in there, he isn't even answering on the feckin' radio...' To gain entry to the premises would require the services of an expert, and one stepped forward out of the group of boys, wearing a completely unexpected Matador's hat. Weatherill gave a low bow, and then strode over to the cast iron gutter downpipe on the corner of the shed. He raised his arm like a stage magician, showing that there was indeed nothing up his sleeve, and then swiftly bent down and put his hand inside the end of the drain pipe. He turned back to the group with his arm aloft- a small bunch of keys held triumphantly in his dripping hand. 'An old trick that I learned from my Granddad' declared "Weatherillo The Great". There was a little confusion, as they tried to work out which key fitted which lock, but eventually they were able to ease open the outer door. 'Better check for booby-traps lads...' Mrs F warned, 'That old fecker has a bit of a strange sense of fun when it comes to uninvited guests'. Slowly and carefully, the team edged inside the inner door, which was surprisingly unlocked. They moved with caution into the first large area of Albert's shed, and noticed an object in the middle of the floor. It was about the size of a cricket ball, and brown. 'Get down!!' shouted Merry: 'It's a grenade!'

Nicky inched forward for a closer look, and reported 'It's a potato...'

He was about to pick up the lone vegetable, when Kendy called out to him 'Don't touch it Shep- just step away slowly...' Kendy himself approached the potato, and produced a small torch from his pocket. He nodded to the group, then shone the light onto, and then up from, the abandoned spud. They could now clearly see the fine fishing line which was attached to the potato- and which stretched up into the beams of the shed. The line ran up to the first roof beam, where it was attached to a cardboard box. Merry was horrified, not so much at the finding of a potato on the floor - but at the fact that he now had a leek in his trousers. Nobody wished to speculate as to what the contents of the box might be, but they gave the booby-trap a wide berth and proceeded up to Albert's rough wooden table. Mrs Finucane began to search the papers which were strewn all across the table top, and the boys looked in the nearby open cupboards for any clues.

Mrs F gave a low whistle and declared 'Jaysus! Oi dread to think what himself has been cookin' up with this little lot'. She held up a sheaf of papers which were roughly stapled together. The boys craned to see them, and made out the title *Hobbyists Guide to Explosives and Demolitions* on the top sheet. Calderman then called over to the group 'It looks like our man Albert is going on a little holiday soon...' The boy showed them what he had found. It was an open airline ticket, the destination being Rio De Janero. Mrs F was staring at the calendar nailed to the wall. It featured a winsome young lady who really should have known better. It also showed the date of November the Fifth, heavily circled in red ink...

Chambers was at his wits end. He had demanded the key to the Head Master's study from Miss Piggott, and it had taken him almost an hour to argue the wretched thing out of her grasp. At one stage, he felt that he might have to wrestle the key out of her grip - and he had been by no means confident of winning that battle. With a scowl and a mouth like a cat's bottom, she had slapped the key into his hand and stomped off back into her own lavender-scented domain. She would be visiting Gerald later, and would be sure to tell him of the behaviour of the Pretender to his throne.

The floor was littered with bent objects. Chambers had tried all manner knives found in drawers, tea spoons, and an ornate letter opener, with which to open the top drawer of the metal filing cabinet - and the small nut deceptively heavy petty cash box which was bolted to the floor. He sat back in the Head's chair, and wiped the beads of sweat from his brow. He knew that there was a hidden safe somewhere within the geographical area of this room, and he was determined to locate it. He began to ask himself some important questions: would there be any incriminating papers in the safe - assuming he could find it? Where would he be able to spot something which had been hidden by someone who didn't want it to be spotted? Where had the Zebra's head gone? The polished wooden shield hung over the fireplace - but was noticeably devoid of anything remotely Zebra-based.

He checked the antique writing desk drawers. His trawling produced a Portuguese phrase book, two seed catalogues, a much-thumbed "Men's magazine", and a confusingly blank desk diary. Had the devious old sod made entries in invisible ink? He turned the diary this way and that, trying to catch the light, but could detect no traces of writing. He wondered: if you regularly used an invisible ink pen - then how did you know when it had run out of ink? Settling back into his task, Chambers poked around every corner of the room looking for secret panels. He pulled back each candle stick and tapped every oak panel, but could find no hidden doors. Winston Alfred Bailey (History, RIP 1916) regarded him from his seat in the leather chesterfield. He felt that this poor boy might need his assistance...

There was a curious knock on the study door. He instructed the purveyor of the knock to enter, and was surprised when Matron slunk over to the desk. She sat on the edge, with her short skirt riding up to reveal a little more Matron than he could cope with at the moment. 'I just called over to see how you were getting on'... she purred.

'Ah, well now, to be honest Dear lady, I am just getting used to holding the reins...' he stammered in reply.

'Good boy!' said Matron, 'bring them with you when you come to see me at three o'clock...'

Chapter Fifteen:

Professor Dick Strangler and his friend and colleague Darwin were enjoying a coffee in the Physics laboratory prep room. In the corner of the room, the "Vortex" continued to display its disco light show occasionally, but had now decided to calm down a little. Darwin studied his digestive biscuit and said wistfully, 'Almost Christmas again- where does the time go to?'

Strangler looked up from his marking and replied 'well strictly speaking, what you are talking about is the relative passage of periods into which we have mechanically divided the days into hours, minutes and seconds. Whilst there is a seasonal change which reflects the movement of the earth into a more wintry climatic presentation, the relevant periods do not in fact vary to a degree that the actual passage of time is significantly foreshortened'.

'Would you like me to pretend that I actually understood the merest iota of what you just said?' Darwin asked his friend.

'Err, sorry old Chap- yes, er, nearly jingle bells and all that tinselly stuff again, as you say' strangler replied. Darwin continued: 'Now that we've got Chambers at the helm, do you think that he will force through all of the cuts that Goodwill was intent on making?' His colleague put down the text books.

'Well I doubt very much if he would want to cut back the Physics Department, especially since we have made so many giant leaps forward recently...'

'Yes, but take for instance, the issue of costs- I mean (he gestured over to the vortex amidst its complex workings) your little "toy" over there must be really eating up the energy, and even Chambers will have a breakdown when he sees the electricity bills...'

'Not necessarily...' said Strangler, with a smile- 'I have the matter fully under control - watch this'. He stood up and took a piece of paper out of a box file. He placed the paper on the table, and began folding it into angular shapes. When he was satisfied, he showed his friend the aeroplane which he had created out of the paper sheet. Approaching the vortex, he casually rolled up one sleeve, and slightly adjusted the "flaps" of the paper plane. He launched the plane into the vortex, where it disappeared with a small "pop". He raised a finger: 'Just hang on a moment...' he said. After a few seconds, the paper plane came soaring out of the vortex, and Strangler caught it in mid-air. He unfolded the sheet of paper, and presented it to Darwin for inspection.

The sheet of paper was actually the most recent electricity bill for the Physics Department. The demand had been for a sum of £758.63. Across the paper, stamped diagonally in red ink, was the legend "paid in full".

'How the bloody hell does that work?' asked the amazed Darwin.

'Don't really know - don't really care!!' said Strangler 'but I have proof of payment, so up yours, Goodwill!!'.

'Would it work with Divorce papers do you think?' asked Darwin.

'Might be worth a try' said Strangler 'Oh do excuse me - I have to let the cat in...' He went over to the French windows, and swung open one side. 'Isn't he gorgeous, he came in through the vortex you know - such good company...'

Darwin pressed himself back in his chair, and said 'He's certainly...I mean he's...but it's- he really is quite fluffy, isn't he'.

Strangler patted the head of his new "friend", and said 'He's just as playful as a little kitten, chasing after a ball of wool'.

'You do realise that he is in fact a '*Smilodon*' do you?' asked Darwin.

'A Sabre-Tooth tiger?, Oh yes of course - and by the way, his name is "Simon"...' Strangler replied. He cooed over the beast- 'Has my little Simey come to say hello to Daddy's fwend den?'.

Darwin's eyes would not physically open any wider: he stuttered 'Well..Ah...err...so what does "Simey" like to play with then?'

'At the moment- mostly First Formers, but he's getting better - he's hardly leaving a tooth mark on them these days!' said Strangler. Darwin swallowed hard, as the big cat rested its head on his knee, and looked up at him with large, happy, and unmistakably carnivorous eyes...

'But where on earth does he sleep?' he asked.

'With those teeth - anywhere he bloody well wants to...' said Strangler.

The Maths lesson today had been a complete shambles. Nicky had so many problematic thoughts bouncing around the inside of his head, that he simply could not concentrate on a single word which the Master had said. What was the "mission" that Albert Brooks was engaged upon? Why were all of the Staff suddenly so jumpy? Why had Dr Chambers not appeared in Assembly for the past few days? What was he supposed to say to Jozza when he saw her again, and he had to explain his non-appearance at her Halloween party? Why was Bannister talking to himself yet again? Whatever the Master was attempting to explain, from the sound of it, it had nothing to do with quadratic equations...The reason for the confusion (as if Bannister needed a reason) was that Mrs Elsie Noakes just could not fathom how to work out her Water Services bill - and had demanded that Miles explain the calculations to her in detail. The question of why his "Spirit Guide" would need to be paying a Water bill for services supplied to her Heavenly residence didn't enter his head. Mrs Noakes did though - and it was interesting to hear the double-sided conversation taking place via one man...

'Madam - my calculations are correct! If you don't agree with the figures, then I suggest that you take it up with the Water People...'

'But I can't have used that much Dear, it's not as if I leave the taps running' she said.

'I thought that you would get your water for free?'.

'Free? And where would all of this 'free water' come from Deary?'.

'Well, perhaps from clouds? They are up where you are, after all'.

'Do you have any idea how long it takes to fill a bath from a cloud? I can't spend time standing about - I'll miss all of my television programmes: anyway, Mrs Timkins needs two showers a day because of her condition...'

'Yes of course...how remiss of me not to have remembered'.

'And then there's the Electricity bill...'

'You have to pay for that as well?'.

'Unless you want to practice the harp in the dark Dear, yes of course you do - which reminds me, do you have any spare 13amp fuses?....'

Bannister sat back in his chair, folded his arms, and decided to let Mrs Noakes get it off her spectral chest. 'And whatever you do - take the day off on November the Fifth - I insist' she said.

Nicky sat bolt upright, now completely alert. Why had Elsie mentioned November 5th?

Doctor Johnathan Darwin of the Biology department had some problems of his own, which were about to wave cheerfully at him over the serene horizon of what should have been a normal day. "DJD" had been summoned to the Headmaster's study, where Dr Chambers was currently sitting at the desk, surrounded by a mountain of escaped paperwork. He knocked at the door and entered on command.

'Ah Darwin...' Chambers said, 'Now what exactly is going on in Biology?'

'Well, there are some promising advances in stem cell research and gene splicing, as far as I am aware, and s -'

'Don't be an arse Man: I mean why am I getting letters from Solicitors, concerning allegations of cruelty to animals within the Biology laboratory?' Chambers demanded.

Darwin was completely caught off guard by this accusation, and could only stand open-mouthed like a salmon stranded on the bank - with no overdraft facility. 'I'm sorry Dr Chambers' he declared, 'I have no idea at all what you are talking about...' Chambers rummaged for, finally located, and brandished a vellum sheet in front of Darwin's face.

'This Man – this! What the hell is all this about?' Darwin fearfully took the sheet from the Deputy Head's hand and read the contents. It was a notice to attend court for the proceedings of an alleged case of assault upon the person of three of the laboratory's mice. They were normally used as subjects in experiments with such things as mazes, but showed little character or spirit. In Darwin's opinion, they were three bland mice. It would appear that during the course of one recent Parents' evening, a woman by the name of Mrs Farmer had been startled by the mice. At some stage, she seems to have been chased by the rodents around the laboratory - and she responded to the threat by actually causing them bodily harm via the use of an extremely sharp kitchen utensil.... The Solicitor acting for the Plaintiffs openly stated that he had never seen such a thing in his life.

Darwin looked up from the letter. 'I'm not quite sure what to say Dr Chambers...' he said.

'And what about this?...' asked Chambers. He flicked a small white business card toward Darwin, who caught it with a deft sweep of his hand. It was printed on one side only. The message on the card stated:

This has been an ODD job.

With the weak winter sun sinking lazily below the western horizon (and heading off to the warmer regions of the globe, where it might possibly be let have a crafty fag in peace), school was ending for the day. The classroom lights were coming on, as Mrs Finucane and her team of specialists began to remove the detritus left by the students and staff alike. Some of the girls complained to Mrs F that the boys had been up to their old tricks again - stuffing food behind the radiators, which would not be spotted until the bad smell became unbearable. This time it was apparently almond cake or marzipan that was leaving traces of its tell-tale odour in the corridors. The smell was particularly strong in Miss Piggott's office- but that could just as well have been the general "Eau d' Emilia", who knows.

Someone who quite clearly did know was now sitting at his table soldering the connections on a remote control unit. Albert Brooks was displaying all of the worrying calm of a man who has been pushed over the edge, taken photographs, bought a tee-shirt or two, sent postcards, and decided that enough was really enough this time. Sacrificing his own free time was not enough then? Nor almost ending up divorced through neglecting his Wife and Family? What about nearly catching his death of pneumonia whilst re-seeding the pitches in the rain at midnight? Had he ever asked for payment for all of the extra-curricular activities he supervised out of school hours? And now the sack. Wasn't this the way with the so-called "Ruling Classes"? Take the labours of the ordinary working man, and pound him hard into the ground, taxing him all the while. If he slacks - beat him: if he falls ill due to over-work, then sack him: if he falls dead on the job - then deduct a day's pay for not giving adequate notice of termination, then use his body as a draught-excluder so that at least you get some work out of the lazy bugger...They would not let him into the Academy, all those years ago, oh no... not him and his "grass roots". He had to be content with cutting their grass, and changing their light bulbs, and hanging their pictures straight, and repairing the armchairs when their lazy fat arses had burst through the seats...

He had once attended a lecture given by that loony Strangler, on the subject of "The Big Bang". He had even worn his suit. And they had laughed - oh, how they had laughed, at the Grounds keeper wanting to educate himself. Well now they were going to get a front-row seat for a big bang of their very own - let's see them all have a bloody good chuckle at that.

Nicky was pleased when the day had finally ended. As his bus had dropped him off on his road at the top of the hill, the cloud which had been nonchalantly following the bus from the town pushed past its brethren and let loose with a burst of stinging rain. The boy held the satchel over his head to keep off the worst of the deluge, and to act as a warning to the leather mugger that no further bad behaviour would be tolerated. Through the misty curtain of falling rain, Nicky saw four dark figures approaching, walking unhurriedly along the path- despite the downpour. Oh God No! - it was Jozza and some of her friends. Nicky desperately tried to calculate if he would have enough time to get to his front gate, without the risk of having to make actual contact with the group. He also tried to estimate if he would be able to run whilst carrying his books, and a leather satchel above his head, without looking a complete tit. Too much time had been wasted on the calculation - the girls and Jozza were almost upon him. Nicky did a double-take as he got closer. The rain had done sterling work- the girls all looked like one would expect Alice Cooper to look like in the shower. He managed to do his best to look cool, with one hand on the gate...

'Hello Jozza...' he stammered, 'Erm, sorry I couldn't make it to your Halloween party- they asked me to help out at the Academy. But erm...thanks for inviting me anyway'

'S'okay- it was crap ...' said Jozza, 'We had to finish it early, because someone (she pushed her friend "Bezza" hard on the shoulder) thought that it would be a good idea to put bubble-gum in the popcorn maker. Dad went ballistic when he saw it, and Mum is still trying to scrape all of the pink stuff off the kitchen walls. We still haven't got it all off the dog...'

'I could give you a hand if you like?' Nicky heard himself offer.

'No, but thanks anyway, Me and the girls are just going to lay down a few riffs - catch you later Mate...' she answered. With that, the dripping band set off up to Jozza's house, and Nicky gradually lost sight of them in the rain.

Auntie waved to him from the living room, and opened the front door so that he could dash in out of the wet. 'I see it's still piss - istently raining then' she said. 'I saw the "Drowned Rat Brigade" just then, was that Jozza and her friends?'

'Yes Auntie, and it's weird - she called me "Mate" in front of her friends'

'I s'pose that's the drugs...' laughed Auntie. She peered through the window in the direction of the departed girls. 'Nothing funnier than the sight of Goths in the rain...' she said.

Nicky was not at all sure how to deal with the fact that his feelings toward Jozza had subtly, and perhaps more importantly, hormonally, veered off in a peculiar direction. It was certainly not a subject which he felt comfortable in engaging his Mum about, and Auntie would no doubt offer him certain kinds of advice which may or may not involve the word "trousers". He had already made one spectacularly unsuccessful attempt to solicit advice on the matter of relationships. Since the elegant yet mysterious writing desk was still churning out strange and wonderful things at an alarming rate, Nicky had decided to "ask" the desk what he should do. His initial query was this: he wanted to know what gift would be appropriate for him to give to Jozza - but which would not make him look too desperate or nerdy. He needed a gift that said, 'I really like you, but we're just very good Mates at the moment - okay?' The message that he certainly did not wish to put across was 'I am seeking your attention, so please talk to me and do not be embarrassed to show me any bits of you which you may consider to be applicable in the circumstances...'He had taken a sheet of Mum's best writing paper, opened the writing desk, and written his plea.

'What do you suggest that I should give her?' was the question.

He had placed the memo in the drawer of the desk, to await a succinct response which would set him on the path to a serious relationship.

Overnight, the force that ruled the desk had indeed come up with a response to his earnest entreaty. He had opened the small drawer nervously, and took out the neatly folded paper. He read the response. He didn't understand it: the desk had replied-

'One behind the Bike Shed...'

Back at St Onans, there was the tell-tale creak of a talkative floorboard. Just for a moment, there seemed to be not just silence, but the vacuum created when an entire room holds its breath. The dead calm was interrupted by one word:

'Pillock!...'

'Sorry Mr Swall...'

Bendy Fletcher and Swall had entered the Metalwork workshop by means of the duplicate key which Figg had provided for their use. The man obviously had no intention of waiting for Duggan to come up with the missing merchandise, and had instructed his accomplices to 'have a little look around' the premises in order to speed up proceedings. Fletcher had furnished himself with a heavy black balaclava for the occasion. It may have helped his progress somewhat, if he had remembered to have cut out a hole in the front of it. Swall tutted, and tore the offending article from the head of his co-conspirator.

'Right - you start at that end of the room, and I'll start here' whispered Swall. 'Look in every cupboard and drawer. Remember - it will be heavy, so don't bother with the light fittings- and if you find anything, then PLEASE DON'T SHOUT!!'. Fletcher began to tip-toe across the room like a pantomime villain, until he received a clip around the ear from Swall. Rubbing his head, he began to ransack the racks, delve into shelves, and rummage through the garbage. He also looked into a lot of storage boxes - but that didn't rhyme quite as well. Swall investigated every side of the old blackboard, to see if there were any secret hiding places. There were not. The two men worked their way around the room like the world's slowest merry-go-round. There was sudden muted call from Fletcher, who was over near the wall (stop it now- you're impressing no-one...).

'Boss...Bosss! Over here!!'. Swall hurried over to where his accomplice was crouching in front of the lathe.

'What is it- what have you found?' he asked.

'Look Boss- I just found a pound coin under the machine!' Swall studied his jubilant colleague, who was grinning like a Cheshire cat at his good fortune. As causes for celebrations go, this man was in the running for the title of "dimmest bulb on the Christmas Tree".

'Hand it over...' demanded Swall.

'Shan't- I found it, an' I'm keepin' it' replied the petulant Fletcher, 'you are always takin' things off me, an' it's not fair. I shall buy a scratch card with this money and when I win a million - then I will retire to my dream Greek island of Domestos...' Swall shook his head, wishing that he could be bothered to shake the head of Fletcher...

Swall and his now rich friend carried on with their searching, although by now, he was getting angry and frustrated. 'Where the hell is it? I mean, all there is here are tools, tools, and more bloody tools. If we go back to Figg without finding anything, I just know that he will talk to us in that calm and disappointed voice of his - an' I hate it when he does that, gives me the creeps it does'.

'Well I don't care - I found a quid...' said Fletcher.

‘Oh, that’s fine then- I’ll just tell him that shall I? I’m sure he will be really pleased for you. Look Bendy, we might as well pack it in for the night, we’re not going to find anything. We’ll just put everything back as we found it, let ourselves out, and go home. We can dispose of the gloves in a bin well away from the school’.

‘Bugger...’ thought Fletcher, ‘that’s what I had to remember - gloves...’

Chapter Sixteen:

There was an old lady from Dagenham
Whose Boobs had developed a sag in 'em
They hung down to her knees
At ninety degrees
So she tattooed a Union Jack flag on 'em...

Hyde-Jones studied the piece of work submitted as part of the class poetry exercise. He considered the imagery of the piece, its underlying theme, the use of rhythm and metre, and the comment on modern day life which the poet was trying to achieve. Having concluded his in-depth appraisal of the work: he decided to give Trevill a bloody good clip around the ear...

The rest of the Staff were standing, sitting, lounging, or practising the art of collapse during morning break. Mr Newhouse looked up from his *Classic Rock* magazine, and solicited the attention of his English-Teaching friend.

'I was just thinking Roy...' he said, 'Do you think that the *Modern Catholic* magazine has a pull-out section?'.

'You require a great deal more psychiatric help than I could ever afford...' replied Hyde-Jones, doing his best to conceal his amusement.

Newhouse continued: 'Seriously Roy - do you think that we're going to lose our jobs with all the cuts that are being planned?'.

Hyde-Jones rose to his feet and extended an arm in a dramatic theatrical pose... 'I may be unemployed, but by Gad! - I shall still wear the Fedora...'

The rest of the Staff looked on. Since the rumours about cuts had begun to circulate, all of the Masters were watching their backs, and being very careful to write on both sides of the paper. They had started to bring in their own tea and coffee, and there was a sudden preponderance of "value range" biscuits to be seen.

The Staff lounge door swung open, and then swung back with equal force. There was the sound of wood hitting bone, muffled cursing, and cries of pain. Dr Chambers entered the room clutching his handkerchief to his nose - which appeared to have absorbed most of the impact. When he had sufficiently recovered his composure, he addressed the assembled Faculty members. 'Good morning one and all (sniff). I have pinned a notice up on the board, which you will (sniff) see is a request for volunteers to help with the (sniff) Bonfire Night festivities up on the Sports Field. If you feel that you can (sniff) help out, then please add your (sniff) name in the spaces (sniff) provided. Captain Brayfield - can I (sniff) please see you for a couple of (sniff) moments outside.. .' He turned and held the door ajar, so that the Captain could follow him into the corridor. Once outside, Chambers produced a rather grubby invoice from Specialist Academic Supplies limited, and showed it to Brayfield. He indicated some items which he had highlighted.

'Sorry to bother you Winston..' he said 'but would you have any idea what these items might be? Brooks the Grounds Keeper has ordered this stuff, but I'm not sure what they are'. The Captain studied the list. Amongst the usual things like creosote, grass seed, liquid polish and similar supplies, were some unusual items. He read the entries again, then declared 'No- I'm awfully sorry Charles, I haven't got a clue what PE4, 808 or 'Cyclonite' might be - sounds like your usual cleaning stuff if you ask me. Maybe Brooks is having trouble getting rid of some nasty residue?'. Chambers looked downcast. 'Ah well - it was only a thought, I was hoping that you would know...still never mind, I'll get the invoice paid'. The Deputy Head (now acting Head) walked off down the corridor.

Well, well...now that was interesting. Captain Brayfield had instantly recognised the mystery items - and knew exactly what they were used for. Brooks could certainly clean out the blocked drains with those compounds. While he was at it - he would clean out the shooting range, changing rooms, generator block, and most of the surrounding houses. The drains would be so clear, that they would leave a ninety-five-foot crater in the ground.

The Vegetarian self-defence class which had been held in the village hall had not gone, shall we say, entirely to plan. The Ambulance was speeding up the road from its depot in the town, weaving urgently between the panicked motorists, as they tried to decide whether to try and outrun it, pull over, or turn up the car radio and pretend that they hadn't seen it. In the driving seat was Brian Johns: a man who had seen every episode of "Top Gear", and had modelled his driving style on what he had seen therein. The vehicle listed dangerously as he forced his way between a lorry and a very frightened District Nurse in a Nissan Micra. His "co-pilot" was one Keith De'Ath. Whilst Brian accelerated up the hill on the wrong side of the road, Keith munched on a sandwich and chatted away to his colleague. 'All I was saying was that I think that Hospital waiting rooms seem to have a certain "St John's ambience..". Brian did not answer. His face was a picture if intense concentration as he leaned into the corners when the ambulance rounded yet another inconsiderate road user. If he could only just get the speed and angle right - then he would really be able to get those tyres to squeal. It should be said, that both men were superb Paramedics. They were knowledgeable, efficient, and caring in their job. What did tend to cause a problem with patients however, was when they regained consciousness, only to see a tall, uniformed man leaning over them- whose name badge said "DEATH".

Brian screeched to a halt outside the village hall. The two made radio contact with Base, to let them know that they were now on the scene. They grabbed their medical kit and raced into the hall. Inside was a picture of Pensioner-based carnage. Bodies were laid all around the room. Those who were not flat out on the floor were sitting up and rubbing various bruises and impact-based wounds. There was a collection of bloody noses, two denture fractures, and Mrs Percy had a badly-sprained wig. 'What the hell happened here?' asked Brian. 'It's that damned Prentiss man!' declared Mrs Parker- 'He gave us all these books on "Toe-Fu".

'So what has been the cause of all of these injuries then?' asked Keith. The tearful woman dabbed at her eyes with a lavender-scented hankie.

'Well - he never told us that we were supposed to take off our boots...'

Uncle Joe was thankfully some considerable distance from the scene of the crime. He had been called in for an appointment at the kind request of the local Magistrate. Since these meetings seemed to occur with alarming regularity, Joe had become firm friends with the Chief Officer of the local Court. Rather than face each other from the bench, the two sat with a cup of tea at a table in a side office.

'What a pleasure it is to see you again so soon Mr Prentiss' the Magistrate said. 'It appears that one or two people have taken great exception to the latest product which you have been marketing, and are seeking to sue you for false advertising under the Trades Descriptions Act...'

Uncle Joe smiled at the man, stirred his tea, and replied 'Well, your Honourable Worshiphood, I think that the criticism of myself and my, if I may say so, brilliant and innovative product is totally unfounded. I went to great trouble to make sure that I described everything properly - like you advised me last time we met'.

'But there does appear to be a certain disparity between the product as advertised, and the actual item received' said the Magistrate. He reached over and picked up a photocopy of the full-page advert which Joe had placed in all of the local papers...

As a gardener and expert vegetable grower, Uncle was constantly frustrated by the damage done to his plants by the local slug population. The slimy little devils were always chewing their way through whatever he planted- turning lettuce into lacework and worse. Joe had come upon a brilliant and innovative idea with which to thwart the invasion of the radish-snatchers. He was only too happy to share his idea with the world. The marketing copy had read:

'ATTENTION ALL GARDENERS!!! Are you sick and tired of your plants being constantly under attack from slugs, snails and beetles? Are your Begonias Battered? Are your Nasturtiums constantly nibbled? Do your Dahlias droop in shame? Well- no more!!!

This brand new product is absolutely guaranteed to keep your gardens slug-free.

YES!!- SAVE ££££££'s IN WASTED PLANTING.

SYSTEM HH20 IS NOW AVAILABLE!!!!

Thanks to a fantastic new breakthrough- we are able to bring you SYSTEM HH20 at the amazingly low introductory price of only £79.99!!

The product is guaranteed completely Eco-friendly and is all-natural.

The unit comes complete with its own tamper-proof security system already fitted.

When not in use- the unit simply rolls up for easy storage.

DON'T DELAY – BUY TODAY!!! SYSTEM HH20 – The Gardener's Best Friend.

'Yep - absolutely brilliant product...' declared the proud Uncle Joe.

'But the buyers have complained that the actual product is not as described in the advertisements' said the Magistrate.

'Oh yes it is!' insisted Joe, 'It is exactly as described- and it really works...'

'That may well be that case Mr Prentiss, but I still have a list of dissatisfied customers who claim that they have been misled...' said the Magistrate.

'Not at all- I have deceived not a single one of my customers' said Joe, folding his arms. The Magistrate looked at the advertisement, then back at the defiant Uncle Joe. He decided to bring the matter to a swift conclusion.

'So, if you will be so good Mr Prentiss- just explain in detail exactly what 'System HH20' really is' said the Magistrate.

'It is a revolutionary system using the power of all-natural sour -'

'Yes, yes - I know all of that. What is it really?'

'A totally eco - '

'What is it....Mr Prentiss?'

'A compl -'

'Mr Prentiss...Let us strive for absolute clarity here. A customer purchases one of your System HH20 units. They pay their money. The product is delivered to them. They open the box - what exactly is it that they see?'

'It's a Hedgehog...'

Since the product did actually do everything which was claimed, there was little that the Magistrate could argue with. He forced an agreement out of Uncle that perhaps any future marketing ventures should be a little more specific as to their actual content. They shook hands, and Joe left the Court a happy man. A very happy man. And why not - he had just managed to sell another three HH20 units to the Magistrate...

Posta had timed it just right. He has been "staking out" the Metalwork and Craft workshop, and was amazed (and somewhat relieved) to have witnessed the two dodgy characters exiting the rooms. He let himself in with the pass key that Mrs Finucane had kindly loaned to him, and very quietly closed the door behind him. The light from the lamps in the street outside cast a broad, bright stripe across the machines and work benches. The light also fell across the edge of the metal filing cab - hang on.... there was what looked like a dirty great hand print on the metal cabinet side. Trying to calm himself down, Posta prepared to collect as many fingerprints as he could. Someone had not been careful, had they! Now at last he had some definitive proof to work with. He already had Duggan's full hand prints on file- but these looked much bigger. A quick search of the Police database would soon provide him with a name to go with them.

Miles Bannister was in conversation with Dr Chambers. Since he had first heard the rumours of Staff cuts, his mind had been filled with the blind panic of a man possessed: literally. He was acutely aware that the constant interruptions and ad-libs from his discarnate Social Worker Mrs Elsie Noakes was a talking point throughout the Academy. He needed to try and persuade Chambers that the interjections of Mrs Noakes in no way prevented him from carrying out his duties as Head of the Mathematics Department. Basically, he was desperate to convince Chambers that he was not completely off his logarithmic trolley. At his age, getting another job as a Senior Maths tutor was sheer Pi in the sky. He had lost a considerable amount of sleep recently, worrying that Goodwill or Chambers, or the Trustees for that matter, would have him sacked, or sectioned- or both. Chambers could see that the man was in an obvious state of distress, and so attempted to calm him down with a cup of tea. Miss Piggott was furious at having to serve her new (albeit temporary) master, and had almost hurled the tea tray onto the desk- causing Bannister to scream and twitch alarmingly. It was rather a shame that Bannister was afflicted by the ill-timed gossip which Elsie supplied. He was a likeable man who got on well with all of his students. He liked them, and they held him in high regard. He had a brilliant mind. The trouble was- he had two of them. It was when the two personalities converged that the problems always manifested themselves. Elsie Noakes was a really lovely lady (is/was, whatever you think works best). Her problem was that she had an awful lot to say on an awful lot of subjects- on an awful lot of occasions. Once or twice she had terrified Bannister unwittingly, when he had woken up in the dead of night with a start - to find himself furiously knitting. There were advantages however, such as the fact that his cooking had improved wonderfully...

Chambers smiled at the nervous man: 'I assure you Miles, that no-one has any complaint about your capabilities. The examination results which your students achieve speak for themselves. We all have our own little "foibles", and there are very few of us that could be considered as perfectly "normal". I assure you, that your job is not under threat, no more than my own, or any other member of the Faculty'. No doubt Chambers had a few more words to say to his colleague, but his attention was focussed on Bannister's tea cup - which was busy stirring itself...

‘Oh no Elsie- please...not now!’ said Bannister. Too late - this was the cue for Mrs Noakes to join in with the conversation.

‘Oooh! Sorry loveys, I didn’t mean to frighten you’ she began, ‘You know that I always like to keep an eye on young Miles, because he does worry so, and apart from his socks he’s a lovely lad. I was just chatting to my friend Mr Hobbley- Miles; you remember Mr Hobbley? He used to go with you and your Dad when you walked down to the railway tunnel. Lovely man- anyway, he had been married to Doreen for forty-nine years until she passed over. Knocked him for six that did - he just didn’t know what to do with himself. Well, he’d always had a passion for steam trains and railways since he was a small boy, so he took up his train-spotting full time. Bless him though - he did get so depressed and lonely without Doreen, that one day he decided to end it all - silly lad. He knew that there was only one real way that he wanted to go, so he went down to the special tracks where they still ran his beloved steam engines, and laid himself down on the line...’

‘Oh, how very sad...’ said Miles

‘Not at all Deary!, not at all - to tell you the truth, he was chuffed to bits...’

Dr Chambers sat in utter amazement. He was not sure what he had just seen, and more to the point, what he had just heard. Befuddlement clouded his academic brain- just what was he supposed to do in these circumstances? He did what he knew he must do. He buzzed through to Miss Piggott - and ordered a cup of Tea for Elsie Noakes...

Detective Sergeant Posta (CID- but currently assistant Master in the History Department) carefully folded the print sheets which he had taken, and put them in his jacket pocket. A Police car dashed past on the road outside, blue lights flashing- but no siren. The sudden illumination of the workshop had startled Posta, and he had instinctively ducked down behind the nearest workbench. In doing so, he caught the edge of a wooden-handled rasp file, which had been left on the bench after repair. The file spun into the air and knocked two pairs of pliers from the top rack of tools. Posta dodged back, as the tools thudded to the floor. He felt like the knife-thrower’s assistant on the spinning board at a circus, as the blindfold marksman hurled projectiles. He bent, and picked up the fallen implements, noting how their sudden absence had broken the regimented symmetry of the tool rack above. The handles of the pliers had obviously been recently renewed, a very neat job. He was glad that the tools had not hit him on the way down, as in his hand, they felt deceptively heavy. The point end of one pair had bent when it had hit the floor- surely; toughened steel should not do that? He carried the pliers over to the side work bench. Fumbling with the plug, he switched on a small spot lamp used for delicate work. Looking carefully in the intense light, he saw that there was a scuff on the end of the pliers- a scuff that showed a yellow metal beneath the paint which was designed to mask its presence.

He took a pen knife out of his pocket. With his heart thumping in his chest, he carefully scraped at the pincer end of the tool. He found exactly what he had been hoping to see. Putting down the pliers on the bench, he climbed up onto the Master's desk in front of the tool racks. He leaned over and up, taking off each tool from the top rack in order, and examining it. Clever Mr Duggan, very clever indeed. If you are going to hide something- the best place to do it was in plain sight. The handles on each of the tools on the top row were moulded plastic. They had all been finished in paint which was the colour of old steel. Under the paint was the real prize. Each of the tools was cast in solid gold...

Chapter Seventeen:

It was a matter of public record that the state of the pavements and public walkways in the town had always been a source of untold anger and frustration. Every week there were dozens of complaints from irate residents in the local paper, which sat shoulder to shoulder with each other on the letters page, like incontinent starlings. The average age of the town also seemed to be increasing steadily, with a never-ending supply of extremely Senior Citizens who blamed all the ills of the world on "The Youth of Today". Whoever this youth was - he or she must be getting pretty pissed off with getting all of the blame. The local Council (motto - 'We run your town- and Serve you right') was under constant pressure to cater for the ageing population, and their ever-increasing list of demands. A recent by-law had been passed after protests from Elderly residents who suffered from poor eyesight. All high street businesses must be fitted with vari-focal shop windows. Extra No-Parking zones were created outside the Bingo clubs, and woe betide the errant motorist who dared to park there for a few minutes - for yea verily: they shall feel the wrath of Bill and Reg who patrol the area with their metal expandable walking-sticks, and who "Fought in the War for you- you cheeky young bugger". Pensioners had also successfully campaigned for the cinema to pause any feature film on show on "concession days" for five minutes every hour - to allow for a toilet break. Fixodent was to be sold alongside the ice creams and drinks during the intermission, and popcorn was strictly banned due to its effect on dentures. Shops were still allowed to sell "alphabet soup" - just so long as it was Large Print...

There were other hard-won victories too, such as Supermarket assistants being forced to sit up straight, and not to mumble. Extra benches had been strategically placed in and around the Market area, so that groups of Seniors could sit together and complain loudly that "no-one has any respect these days" and "things were much better when I was a child". One elderly gentleman (with a highly-skilled engineering background prior to retirement), had doubted this statement. Since his memory was beginning to let him down, he decided to put the statement to proof. He constructed a time machine, and travelled back to his wartime boyhood in order to see if things really were better. He returned from his travels, immediately bought tee-shirts, jeans and trainers: went hang-gliding, bought a red sports car, enjoyed five-course dinners with wine, signed up for Space

Tourism - and declared the phrase in question to be the biggest load of bollocks that he had ever heard. He has since retired to Malta, where he runs a highly profitable rock music club, and owns an eighty-five-foot yacht.

With the advancing plague known as the mobile telephone (where people meander around with their hand clasped to their ear like demented folk singers), came another decision which had been taken at a Council meeting. The general public had formed the opinion that far too many mobile users and Pensioners were forming impenetrable barriers for the everyday shoppers, and people who, well, actually wanted to be able to get somewhere before dusk. Sick of dodging right and left like drunken rugby players, in a vain attempt to avoid collisions with the coral reefs of gossiping fools - the people had spoken. The innovative idea was to paint lines on the pavements in order to put the ditherers, chatterers, phone zombies and double-buggy wielding maniacs out of the way of people who actually needed to get somewhere. A system of "pavement lanes" was introduced, in order to attempt to keep the pedestrian traffic flowing- and keep the 'Meanderthals' out of the bloody way. Uncle Joe's network of contacts had made him aware of the plan, and of course, he wanted in on the action. He immediately put in a tender for the work (having fully costed his bid on the back of a lottery ticket), and sought out the assistance of his painting supremo from the Emerald Isle - Seamus Murphy O'Shaughnessey. This time, Seamus would not have the usual problems associated with his dyslexia, as there was no letter P or B to cause him trouble. After much lack of deliberation by the Council, Joe was awarded the tender, and the work began on the high street. Seamus turned up bright and early, whistling to himself happily, and began to paint the first of the lines. He began at the very far end of the street, and worked accurately and diligently throughout the whole day. Little by little, the long line began to creep up the high street as had been planned. It was on day four that Joe asked for a quick meeting with his friend. There seemed to be a serious problem with the job...

Joe stopped his friend in mid brush-stroke, and said to him 'Look, I'm sorry Seamus, but this is not working out'.

'Is dere a problem Sorr?' Seamus enquired.

'Indeed there is. It's a problem with your work I'm sorry to say' said Joe.

'But I am doin' me best on dis job Sorr, as I know dat it is important...' answered a rather shocked Seamus. Joe explained: 'Look

Seamus, it's just that your work has really fallen off in the last couple of days, and we are getting behind schedule with the job'. Seamus looked horrified - 'But Sorr, I'm workin' hard, so I am, and not slackin' at all'.

'Okay Seamus, let me explain the problem' said Uncle, as kindly as he could. 'On the first day - Wow! You painted nine hundred yards. On the second day, you painted another seven hundred and sixty-five yards. On day three, well, you only painted a total of five hundred yards - and yesterday you only completed three hundred. You seem to be painting less and less every day- is there some sort of problem? Because if you can't get more done in a day, then I'll have to take you off the job...' Seamus regarded Joe earnestly and replied 'Well Sorr- de reason dat I'm not gettin' so much done in a day is dat it's an awful long walk back to me pot of paint...'

So then, the next thing for Nicky to begin to worry about was the approach of Bonfire Night. "Please to Remember the Fifth of November - Gunpowder, Treason and....spots". With predictable inevitability, his teenage face had decided to rebel - against himself, it would appear. He seemed to have developed the beginnings of a promising crop of acne, which would no doubt bloom into splendour just as he needed to ask Jozza if she might accompany him to the fireworks celebrations. How could he possibly face her with a mush like a pepperoni pizza? And how could she face his face, whichever way he was facing. Getting up the nerve to ask the girl if she would go to the bonfire with him was bad enough, but having to contemplate doing so with a face like a Welder's bench was beyond all reason. Mum was consulted immediately, and came up with a bewildering variety of herbal washes and cures that might aid his problem. There was the usual soap-wash-rinse-scrub routine, as well as the more extreme solutions, such as the emergency cheese grater and homeopathic sandpaper. Auntie had come back from a trip up to the village shops, and presented him with a stout brown paper bag. 'You might like to try this...' she told him. Nicky thanked her for her kind thought, and then opened the bag. It was empty. He looked at Auntie with a confused expression. Auntie said 'If all else fails Lad: just cut out holes for your eyes and mouth - and pop it over your head...' She disappeared into the kitchen in fits of laughter. Actually, a Guy Fawkes mask might be the answer to his prayers! But No! Dammit...what if the unthinkable really happened, and there was the chance that he might actually get to kiss the Gothic Princess? He would have to remove the mask - and blow his cover. Surely there was no physical way of keeping the mask in place, and yet still achieving the desired result? What was a boy to do… for Fawkes sake?

There was still the unavoidable hurdle as to how he should actually ask the girl to come to the fireworks display. If he didn't act quickly- then she might make alternative arrangements, and might place herself out of his reach. The only other alternative was actually presenting himself at the door , and asking her out in front of a possible "audience" of her younger sister and the family. When she turned his invitation down, he would have to try and make a dignified exit. A dignified entry was also going to be a problem - as their dog and Nicky seemed to have a mutual dislike of each other. He chose to take the easier option, and put a brief note under her front door, asking if she would care to go to the firework display with him, written in a manner which he hoped was inviting, yet sufficiently casual not to appear too eager. He put the note in an envelope, put on his jacket, and set off to walk the short distance up to number 27. Approaching the front path, he flicked up the collar of his jacket to present a more "playboy" image to any casual observer. He put on his best nonchalant slouching gait, and walked up to the front door. The letter box was set at floor level on the door, and Nicky had to crouch low to insert the envelope. He pushed the brass flap slightly open and put the note into the slot. He then turned and walked off in the confident knowledge that he had made her an offer that she couldn't refuse.

Well: that's what the scene had played out like in his head, but actual events were somewhat different. He had pushed the envelope well inside the letter box. Upon hearing the sound of someone delivering post, their dog had leapt to the door, and grabbed the note, and more importantly, his hand. The hound now had a sharp grip on his fingers - and pulled at the intruding limb with some force. Not wanting to suffer amputation of his fingers, Nicky pushed his hand forward, as the dog pulled back. The dog suddenly loosened its grip on his fingers, and the boy quickly took the opportunity to pull his hand away. Or rather, he didn't. Nicky found that his hand was jammed in the letter box at the wrist. He was now lying flat out on a wet path, with his hand inside the front door letter box of a neighbour, a growling dog swinging merrily on his sleeve which protruded inside. Just as it began to rain, he heard footsteps behind him.

‘And what is going on here, may I ask?’ enquired Mrs Hislop in her most outraged tone of voice.

‘Erm...I appear to be stuck in your letter box- sorry’ said Nicky.

Turning his head as far as he was able to his left, he could see the entire Hislop clan staring at the spectacle of a prostrate youth with his right hand inside their property. Mrs Hislop glared at him: Mr Hislop looked at him in disgust, and the Hislop sister regarded him with contempt as only a younger sibling can achieve. Worse than that was the fact that Jozza was with them - and she stood laughing at the boy as he began to blush. ‘Are you attempting to burgle our property?’ demanded Mrs Hislop. ‘No, No, God No.’. Nicky stammered, ‘I was just - and I put - and your dog - and I’m stuck’. Jozza removed her headphones, tucked them inside her tee-shirt, and bent down to speak to the trapped boy. ‘I was just going to come down and see you’ she said casually, ‘I just wanted to know if you fancied taking me to your School’s bonfire party? - if you’re not too busy being a ghost, that is...’

‘Nnnf...Grnnh...Yes please...’ said Nicky, as the circulation in his right arm began to be cut off.

‘Good- sorted...I’ll phone you later’ said Jozza ‘Dad will get you out of there if you hold on a moment’. Not holding on a moment was not an option for him, but he wished that the dog that was still swinging on his shredded sleeve might take the hint.

While the unfortunate boy lay spread-eagled on the concrete, Mr Hislop ambled down to his shed, and muttering curses under his breath, returned with the tools necessary to remove the letter box and its human attachment. When the brass fitting had been removed from the door, Nicky was finally freed by means of soapy water- which was applied to his now bruised wrist. He thanked Mr Hislop for releasing him, and then made a quick retreat as tactfully as he could. It was some time before he realised that Jozza had in fact completed the actual mission which he had set for himself. Wow!! She had actually asked him to take her to the firework display...Mum was not at all happy about the damage to his jacket cuff, and whisked it away from him for repair. ‘How did this cuff get so badly chewed up?’ she asked. ‘It was the Hislop’s dog again; he replied. ‘Right then...’ declared Mum ‘I’m going to write a stern note to that woman- and complain about her keeping a dangerous animal on the premises. I will write it now- and you can go up to their house and put it in the letter box’. Nicky was still too traumatised to explain why this was a bad idea, so he popped the letter in his pocket for later disposal. Auntie was told the full story, with no gory detail left out. When she had finished laughing at the sad tale, she wiped her eyes with a tissue. 'If you repeat the story to anybody else' she said, 'then I advise you not to tell them exactly what you were doing'. Auntie began to giggle again, her shoulders shaking with mirth - 'and if I were you, I would definitely not use the phrase "I got my hand jammed in Jozza's box" under any circumstance'. Not really understanding why, Nicky decided to be guided by Auntie the wise.

Back at the Academy, very similar to Cousin Sheila when she was in the act of removing her makeup: things were about to get ugly....

Chapter Eighteen:

Mrs Finucane was unable to apply herself to any work. She was not able to concentrate at all on the tasks of the day, as her mind was filled with dread at the thoughts of what her friend and fellow conspirator Albert Brooks was planning to do to the Academy. She had seen him incandescent with rage at some of the strokes pulled by the Staff over the years- but never before had she witnessed his bubbling anger boil over into violent protest. The trouble was that any chance of stopping Albert from exacting his terrible revenge upon the place was diminishing by the hour. The clock was ticking- and she wished that she hadn't thought that, as it was all too real. Who could she turn to for help? She regarded most of the Staff as 'A right bunch of Dozy Feckers', which meant that her choices were limited. Her only chance was to grab hold of some of the lads, when they turned up for the bonfire party- they would know who the best people to help were. She was so distracted, that she didn't notice as she ignored the kettle, and poured the boiling water into the sugar tin. Maybe she was blowing this up out of all proportion - oh feck!! That's another thought which she wished that she hadn't had...

Captain Brayfield too, had more than a rough idea about what the Grounds Keeper had planned. His long Army service had brought him into contact with all manner of explosives, and he knew only too well what their cumulative effect would be if detonated within the confines of the Academy corridors. He thought of Brooks- had the Bounder no conscience? Did he have no pride in the Institution which had cared for him and nurtured him for all these years? Had the man no thought for the centuries of History which would be reduced to rubble by his actions? Ye Gods!! This was his Academy, and he would lay down his life to defend it if necessary: well, be instrumental in deciding who else should actually lay down their lives - he was, after all, a Captain, and the lower ranks would normally deal with that sort of thing.

Gregor Duggan was walking stealthily around the narrow street corner, before turning into the main road and entering the Academy via the side entrance. He glanced up and down the street, then approached the covered archway door. "Scuse me Guv- 'ave you got a light?' said a voice behind him. He half turned toward the source of the voice. Duggan began to pat his pockets in search of a lighter, when suddenly, a car screeched to a halt right opposite him, and a black hood was thrust over his head. The car door slammed, and there was another scream from the tyres as Duggan was driven away...

November the Fifth was beginning to have the rather odd feeling that certain celebrations throughout the year all seem to have - in other words, a kind of "something special is happening but not until tonight" sort of feel. (Halloween is a bit like that: turn up on someone's doorstep at two-thirty in the afternoon in your skeleton mask and black tights shouting, 'Trick or Treat!'- and they will think you are a first-class tit).

Which leads us nicely into the current predicament of the Reverend Felchingham. He was sitting uncomfortably in the worn armchair in front of Dr Chambers, who regarded him across the Head's desk. Highly-strung at the best of times (and according to Stan, he should be...), the Rev was terrified at the prospect of being called in front of the Acting Head Master, for reasons which he was unaware of. Chambers spoke first:

'And so, Reverend, the Trustees have decided that since it would appear that we are moving towards an increasingly secular society, they are forced to review the current expenditure for what they term as "non-essential" subjects. I would point out that it is not just your Department that is coming under financial scrutiny- but all sections of the academic curriculum which may be viewed as unproductive in the long term. The reason for the review I can assure you, is financial, rather than personal'.

The Rev had turned a whiter shade of panic. 'But...but...I have always done my very best to teach and promote Comparative Religion to all of my students' he said. 'And some of your comparisons are, I hear, a little "extreme" to say the least' answered Chambers.

'But the boys need the education which I provide!' said the Rev, almost shouting, 'Religion gives us a strong base in Life, and if we have faith, then we can have faith in both ourselves and others. I do my best to teach my students about all other Religions, so that they can make their choice of which tea- which one to follow, should they so choose. I am attempting to open the spiritual door to their enlightenment. I see myself as the device which I hope will make this happen. Enlightenment is the door; and I am the kno -...' The Rev began to cough and choke as he realised what he was about to say. Chambers looked around him, as he could have sworn that he heard a throaty chuckle from somewhere...

Gregor Duggan blinked and turned his head away from the blinding light which was being shone into his face. 'Whut the bloody hell is gan' on here?' he demanded. He peered into the room through half-closed eyes, trying to determine the identity of the dark shapes that he could just see beyond the flare of the lamp. He had been tied to a rickety wooden chair. His bound hands could feel the splinters on the back spindles, and he silently cursed the craftsman who had omitted to smooth off all surfaces before selling. There was a loud cough from behind him, and one of the shadows (it might even have been Cliff- he couldn't see) detached itself and walked around to a position in front of the chair. The voice that spoke next was all too familiar to him: 'Well well, if it isn't our good old friend Mr Duggan. Isn't it a small world. Fancy running into you here, especially as I was only saying to my colleagues just this very morning, that we hadn't heard from you in ages. Mr Fletcher: do you know what time it is? Mr Swall - can you tell me what your watch says? Well Mr Duggan, my own watch says that the time that I gave you to come up with my merchandise has expired. Whatever am I to do? Now this puts me in a bit of a predicament with The Boss - who has been ever so worried that some devious little toad has been holding out for a bigger cut of the loot. I hope, oh I do so hope Mr Duggan, that this is not the case, because The Boss and I would be so disappointed...'

'Noo- see here, ye ken..' began Duggan. 'No Mr Duggan, YOU see here- welcome to Bannockburn...'

Chapter Nineteen:

Why is it that whenever you want the time to pass quickly, and the chores of the day to hurry past so that you can get on with what you really want to be doing in the evening, that the hands of the clock appear to swimming through treacle? The only events which create the temporal opposite of this well-known phenomenon are exams and dentist appointments.

Nicky had spent all day watching the clock. It had done nothing interesting. There was a conspiracy afoot, where all timepieces had decided to engage in a "go-slow". At the sound of the old bell which signalled the end of the last period, spontaneous euphoria had broken out, with boys dashing off as quickly as possible (and some dashing off to check the dictionary for the correct spelling). Nicky needed to get home as fast as possible, get changed into "normal" clothes, and hurry back to the Academy. Jozza had put a note under the door which stated that she would meet him outside the entrance to the school sports fields at seven thirty. The fireworks would begin around eight o'clock: so that should leave him time to calm down, think of something witty to chat about, and most importantly - use the lavatory. It would do his chances no good at all if he had to break off mid-sentence, and make a mad dash for the bushes.

The boy finally dashed through the front door. He sprinted up the steep stairs three at a time, and dived inside his bedroom, where he changed his clothing faster than Clark Kent on steroids. Mum fussed over him as usual, insisting that he had something to eat before going back out. Auntie said that she and Mum might come down to the bonfire later on, adding 'Mind you - I expect that you will be too busy trying to get a look at Jozza's sparklers...' Honestly, there were times when Auntie could make "Good Morning" sound suggestive.

When Nicky stepped off the bus, he could see the "flaming torch" lanterns that lined the path from the entrance of the sports field. As he neared the gates themselves, he could also see a cluster of extremely worried-looking faces illuminated by the flickering torchlight. Calderman, Merry, Kendy, Davis, Jackson and Weatherill were all there - and boy, did they look scared. In the centre of the huddle of boys was Mrs Finucane, who looked even more apprehensive than the gang did.

'Hello Chaps! What's up?' asked Nicky.

'We need to get down to the Academy a bit sharpish...' said Calderman - Mrs Finucane cut in: "Tis Himself that's gone mad...he's put a bloody great bomb in the school, and...and- we'll all be blown to shite so!!!' Kendy chipped in 'Well technically my friends, as we are all here, we are in no d -' Weatherill stopped his friend in mid-sentence 'Look - we don't have time for this, we need to get down there now and see if we can stop it. Jackson - you have your bike here: you can give Mrs F a lift, and me and the gang will leg it through the estate and back to the Academy'. There was no further comment. Jackson got onto his bike, whilst Mrs Finucane clambered onto the seat behind him. They set off at a furious pace, with Jackson pedalling hard, and Agent J-Cloth frantically crossing herself. The rest of the boys ran as fast as they could past the houses in the narrow tree-lined streets that led back to the Academy. They arrived in a breathless huddle, just as Jackson helped a windswept Mrs F to dismount, and hurled his bike behind the bushes. 'What do we do Mrs F?' wailed Merry. 'Follow me to the Head's study- dere's the big box on the wall dat controls all of the CDBBCVTC camera thingies, we'll try and switch off whatever dat silly bollocks has rigged up' Mrs Finucane answered. The group ran to the study corridor, almost kicking over the small red moped belonging to Keith the Raven. He shook an angry wing at them as they went past at speed. He was Raven mad...

Mrs F produced the key which unlocked the main security camera control box. The grey metal door swung open to reveal what looked like a small black digital alarm clock taped to the back of the box. The display showed 14:04. 'Well dat's a relief..' said Mrs F 'the thing is not set to go bang until four minutes past two'. Nicky stared at the device. 'I don't want to worry you Mrs Finucane - but that thing is a timer, and it's counting down...We have just over fourteen minutes to try and switch it off before it blows up!!' The lady reached up as if to pull the timer out of the box 'DON'T TOUCH IT!!!' the boys all shouted at once. Mrs F jumped back from the box, flattening herself against the wall. 'Sorry Mrs F...' said Nicky 'but there may be a booby-trap wired up to it - if we try to remove the timer, it will blow up immediately'. The outer door to the corridor suddenly came open, and Hyde-Jones and Mr Newhouse came into the passage. 'What are you lot doing here?' asked Newhouse. 'Tell him Mrs F...' said Calderman- 'we don't have much time left'. She explained to the Music Tutor all about Albert Brooks' little "revenge", and that oblivion was about fourteen minutes away. Hyde-Jones leapt into action: 'Right - get down the corridor quickly, and see if there are any more "surprises" inside the camera boxes - and for God's sake be careful'. The boys sped off down the corridor and looted chairs from the open rooms. Standing on them, they gently pried open the camera boxes. From down the passage came shouts of 'One here!' 'Here's another' 'Got one' and 'One here too...' So then - Albert had been a busy boy.

The outer door was opened again - this time, the "visitors" were Miles Bannister, Mr Thwaite, and Betty Bradley. 'What the bloody hell do you lot want?' asked Mr Newhouse. 'We, ah, erm, were just coming to see if the Head's study was open - and if it was, then -' 'Then you would have a good old rummage through his drawers looking for evidence that he might be going to get rid of you?' said Newhouse...The next figure through the door was Dr Chambers. 'What the bl-'

'I just did that bit' said Mr Newhouse.

Chambers looked at the ashen terror in the face of Mrs Finucane; he looked down the corridor at the boys spaced out at intervals, standing on chairs. He demanded an explanation. He got it. Mr Thwaite screamed. At that point, there was a sound from the other end of the corridor. Smelling strongly of self-assembly furniture, Dr Matthews emerged smiling. 'What the bl-' chorused the Masters.

'We've done that - twice...' said Newhouse.

Matthews, glass in hand, gave a respectful bow to the assembled throng. 'I heard that Goodwill had a few bottles of twenty-year old Scotch in his office, and I thought that since he is going to be 'in dock' for a few more days- then I should do my duty and keep them safe for him...'

07:54

'Right!!! Everyone shut up now!' shouted Hyde-Jones. 'Loopy - help me with this chair. I'm going to have to cut the wire...'

'Should we be doing this?' asked Thwaite

'Are you sure that you know what you are doing?' said Chambers

'Perhaps we should stop for a little drink?' said Matthews

'Would anyone care for a sausage roll?' enquired Betty Bradley

'Does anyone require Medical attention?' said the Matron, who had suddenly made her entrance, wearing an extremely skimpy and revealing Nurses uniform - complete with white stockings and matching stiletto heels. 'I have a blister...' said Newhouse, eagerly.

'No you bloody well haven't! - get over here and hold the chair while I cut this wire: Damn it! - has anyone got a pair of scissors?' asked Hyde-Jones.

'There's bound to be some in Miss Piggy's office' replied Bannister. The whole gang of nervous people rushed in a mobile huddle down to the Secretary's office, and blocked the doorway as they all fought to get inside at the same time. There was a mad scramble for the desk drawer, and a shout of triumph as a pair of scissors were located.

06:44

The mass of nervous humanity rushed back up the corridor. Across the road from the Academy - quite a long way, and behind some very thick bushes, Albert Brooks sat laughing at the progress of the would-be heroes. He was observing the whole drama on a hand-held device of his own construction. He was highly amused when Hyde-Jones' foot went through the seat of the chair, plunging the man to ground level. He laughed loudly as Bannister rushed to obtain a replacement chair, especially when he trapped the head of Mr Thwaite in the door.

Hyde-Jones was gently lifting the coloured wires away from the timer unit, sweat now trickling down his face and neck. Newhouse was humming the theme from "Mission Impossible" - much to his friend's annoyance.

'For Pete's sake stop buggering about Loopy!' he called out - 'I need a pair of tweezers...'

'I may have some in my bag!' said Mr Thwaite, happy to finally be of assistance. As he rummaged around in the receptacle, Newhouse regarded him with suspicion, 'Is that a handbag?' he asked. 'It may indeed be – a handbag' replied Thwaite, earnestly. The tweezers were found, and passed up to Hyde-Jones. Elsie Noakes (Bannister's constant companion and commentator) could not contain herself any longer 'Oooh! - it's exciting isn't it! It's just like in those James Bond films'. Bannister answered her, his voice quivering with fear - 'Madam, we are about to be blown to very little pieces: does that thought not worry you at all?'

There was a short silence, then Elsie replied, 'I'm a ghost Miles - what do you think?'

05:49

Chambers called up to Hyde-Jones: 'Look - do you think that we will be able to hush all of this up?' The English Master wiped the sweat from his eyes and replied 'Hush it up? When this lot goes up - they'll hear the bang in Lincoln!!' Chambers looked defeated. 'Do you suppose that Third Party Insurance will cover it?' he asked. 'If I were you, I would be more concerned with how we cover a half-mile wide hole in the ground Matey!' said Newhouse. 'What do we do about the booby-trap?' asked Matron.

'Take it off - and I'll hold on to it for you, if you like...' replied Newhouse.

With activity around the control panel intensifying, Matthews drew up a comfy chair and poured himself a generous measure of vintage scotch. 'Reminds me of the time me and old "Trousers" Wenderby broke into the Officer's mess and wired up the barman to the lightning conductor - glorious times...' he said, to whoever was listening.

04:50

'I can't get a decent grip...' said Hyde-Jones.

'Life can be like that sometimes...' said Newhouse, still staring over his shoulder at the Matron.

'I need something to hold the wires up away from the timer, so that I can see the connection, said Hyde-Jones. Newhouse acted decisively, and passed one of Mrs Bradley's sausage rolls up to the struggling technician.

Matron was still concerned: 'Now I realise that we are all under a little bit of stress at the moment, so if anyone does begin to feel at all unwell, then please let me know immediately - and I will attend to them' she said.

'I seem to have developed a localised swelling...' said Mr Newhouse. 'No you sodding well haven't! - and keep the damn chair still Loopy!!' shouted Hyde-Jones.

03:36

'Can you see the connection?' asked Mr Newhouse. The corridor had fallen silent. Nicky was suddenly overcome with a crushing range of emotions. When he first arrived at St Onans, he had experienced the acute sensation of separation which a new school can bring. Even when he began to settle in, and make new friends, there were regular periods when he would happily see the school blown to pieces just to put an end to his misery. Two years down the line, he had miraculously formed a "connection" of his own, not just with his fellow students, but with the crusty old buildings which kept them secure within. Try as he might, he was unable to decide what he would miss the most. Once, he had hated the thought of attending this Academy. Right now, he hated the thought of it being whisked away from him. If the Academy were reduced to rubble - where would he go? What would happen to the Masters with which he had made friends? And what would become of Bernie in the Biology Lab? Even if Mum and Auntie would let him move in with them - finding bunk beds which would fit him was going to be a real problem. He felt a strange wave of calm wash over him, as the prospect of the cloistered world of St Onans being blown sky-high seemed to somewhat overshadow those other little concerns. He looked at his friends - were they thinking the same as him? Probably so, because Weatherill was wearing his Army tin helmet. No-one mentioned it, but they were all staring at the timer unit as it counted down what might well be their last seconds of existence.... 'I haven't finished my French homework!!' wailed Merry, 'Madame will kill me...'

Nicky looked up at the timer clock. 'Unlikely...' he said.

02:49

'Right- I can see it. I'm going to cut the wire now' said Hyde-Jones

'Which one?' said Newhouse

'The blue one. I've seen all of the films, and it's always the blue one. Okay - here we go...'

'Unless it's the Red one...'

'What did you say?'

'I said - unless it's the Red wire, I mean, it could be?'

'No. It's definitely the Blue wire. Now let me concentrate...'

'Or maybe the Yellow one?'

'Look: any second now, my arse is going to shake hands with my eyebrows at approximately three hundred metres per second - flicking through the *Dulux* colour chart at this moment is really not helping....' said Hyde-Jones.

'Only trying to assist, Roy...'

'Yes, I know - sorry if I was rude, Loopy. Whatever: it's been a pleasure to know you and work with you. Get me a pint in at the "Pearly Gates" bar my Friend...'

The English Master hesitated as if frozen solid.

01:47

Brooks watched the small screen on his device as the last seconds poured away. He fished into the pocket of his camouflage jacket, and produced another small metal box. This one had a single red button on the top of it. His thumb hovered over the firing switch...

'Roy - for God's sake do something!!' called Mr Newhouse.

'Did you have anything in mind?' asked his colleague

'Do something technical - and do it NOW!!!'

'Okay - Eeny, Meeny, Miney, M-'

Newhouse dived up onto the chair, grabbed the scissors, and cut the White wire. He fell back to the floor. Hyde-Jones grabbed Betty Bradley, Thwaite grabbed his handbag, Chambers grabbed the petty cash box, and Newhouse firmly grabbed Matron...There was a deep "clunk" as the timer reached the sixty-second point, and the visual display changed from green to red.

Matthews topped up his glass, and raised it to his colleagues.

Davis finished the last of the sausage rolls. The boys all looked at each other as if seeing their friends for the very first time.

00:10

Nicky turned to Calderman and the gang: 'There was something which I think we need to do...' he said.

'What's that Mate?' said his friend.

'LEG IT!!!' screamed Nicky.

00:09

The Masters who had dived for the safety of the carpet slowly sat up. They looked up in horror at the timer as it impassively counted down the last seconds.

00:08

The boys hurtled down the corridor and through the ancient portal out into the quad. They were most surprised to be overtaken by a sprinting Mrs Finucane, skirts held aloft as she ran, who from somewhere, had developed the stamina of an Olympic athlete.

00:07

Albert's thumb hovered over the button. Not long to wait now...just a few more seconds...

00:06

'Oh Blast- I don't think that I remembered to lock the car' said Chambers.

00:05

Matthews gave up on the glass, threw it over his left shoulder, and tipped the bottle into his open mouth...

00:04

The boys and Mrs F paused halfway through the row of houses, peering back at the Academy buildings from behind a stone wall. 'Do you think that we're far enough away?' said Kendy.

'If we're not- then we soon will be' answered Calderman.

00:03

'Sorry Miles - I've got to dash; I'll see you later' said Elsie Noakes. She departed for whatever spiritual task she had lined up. Miles Bannister had never felt more alone...

00:02

00:01

ZERO.

Brooks pressed hard on the red button. He had worked hard on putting together this device - it had better work.

In the corridor, the Staff members covered their heads.

Without warning, there came the ear-splitting sound...

- of a raucous fart.

When the horrendous noise had ceased buffeting the air around them, the people in the corridor slowly began to stand up, as the realisation that they had not been vaporised began to sink in. Hyde-Jones was the first to break the silence...

'Is everyone okay? Mrs Bradley? Bannister? Thwaite? Loopy? Loopy...LOOPY - YOU CAN LET GO OF MATRON NOW!' Newhouse grinned as he clung onto his own private medical representative.

'Sorry Mate - can't hear you, I must have been deafened by the blast...'

'Loopy- get up, there wasn't one' said Hyde-Jones.

'Blast...' said Newhouse, 'there- have that one on me!'. Matron arose from her recumbent position, adjusting her dishevelled clothing, where it had clearly and deliberately been "shevelled" by the application of a Music Tutor.

'My God!...' said Bannister - 'there was no bang...' Hyde-Jones shot Newhouse a look of the 'don't you dare say it' variety. The Music Master in return, gave him the specialist grin that would have him forever barred from becoming a priest....

The group of Masters slowly dispersed. There was little else that they could do tonight. Nothing had exploded, there were no injuries (although Mr Newhouse had insisted that Matron make absolutely certain of that fact, by giving him a thorough physical), and the only boom had been the thunderous sound of a pre-recorded fart.

The boys followed Mrs Finucane back to the Academy, curious to see exactly what had occurred, and glad that it was still intact. Albert Brooks lay on his back in the grass, convulsed with laughter.

In the corridor once more, Agent J-Cloth and the boys carefully approached the open control panel. The sweet odour was now even stronger in the air. Mrs F climbed up onto the chair. She prodded the lump of material which was stuck to the back of the box, flinching slightly. She held the exploratory finger to her nose. Hesitantly, she licked it.

'Yous can go to yer bonfire Boyos...' she said to the gang, 'It's perfectly safe'.

As the boys walked away, she closed the door to the control box. She then noticed the business card which was stuck to the inside of the box door. The script was familiar.

'The Auld Fecker!...' she said aloud '.... bloody marzipan...'

Chapter Twenty:

At the far end of the sports field stood an immense wooden structure, which even in the dusk seemed to compete with the tall poplar trees which thrust skyward on the field edge. It was lit from the side by a bright lamp, and resembled a Space Shuttle about to be launched from Cape Canaveral, excepting the fact that it was constructed from timber- give or take the odd sofa or wardrobe here and there. It could only be hoped that the residents of Narnia had been astute enough to purchase adequate fire insurance. The boys approached the ligneous pyramid and gazed up at the summit. Rising from the grass, almost up to the very top of the construction was a long wooden ladder. By this means, the unfortunate effigy of Mr Fawkes would be raised aloft to his doom. Master William Trevill surveyed the wooden leviathan, and gave his considered verdict: "Ere Lads. It do look loike that there Great Pyramid of Geezer...'

The gang were milling around with the crowd, discussing the non-destruction of the Academy by confectionary. Nicky suddenly let out a gasp- 'Oh bugger! - I forgot about Jozza!!' With the pandemonium which had just taken place, he had completely forgotten that he was supposed to meet the girl at the sports field gates. He immediately raced up the gravel path towards the entrance, but of his would-be companion for the evening, there was no sign. He trudged dejectedly back up the path (well, as dejectedly as is possible, when you sound like you are walking through Cornflakes). Davis tried to cheer up his despondent friend- 'Never mind Shep - let's go and have a hot dog'. Kendy was outraged at the suggestion, and had to be taken over to the stall, where the vendor gave him reassurances, and a dissection confirmed - that at no previous time had the filling of the bread rolls ever chased after a stick...Fido or not, Davis had three.

The attention of the crowd was drawn to the right hand side of the unlit bonfire, where two men were struggling to manhandle a "Guy" to the foot of the ladder. 'There's Fletcher and Swall' said Calderman, 'keep an eye on your pockets!'. There seemed to be a heated argument taking place as to who should have the dubious task of climbing the vertiginous ladder and placing the guy on the top. Fletcher spun a coin into the air -Swall caught it, and declared "Heads". Fletcher heaved the life-size effigy onto his shoulders with considerable effort, and slowly began to ascend the ladder. 'That Guy looks a bit on the scruffy side' said Weatherill - splendidly attired in a high Tudor hat.

'He should do- that's Fletcher...' said Nicky.

'No, I didn't mean that guy, I mean the guy carrying the Guy - I think?' laughed Weatherill. 'That jacket on the guy looks about as threadbare as the one that old Duggan usually wears' said Merry, 'Burning might be the kindest thing for it!'.

Across town, Duggan's Landlady wondered why he had not come back for his dinner.

Strangler and Darwin were circling the bonfire, lighting it in various places. All this took place under the watchful eye of the small crew of local Firemen, who had turned up in their shiny red engine to ensure safety at the event. Merry had enquired if all their fire engines were called "Dennis", as it said on the front. The hunky fire crew were enjoying the attentions of the female section of the crowd... Neither Strangler nor Darwin had thought to check if Fletcher had come down the ladder, and the man was forced to slide down the last few feet, before landing in a heap at the bottom. Very slowly, the fire began to take hold. Crackling alarmingly, the flames began to lick upwards as they consumed their meal of discarded timber. Nicky could not help looking at the furniture that was heaped randomly throughout the burning structure. What sort of family had last sat on that sofa? What conversations had been had around that old table? Whose clothes had hung alongside their "Sunday Best" in that wardrobe? And what television or radio programmes had been enjoyed by whoever sat in that torn armchair?

The fire had now really taken hold, with sparks drifting up and up into the night air. The faces of the crowd were illuminated in flickering orange by the bonfire. The circle of people looked strangely ritualistic. Why are we always drawn to fire? Is it a memory of the safety that we sought as primitive man, wanting to frighten away predators? Could it be memories of when we relied upon fire to be a warning, or a beacon to light the way home? According to the great historian Davis - it was to roast marshmallows. Nicky watched glumly as the flames reached the guy on top of the fire. Trevill had noticed his friend's despair, and sidled up to him. 'Don't Ee bother Chum!' he said 'We'em 'avin' a few bangers in a minute or two!'

'Not really in the mood, for some reason' Nicky answered. Trevill regarded his mate as a Craftsman would look at a young Apprentice. He laid a brotherly hand on Nicky's shoulder and told him: 'Now just you see 'ere, young Shepherrd. As Ee may well be aware, Oi 'am considered (boi those in the know), to be a Man of the World. In moi vast and varied experience of Womankoinds, Oi can tell 'Ee that Women is a lot loike fireworks - if Ee think that you'm lit the fuse, but nothin' do seem to be 'appenin' - then don't Ee go back near it, in case She'm blow up in yer face!!'.

With the wise teachings of the Relationship Guru Trevill still ringing in his ears, Nicky stood back and watched the firework display. Which actually turned out to be pretty good. Things on sticks went "Whizz", spinning things twirled and sprayed out golden sparks; some things went "Fizz" and then shot other things into the air which went "Boom". The audience was illuminated as the huge silver and gold showers blossomed above their heads, and girls shrieked (as did Mr Thwaite) as loud bangers concussed the air.

Across the field, at the side of the tall trees, was the wing of the local hospital. Dr Goodwill lay face down on his bed. A smiling nurse had asked if he would like her to open the curtains, so that he could have a good view of the firework display.

There was absolutely no need for him to have used language like that...

The display ended with a "set piece" which was intended to depict the outline of the Academy. It began well - but then sections of the piece refused to ignite in sequence. This left the central pillar of the Dark Tower illuminated in the middle-flanked by two structures on either side, which were supposed to depict the Dining Hall and Library. The end result was something rather phallic, which drew laughter from the crowd of onlookers. When the "roof" of the dark Tower shot out its final shower of sparks, there was loud applause, and sniggers as it drooped to the left when it had finished. Dr Chambers bade everyone a good night via a megaphone, and the crowd began to troop homewards. As the fire engine slowly drove up the gravel track toward the road, no-one appeared to notice that one of the crew seemed significantly shorter than the rest. He was peering out from beneath a helmet that almost covered his entire head. A casual observer would have noticed a striking resemblance to that serial escapee: Master David DeVere...

The bonfire continued to burn away the last remnants of its fuel. There would be no trace of the guy left in the ashes by morning...

The gang had thoroughly enjoyed their evening. There was much light-hearted pushing, shoving and general mickey-taking. Davis had even struck a deal with the hot-dog vendor for leftovers. Nicky however, was anything but light hearted. He had blown his second chance for an evening with Jozza, and he could see no likelihood of chance number three ever becoming a reality. He decided not to wait for the village bus, and set off to walk home up the hill. He slouched along, contemplating the bizarre combination of heart-stopping terror earlier in the evening, and acute disappointment of a bond not cemented. Cursing his luck, he ambled between the street lights, trudging miserably from one pool of weak light to the next. His young mind was so occupied, that he did not see the pothole on the footpath, and received a rough tarmac greeting to his face when he fell. Bleeding, battered and emotionally bruised, he plodded on. Just to add insult to minor injury, a vindictive owl vacated onto his shoulder.

It seemed an age before he reached the comfort of his front gate. He opened the door and went into the front room. He was confronted by the sight of two Police Officers sitting on the sofa, drinking tea with Mum and Auntie. 'Well, that's about it- sorry to interrupt your evening Mrs Shepherd, we'll go now if that's alright with you' said PC 3037 Harris. He and his female colleague stood up, gave the boy with a shoulder covered in owl shit a strange look, and made their way out of the front door. Mum said 'Well, weren't they pleasant...so well mannered, although the young lady was a little muscular..'

Auntie chuckled 'Yes- I wonder how long ago it was, that she was actually a man?' Nicky was confused, which was fast becoming his "default setting" nowadays.

'The Police came to inform us about Cousin Sheila' said Mum. 'What has she done now?' asked Nicky. 'Oh, she hasn't done anything. It seems that she has been taken to hospital. The Policeman said that there had been a pit explosion'.

Nicky stared in disbelief at his Mother, while Auntie was bent double with laughter in the armchair. 'But that can't be right...' said Nicky 'I mean- Cousin Sheila lives a good sixty miles away from the nearest coalface?'

'No Dear...' said Mum 'It appears that her armpit blew up...'

Chapter Twenty-One:

Nicky sat in front of the imposing polished (thanks Mum) writing desk, gazing absent -mindedly at his copy of the *Oxford English Dictionary*. It had been a birthday gift from his Mum. It was thick, austere, and crammed full of important knowledge (the book that is - not his Mum, who was a lovely Mum -shape, very friendly, and also crammed with important knowledge). Just why he needed this book was a mystery to him - because he already knew how to spell "Oxford". To be fair though, his "Thesaurus" had not been made extinct due to a meteorite strike, so it sort of balanced out, didn't it? His homework already completed, the boy sat at the desk and replayed some of his most treasured daydreams (some with quite good graphics). His head seemed to be crammed to bursting with the cavity-wall insulation of recent events. What would they do about the so-called "bomb plot"? Would the Masters reveal all to the Authorities? If so, could you actually be prosecuted for the malicious act of supplying confectionary with menaces? What was it that the Staff all seemed to be so worried about? What was he to do about the problem of Jozza? And perhaps most importantly, now we were at this particular juncture of the calendar - should he write a letter to Santa?

What could it hurt? But then again, he knew that he was a little too old to even contemplate such a childish act. Certainly not. What a ridiculous idea.

"Dear Santa" he began...

Auntie was sitting in the big armchair, idly scanning the local paper for known shoplifters. She rested her reading on her lap and said 'Monday, Tuesday, Wednesday, Thursday, Friday, Saturday and Sunday...' Nicky turned and stared at his Aunt. 'What was that Auntie?' he asked. 'I was just thinking...' she replied - 'those were the days...' He finished off his letter to Santa, and signed it - making sure that he kept the message well hidden from prying eyes. He carefully folded the sheet of paper and placed it in the small drawer, suddenly feeling seven years old again. The desk had never let him down so far, so all that he had to do was wait...

He began to think about Christmas. The Festive period was always the bringer of fun, laughter and good times to the family. It was as if a comforting "blanket of niceness" descended upon the house at this time of year. Ever since he was a toddler, Nicky had lovely memories of smiling faces and a lovely warm glow to the house all through Christmas. They may not have had much in the way of money - but somehow the gift of Family was the best present possible: it was cheap to wrap, and came with batteries that lasted forever. Even when Uncle Joe's Origami business had folded - it failed to put a damper on the spirits of all those who lived in, or visited their house. There was a magical, expectant feeling in the air, and Nicky could sense the beginnings of it starting to emerge. On Christmas morning, his world had been the living room carpet, where toy cars were raced under furniture, aeroplanes would take off and land, and where smaller parts to games would make their bid for freedom- hiding at the periphery of the living room, hoping to escape detection. He remembered how they would make their own Christmas decorations with coloured gummed paper, which hung in glorious festoons, bisecting the room with lurid colour. There was the magical, mystical moment when Mum or Auntie would lift him up so that he could place the star on top of the Christmas tree. Afterwards, he would stand gazing up at the tree for ages, basking in the gentle pastel glow of the fairy lights. It would be impossible to sleep on Christmas Eve, as he liked to lay awake and listen for the distant sound of sleigh-bells. Some wonderful adult had made sure that he had heard them too! Such were the dreams of a small boy - and memories that would never, ever fade. On Christmas Day, the whole house would have the smells of sherry and Brussels sprouts, but then again, so did Cousin Sheila...

The next morning in the Staffroom, there was a meeting of the great minds which one could say was, just a little tense. Chambers had called all of the Staff together, with a view to covering up the whole "exploding Academy" incident. Whenever the entire collective of Staff was called together, there was the usual jostling for position, not merely who thought that they should occupy top position in the educational ranking, but who was of a sufficiently sober disposition to be able to make the most coherent and positive contribution to the proceedings. This was liable to take up some time.

Dr Chambers had made an impassioned plea to all of the Staff that any disclosure concerning recent events would lead to ridicule in the local press, immediate and certainly punitive action being taken by the Board of Trustees, and in all eventualities, a full and embarrassing investigation by the Police. Quite what the possible charges might entail, he was not sure, but it would be a major blight upon the reputation of St Onans Academy if it became public knowledge that they had been threatened by almond-flavoured confectionary.

Gideon Rundell the Latin Tutor was of a completely different opinion. 'I wish to register in the strongest possible terms Dr Chambers, that I am vehemently opposed to the perpetrator of this act being allowed to walk away "scot free" as it were. The man Brooks is obviously unbalanced, and thus completely unfit to carry on his duties as a member of this Academy. He must be brought to book immediately: and taken to task over his actions. I insist that nothing short of his immediate dismissal is called for'.

Chambers gave his colleague a sympathetic glance. He knew that there was a pinch of truth in what Rundell had just said, but calling for Brooks to be sacked might just open up a whole new can of worms. He had received letters of complaint from Parents whose precious offspring had apparently been "abandoned" on the Derbyshire Moors by himself and Rundell on a recent Academy out-of-school venture. By means of stealth, covert filing, and pure good fortune, he had managed to "bury" the written calls for the resignation of Rundell (and himself). He would seek an opportune moment in which to have a quiet word with his colleague, and perhaps remind him that those without sin should be the only ones to consider throwing marzipan...Hyde-Jones had pointed out that there was no physical proof that Brooks had actually tampered with the camera system at all, and that the whole thing was just a major prank played by the "practical joke society" which they all knew operated regularly within the Academy. Sure, the incident had been terrifying for all concerned - but no more frightening than the dread that they had all attempted to visit upon the participants of the "Ghost Walk"?

Bearing in mind that during the incident, Chambers had managed to "liberate" some rather incriminating documents outlining Dr Goodwill's financial malpractices, he decided to go for the soft option of speaking to Brooks privately (not that this would get him very far - as he well knew Brooks' attitude to all forms of Authority). 'Very well Lady and Gentlemen...' he stated 'I will take appropriate action, as we have agreed - please leave the matter with me. Please be mindful that we must at all costs avoid any repercussions...'

'Well stop setting your drum kit up in here then...' advised Mr Newhouse. Hyde-Jones collapsed in fits of giggles, Thwaite didn't get the joke, Darwin turned to face the window with his shoulders shaking, and Rundell stormed out of the room.

In addition to the generally light-hearted banter and rivalry which played out on a daily basis between boys at the Academy, there was always the ever-present threat of an attack from pupils of one or other of the town schools. Students from other educational establishments seem to consider it their duty to pick on the boys from St Onans, wherever and whenever their paths should cross. This had led to many "stand-offs" in the shops of the town. Nicky and all of the boys in his year remembered only too well the dreadful "spring roll" incident, which took place outside their favourite Chinese Takeaway. This was an establishment that was just around the corner from the Academy - and was very popular with boys who did not wish to partake of the fare on offer from Mrs Bradley and her team. The owner, Mr Yin, was a jolly little well-respected member of the local business community. When he had first bought the premises, he had been in a state of dismay, as he did not yet have a name for the shop. After much deliberation, he had decided to name the takeaway after what he had heard the local people declare when they turned up at the door, and found that the shop was not yet open. He had christened the business "Ah Fook". Mr Yin had been very helpful in the removal of the spring roll from the anatomy of a local youth who had thought that it was a good idea to pick on Nicky's classmate Johnny Ashman.

Such incidents were an all too often occurrence - though thankfully, not all would involve the insertion of an item from the "extras" section of Mr Yin's menu.

It was lunch time. Nicky and the boys had decided to take a walk in the local park and enjoy the crisp sunshine. Since Trevill had not quite completed his English Poetry exercise, he sat on the park bench and pored over the verses in his text book. The rest of the gang were some way off, and did not notice the approach of a raiding party of boys from the local "Central College", who also frequented the park on a regular basis. These lads had approached Trevill from behind, and had decided to have a little fun at his expense.

'Well look what we have 'ere Lads!' said the first tormentor 'We got a little Toff readin' his poetry book - how sweet!' The boy snatched the book from Trevill's hand, and proceeded to flick through it. 'Cor! - this is top readin' this is...look 'ere lads - 'Ode to a Nightingale' and 'Daffodils', and this sounds like a real scorcher - 'Isabella and the pot of Basil'. They sure give you Toffs some excitin' stuff to read at your Pansy Academy school!'.

Trevill stood up and approached the boy.

'Roight then, you'm 'ad yer laugh at moi expense, but Oi wants me book back 'cos Oi'm workin' on it see?'. There was a sudden movement by the other boys, and now Trevill was surrounded. They began throwing the book of poetry from one to the other, just over Trevill's head.

'What sort of stupid Redneck accent is that then, Farmer Giles?' said the sneering boy.

'Moi accent comes from Dorrset...and Oi am proud of it!' declared Trevill.

'I bet that the only reason that they let you into your school was to make sure that they had someone to clean the boots!' said the bully. 'Anyway -I didn't think that you Dorset peasants could actually read!'.

'Arr- an' Oi can do it without moi lips movin' at the same toime!' said Trevill.

The boy stopped smiling. The circle of boys opened up and formed a line in front of him, with the biggest taking up a central position. By now, Nicky and the lads had seen what was taking place, and had quietly walked over and formed a line of their own just behind the Central boys. 'Shall we jump on 'em?' asked Merry.

'No- hang on a moment, I think our Chap is about to get creative...' said Nicky.

Indeed, he was. Trevill walked forward until he was a few inches away from his chief tormentor. He reached up and took the poetry book from the hand of the Central boy. He then walked a little way back, and climbed up onto the park bench. He cleared his throat. He held the book out in one hand, and placed his other hand on his heart like a Bard at an Eisteddfod. 'Oi will show 'ee the magic of poetry...' he declared. With that, he began:

'Oooooh -
Ye Foul Bunch of Turds
Wot pour scorn on Moi Words -
And speak Vile Abuse as Oi wrote 'em
Where Friendship 'as failed,
A new Plan is unveiled -
I'll apply moi right boot to yer scrotum...'

There was a blur as Trevill launched himself down from the park bench at took his revenge on the boy in front of him. The bully received a good hiding - culminating with a crippling kick in the fork.

With their leader incapacitated, the other Central boys panicked - as the Dorset Tornado was now heading in their direction. They scattered, with Calderman, Merry and Nicky picking off one or two stragglers who were not quite clever enough to realise that escape would be the best option. The tormentors ran off for the hills- with their "leader" doing his best to follow them, as fast as his crouching gait would allow. It would certainly be some time before Central boys decided to pick on the lads of St Onans again - especially when word got out about the "Wild Bard of Wendham Park".

'Ah- the power of the spoken word...' declared Calderman.

The soon-to-be legendary poem of the Bard Trevill was duly presented in the afternoon's English class. It received great acclaim from the boys, especially when presented with the full story of how it came to be written. Mr Hyde-Jones had joined in the applause, awarding Trevill a high mark of A minus (it would have been 'A plus'- but HJ felt that he must take a stand as regards the punctuation).

As if they hadn't already had enough - there was yet another Staff meeting as soon as lessons for the day had finished. The purpose was to allocate stalls and pitches to the various Staff members who had volunteered to help out with the "Grand French Market". Madame of course, would be hosting the event, and showing the visiting Dignitaries around the Academy. Dr Chambers would be assisting her. Captain Brayfield sat at the back of the room, and pulled fierce and defiant faces. Here was a man who suffered acute acid indigestion at the mere mention of "French Chalk". His personal fury was such, that at the mention of flying the flag of France from the Dining Hall tower - he bit his fountain pen in half. Doctor Matthews could not have been happier. The great God Bacchus had looked down into the realm of mortals, and had played his trump card. Perhaps out of pure mischief, or a misplaced sense of trust, he seemed to have been given him the task of running the wine stall.

When Nicky got home that evening, it was to find a three-person business meeting in full swing at the kitchen table. He eased the killer satchel from his shoulder, and subdued it behind one of the larger cushions on the sofa. Sofa, so good, he thought. His curiosity concerning his letter to 'The Festive Gentleman in Red' was niggling at him. It was plain to him that he would not be able to wait until morning in order to see what result the Desk had conjured up for him. He greeted Mum and Auntie - who gave him a 'just wait until you hear this one' look.

Uncle Joe sat at the head of the table. He had at last decided that no longer would he be restrained by a lack of technical expertise, as regards the world of computers. At length, and in meticulous detail, he explained about his latest venture into the field of commerce. He had researched, designed, and marketed a very special range of chewing sticks - which were black pudding flavoured. He had rushed his product onto the Internet. To ensure that sales would really "take off"; he had released the product in the Yorkshire area. To his utter amazement, and no little measure of utter dismay - his innovative new product had failed to sell.

It would appear that no-one was buying Uncle Joe's E-Bay Gum...

While Mum served dinner, and Auntie tried her best to resist the urge to stun Uncle Joe with the heaviest kitchen implement that she could lay hands on, Nicky crept back into the living room. He approached the Desk, all the while mentally apologising for his undue haste in seeking a reply to his letter to Santa. Reverentially, he sat at the chair and pulled down the writing shelf. Nervously, he reached for the small middle drawer, and gently pulled it out. There, in the drawer, was a small rolled scroll tied with a festive red ribbon, and an imposing-looking wax seal which bore the legend 'North Pole Post'. Wowee!! This was it! With trembling hands, he slid the ribbon from the rolled vellum. He stretched out the sheet and read his response, which was written in a fine italic script, it said:

'I know exactly what it is that you wish for Christmas, and furthermore, *exactly* what it is that you would like to unwrap...'

Damn! Now he knew that he was probably on both the "Naughty" and "Nice" lists. There would be no chance of fooling Santa - as he would have read it twice.

Nicky decided to have a refreshing shower in order to take his mind off the fact that one of the Elves had obviously grassed him up. Recently, any bath night had become a matter of some concern. Along with her other numerous talents, Auntie had decided that she should fit a shower above their bath. He had faith in her abilities as an amateur plumber, but not in the actual shower unit itself - which seemed to produce an alarming chorus of gurgles and thumps every time Nicky attempted to use it. It hung on the wall like a perforated cobra, just daring him to touch the temperature dial. Well tonight he would do battle with the lurking beastie. He collected a large bath towel, which was still warm from the airing cupboard. Closing the bathroom door, he hung the towel on the hook. He stared into the mirror - oh dear me, that beard was beginning to take over his face: perhaps now was the time to attempt one of the benchmarks of Manhood. He ran a sink of reasonably hot water, and washed his face. The mirror was now misted up, so he had to wipe it off with the edge of the towel. Shaving gel and razor had been provided by Auntie, who had thoughtfully hinted that the time was fast approaching when he may not wish to look like a wino.

He read the instructions on the can. Squirting a blob of gel out of it, which was perhaps a little over-generous for the task in hand, he applied it liberally to his face. Looking back at him from the mirror was the face of Santa, which panicked him for a second. He was sure that he had just seen a hooded elf making crude gestures at him out of the corner of his eye - but on inspection, this turned out to be only the shape of the hanging towel. Okay then - here goes.. He picked up the razor and made tentative downward strokes on his cheek. The foam came off in great dripping mounds, but disappointingly, the trainee beard remained. He tried again, only to achieve a similar result. He now had an apprentice beard on his cheeks - with a white goatee in the middle. He made as if to try another attempt - and the razor spun out of his hand, and onto the bathroom floor. As he picked it up, he was about to take another lunge at his face, when he noticed (just in time) the silver, sharp edge of the blade. Ah - so you had to remove the cover first then. Right, got it. Here we go...carefully. Nicky carefully completed his very first full shave, including pulling the "Bloke shaving" faces that he had seen on the television. He washed the razor and dried off his face, turning back to admire the results in the mirror. Not bad for a first attempt! Not bad that is, if you had just been involved in a gangland razor-fight with a dozen thugs. He now needed two things: some toilet paper to put onto the cuts, and the telephone number of the nearest Blood Transfusion Centre...

The boy decided that he would deal with his self-inflicted wounds later. First, there was the matter of the shower. He stepped into the bath and confidently reached out for the temperature control. He set it to "medium". Now, it was on with the water. There were no sounds of complaint from the system, no pops, gurgles or groans. No water either. Turning the dial this way and that produced nothing more than a tepid drip into the bath. He reached up and unhooked the shower head from its resting position. He gave the unit a good shake, just in case, then turned on the water again - this time increasing the setting on the dial. There was a sound as if someone were trying to ride a donkey whilst wearing tin trousers. Nicky looked into the upturned head of the shower. There were many reasons why this had been a very bad idea. Perhaps the worst of these was the sudden jet of water which shot out of the shower into his face. Not only into his face, but up into the air - where the water made contact with the hot light bulb in the ceiling fitting. There was a loud "bang!" and the boy found himself in darkness, in the bath, surrounded by broken pieces of the exploded lightbulb, and still with cuts to the face. His instinct was to shout for help, but the towel was hanging far off on the bathroom door. To reach it, he would have to walk over broken glass. He didn't want to call out for his Mother - as he didn't want another of those awkward conversations which go 'Yes Mum- but it's mine...and I am entitled to wash it as fast as I like...'. There was only one thing that he could do. He attempted to hide as much of himself at waist level with the small flannel - (secretly disappointed that what he was seeking to conceal was so easily hidden). He called out to Auntie, who appeared at the door and looked aghast at the vision of the foam-flecked, face hacked, naked boy standing in the dark in the bath, surrounded by broken shards of glass, wearing a small paisley-pattern flannel.

'Could you give me a hand please Auntie...' he asked, pleading…

Auntie grinned, and supplied the applause which he had requested.

Chapter Twenty-Two:

Ah Well: it is said that 'Cometh the Hour - then Cometh L'Homme'. The eagerly-awaited event which was due to pass into legend as "The Grand French Market" was now upon them. Friday night had seen the beginnings of the transformation which would change the quadrangle into "Le Quatretangle" for the celebration of all things French. Stall frames had been erected (without the help of Matron), and boxes of bunting plus various other weird and wonderful items had been stored in the Geography classroom. Early on the Saturday morning, the whole area began to fill up and come alive with Gallic expectation. Quite a lot of money had been spent to ensure that the visiting Dignitaries and the public would be treated to an enjoyable spectacle. Dr Chambers was hoping that the expected crowds would spend quite a lot of money too - and had seen to it that prices were hiked up accordingly. At least they would not be pestered by those bloody Morris Men at this event. This troupe of local nutters took it upon themselves to insinuate themselves into any such gathering - but had been told in no uncertain terms by Chambers that since they were not French, nor had any connection with France, that they should bugger off...

As the early morning chill began to dissipate, it had all the makings of a lovely day. Mrs Bradley had already been round with a laden tea trolley, supplying drinks for those who were busy setting up the stalls. Madame had not yet arrived, and was presumably getting one of the local garages to spray on her makeup. Chambers hoped against hope that she would arrived dressed in something which would at least make the attempt to restrain her enhanced frontage. At least there would be no Dr Goodwill here to ingratiate himself with the French visitors in that oily way of his, or tut-tut loudly at anything which Chambers himself did. The Acting Head decided to have a leisurely walk around the quad and see how the various "attractions" were coming along. There were several stalls that had been set up for (hired out at exorbitant rates to) Businesses such as Air France, Renault, Le Coq Sportif, and one which seemed to be displaying a life-size cut-out of Britney Spears (he assumed that this should have been hired to Brittany Ferries, but hey-ho..).

Already fully set up and ready to go was a booth constructed from study sheets of thick plywood. There was a counter-like arrangement at the front. Above the "serving window" was a large sign which bore the legend 'Plus Ca Change' This was where the visiting dignitaries from across the channel could convert their Euros into Sterling, which would be spent at the stalls. If Chambers had his way, it would also convert quite a bit of cash into linings for his pockets. Across the quad, the Academy band were setting up on their own small stage, to play for the crowds, God help them.

Entering the quad, the first stall that the public came to was the one given over to all things St Onan. The table was crammed full of badges, ties, sweatshirts and a positive cornucopia of products which all bore the distinctive logo of the Academy. On the back wall of the booth was a large copy of the most recent photograph taken of the whole school. The boys and Staff stood or sat in their rows, dressed in their finest Academy attire. Chambers winced, as his eyes zoomed in one particular boy at the back, who was not dressed in his finest - in fact he was not dressed at all. He nodded to the stall proprietor Miss Piggott, and moved on hurriedly. Striding along to the next tented unit, he was greeted by a somewhat over-enthusiastic Mr Thwaite, who dashed up to him and stood in front of his "pitch", as if awaiting some gesture of approval. Chambers stepped away from the man. 'Did we agree that the stallholders should all wear fancy dress?' asked Chambers.

'Oh no Sir!' gushed Thwaite- 'but since we are supposed to be a French Market - I thought that the least that I could do was to dress as Edith Piaf...'

'Do you think that was a wise decision?' said Chambers, picking up a very strong scent of Chanel number five.

'I regret Nothing....' answered Thwaite, haughtily.

The eyes of the Acting Head master were suddenly drawn to the collection of objects which hung bunting-like from the top of the stall. A large collection of small knobbly rubber items were swinging gently in the breeze. He raised a shaking hand, pointing an accusing finger at the objects 'What the Blazes are those things doing strung up there?'.

'I did exactly what I was told to do, and followed my instructions to the letter' said Thwaite. 'That cannot possibly be what you were asked to put up' demanded Chambers.

'Indeed, it was - Madame said I should hang up a string of them in honour of our French visitors...' Chambers stared at the man. It was a few seconds before his mind deduced the flaw in the supposed instructions that Thwaite had been given.

'I am certain that what Madame instructed you to display were French TRICOLOURS...'

'Ah...not 'tick-'

'Thwaite- please remove them'.

Chambers walked off in search of a cup of coffee. A very strong one.

At precisely eleven o'clock, the gates of the Academy were thrown open to admit the great, the good, and the curious. Some had come to buy up a range of French produce, some were merely killing time before their lunchtime boozing session, and some had come for a good old nosey at "Toff City"- as the Academy was often referred to. Whatever their particular calling, the iron twin-set clad figure of Miss Emilia Piggott ensured that no-one gained entry to the Market without having paid. The trickle of "guests" at the gates soon became a flood- and Darwin and Strangler had to rush over and lend assistance to the Secretary, who they discovered had one teenage "non-payer" in an armlock. The quad and the areas between the stalls began to fill up with people. Chambers looked out at the scene from his office window, and concluded that it might well turn out to be a profitable day after all. From the car park, Captain Brayfield regarded the spectacle through his field binoculars - which he held in one hand. This was intolerable - a positive invasion damn it! The place would stink of Dalek-Garlic or whatever the wretched stuff was called, for weeks. His other hand gripped the steering wheel of his car so hard, that it left indentations in the wheel...

From the central podium which had been set up, came the announcement of welcome from Madame Dreadfell. She had draped herself in furs for the occasion, the fox wrap that she wore looking like it had barely survived a recent battle with a much larger predator. She looked nervously toward the entrance, and then nodded urgently to Phillip Whiggley, who was conducting the group of would-be musicians masquerading as the Academy Band. He hurriedly tapped his baton on his music stand- the baton flying out of his grip, and poking the trombone player in the eye. He waved his hands in panic - and the strangled strains of what was supposed to be the French National Anthem began to rise from the band. At the same moment, a sleek, black, Citroen D car swished into the quad, scattering the crowd. It pulled up at the side of the podium, and five bodies emerged.

Madame rushed over to greet them, and began to kiss the cheeks of all concerned - managing to include the driver, who was most grateful. The French deputation lined up on the podium, which was draped with the French flag. The head of the party was the Town Mayor of St Gussette - Jean-Claude Derriere. He was accompanied by his small and sour-looking wife Brigitte, and the Mayor's "Secretary", Mademoiselle Denise LeBuste. There was a small scuffle as the wife of the Mayor proceeded to elbow her rival away from her husband's immediate vicinity. Also along for the jaunt were Pierre Noblong, and Armand Coustarde. Armand wore a furious scowl. He had been a rival for the post of Mayor, and amidst accusations of corruption during the election, had lost the role by a mere two votes. He was still extremely bitter. Oh - bitter, bitter Armand...

Madame returned to her position on the podium, and introduced the visiting dignitaries to the crowds. There was muted applause from the public, although Madame clapped like she was on some severe medication. The Mayor announced that it was 'Ver-ee wonder-ful to bee 'eer today, and I thank you for giving to me the clap...' This brought a large cheer from the crowd - and the Mayor beamed with Gallic pride. Madame signalled to the band leader again, and another rendition of the *Marseillaise* struggled into life. Back in the car - Brayfield was furious. 'My God and all the Saints in Christendom!!' he shouted, 'They're only playing their National Anthem - Right then Frenchie: if that's how you want it - that's how we'll play it!'. He started the car, grinding the gears terribly, and screeched off to prepare his revenge on the invading forces from across the Channel.

Chambers had now joined up with Madame for the walk-around with the French contingent. The party began with a stop at the Academy tent. Miss Piggott curtsied primly to the Mayor, and blushed like a schoolgirl when he leaned over and kissed her hand. Out of sight, his wife leaned over and trod heavily on his foot with her stiletto heel. She was not happy - she had already noticed when her husband appeared to be trying to remove stray fibres from the skirt of Mlle LeBuste. For a "Secretary", she did not seem to take an awful lot of notes, and the silly girl would often emerge from the Mayor's office with her blouse untucked...Madame Derriere had noticed the Academy photograph, and asked 'Zat boy – why 'as Ee got no cloths on?' Chambers panicked - then rallied: 'Episcopalian Church of Kidderminster Madam, very strict observer - excused clothing on

Wednesdays'. He quickly steered the group away and on to the next stall.

Miles Bannister had been put in charge of the French food stall. The rear of the stall was stacked with bread of all descriptions, Golden Delicious apples, croissants, pate, preserves of endless variety, and a plate of snails. Actually, there were two plates- but only from one of them, had the occupants made a bid for freedom. As the group approached, Bannister could be heard engaged in a furious row with himself. As the bemused visitors looked on, Mrs Elsie Noakes raged on about the cruelty involved in the consumption of frog's legs - 'I mean to say Miles, the poor little things don't have much of a life as it is, and just because some foreigner thinks that their legs are a delicacy, they are condemned to spend the rest of their time in a wheelchair? It's barbaric - that's what it is!! And I just hate to think of all those tiny pairs of unusable socks - just piling up...'. Bannister stuffed a whole brioche into his mouth to mute the sound of Elsie's lecture, and the group moved swiftly on.

Linked to the stall of Bannister on a semi-detached basis was a unit stacked from floor to ceiling with French cheeses. A large "wheel" of soft cheese rolled away to reveal the grinning face of Professor Strangler - munching on a cracker topped with a fine variety of "Combat Camembert" (cheese that fights back). He waved a small French flag on a stick in welcome. Sitting next to Strangler on a deck chair, was an apple-cheeked young girl of about sixteen years of age, wearing clothes that clearly belonged to a Victorian Housemaid. The group looked from one face to the other, and Strangler explained: 'Oh I do beg your pardon - let me introduce Mollie Soggins' (the girl rose and gave a polite curtsy) 'She pops in now and again through the vortex to get her laundry done. I thought that I would let her come to the Market today - as it's her day off' (the girl covered her mouth and giggled behind her hand). 'I am veree please to meet wiz you Mollee...' said the Mayor, eyeing the girl's ample bosom. The man received two looks of fury - one from his wife, and another from the "Secretary", who still hadn't taken a single line of dictation. The attention of the party was caught by a loud voice shouting 'DOWN SIMEY! - Down I say!..'

They peered behind the cheese emporium, and saw a long rectangular area which had been covered in sand. 'What's going on here?' demanded Chambers - striding around the back of the tent. He came to an abrupt halt. There was Dr Darwin, and Albert Brooks - but more to the point there was "Simon" the Sabre-tooth, who appeared to have put the sanded rectangle to use as his own personal litter tray. The Mayor stood fascinated at the sight, his mouth open. 'What iz zees going on 'ere?' he asked.

'Balls!...' came the swift reply from Brooks. Chambers looked aghast. 'I think he meant to say "Boules" Mr Mayor' said Madame, quickly. The Mayor was impressed - 'Ah..ze Boules- Tres Bon!! I will give you ze game?' He looked down to the end of the "pitch", saw Simon, saw what Simon had almost finished burying, and said 'Per-'aps later, Non?'. As the visitors were guided swiftly away by Chambers, Mlle LeBuste made a bee-line for Simon, who obligingly rolled over for her to tickle his tummy...

Hyde-Jones and Mr Newhouse had turned up slightly late, after a night out at a local Hostelry, where they had turned up surprisingly early. After both waking themselves up with a strong coffee, they had decided to be guided by their own subconscious radar- and had somehow gravitated to the tent of Dr Matthews. The good Doctor had really entered into the spirit of the occasion, and a good deal of spirits had already entered into the Doctor. He was busy mixing mind-numbing blends of liquids, in search of a suitable cocktail to serve to the visitors. He peered at his latest creation and declared - 'Oh bugger...'thought I'd got it just then...I was trying to make a cocktail that is blue, white and red. This damn thing is red, white and blue'.

'That's because you are upside down, Gus...' Mr Newhouse helpfully reminded him.

The happy cocktail expert righted himself, and sat down alongside his friends. Behind and around the three men were staggering arrays of bottles. There were fine wines of all types, such as might only be found in the very best cellars (they were - all liberated from the Academy's own stocks). There was Pernod, Napoleon Brandy, Armagnac, Champagnes of all sizes, Vin Blanc, Vin Rouge and Vin Rough. Chambers and the guests arrived in front of the stall. Newhouse and Hyde-Jones immediately plied their visitors with glasses of Champagne. Then Cognac. Then another spot of Champagne with a smidgen of Armagnac to help it go down. The two Masters took it in turns to raise a toast to everything from the town of Saint Gussette - to Mr Newhouse's new pants. Never was there an Entente so Cordiale. Mlle LeBuste looked into the Master's fizzing glass, and declared to Mr Newhouse 'I like to see your bubbles, Meester Loopee...'

'And I am looking forward to perhaps catching a glimpse of yours, Mademoiselle...' replied Mr Newhouse.

Hyde-Jones had sunk to the floor, where he was calling out 'Loopy...Looopy- I can't feel my legs!!'. Chambers looked around the stall, and discovered a frightening quantity of empty bottles. 'Matthews!' he demanded - 'Where the damnation has all the wine gone?' Matthews raised an admonishing finger, 'Ah Yes; you see Dr Chambers, Madame told me that the wine, when opened, must be allowed to "breathe"..'

'So why are all of these bloody bottles empty Man?' said Chambers. Matthews smiled, 'Ah well Dear Boy, I checked on each and every bottle. It appeared to me that they were having great difficulty in breathing - so I gave them mouth-to-mouth...'

As the honoured guests staggered away from the Alcoholic Emporium of Dr Matthews, their progress was halted by a very large group of male members of the public, who were all pressing to gain entry to the Boarding House doors. Clearing a way through the crowd, Dr Chambers led the delegation through the melee. The doors to Matron's quarters had been augmented by a red, white and blue awning, at the side of which was a sign with large printed letters in several languages. The notice declared to one and all: 'Bonjour!! Madame Lucretia's European Massage and French Riding Lessons'... At the door stood Matron, casually dressed in a skimpy French Maid outfit- in rubber. What was said by Mme Derriere to her husband the Mayor was not recorded - but even a complete non-French speaker could tell that her comment was of the "Make one move toward that door - and you're dead Chummy.." variety. From the rear of the group came the sound of Mr Newhouse's jaw dropping. The group were rapidly spun around by Chambers, and herded along, where they came upon what could have been a typical street scene in Paris. Sitting in his smock and beret was the Art Master Bell-Enderby, who was painting portraits of willing sitters in the Impressionist style - for cash, of course. The Mayor passed an expert eye over each of the drying portraits. Chambers looked over his shoulder. Oh good grief! - this one was going to take some explaining. It would appear that Bell-Enderby's obsession with certain aspects of the Female form had resurfaced. All of the subjects painted had been depicted with enormous breasts - including two of the men who had posed. Bell-Enderby looked up from his work and said 'Ah Bonjour Monsieur Mayor. Can you please answer me a question?'

‘I weel try, of course..’ said the Mayor.

The Art Master continued- ‘The area of France where they make all of the springs that go into mattresses- is it by any chance the place known as “The Dar-Doing?” ...’

Little did they know, but much worse was to come...

Chapter Twenty-Three:

The cluster of nervous men had assembled around the corner of the Arts block, and out of sight. In silence, they had donned their equipment and uniforms. Specialist items of kit had been quietly affixed to ankles, waists and cuffs. Their assault on the event would ensure that they were regarded as a force to be reckoned with- if only Barry could keep his trousers up. The leader surveyed his troops, adjusting pieces of their uniform here and there. He was satisfied- now they were ready to make their mark. The squad formed up into two lines of five, with the "Commander" at the head. He raised his hand, and at his signal, the men marched into the quad...

At the sight of the squad of men making their entry into the Market, Chambers had dropped his French bread and pate, and run over to head them off. Newhouse and Hyde-Jones had dashed over with him (Hyde-Jones a little unsteadily) to lend their support. The Acting Head waved his arms at the Leader, and the two men faced each other nose-to-nose at the end of the quad. 'What the Ruddy Hell are you lot doing, turning up here?' demanded Chambers. The Leader folded his arms and declared 'I was given a verbal agreement that our services would be required, nay needed, at this event'.

'Right then Gordon...' said Chambers 'You are a bunch of –'

'Tossers!!' added Mr Newhouse.

'Thank you Mr N: as I was about to say, you purport to be a group of Morris Dancers. The tradition of Morris Dancing (God help us..) is cemented in English history. This event is a "French Market"- and you have no place here' said Chambers, angrily. A hurt sounding voice from the back said, 'But we've got French ribbons, and I've re-painted my bells especially...' Chambers ignored the entreaty, 'Nothing about your attire, nor your performance - if that's what it is called, is in any way connected to the People or traditions of France...'

'Oh yes it is!' replied Gordon.

'How do you intend to justify that statement?' asked Chambers. There was a pause... 'We are in fact not 'Morris Dancers' as you so crudely put it. Today- we are "Les Danseurs Maurice..." said a proud Gordon.

Chambers looked to the heavens, as his colleagues chuckled. 'Give me just one good reason why I should allow you into this event' demanded Chambers.

'We have an Accordion' said Gordon.

Chambers leaned forward, causing the Leader to lean backwards and jingle slightly. When he spoke, it was a hiss through firmly gritted teeth: 'I couldn't care less what wheezy instrument you have dragged along here - or who may or may not have asked you buffoons to turn up. It says "*Goodyear*" on the tyres of my car - but thanks to idiots like you, I do not seem to be having one...'.

Mr Newhouse stepped into the fray: 'Right- you heard the man...Allez you lot, and be vite about it, or you'll get a kick in the jinglebells'.

Shamed and defeated, the troop turned and sadly tinkled off into the distance.

Behind the changing rooms up on the sports field, Captain Brayfield checked and tightened the girth around the belly of his best friend- his horse Montgomery. There were certain things that he was not going to stand for: and this foreign farce was certainly one of them. Now that he thought of it – the only thing that he would certainly stand for was the National Anthem - and that would be the ENGLISH National Anthem at that. What they were doing today, well, it was the straw that broke the Camel backwards - a Bridge Too Far from the Madding Crowd. He patted Montgomery and straightened his tie. Placing one foot in the gleaming stirrup, he rose into the saddle, seating himself comfortably and pulling down the peak of his cap. The ears of the horse twitched as he heard his master begin muttering to himself 'We shall have our day...and did those feet in Ancient Times....on English lawns...not in sandals by crikey...borrowed my mower and never returned it...tomato sauce on his cornflakes...' Digging his spurs lightly into the horse's flank, the warrior rode off to battle...(actually, not to Battle itself - which is near Hastings: and best not to get him started on the subject of 1066, because they have only just got the last of the blood off the Staffroom walls...) Let's just say that he trotted off determinedly in the direction of the Academy...

The French contingent seemed to have split up- and were going around the stalls individually. The Mayor had pushed his way through the crowd in order to greet what he thought was a Gendarme- only to be treated to the sight of the boy Weatherill wearing a "Kepi", and tucking into a bag of chips. He was happy to share these with the Mayor, and the two struck up an immediate camaraderie. The driver of the sleek French car leaned back on the vehicle, and lit a Gauloise cigarette, blowing an elegant cloud of smoke into the air. He had not noticed that a small sandy-haired boy had climbed into the boot - closing the door from within.

Madame was trying to lever the wife of the Mayor out of the clutches of Bell-Enderby, who was insistent that she let him immortalise her on canvas. Since it was not the warmest of afternoons, she could not (bad translation permitting) see why the man was urging her to remove her blouse. There was no sign of Mr Newhouse...the last positive sighting of the Music Tutor had taken place some time ago on the far side of the Wine tent, where he had been seen in the pleasant company of Mlle LeBuste. The two had slid out of sight behind the tents, heading toward the Music room - where he may well have been intending to show her his quavers, or if she was very lucky, maybe his crotchet.

Armand Coustarde was having a lie down. He had little choice in the matter - as he was being pinned down to the floor by "Simon", who was attempting to lick him to death. Darwin and Strangler were doing their best to extract the poor man from his Sabre-tooth carwash, but when a cat the size of Simon is having fun - it might be best to let him play.

Our own French Ambassador, Madame Dreadfell, was in a state of panic as she tried to locate and keep together the visitors. She had arranged a special prize raffle, and wanted the Mayor to make the announcements of the winners. Last time she had caught sight of him, he was standing with Weatherill, throwing gherkins into the air, and trying to catch them in their mouths. After helping her to escape from the clutches of the Art Master, she had given the wife of the Mayor a Valium. She now stood at the side of the podium, with glass in hand, and a distant look upon her face. Around the corner appeared Mr Newhouse, arm-in-arm with Mlle LeBuste, who looked rather flustered. 'Where have you been?' asked Madame 'It's almost time for the raffle...and did you know that you have your jeans on back to front Mr Newhouse?'. Hyde-Jones had managed to sober up, and had helped to re-assemble the French Delegation at the podium. He nudged the Mayor, 'Who's that woman there?' he asked. 'Which ees the woman to 'oo you refer?' said the Mayor. Hyde-Jones pointed to Mrs Derriere, 'Her - Joan of Arse there, standing by the stage...' The Mayor laughed, and confided 'Zat ees ma wife...!' 'Oh, I'm so sorry Dear Boy' said Hyde-Jones.

The Mayor turned to the English Master with a sorrowful look on his face, 'So am I Mon Ami- I married 'er...'.

Madame Dreadfell straightened her bolero jacket, and stepped up to the microphone which was set up at the front of the stage. After a lot of squealing feedback from the microphone, the sound settled down, and she addressed the crowd: 'Monsieur Mayor, Lady Mayoress, Honoured Guests, Ladies and Gentlemen...We now come to the raffle draw for our terrific list of prizes. So without further ado- please get your tickets ready!' There was a general rustling as the crowd sought out the fragile raffle tickets which had been bought grudgingly, and stuffed into various pockets. Chambers stood behind her, turning the handle of a machine which caused a barrel to rotate. Inside were all of the raffle tickets. He opened the small door in the barrel, and handed her a green ticket.

'This lucky winner will receive a year's supply of Brie!!' she exclaimed. The crowd looked on non-plussed. 'And the lucky winner is.....ticket two-six-nine'. A little elderly lady made her way to the front, and waved her ticket under Madame's nose.

'I got it...' she declared.

'Can we have a round of applause please for our lucky winner!!' said Madame. She handed the wedge of cheese to the lady. The lady looked at the cheese. She bent over and smelled the cheese. 'It stinks!...' she said. 'That is Best French cheese Madam!' answered the French Mistress. 'Well best give it back to 'em then!' said the woman, who slapped the cheese firmly back into Madame's hand, and stomped off into the crowd.

And so it went. The couple who won the case of wine found that four of the bottles were empty; the prize tickets for the weekend in Paris had gone missing, the delicate and expensive perfume was won by a six-foot-three hairy garage mechanic, and the five-course beef dinner for two at a local French restaurant (with fine wines included) went to a couple of Vegan tee-totallers. Madame was somewhat relieved when it came time to make the draw for the last (and "star") prize. 'And now Ladies and Gentlemen- the moment that you have all been waiting for...a drum roll please!! (a stale bread roll was spun across the stage). The holder of this ticket will win a brand new Citroen car - which has been donated courtesy of Messrs Gymp and Clarke - your local prestige car dealership'.

The crowd fell silent, all eyes on their tickets...

Chambers opened the door in the machine, and handed Madame a ticket stub. She extended her arm to her left, and stated 'And the number of the lucky winning ticket for our Star Prize will be announced by my very good friend- Monsieur Jean-Claude Derriere, the Mayor of the town of Saint Gussette...' Nervously, the Mayor stepped up onto the stage, and gave Madame the traditional French greeting of kissing on both cheeks. Another stale roll hit her on the back of the head at this point, which may, or may not have been launched by his jealous Wife.. The Mayor prepared himself. He smiled cautiously at the crowd, then took the ticket from Madame's hand, and announced...

'And eet give me greatest pleasures to announce, that thee winner ticket is -...'

The screaming began as a tall man mounted on a huge white horse galloped into the quad, wildly swinging his cavalry sabre left and right. He wore a white silk scarf over his face. He was wearing a Union Jack waistcoat. The horse wore an identical garment...Thundering down on the crowd at full speed; the mad charger hacked and sliced at the stalls as he passed, scattering the terrified people, who dived for cover under the nearest available solid-looking object. In the case of Mr Newhouse, this just happened to be the Matron.

Wheeling and turning: thrusting and slashing - into the valley of the Market rode the er, one. The Captain was shouting loudly as he rode through the stalls 'I'll make yer plead for Merci...serve you right for calling your car a "Lemon"...Confiscate my Duty-Free will yer!?...' A man stepped bravely out in front of the massive horse.

The Captain halted... 'Hoi You - are you one of these Foreigner Types? - what's yer name?' demanded the Captain.

'Norman...' said the man.

'Thought so -' said the Captain...and punched him.

The Avenger on horseback set off again, circling the stalls and laying waste to anything which came within reach of his sabre. He twirled the sword above his head in order to dislodge a large cheese which had become impaled. The cheese flew in a beautiful parabolic arc over the food stall- where it struck Mr Thwaite and rendered him unconscious.

Brayfield reigned in his steed, and trotted to a halt in front of a stall which had a copy of the Bayeux Tapestry hung on its wall. As he snorted his displeasure, he leaned over and cut a name into the cloth with swishing strokes. This done, he pulled on the reins, and his horse reared up and struck out at the air with its front hooves. He held his sabre aloft and shouted, 'For Saint George- and England!!', before galloping off into the distance. Slowly, the people began to emerge from their hiding places. A man watched him go, and said to his wife 'Who was that Masked Man?...'

She studied the cuts made in the tapestry - which seemed to spell out a name. Due to the difficulty of cutting a name into thick cloth with a cavalry sabre whilst on horseback, the name was rather indistinct.

'It looks like "Zolpo"...what do you think Hilda?'

'Nah - it's more like "Zippo" from this angle' she said.

'But what can this possibly mean?' asked the man...

'Well I'm no expert - but we may have just been attacked by one of the Marx Brothers...'

Chapter Twenty-Four:

Of course there was an enquiry. What had supposed to have been a jolly event which may have cemented Anglo-French co-operation for the Academy had descended into chaos and mayhem, with a side order of fracas, and just a hint of Brouhaha. Madame had tried to calm the frayed nerves of her Gallic guests to no avail - and finally had to resort to extremes by "maxing out" her credit card on hotel accommodation for them: somewhere luxurious, quiet, and more importantly - well out of the way of the Academy.

Captain Hercules Brayfield denied all knowledge of the desecration of the Market, despite the fact that there were not too many men of his stature who were a) ex-Cavalry officers, and well versed in swordplay, and b) owner of a dirty great white horse with hooves like car seats. 'But the man was masked!' he had said 'And these days, I believe that the hire of a white horse can be very easily achieved via the "Interweb", or some such nonsense'. Chambers was having none of it, 'Your actions have brought disgrace upon the Academy - heaven knows what the Trustees will do when they get wind of this little caper' he declared.

True, there was no actual physical proof which would link Brayfield directly with the incident, but come on now - I mean, really? As it was, Chambers was baffled to see what action he could possibly take, without causing the Captain to ultimately take out a law suit for unlawful dismissal against St Onans. The two men stared at each other across the desk. Brayfield's iron pride won the day, and it was Chambers who blinked first. Here was yet another incident which would have to be carefully and efficiently filed under "L" for "lose behind the filing cabinet in the back office under last term's petty cash receipts". To be frank- the Captain might well have got away with it scot free, had he not risen like a bad kebab after six pints on a Friday night, and declared indignantly 'I mean - what sort of damn colour is "Sacre Blue" supposed to be anyway'?.

Oh, Ye Gods! - it was all collapsing around his ears. Five minutes ago the Institution over which he had been given control had been threatened by the placement of deadly marzipan. Now a jolly gathering had left the quad resembling a war zone - after the surprise guest appearance of Genghis Khan and his rampaging "bijou hordette" of one. To add further misery to the rising pile... that wretched DeVere boy had apparently escaped *again.*

Up in the village, another meeting had taken place - one with a completely different agenda. The single topic of discussion here was the conservation of the planet's natural resources: to whit, the imminent destruction of five rather aged elm trees adjacent to the "bomb crater" in the big field. Nicky had decided to assemble a brain-storming collective of the finest eco -friendly minds which he could muster, and so had contacted his village friends Mikey, Squiddy, Stuart and Pete. He had augmented the Team with Calderman, Kendy, Merry and Mark Davis from St Onans. Agent Trevill would possibly be brought into action later - as a secret agent, or possibly as Group Spokesman. Much against their expectations, the village boys had struck up an immediate friendship with the lads from the Academy. There seemed to be nothing snobbish at all about the Academy boys, and Squiddy had even felt confident enough to ask Calderman what exactly was the difference between a serviette and a napkin. 'If you blow your nose on both of them - then the one which makes your Mum shout at you the loudest is probably the napkin...' answered Calderman. Okay – that's etiquette sorted then.

Nicky steered the topic back to the subject of saving the trees. 'What I am trying to say lads, is that these trees are just as old, if not older, than the village itself. They are just as much of an historical landmark as, say, the old Blacksmith's Arms pub at the top of the hill. What would people say if they pulled down the Church, for instance...Someone needs to take a stand against the wilful destruction of our natural heritage - and that someone, Gentlemen...is us'. This drew an enthusiastic round of applause from the group, all apart from Stuart, who looked unhappy.

'The problem is...' he began 'My Granny can't live in her old house at the top of the village any more. Since Granddad passed away, the house is too big for her - and we're always worried that she will fall down those steep stairs and do herself a mischief. She will be able to have a nice new bungalow when the site is developed, and there will be plenty of people around who can help her if she has a problem' he said.

'But the trees are really old' said Nicky.

'So's my Granny.'

'The trees need the land to live'.

'But the old people need the land so that they can live safer lives.'

'The trees give shelter to other creatures'.

'Granny has a poodle and a canary...'

'Where will all of the rabbits and owls go to?'

'The new bungalows will all have a shed...'

(There was a pause as the group pictured the chaos that would ensue as an elderly resident casually opened the door to their shed, and was besieged by woodland wildlife...)

'Can't they just transplant the trees?'

'Good idea - has anyone got a twenty-five-foot plant pot handy?'

'Why don't we go and cut them down during the night, and hide them somewhere?'

'Can anyone else spot the deliberate mistake in that sentence?' said Davis.

'Are there any protected or rare species around?- you know, things that need saving?' asked Pete.

'Yeah - my Granny for one...' said Stuart.

'No - I mean Great Crested Newts or something *exotic...*' said Pete.

'Granny once went on holiday to the Isle of Wight.?.' said Stuart.

'Could the people and the trees not peacefully co-exist?' asked Kendy.

'Can't see my Granny wanting to live in a tree-house, and it wouldn't do her arthritis much good' said Stuart.

'I still say we go and buy a big box of Newts...' said Pete, looking hopeful.

The discussion went back and forth for several minutes, until it settled upon the basic notion of "First come, First saved". They were all aware that their protests would probably end in failure, but all were agreed that some kind of direct action simply had to be undertaken. Nicky was rather hoping that the matter might find its way into the local papers, where Jozza would be bound to see her would-be suitor the Eco-Warrior proudly standing at the top of one of the trees, waving his banner. The realist in him was hoping that it wouldn't be raining on that day. And so it came to pass that the gathering didst agree that on that very night, under the cover of darkness, they shouldst verily pull up all of the marker posts which the Contractors had placed near the trees - and so shall sling them over the nearest hedgerow. And the boys saw this plan, and agreed that it was good. And yea verily didst Davis see that there were three chocolate mini-rolls left on the plate, and this too was good.

The door to the Metalwork room clicked open. Mrs Finucane opened the door and held it open whilst the "Gentlemen" visitors filed into the room. Mr Posta began to explain to his superior officers how he had obtained numerous fingerprints from the surfaces and equipment within the room- and that he now had positive evidence which linked Swall and Fletcher to the gold thefts. He confidently strode over to the tool rack on the wall, pausing for dramatic effect in front of the neat rows of equipment. 'And so Sir, after considerable effort and painstaking detective work, I have used all of my training to uncover -'

'For God's sake stop piddling about Posta - just show us whatever big secret you seem to have found' said his Chief Inspector. Posta grinned the grin of the eternal smartarse - and reached up to the top row of tools on the rack. He selected a fairly hefty pair of pliers, and handed them to his superior. 'Right Sir- now take a pen knife or a small file, and just scratch at the metal end of the pliers' he said.

'Look- I really don't have time to p-'

'Just indulge me Sir, if you don't mind- just tell me what you find...' said Posta. The Chief Inspector looked at his assistant, who shrugged her shoulders, and handed her boss a small knife. He began to scratch vigorously at the metal, whilst Posta stood grinning at his assistant, awaiting the approval of his boss for a job well done. DCI Parker (his rank - not his initials) was still scraping at the tool nearly a full minute later.

'Good God!...' he said, 'That is absolutely unbelievable!'. Posta stood and beamed with pride, 'I told you I had found something remarkable Sir...' he said.

'Well, I take my hat off to you Detective Sergeant. In a Metalwork room - the very last thing that I expected to find was a pair of pliers made from hardened Steel...' Posta raced over to the bench, and snatched the tool out of his superior's hand.

'But these were - they were made of - last time, I found - someone's obviously...' he stuttered in disbelief. Parker stood up to his full height and straightened his tie.

'Did you hand in your Police waterproofs Posta?' he calmly enquired. 'Why do you ask Sir?' quavered Posta. 'Oh I don't know...I just get this feeling that you might be needing them. You know how wet you can sometimes get when you are on Traffic Duty...'.

As the poor young Police Officer who had been placed on Traffic Directing Duties at the busy junction was waving his arms ineffectually, whilst confused motorists swerved and screeched around him, a car turned a hurried circle in the road in front of him - taking the most direct route, which just happened to be over his right foot. Bent double with the pain, the unfortunate Officer was unable to get the registration number of the vehicle, which would have been pointless anyway, as it was a stolen plate from a milk float.

Inside the car sat three occupants with severe scowls on their faces (apart from the passenger in the front, who was making a desperate attempt to read a road map. This was fated to be a futile exercise - as it was in fact a road map of Cardiff...) The passenger in the rear right hand seat was busy gazing out at the town as it sped past his gaze, and even waving at one or two shoppers as they went about their business along the pavements.

The driver looked up into his rear view mirror briefly, and addressed the nonchalant sitter in the rear. 'Youse 'ave been told often enough Chummy...now it's time that you were arsked a few more difficult questions. We're takin' you to see the Big Boss - so you 'ad better get your smart Alec answers ready...'

'I like to get out and meet new people...' said Duggan.

'You ain't gonna like it as much when the Boss 'as finished with you Mate!' said "Bendy" Fletcher. 'Trust me- when the Boss tells you to jump, then you don't squeeze lemons into the soup...' The other members of the Gang looked at Fletcher, whilst their brains performed gymnastics in an attempt to make sense of that statement. They were not awarded top marks.

Fletcher continued to grin horribly, and turned on the car radio. The station that blared out was playing a ghetto Gangsta tune:

'I'm gonna hunt you down
Gonna cut you good
Gonna leave bits of you
Hangin' round the neighbourhood...'

'What the hell is that rubbish?' asked Swall...The DJ then cut in for the traffic news, announcing 'And that was the new single from the East End MC - Jack the Rapper...'

The car pulled up outside a rather swish apartment block on the outskirts of the town. Duggan was bundled out of the car and pushed up the pathway to the polished entrance doors. Figg gave him an extra shove for good measure, and then pressed the call button for apartment number seven. 'Hello...Hello...it's us Boss'. There was a pause, then a tinny voice answered 'Ye Whut?..Speak up ye daft scunner..'

Figg leaned closer to the panel and repeated 'It's us Boss - we've got the package that you wanted us to collect...can we come in?'

'Did ye forget something, ye daft spanner?' said the voice

'Sorry Boss - can we come in PLEASE...'

'Aye - ye can noo, just push the door'.

Figg opened the door, and Duggan was herded up the wooden stairs by the men. The gang of four came to a halt outside the very elegant door of the apartment, with Fletcher at the back colliding with the others. Figg turned and aimed a threatening leer at Duggan. 'Now you're for it Pal..' he declared, 'if you think that we're bad - just you wait 'til the Boss gets a hold of you...'

'Who is the Big Boss then?' enquired Duggan innocently.

'None of your damn business, that's who' replied Figg. Fletcher folded the comic which he was reading, and asked 'Yeah - I bin meanin' to ask that meself as it 'appens, how come we don't know who the Boss is? And why have we never met him?'

'Because we don't need to - and because the Boss don't like people who ask questions...' answered his annoyed colleague. Fletcher thought for a moment, and all of the men could see the mental struggle taking place as his under-used grey matter fought to construct a response. Finally, he turned to Figg and said 'But you said that the Boss said that if we did as we was told, then we would all be Millionaires. So if the Boss don't like questions, then if he goes on that "Who Wants to be a Millionaire" show- then how can we get our 'ands on the cash if he don't like questions?'

'That is a very good point' said Duggan.

'Shut it You...' snapped Figg 'You need to keep your mouth shut'.

'How is that supposed to work if the Boss wants answers to questions from me?' asked Duggan.

'You could write it down - I've got some paper and a pen in my pocket' said Fletcher, with a helpful smile. Figg did not take the suggestion well.

'Look- just shut up the bloody lot of you. The Boss will ask the questions, and you will supply the answers Duggan, whether you like it or not'. There was another menacing silence. 'You could always try Sign Language I suppose?' said Swall. Fletcher nodded, and patted his friend on the back for his helpful suggestion. Duggan began to laugh silently. Figg looked up at the ceiling and shook his head sadly, and noticed a rather large spider above the doorway- which made a very rude gesture at him. The men all jumped in shock as the door to the apartment suddenly swung open without warning.

Duggan was pushed into a plush room, and forced down into a leather chair which sat in front of an elegant desk. 'Right Matey...' said Figg, with as much menace as he could muster, 'You sit here like a good boy - and wait until the Boss comes in. Don't even think about tryin' to escape - coz' me and the boys 'ave got all of the doors covered. I was goin' to say Good Luck to you - but your luck seems to have run out...' Figg left the room laughing like a mad professor, his sinister exit being ever so slightly spoiled when he shut his fingers in the oak door on the way out. Duggan looked at his surroundings, which were opulent and very tasteful. Even the potted palm in the corner seemed to hold itself up in a haughty manner. He fished in his jacket pockets, and took out a peppermint, which he rolled around his mouth whilst he awaited his appointment with fear...

The door on the right hand wall eased itself open, and a figure entered the room without casting a glance at the seated man. The Boss gently closed the door. Duggan watched as the Boss approached the desk, and removed the heavy fur coat - placing it carefully over the back of the chair. The figure sat down in the chair, and turned to stare at him. There was no expression on the face that Duggan was looking into. The Boss leaned forward, placing both elbows on the leather-covered desk top, produced an ivory cigarette holder, inserted the expensive foreign cigarette into it, and after lighting the end with a slim gold lighter, blew a cloud of expensive smoke in Duggan's direction. Having satisfactorily set the mood, the Boss spoke in a calm voice...

'So...at last I get to meet up with you, Gregor Duggan. I must say that I am verra' disappointed at the fact that ye seem to have been avoiding me for so long. Ye ken that I have been most anxious aboot ye, and I am awfu' sorry that ye had to be brought here today. I would have thought that ye wud have come under yer ain steam, so tae speak.'

Duggan took out another peppermint, and crunched it apprehensively.

'I wud like tae ask ye whut ye have done with the gold which I have got that bunch of scunners to provide ye with. I want tae know where ye have hidden it, and what ye intend tae do about concealin' the matter from the attentions of the Polis- who I hear are sniffin' aroond the place like a wee doggie with three noses. I need to know just whut ye intend tae do with all of the money from our wee 'project'- and whether I can trust ye tae continue in oor little enterprise wi'oot raising undue attention and suspicion. I have some big decisions tae make for my sel' ye ken- and I need tae be reassured that as a great Church-goer, we are all a-singin' frae the same Hymn sheet'.

Duggan nodded, and folded his hands in his lap.

The Boss leaned further forward, and stared intently into his eyes.

'Weel noo - come on then Laddie...whut have ye got to say fer yersel'?' asked the Boss.

'Happy Birthday Mum...' said Duggan.

Chapter Twenty-five:

'Biddie' Duggan was still, at the tender age of ninety-three, a five foot four package of Glaswegian fury. In her slightly younger years, she had ruled the tenement block in which her family lived with a rod of iron, and on one notable occasion, a steam iron (still set on "steam"). She possessed the stealth of a Ninja, and a right hook which had felled a professional heavyweight boxing contender who had failed to hold the door open for a sweet old lady in a bar.

Biddie had slaved away at a variety of poorly-paid jobs, in order to ensure that her two children Fiona and Gregor could go to a decent school and "better themselves". Fiona was now a respected doctor in Glasgow, and younger Gregor (as we all know) had become a Teacher - specialising in metalwork and craft studies.

When she had been "retired early" from one of her jobs as a School Crossing Supervisor (also teaching boxing in the gym every alternate Wednesday), she had volunteered as a Prison Visitor to one of Glasgow's toughest penal establishments. She took her work very seriously, and after an incident where she had single-handedly quelled a prison riot armed only with a hairbrush - the same respect was given to her by every one of the inmates.

It was in one of these correctional establishments that she had first encountered a Mr Norman Figg, and a fellow detainee by the name of Adrian Swall. She taught Figg and Swall Literacy, Manners, and Etiquette - and they in return taught Biddie all that they knew about the workings of the Criminal mind, and just how to profit from the hard work of other people. Despite herself, Biddie found that she was developing an ever-increasing interest in gold, never before having had the luxury of being able to afford jewellery. When the two men had paid their debt to Society, she had asked a "contact" of hers to look them up. Ideas had been tossed around like drunken punters on Karaoke night, and a long-term plan had been put together, which would provide financial security for a Dear sweet old Lady and her friends. Biddie was oh so careful not to have any direct contact with her criminal gang, so that any looseness in the tongue department did not lead to pointing of the finger section, as it were. Telephone instructions would be perfectly adequate.

And so when gold needed to be "acquired" - off went Figg and Swall. When the gold needed melting down into something untraceable and a bit more manageable, why of course! Who better to lend a helping hand than her Metallurgist Teacher son Gregor? Fletcher had been acquired along the way, in much the same way that a newly-washed car quickly acquires bird poo....

Duggan reached into his jacket and took out an envelope, and two carefully-wrapped packages, which he handed to Biddie over the desk. 'Just a little something for you Mum, to wish you a very Happy Birthday with all my love...' he said.

Biddie opened the card, and smiled at her son. 'Oh that's lovely - whut a very thoughtful boy ye are...' she purred. She then opened the two wrapped gifts, and was delighted to find that they were an egg-cup and matching plate. Cast in solid gold.

'Och, Bless ye Gregor- it's just whut I wanted!, and it will match the dinner service that ye gave to me last birthday. I'm verra lucky to have such a thoughtful Son...'

Duggan stood up, walked around the desk, and gave his Mother a hug. 'Now- what was that ye said about "Big Decisions" concerning yourself Mum?' he asked.

Biddie Duggan smiled at her son.

'I've decided to retire...' she calmly stated.

Back at St Onans, there was someone who was at the point of wishing that he too, could retire, if only to escape the mayhem that was breaking out like a teenager's face all around him. Chambers had asked Professor Strangler to assist him in the mystic task of obtaining access to some of the "locked" files which he had come across on Goodwill's computer. The passwords had given him some trouble, and it wasn't until he accidentally knocked the Head Master's ancient cricket ball off its display stand on the desk, that the penny had dropped. Of course - since the Head had a passion for all things cricket, the required passwords would have to be something based around his favourite sport! He had typed in the passwords "Googly" "Silly Mid-on" and "Leg Break". These terms had eventually permitted him access to the darkest hidden rooms of the data fortress. The process had taken him well over an hour and a half - and he was now at the point of wanting to break the leg of, smite severely in the googly, and physically inconvenience whichever silly bugger had set up the system. What he did discover was truly disturbing. From an account only identified as 'FSF Ltd', the Academy was receiving very large sums of money on an irregular basis. More worrying was the fact that these sums were then being immediately transferred out of the Academy accounts, and into the coffers of one individual recipient.

The account holder was a certain Doctor Gerald Goodwill.

He read and re-read the total balance on the accounts five times, both with and without glasses. It was another half an hour before his hands stopped shaking...

Knowing that it was important, but not completely certain as to why he should be doing it, Chambers hunted out a memory stick from the drawer of the desk, and made a hurried copy of all of the data which he had uncovered. He placed the memory stick into an envelope and sealed it with sellotape, then addressed it to the head of the Venerable Board of Trustees (who ironically was named M. Bessler, so it just goes to show...). He stuck a stamp on the corner of the envelope, just as he became aware of the sound of happy, inebriated singing echoing up the corridor. Chambers leapt up from the chair and wrenched open the door, where he was confronted by a smiling Dr Matthews, who was just finishing the verse of the song that he was singing - which apparently involved the combination of a Young Maiden, a large and much-admired prize vegetable, and some indistinct reference to a goat and 12-volt batteries. Checking the corridor for eavesdroppers, Chambers pulled the singing man into the doorway, and thrust the envelope into his hand.

'Quick Matthews - I need you to do an urgent favour for me...' hissed Chambers.

'AAAAnd they couldn't get it out until the swelling went dowwwnnn...' sang Matthews.

'Matthews - please listen to me, I need you to get this out of here as fast as you can...' said Chambers, doing his very best to get the attention of the History Master. Matthews looked down at the envelope that had been placed in his hand. 'Is it dangerous?' he asked. 'To one person - yes...it could be absolutely catastrophic' answered Chambers. Matthews cleared his throat, tucked his thumbs into his waistcoat, and began another bawdy song in a rich tenor voice 'OOoooh...I dined with a fellow from Ongar - who wished that his wi-'

'- Look, stop buggering about and listen, Matthews...' Chambers hissed. 'I want you to get this into the post NOW- not later, or when you remember, or when it falls out of your pocket, but NOW..'.

'Got it Dear Boy...urgent...secret mission...confound the enemy...new socks...that sort of thing, is it?' said Matthews, tapping the side of his nose to indicate secrecy. Chambers spun the man around, holding both shoulders, and spoke calmly but firmly into his smiling face. 'Dr Matthews - please listen to me. It is vital that you get this letter into the post. Do you hear me? Take the letter and for God's sake GIVE IT TO THE POSTIE!...is that clear?'

'Absolutely...got it...Postie...no delay...cabbages...' replied Matthews.

'Thank you, Matthews, - and remember...not a word to anyone' said Chambers.

'When exactly was the last time that you saw an Elk?' asked Matthews.

'Matthews – letter – Postie – now – GO!...' instructed Chambers.

Matthews tucked away the secret communication, and hurried off down the corridor to carry out his mission. He managed to find the door at the fourth attempt. Now standing in the fresh wintery air of the quad, Matthews drew in a couple of deep breaths, and checked his watch. 'Good Grief!!' he exclaimed, when the hands eventually swam into focus 'It's almost Scotch o'clock already!!'. He straightened his tie, and strode off purposefully. Before he had entered the new block on his way to the Staff lounge, he met Mr Posta coming out of the door. To Mr Posta's shock and surprise, Matthews pulled him over to the side of the door, and waved a buff envelope bearing the Academy crest in his face. 'Thank God I've caught you my Dear Fellow...I've just come from Orifice Head - no, Mister Head Otter - oh bugger...yes!! that's it - the Headmaster's Office...and Dr Chambers said that it is vital that I give you this letter straight away..'

'But it's not addressed to me...' said Posta, confused.

'Can't help that Dear Boy...' said Matthews, 'Chambers told me to give it to you urgently- he was most specific. Tell you the truth; I think the fellow was a bit drunk - because he was rather wobbly and blurred...' With another conspiratorial tap of the nose, Matthews swept past the startled Mr Posta, who stood in the doorway clutching a letter that he had no idea why he had received. Okay - if Chambers had said that it was urgent, then he would look at it later, when he had worked out how to save his career and credibility. If only he could get a hold of something that would get him back in the Boss's good books.

Matthews staggered in to the Staffroom. He fixed the figure sitting in the corner near the coffee machine with a quizzical eye. 'Ye Gods!!' he exclaimed, 'Who has invited a lady into m'rooms then?' Mr Thwaite looked up from his magazine, flicked the long hair out of his eyes, and adjusted his sitting posture to allow for the leather skirt which he had dared to wear today - without comment, until now, that is. Leaning on the opposite wall near the lockers was Mr Newhouse, who was engaged in what sounded like a rather defeated conversation with Bannister the Maths Tutor:

'So that's why I thought that I would try and get some fresh faces into the Orchestra. We don't have long before the Christmas Carol Concert in the Big Church - and I really want to put on a good show this year. There's a rumour that *Songs of Praise* are going to record their Christmas show here...' said Newhouse, sipping his coffee.

'Where did you get that rumour from?' asked Bannister.

'I started it...' said Newhouse. 'But the whole point was to try and get the guys interested enough that they would want to take up an instrument'.

'But the Orchestra are already very good' Bannister stated.

'Yeah - I know...but this year I want something bigger, better, louder and more "edgy" than before' said Newhouse. 'Some of the kids have been in that Orchestra since the first year. Several of them will be leaving next term - and one kid is already drawing his Pension. Things have gotten a bit stale. Some of the lads think that a "Lad's Mag" is a DIY catalogue - we need some new blood'.

'Have you advertised for new members?' asked Bannister.

'Oh yes indeed...I even asked young Davis if he wanted to join'.

'And what response did you get?'

'I asked Davis if he wanted to be a part of the new Orchestra. He didn't really seem to have much enthusiasm, so I thought that I would try and build up his interest' said Newhouse.

'And how did it go?' enquired Captain Brayfield.

'Not as well as I expected...' said Newhouse. 'I showed him the full range of instruments which he could learn to play. I thought that a large lad like him would be a cert to go for the tympani, or the double bass, or at least something big and noisy in the Brass section'.

'He didn't show any interest at all?' asked Bannister.

'I stood with him in front of the whole range of gear. I put a friendly arm round his shoulder, and asked him – "go on Davis...tell me- what is your favourite musical instrument?"

'What did he say?' asked Bannister.

'The bloody Dinner Bell...'.

As far as arguments go, this was one that Nicky felt that he was not, however logical or factual his points may be, going to win at any cost. Kendy was his dear friend, and more like a brother to him, but he had the knack of taking the salient points in any given argument, and subjecting them to his own brand of intensive scrutiny. With the point of view of a genuine "outsider", he would analyse the essential truth or falsehood contained in any given statement. What made it much worse, was the way that he displayed his default facial expression of quiet interest, and could be so unreasonably, well...reasonable. The argument had begun when Nicky and Calderman had been discussing the plan to disrupt the work of the Construction Teams, and save the village trees. What had started out as a jokey remark from Calderman had already led to half an hour's worth of intense discussion. Kendy had already been fully briefed on the Seasonal applications of, and duties pertaining to, Santa. It was a separate Clause entirely, which was causing the problem. Kendy sought clarification:

'I hate to be pedantic on the matter, but I feel that there may be a larger question embroiled within the contractual implications, which we are failing to address here...' he said.

'Such as?'

'I totally accept that the onus of gift distribution must, by nature of convention, fall upon Santa to perform. This is, in my humble opinion, without problem and not open to question. What I wish to clarify is why a single individual should be automatically delegated the right with which to enact a system of segregation between recipients of equal status. It seems to me that the individual is being given the power to arbitrarily determine the qualifying status of others- who may be quite unaware that their conduct may be being judged. To make matters worse, you have unequivocally informed me that the segregation by behavioural merit is actually recorded in writing by the individual...'

'No Mate...what I actually said was "do you think that if we take action against the Builders and save the trees, we will end up on Santa's 'Naughty' list?" 'said Calderman.

'Yeah - there's no need to get so worked up, Kendy' Nicky added.

'But we have no way of guessing whether our planned actions will be regarded as "Naughty" or "Nice"- and you already informed me that Santa will be taking *two* opportunities to review the list...' said a rather concerned Kendy.

'Look - don't worry old Chap...' said Nicky, 'I'm sure that Santa will be well aware that whatever we do, we are doing it for the very best of motives'.

'Yes, but anyone who has gone to the trouble of observing me when I am asleep - and knows when I am awake, may well take a more severe view when transferring candidates from one list to the other'.

Calderman placed a reassuring hand on the boy's shoulder, and informed him 'Trust me Kendy - you have been good enough to qualify for full gift delivery, and Nicky and the rest of the lads will happily appear as character witnesses for you, should the need arise...'

Kendy thought about this. The boys could see another problem forcing open the door in Kendy's storeroom of logic...

'What really concerns me, is the fact that there seems to be absolutely no appeals system in place...'

It was Nicky that provided the killer fact - 'Just make sure that you leave out a glass of sherry, a mince pie, and something for the reindeer, and you should be in the clear...'

'But I have concerns about the man being given alcohol, and attempting to operate a complex flying vehicle, especially as the process is likely to be repeated in homes throughout the world...'

'Kendy...just be good- for goodness sake' said Nicky.

Although computers and new technology (fire, the wheel, flint axes, yo-yos and safety matches etc..) were not only frowned upon, but openly ridiculed and ultimately forbidden within the environs of the Academy, what a body chose to involve themselves with out of school hours was their own confusing business. There are some individuals who have the innate ability to absorb technology like a sponge, and there are some whose brains, when faced with such computing wizardry - turn into one.

Posta had convinced himself that along with his rise up the greasy pole of Police rank to the dizzy heights of Detective (albeit probationary), he should equip himself with the very latest in laptop gizmology, as befitted his new-found status. He visited a very modern computer emporium, and was sold the very latest in digital communications by a salesman who had one eye on his coming commission, and one ear on his mobile 'phone- where he was already booking a tropical holiday. Such was the hypnotic effect of the shiny merchandise on offer, that Posta did not note that he had fillings which were older than the salesman...

Clutching a large box to his chest, (which contained everything which he was never likely to need) Posta returned to his rented flat. Cardboard was hurled hither and thither in his frenzy to get the computer set up, plug in the mouse (which had no lead, or plug), and remove a particularly persistent and incredibly adhesive piece of sellotape from his finger. Now some people take to computers like a duck to water. Posta took to technology in all its forms as a duck takes to a shotgun...

An hour later; the machine was not only displaying the looted information concerning the Academy, but he had actually managed to get connected to the Internet (the discovery of the "Power" switch on the unit had been a revelation...). He now needed to use all of his great detective and analytical prowess to determine if any of the Board of Trustees might be embroiled in Goodwill's little "venture". The e-mail addresses of each member of the Board were very easy to find. The ever-helpful Miss Piggott (she of lavender water and a face like a recently - smacked arse) had been very neat in setting out all of the details. Posta felt his chest swell with pride as he located the "copy" function. He pressed the key with all the consummate ease of a real IT professional. Upon reflection, there just might have been a couple of missing letters just before the "I" and "T". Posta gaped in horror as he saw the legend "Files sent successfully" appear in a neat little box on the screen. Okay - no need to panic, all that had happened was that he had just sent each and every member of the Venerable Board of Trustees a full copy of the financial information, including the "special bonus prize" of a file featuring "Goodwill's Greatest Hits".

Ah...

Chapter Twenty-six:

'Twas a veritable week of incidents.

It was the week that saw the haughty and posher-than-thou Gideon Rundell of the Latin Department extend the unexpected hand of friendship to Miles Bannister the Maths Supremo. Rundell had offered to accompany Bannister to a local book store in order to purchase some literature as a Christmas gift for his Mother. Now this was no ordinary book store, oh my good golly no: this was the upper class dispenser of tomes to the Rich, known as "Weddlestones". If you worked hard at school (the right school, of course) and passed all of your exams to attend Cambridge University, then sat an acceptable "post-grad" qualification (achieving an acceptable grade, naturally), then studied to become a Doctor in your chosen subject, were given a title, wore Saville row suits, married well and owned land, and had talked the Bank into giving you an overdraft the size of the national debt of Batanaswazia: then, and only then, would you be considered fit to hold open the door of Weddlestones for one of their established clientele.

Rundell strode into the store, nodding imperceptibly at the doorman. Rundell assumed the nod to mean "welcome again, valued client", when in fact it was unspoken code for "bumptious little tit". Bannister had been given strict instructions as to what sort of books to purchase for his Mother. It was to be 'something historical - preferably on the Tudors'. She would also like a celebrity biography ('not anyone I can't stand, not her with the teeth, that camp-looking one in the velvet suit, not that big-headed idiot who always has his shirts undone, and not that greasy one who talks down his nose - and no ruddy footballers neither'). Rundell helped his colleague select a suitably bloodthirsty book on HenryVIII, and a fairly lightweight and possibly ghost-written autobiography of one of the more long-lived soap stars. They queued politely as required behind the heavy maroon plaited rope barrier. Just as they were about to be served, the door burst open, hurling the doorman into a stack of detective paperbacks. Into the shop came Weddlestones' worst nightmare.

The young woman thrust customers aside as she approached the counter, causing several flesh wounds due to the double buggy which she was pushing. She was chewing gum at a furious pace, creating a sound like a slug in a blender, and screeching into her mobile phone at the same time... 'ANG ON OUR KAYLEY - I'M IN THE SHOP...I'LL CALL YER BACK'.

She ignored the queue of customers, and pushed her way straight to the front of the line. "SCUSE ME MATE...' she bellowed 'I NEED A BOOK FOR MARILYN MY YOUNGEST - SHE NEEDS IT FOR SCHOOL...' The sales assistant did not show any sign of distress, and merely stated 'If Madam would care to join the queue, I will be happy to attend to her requirements'. Opening a can of caffeine-loaded energy drink, the woman took a huge gulp and repeated her ear-splitting request 'IT'S URGENT MATE – SHE'S GOTTA 'AVE THIS BOOK 'COS THEY'RE DOIN' IT AT 'ER SCHOOL SEE...'. Bannister leaned over the counter and spoke quietly to the assistant - 'Look, don't worry, it's quite alright if you want to serve this young person, I'm not in any great hurry'. The server gave him a grateful look, and turned back to the woman, who was now blowing a bubble with the gum. 'And what book is it that you actually require Madam?' he purred.

'IT'S BIN A FILM AN' EV'RYTHING...' she shouted, as her mobile shrieked out a tinny "dance" tune as it rang.

'And the title of the book is...?' asked the patient assistant.

'I FINK IT'S CALLED - 'LIONEL RITCHIE AN' THE WARDROBE'...'

There was a scrum at the door as all of the other customers tried to flee the shop at once. In the street, a woman began to thump the back of her husband, who appeared to be choking, and various people were holding their sides - some bent double in fits of hysterics.

Nicky had been extremely impressed when Auntie had announced 'I'm going to make a big special dessert for Uncle Joe to take up to his Senior Citizens' meeting at the Village hall'. Now this was quite a rarity. It wasn't that Auntie couldn't cook - she was quite skilled in the kitchen department, but it was rare that she ventured into the mystical world of puddings. Without making it too obvious that he was observing, Nicky took a ringside seat for the event. She had already prepared a large pie base. She took four eggs and cracked them- separating the whites from the yolks. These went into a large bowl, into which she put quite a few large spoons of sugar, and then squeezed the best part of a whole fresh lemon into the mixture. Auntie then set about the bowl like a thing possessed - whisking the mixture up with the same amount of fury that Nicky put into his drumming, which was rather scary to watch. After what seemed like ages, and with no reduction in effort, Auntie seemed satisfied that the mixture was as it should be. She lifted the whisk out of the bowl, leaving a white peak or two standing proud like sugary little Alps.

Into the pie case went the beaten and fluffy mixture. Nicky was fascinated by what happened next. Auntie placed the whole dessert on a baking tray, and placed it lovingly into a pre-heated oven. Very professional Auntie - he thought to himself. She then took one of the kitchen chairs and sat down facing the glass oven door. After a few minutes, she began to shout at the oven, and there was judicial use of some quite specific nautical and medical terms. She carried on abusing the dish, until it had apparently risen to her satisfaction. Nicky had sat spellbound by the bizarre actions of the cook. Auntie then turned off the oven, took out the creation (which had an ever-so-slightly browned top to the small "mountains") and placed it reverentially on the kitchen table.

'There we go...' she declared, 'Lemon harangued pie...'

The pie had been delivered up to the Village Hall, where Uncle was holding court with a group of the more Senior village dwellers. It was then taken back round to Joe's house, as the meeting had to be relocated due to part of the hall ceiling having fallen in, and some unfortunate part of Mrs Dilley having fallen out. It didn't take too long for Uncle Joe to get everybody comfortably seated, and duly plied with tea - or something a little stronger by special request. Mr Mallett, now in his early nineties, but still a tremendous mechanic and vintage car enthusiast, had asked Mrs Colley to get him a DVD of *Pimp My Ride* for the group to watch. He would tell them all about the old cars that he was restoring, and the television programme would let them all see how "customisations" were carried out on motor vehicles. He had given clear instructions to Mrs Colley. The slight problem was that dear, smiley Mrs Colley was rather deaf. And forgetful. And as endearingly barmy as a wasp in socks. Her Daughter had taken her to town. She had asked for the title which Mr Mallett had suggested. Well - almost.

The group had settled down to watch some skilled men in action, and getting dirty in the process. Whilst Mr Mallett said a few words about cars, the group watched the DVD. He explained to the people that 'What you can see is a lot more advanced than I usually get involved in - but the theory is basically the same sort of thing...The tools, of course, have changed a little over the years...'

The group had shown a good deal of interest in the programme shown to them. In some cases, there had been a very great deal of interest. Mr Mallett turned to look at the television screen in order to explain a particular point. The bodywork which he noticed was considerably different to that which he had been anticipating. He picked up the DVD case and stared at the title. Well...that would explain it then.

However well-intentioned she had been, it seemed that Mrs Colley had actually somehow managed to return from the town with a copy of a programme from the "special interest" section as instructed. The DVD which she had brought back was titled "*Ride My Pimp*" ...

When the Seniors had eaten Auntie's dessert, they all took a vote to let Mr Mallett choose another film for next week.

Duggan was still confused as to why Biddie had suddenly decided to retire from her life as the Queen of a small but incredibly lucrative crime syndicate. They had quite an intense discussion in the living room of the luxury apartment that Biddie had rented so that she could pass on the news to her son. The wily OAP had lived for many years in the same rebuilt tenement block that Gregor had loved as a child. Many of the original families still lived in the block, happy to stay amongst familiar faces and surroundings in their later years. Most of them had no idea whatsoever that it was their neighbour Biddie that had funded all of the improvements to the block - in fact she had bought the building many years ago, following some intense negotiations, and a good few knuckle sandwiches handed out to potential competitors for the property.

She was always fiercely proud of her working-class roots, as she would regularly tell the chauffeur who collected her in the white stretch limousine to take her to bingo on a Friday night. Biddie was still the home-loving girl that she had always been. Although others around her may have drastically changed their lives if they suddenly found themselves with a bit of spare money, she was not about to start giving herself "airs and graces" - she was proud of who she was and how she was. This was a conversation that she had on many occasions, with her friend Dougie - the pilot of her private jet. She had a strong connection to her humble "roots", and always felt a little lost when she was away with the group of ten or so of her friends - who she took on

Caribbean cruises at least twice a year. What use was money anyway? You could only use it to buy things with, and she already had all the gold taps, door handles, and towel rails that she could ever need. Jewellery was nice to have, but even with her permanent security guards behind the door twenty-four hours a day, an old lady was bound to worry. I mean - there were so many criminals around these days, it made you nervous just to read the local papers. The fact was, Biddie had such a collection of opulent jewellery, that the local traders often referred to her as "Oldfinger". There was even talk that the lady had bought her own discreet island in the Indian Ocean, but this may possibly just have been a Mauritius rumour...

'So noo, I wants ye tae take over the business, wee Greggie...' she said.

'But Ma - I'm verra' happy just doin' whut I do at the Academy' he had replied.

'An' I'm proud o'ye Son…' she said, 'But I need tae know that my savings is in gud hands - and that ye'll run the business in a fit and proper manner'.

'But Ma - whut if I cannae do it?' he had said.

'Then I'll have tae use my alternative plan...' she said.

'Whut might that be?' he hesitantly enquired.

'I'll have tae break yer bludy knees for ye...' declared Biddie. 'Ye ken, it's aboot bloody time that my money went oot an' started tae meet people'.

'What people are we talkin' aboot Ma?' he asked.

'Any puir wee nadger that may be in need of it!!' she laughed. 'I may have been a bit naughty in the past Son - but frae noo on, we'll bring a little sunshine into the lives o' them that only sees clouds - what de ye say, eh?'.

'Ma...ye're on!!' said Gregor Duggan, the newly-appointed Robin Hood.

Perhaps the most eagerly-awaited and cherished incident was the arrival of the first winter snow. As soon as the flakes changed from a light dusting of icing-sugar promise, to great soft downy slivers, it was enough to send people of all ages to their windows in order to marvel at the spectacle. These were what Nicky's Mum always referred to as "Horse feathers", and they soon began to cover and soften every sharp edge of buildings - and put a layer of cold, white insulation upon the branches of trees, where they drew their own Christmas card scenes.

Sparrows were already swiftly flying home in order to dig out their scarves from the bottom drawer…

Uncle Joe sat disconsolately once again at the kitchen table. He was bemoaning the fact that he must have been cursed by some Witch in the past (it wouldn't surprise him if it was that miserable old crone that lived opposite him, you know, the one who smelled of cats and stale biscuits). Whatever he had put his hand to recently seemed to have gone epically wrong. Even when he had decided to spend a leisurely Sunday morning delivering hot meals to some of the less mobile of the village's residents, there had been a problem. How the hell that badger came to be asleep in the boot of his car, he would never know.

As part of an "arrangement" which the Magistrate had kindly made for him, as recompense for some previous misdemeanour, he had set up a separate wing of the RSPB (or a Lapwing, if you prefer). Joe had thrown himself into the world of avian protection. He collected funds for his feathered friends, he built bird tables and feeders, he renovated nesting boxes, and left part of his garden wild - so that they had a natural feeding area. For the past week or so, he had been regularly found in the market place, where he was selling self-printed tee-shirts to raise funds. The shirts bore the logo of his newly-founded group, which promoted the conservation, rescue and protection of birds. In his haste to get the shirts ready to sell, Joe failed to consider that the use of initials might just not be a good idea in this case. He soon discovered that although people gave lots of donations to his cause, not many people were willing to walk around the town wearing a tee-shirt which bore the legend "Bird C.R.A.P".

As he had told his sad tale, Mum and Auntie had listened with sympathetic ear, but Nicky could still hear them both giggling later, upstairs in the bedroom.

All was not harmony in the world of Figg either. He and his fellow petty criminal masterminds had suddenly come across a major problem…

"Ere…we ain't been paid!' wailed Swall- 'we need to get on to the Boss…'

'The Boss is busy dealing with Duggan' said Figg.

'Well oo's in charge at the school then?' asked Swall 'If old Goody Two-Quid is still in the 'ospital, then who do we have to grab by the throat to get our wages?'.

'Chambers has taken over until the old scroat comes back…' stated Figg.

Fletcher stopped picking his teeth, and considered this. As his seldom-used brain went into gear, the other two men could swear that they could smell burning...'Well who is second in command then?' he eventually managed to articulate.

'I think it's that old fart from the History Department' said Figg. The men grinned at each other. Swall came up with a plan, and they all shook hands on it.

'Right then gents…' said Figg, 'so the plan is this. We will get hold of Matthews from the History department, and have a little meeting. We'll get him good and drunk - and then when he starts to talk, we will find out about where our money has gone to, and how we get more of it. He's an old feller - so a couple of large sherries should be enough to do the trick - well done boys…it couldn't be easier'.

As birds take the cue of the first snows to assemble - ready to fly south for the winter, so the falling of the white stuff triggered a similar annual event in the Shepherd household. This was the difficult task of "the writing of the Christmas cards". Now I am sure that you are all aware that there is a certain amount of politics involved in the sending and receiving of Christmas cards. Mum and Auntie were already in deep discussion as to which type and size of card should be sent to whom. There were certain far-flung sections of the Clan who did not merit a "top of the range" greeting. There were also some of them that would struggle to read the card - whatever size or type was sent. To receive a card minus dribble, tea or coffee stains or worse, was considered to be a definite bonus. Some were even in joined-up handwriting. Mostly, they appeared to be in foot writing, or worse.

So then, it was the large, traditional "snow and pheasant" cards for close family or favoured cousins and good neighbours, then smaller "Merry Christmas" offerings for those people who had only committed minor misdemeanours, such as sending a crappy card last year, then very small "Seasons Greetings" cards to the also-rans. Mum was bemoaning the fact that some of the more expensive cards (from the so-called 'better class' of shops) had shrunken in size over the years, and were now only marginally bigger than the stamp. On the matter of stamps - Auntie had come up with the reason that her arch-enemy Seaton had never appeared on a postage stamp 'Because you wouldn't know which side to spit on…' she had explained. There were also cards for neighbours who you weren't particularly fond of - but who would talk about you if you didn't send them a card, and so the whole discussion rolled on and on again… Nicky was pondering just exactly what sort of Christmas card he should send to Jozza. "Santa" cards might make him look rather immature, and snow-covered robins on a gate could possibly cause her to think that he was a boring old git. A "special" card would perhaps send the wrong signal entirely - or merely make him look desperate. He toyed with the idea of sending a card which said, "Happy Easter" or "Congratulations on your Bar Mitzvah" for comedic effect. If he did so, he knew that he would receive a card in return which would read "In deepest Sympathy", just before, or immediately after she had punched him. Much, much worse - should he write "Best Wishes" (not enough), "With Love and Best Wishes" (too much), or simply "From" (non-committal). Either way - he would have to write the card out of the way of prying eyes…

At the Academy, cards and Good Wishes were already being exchanged. All of the Staff had given each other cards (although Mr Thwaite appeared to have mislaid his...) and one or two pre-Christmas gifts had changed hands, some in plain wrappers. This afternoon, there was due to be one of the most eagerly-anticipated events on the Academy calendar- the switching on of the Christmas lights, which were already in place on the huge tree in the quad. Strangler and Darwin were gazing dreamily out of the Staff lounge window, looking out over the ground which was now covered in snow.

'It really is amazing…' said Darwin.

'What- the way that a little bit of snow can transform the usual scene into a winter wonderland?' asked Strangler.

'No…' said his friend, 'I mean the way that Bannister always manages to fall on his arse in exactly the same spot…'

The two men watched as their colleague made unintentional "snow angels" in the quad, then began to hunt around under the snow for dropped pens and other fallen personal items. 'I know he claims to have a "spirit guide" said Darwin, 'but I can't help thinking that what he really needs is a spirit *level* - and perhaps a guide *dog*'.

The poor Master eventually made his soggy and bruised way into the Staff lounge, with his standard "I'm embarrassed - so I hope that no-one saw what just happened" look on his face. Too late Miles - miles too late, they did. Newhouse and Hyde-Jones had held up cards at the window which showed that they had both given him six points for artistic merit. As they were still laughing, Chambers swept into the room.

'Gosh- it's getting cold out...' he declared.

'Well better put it back then...' said an unnamed voice at the back. He glared around the room for the ad-lib culprit, but since no-one was likely to be owning up any time soon, he carried on. 'Right then you Fellows - when you have all finished your teas, it's coats on and out into the quad for the switching on of the lights. In the absence of the Headmaster, I have asked Miss Piggott if she will kindly do the honours for us'.

'That's the nearest that she'll get to being turned on this year...' whispered Hyde-Jones. The ritual high-five with Mr Newhouse was exchanged and performed with glee.

Having donned their protective garments to keep out the snow (which had now put in a written application for "blizzard" status, just in case), the Staff formed a jovial procession out into the quad. They assembled at the far end, in front of the tall Christmas tree, one of Norway's finest. (it had in fact been a present in a roundabout way to the Matron, who had recently obliged a truck driver with a small favour just off a local roundabout). Chambers turned up the collar of his tweed overcoat and addressed the gathering.

'It is with great pleasure that I find myself once again engaged in the ceremony of illuminating the St Onans Christmas tree. I hope that our Pupils may all come to regard this tree as a symbol of how through continued effort and steady application, they may indeed rise to the very top of the tree'.

'And become a Christmas Fairy!!' called out a voice from the back. When the laughter had subsided, Chambers turned to his right, and gestured to a small figure which appeared to have been completely hand-knitted.

'It now gives me the greatest pleasure... ('you'll go blind!!' called the voice again) to ask our own Miss Piggott to switch on our Christmas lights'. He began to clap, but when no-one else joined in, looked rather like a tweed seal pleading for another herring. Miss P stepped forward demurely, and took a white plastic connector in each of her mittened hands. Gazing up at the top of the tree, she smiled and brought the connectors toward each other. She paused, causing a comment of 'Go for it Pigster!!' to ring out from the crowd (it may or may not, have originated from the area around the Music Tutor). Now the more astute observers amongst you will already have deduced that the combination of mains electricity, slippery plastic connectors, and wet woollen mittens, is not a combination which bodes well. There was a flash, a bang, and a sudden smell of singed knitting patterns. Miss Piggott was hurled several feet backwards, where she did in fact cause bruising to several feet. Chambers dived forward and grabbed the two connectors, jamming them together with considerable force. The tree lit up in a cascade of beautiful white lights, much the same as Miss P had done, just seconds before. The crowd all applauded wildly, and festive cheers rang out across the quad. Once a couple of minor fires had been put out on the person of Miss Piggott, she was gently led away to her office and given emergency brandy.

Reverend Felchingham stood and stared at the tree in all its radiant glory. As his eyes took in the full vision of the tree, he was suddenly aware of the laughter that was coming from the assembled Staff behind him. He knew only too well what had caused their amusement.

Considerable time and effort had been taken to get all of the lights spaced out so that they covered all of the massive tree equally. Whoever did it had done an expert job. What the Reverend wanted to know was who, (and he had more than a reasonable idea who that might have been), had then re-visited the tree and rearranged certain lights into the positions which they now occupied? The tree thrust its Christmas joy skywards for all to see and admire. There, quite plain for all to see, and set out in lights, was the word…

KNOB.

Chapter Twenty-Seven:

Picture, if you will, a scene where thirty or so bodies are attempting to occupy enough chairs for a maximum of ten. Such was the spectacle at the meeting of the Groundlings in their Great Hall (even the ones who wore contact lenses). For some time, they had been rehearsing their twenty-strong choir in readiness for their appearance at the Academy Carol Concert. The choir were already perfect. The harmonies were clear and sweet, with all vocal parts a sublime blend of combined sound. They were also a good deal cleaner than the boys' choir above ground. Jedekiah the conductor lay down his baton, and wiped away a tear from the corner of his eye.

'And HoBi saw that it was good…' he said quietly.

'Father Elder - is it true that *Songs of Praise* are going to be filming the Carol Concert?' asked one of the younger members of the choir.

'I know not if it be truth or falsehood - for 'tis the nature of rumour to lead us down paths of uncertainty…' he stated.

'So…is that yes or no?' queried the boy.

'Hath HoBi not told us that he who should by repetition ask the same question, earn for himself that which is called "a clip 'round the ear'ole"?'.

'Verily Brother - but will the enquiring mind not by question seek the true path?' said Ezekielvis, brushing back his well-oiled quiff.

'Silence may yet be the path to understanding…' answered a rather annoyed-sounding Jedekiah, 'and yea…I shall give thee such a ding round the head if thou does't not drop it...'

'So we'll take that as a "Yes" then? Shall we?' said the boy.

Since their presence beneath the Academy had become common knowledge (that is - known by most people, not just people who live on the common, or common people, come to that) the Groundlings had enriched themselves with as much contact with the "above ground" world as they felt would benefit the group as a whole. They no longer felt the compulsion to remain hidden from view, but chose to do so in order to retain privacy, and a certain "distance" from what they considered to be the worst aspects of life on the surface. Mercifully, this had included velour tracksuits and tank tops.

Betty Bradley had been "adopted" by the Groundlings as their unofficial mascot and cookery tutor. She had worried about their somewhat Spartan diet, and had set about giving them the benefits of her many years of experience in the Academy kitchens. Their cookery skills now matched her own - although the younger children still pinched the odd pie now and again, just to keep her on her toes. So successful had her instruction been, that some of them had recently won a competition organised by a magazine, where they cooked the perfect Christmas menu. The food was featured in the glossy pages of *In Digestion* magazine - along with Betty and the proud Groundling team of chefs. In accordance with their strict and moral upbringing, all of the group now cooked meals for the homeless - which they would distribute at Christmas. A revolutionary idea had come from Mark Davis in Nicky's form, who had the brainwave of making edible hats out of rice paper.

There was also an underground rock music club and bar set up in the old wine cellar, which was doing very well, thank you. The Groundlings had also been given the main role in organising the "Ghost Walks" through the Academy. Once the "extras" had got used to the fact that they should go 'WHoooo!' and not 'Get thee hence, fiends from Hell!', things went along swimmingly. Betty continued to teach them what she called "Gordon Blew" cooking - and they all admired her puddings (oh really….stop it).

In the secret meeting room within the shooting range on the sports field, something else was being cooked up by the senior members of the ODD. Now that the dust had settled following "marzipangate" as it came to be known, Albert Brooks was feeling confident enough to be planning a few more "little surprises" for the Staff, based of course on a festive theme. Mrs Finucane sipped her tea, which was heavily laced with Irish whisky, and chuckled as Albert told her what he had in mind.

'Bangers…' he said. 'What's unusual about a feckin' sausage?' she enquired.

'I mean something with a REAL bang!' he laughed.

'How's about exploding Christmas puddin'?' Mrs F suggested.

'Laxative Brandy Butter?' said Brooks.

'Well now - ye'd have to get the consistency just right, or it wouldn't run' she said.

Albert gave an evil grin…'No - but those buggers certainly will…!!!!'

With his particular "leanings" toward the darker side of things, Christmas shopping had always been somewhat of a trial for the poor Reverend Felchingham. He had a very clear view in his warped mind's eye as to what particular presents he would like to buy for his friends and colleagues, but knew only too well that his choices might give the game away, and condemn him to even more severe isolation. For instance, he knew that for some reason, Madame Dreadfell was actually quite fond of spiders. His idea was to buy her one as a gift. This had proven to be quite a task, as the local exotic pet shop was insisting on charging a vast amount of money for such a creature. He wondered if it might be cheaper for him to get one from off the Web?

Although his list of "friends" was not shall we say, extensive: he didn't want to be thought of as mean spirited, and so he had trawled the shops for some suitable and yet affordable token gifts. The problem was, his constant contact with "The Darker Side" had caused him to develop a strange compulsion. The whole process had almost driven him insane, as he had found it hard to purchase gifts to the value of £6.66. His food shopping had come to a total of £66.60- which was acceptable, but the rest of the shopping would be a struggle. If he was unable to achieve the required price- then he would go for titles instead. So far he had purchased a bottle of 'El Diablo' wine for Matthews, 'Devil's fudge cake' for Madame, 'Demon' aftershave for Strangler, Darwin, and Hyde-Jones, a bottle of 'Possession' perfume for Mr Thwaite, and a copy of the biography of Evel Knievel (as near as he could get with that one) for Miles Bannister. He knew that Mr Newhouse would be happy with a CD from either Ozzy Osbourne or Iron Maiden. Dr Chambers was a bit of a problem though, as the Rev desperately wanted to get into his good books (if he would pardon the phrase). Miss Piggott would be given a year's subscription to *Which* magazine (the spelling was near enough - and there was every chance that she would one day appear in it as the centrefold...). He eventually had the brainwave of buying the Deputy Head a massive box of chocolates. At least the name fitted his requirements - 'Black Magic'...He had been very disappointed with the book shop however, as even the Venerable "Weddlestones" could not supply him with a copy of *The Lord of the Rings* - as written from the Dark Lord's perspective. He returned home quite satisfied with himself, and spent an enjoyable hour or so fixing marzipan horns and forked tails onto a box of Christmas Gingerbread men.

Dr Matthews had been taken aback when he had been approached by the men who regularly helped out with the Archaeology Society field trips, and invited for a pre-Christmas drink. Although the three seemed rather uncultured fellows - a tincture or two at any time was not an offer that he felt inclined to refuse. He now found himself sitting in the lounge bar of the "Three Crowns", sipping a very large scotch which the taller of the men had thoughtfully provided for him. He raised his glass in a toast, and said 'A Merry Christmas to us all - and here's to discovering the Past in the Future!'. Figg took a small gulp of his half pint of shandy, and turned to Matthews. 'It's about the future that we wanted to speak to you, Dr Matthews…' he said calmly, 'We were just wondering if you had heard anything about our mutual friend Dr Goodwill - only it seems that there has been some sort of financial oversight, which has left all three of us: well, how can I best put this? Rather out of pocket'. 'I'm dashed sorry to hear that…' said Matthews - 'do let me get you another round in…'

He sped up to the bar, returning with a tray of drinks, which Figg noticed, were all triple whiskies. 'Cheers!!' said Matthews... 'now do tell me how I may assist you'. Swall knocked back his drink, and said 'well see…we was all wonderin' if Goodwill 'ad asked you to give us any money in his absence? He usually makes an arrangement to pay us directly'. Matthews stared at the man and smiled 'Good Lord - you haven't got a drink! Shall I do the honours?' It was a grumbling Fletcher that was sent to the bar for another round. He placed the drinks in front of each of them, and noticed that by the time he had put down the last glass - Matthews' drink had already disappeared…'Same again, Doctor?' asked Figg - and Fletcher was sent back to the bar.

The drinks continued to flow, and the questioning continued. It was as if the scene had been filmed, the tape loop being played over and over again. Figg paid, Fletcher collected - and Dr Matthews swallowed. After four drinks had been consumed, Swall slowly but inexorably slid from his seat onto the plush carpet of the bar, where he slumped against the table and began to snore. The meeting was not going to plan. Figg was suddenly finding it quite difficult to formulate the right questions in his mind, and having great problems in articulating them when he did. Matthews however, had settled in comfortably, and was thoroughly enjoying his evening. 'S'thing is…'ting isz...you see…Goodwill pays us...pays us to...'coz we know like…he's on the fiddle- oh yess!' slurred Figg.

'How interesting…' said Matthews, ordering another round of drinks, 'do tell me more- what does he pay you to do exactly?'.

Figg tapped his nose and leaned closer over the table, his elbow slipping off and catching Fletcher in the groin: 'Now yer see Doc- yer Man is on the take see…he's bin robbin' the School for years...got it all goin' into his own little account he has Sssshhh!'

'Well I never!' said Matthews, 'well I think that it's most unfair to leave you decent fellows financially embarrassed - not the done thing at all - here, let me get you another drink…'. Matthews sat and listened, while Figg attempted to explain the finer points of their involvement in the Head's scheme. 'So…so see…all the gold don't get to the Musee – Musmee - Museum…we gets the Boss to get it melted down, an' we gets a cut of the prop- the perf - the profits see…. The gool - the gold is from rubbery - from rabies - from robberies what we does…an', an' what we manages to dog - to dig up when we 'elps out your Archer - your Armpit - your Arse - you lads wot dig things up…' he said.

Figg made hard work of the story. Matthews made notes. Swall made noises like a hedge trimmer from under the table - where he had been joined by Fletcher. As Figg fell forward onto the table, Matthews was the last man standing. He put away his small note pad, looked sadly at the three sleeping beauties, and ordered himself another round of drinks. This was certainly a startling revelation, and not something that he could keep to himself if it was true that the Head Master was engaged in criminal activity. He would mention it to that "Posta" chap when he saw him - he looked like the sort of fellow who could keep a secret.

Matthews stood up and approached the bar. He had one final large whisky (and asked the barman to join him), and then with one sad look back at the heap of former drinking buddies on the floor, bade the bartender good night and headed purposefully off in the direction of Posta's flat.

Someone somewhere had decided to take a vote. When all of the crosses had been counted, and the "spoilt votes" been duly hurled into the nearest litter bin, it was announced that the democratic decision was that it should continue to snow. There would be further discussions held in a side office later, with a view to the phasing-in of ice and blizzard conditions at an agreed time, but for now - down came the white stuff with a vengeance. Against all common sense, Dr Chambers had decreed that the Academy should remain open for business as usual, and so pupils were obliged to make their way into the town, braving drifts of all sizes. One of these drifts proved to be Dr Matthews, who rose up out of his wintry covering, shook himself, and headed into the school as if waking up in a snow drift were an everyday event.

The Staff were already gathered in the lounge for yet another hastily-called meeting. To have two meetings in the space of two days was never a good sign, and the Masters were all worried that today might just be the day when Chambers would announce exactly where the axe was going to fall. Although things had not quite yet reached the argument stage, there was a lot of rather heated discussion taking place between Staff members, and much talk of redundancies to come.

'So come on then Newhouse- who's got the sack?' asked Rundell.

'Santa…' answered the Music Master.

'Oh do shut up…this is no time for levity!' said Madame Dreadfell.

'Thus spoke the Ghost of Employment Past….' said Mr Newhouse in response.

'Will everyone please just calm down…' said Miles Bannister, who was handing out drinks, 'Sherry?' he said, to Mr Thwaite. 'No- I think that I will stick with "Geraldine", but thank you for the drink…' the Geography Master answered.

'Well I wish that the fool would just spill the beans and put us out of our misery...' said Rundell. Mr Newhouse was ready for him:

'I wish that he'd put us all out of your misery, at least!' he replied.

'Advantage Loopy - new balls please!!' stated a voice from the back.

Before matters had a chance to escalate, Dr Chambers emerged through the door flanked by Miss Piggott, and three rather travel-weary men in suits. The three entered the Staff lounge and stood to one side looking oddly uncomfortable, as if all of them had just discovered that the previous visitor had used up all of the lavatory paper…

'Good morning Ladies and Gentlemen…' began Chambers 'May I introduce three Senior Partners from the Wiseman Corporation - Mr Casper, Mr Melchett, and Dr Balthesari. These gentlemen have travelled all the way from I believe, Eastbourne. They have come here to bring exciting news which I hope will excite you all: they have in a way, come bearing a gift for the Academy. I will hand you over to Mr

Casper - who will explain in better detail the exact purpose of their trip…'.

Mr Casper reluctantly stepped forward, his gaze temporarily distracted by Mr Newhouse at the back of the room - who was busy filling the jacket pocket of Gideon Rundell with tomato ketchup. When the man finally spoke, it was in a high nasal whine, as if a bee was attempting to read the news whilst wearing a stocking mask...

'Well...Firstly may I say Good Morning to you all, Ladies and err...Gentlemen (he paused to glance at Mr Thwaite, resplendent in high heels and twin set). It is a genuine pleasure for my Colleagues and I to visit you here today - at what is one of the most respected Educational Establishments in the country (there was a noticeable snort from the back). As you will no doubt be aware, your Academy has for some considerable time been a part of the Middle Eastern Student Exchange programme. This, as I am sure you are aware, is a scheme which admits students from abroad into first-rate academic institutions, where they have demonstrated particular educational excellence- or in cases of urgent circumstantial necessity.

'I had that done when I was a baby…' said Strangler. He was "shusshhed" into silence by Chambers.

Casper continued - 'Under the terms of the agreed scheme, we have come to inform you that you are to receive a student who has shown great promise in his Native land. We are confident that he will have a great future - and will achieve many wonderful things. I will hand you over to my esteemed colleague, Mr Melchett, who will explain a little of the lad's circumstances...'

Mr Melchett now stepped two paces forward. He spoke with a rich, deep baritone, but the overall effect was somewhat spoiled by the fact that he had a face resembling a kipper which had lost too many boxing contests. 'The boy's background has quite humble origins...' he explained, 'His Father is the head of a very successful timber exporting and bespoke carpentry business. The boy needs to board here due to the fact that his Father is having to relocate and travel from their home town due to tax reasons. The Board considered that under the terms of the scheme, this might the ideal chance to place the boy with yourselves'.

Chambers paused for consideration, then asked 'Would there be any pecuniary easement being made available, to ensure the smooth transition of the individual into the environs of the Academy?'

Melchett looked blankly at the Deputy Head.

'He means - how much is the Transfer Fee?' Hyde-Jones helpfully stated.

'I am given to understand that appropriate, and not insubstantial remuneration is to accompany the young man, in order to assist his settlement. Once he has established this Academy as his new "base" then the funds will of course be released…' said Melchett.

'Sounds like the bases are loaded...' laughed Darwin.

'Well, I am sure that the young Gentleman will be welcomed here with open arms' said Goodwill.

'And open wallets' said Mr Newhouse, quietly.

Chambers spoke up again - 'Well I would like to thank you Gentlemen on behalf of us all, and I think I can speak on behalf of the whole Academy when I say that we will be proud to welcome a new Onanist into our banks - sorry…ranks. May I offer you our hospitality as regards lunch? Should the weather make your return journey hazardous, then might I humbly suggest that you stay with us in our Boarding House -? I am sure that Matron will be more than happy to squeeze you in…' (there was a loud outbreak of coughing at this point, which seemed to be especially contagious in the area of Newhouse and Hyde-Jones).

The last of the visitors, Dr Balthesari then spoke up:

'Well thank you Dr Chambers, for your kind words and warm welcome. To tell you the truth, we very nearly didn't get here at all today - we got rather confused in the quaint back roads around the town. By pure luck, we got here by following one of your local buses- "Star" coaches, I think it was, otherwise we would have got completely lost…'

So it was on to the tea, biscuits and limp handshakes, as the three men mingled with the Staff. Chambers was rather quiet, and was thinking to himself "play this one right - and it could be a gift from heaven…". The visitors were offered a whistle-stop tour of the Academy, which they seemed overjoyed to accept. It was a strange time of year to accept a new student, but then if you could point out a single day at St Onans that was any less strange than any other day, then you were a very clever and astute person indeed.

As the trio were escorted out of the Staff room, Chambers invited them for a glass of sherry in his study. Miss Piggott pointed out that it was only his "temporary" study. No-one had pointed out that Dr Matthews had called at the Head's room previously, and that the only dry thing left in the wine cabinet was now the empty decanters.

Chambers was making small talk with the three as they walked - he was quite clever like that; you can do two things at a time when you've been to Oxford…

'Can I ask- what is the name of our soon-to-be new student?' he said

Mr Casper consulted his papers…'Ah yes, the boy that you have joining you is called Christo - Jez Christo…'

Chapter Twenty- Eight:

See amidst the winter snow- six schoolboys and five Senior Citizens (four calling birds and the three French hens etc. came along a little later, just thought that you might want to know…) wrapped up warmly in whatever they could get for under a fiver from the last Church Jumble Sale. The teams from both ends of the age scale were huddled between two portable cabin units, which had been deposited a short distance away from the five ancient elm trees. It was this little cluster of arboreal majesty that had caused them all to convene on this night of bone-piercing cold.

Mikey, "Squiddy", and Pete from the Village had joined up with Calderman, Nicky and Kendy, to put their plans into action. Davis would have joined them- but his Mum had just ordered a pizza, and you know how it is…The more "bingo friendly" members of the Team were Mr Leonard (retired Marine Commando), Mrs Sidney (retired Schoolteacher), Mr Jenkinson (retired Lorry Driver), Mrs Timpkins (retired due to industrial deafness) and Mr Snell (retired 353 not out…).

Prior to this auspicious gathering, a meeting had taken place at the village hall, where Nicky and his gang had divulged to the older folks the reason for their plan to take action in order to save the trees. It was important that the potential residents of the planned bungalows were made aware that the action was not being taken to in any way prevent them from enjoying a comfortable new home. Nicky and Squiddy had explained at some length why they thought that the trees should be protected. The response which they had received was certainly not (apart from the odd flatulent ad-lib) the one which they had been expecting. Re-settling his troublesome and highly mobile dentures back into place, Mr Jenkinson had told them 'Well Son…I'm more than 'appy to 'elp you strike a blow against the Authorities. I have lived in me 'ouse for fifty-seven years, and apart from the subsidence, burst pipes every winter, faulty wiring in the kitchen, a cracked bath, the landing ceiling falling in, and the odd tile coming off the roof - there's not a damn thing wrong with it. I've just got the place just how I like it mind you - when we all gets a snotty letter from the Council to say that we are goin' to be moved out lock, stock and barrel, into some new-fangled bungalows which are miles from the pub and the shops. How am I supposed to fit the new carpet which I bought for the upstairs front bedroom, in a bungalow? So I 'ad a word with my friends here, and we're all agreed that we're quite 'appy where we are- ain't that so?...'

There was a loud murmur of agreement, and another windy repost which could possibly be taken as a "yes" vote.

Mrs Sidney took up the baton: 'Well I told 'em flat, I did, "don't you even think of shiftin' me around at my time of life, or I'll get the Council on you…" Of course, they wrote back and reminded me that they WERE the Council, and it was entirely for my benefit. I wrote back to them and told them that I don't claim benefit - so they needn't take that tone with me. They wrote back and said that they had made studies - studies if you like…that proved that the new accommodation would be more comfortable. I wrote back and told 'em that my old pants were "more comfortable"- but I still had to chuck 'em out when the elastic broke…I told 'em that I was not prepared to bandy legs with them any more - and that I was going to consult my late Husband, Mr Sidney. They wrote back to me and said that they were sorry to have caused me any distress, and that they sent their deepest sympathy on the loss of my Husband. I wrote back and told them that he was certainly not "Late"- just late getting back from the pub. It was just after that when Mr Jenkinson told me that he had got a letter too, and we all decided to dig our heels in. That's apart from Mrs Timpkins of course, as the poor old dear has only got the one leg. She'll just be digging in the one heel for the time being…'

'I certainly ain't about to move…' said Mr Snell, taking a generous pinch of herbal snuff, 'An' I don't want anyone messin' around with my house either – I remember a few years back I 'ad some foreign firm come over and do some demolition work. Time after time they came back - and they made a right bloody mess they did…'

'That was the Luftwaffe, Mr Snell…' said Mr Leonard.

The discussion broke out into the Brownian-motion random conversation of Pensioners everywhere…

'Well I'm not movin' down the other end of the village - it's too far from the pub'.

'Well I need to be near Denise and my Grandkids…'

'My cat will go spare, he's already a bit delicate…'

'I need the lavatory…'

'Where will I be able to park my new car?'

'The Milkman won't know where I've moved to, and I owe him £3.20'.

'I really, really do need the lavatory…'

Eventually, Nicky and the boys had regained order, and a consensus was reached that they would all meet up at the site and take offensive action. Mr Snell took action, and did in fact get to the lavatory. He was almost in time, too…

So that, roughly, is how a group of boys and a team of Ninja Nonagenarians came to be standing in a freezing field. The plan was to remove all of the "marker" posts that the Contractors had set out again. Nicky and the boys noticed that there was a new hazard for them to negotiate - as drainage trenches had been dug along the approach to the trees. The boys were worried that the eyesight of their Senior conspirators might just lead to them falling headlong into any of the open trenches. It would be a safer idea to have the Elders keep watch, and maybe just remove the odd wooden stake here and there. Things started off quite well (once Mrs Timpkins had been released from some vicious barbed wire), and soon, wooden posts were flying up and over the hedges, accompanied by whoops of glee from the Wrinkly Warriors. After a while, Nicky and the lads realised that things seemed to have gone a little quiet, and the Seniors were nowhere to be seen.

A short search ensued, and the Pensioners were found at the side of another cabin - gazing in through the window. The boys approached the group: 'What's going on…?' Nicky asked.

'Shhhh! Look! - he's got a flask of hot soup in there!' whispered Mrs Sidney.

The Pensioners were gazing longingly at the table inside the cabin. On the table was indeed a steaming mug of what even from outside, smelled like minestrone soup. At the table sat an extremely conscientious Night Watchman in uniform - who had fallen soundly asleep, his cap over his eyes, and the aerial of his walkie-talkie radio almost up his left nostril. In the corner of the cabin, a tiny black-and-white television was showing some foreign game show, and the well-endowed sequinned hostess was busy displaying a couple of the prizes that were definitely not on offer. Nicky urged the OAPs away from the window, and the group were just tiptoeing away, when they were confronted by a huge figure in a high-vis jacket.

'What the bloody 'ell are you lot doing on my site?' he shouted, 'don't you know it's dangerous to be clamberin' all over open trenches in the dark? You could break your bloody necks, the lot of you. Right - you just stay where you are…I'm calling the Po – '

'No you're bloody well not, young man!' declared Mrs Timpkins, who had removed her artificial leg and dealt the man a biblical smite across the back of the head with it. 'The sign says "Hard hats to be worn" for a reason, you little bugger…' she added.

'Nice one Mrs T…' said Squiddy.

Whilst she reattached her weapon of much destruction, Kendy had an idea:

'Guys - prop him up against the big digger wheel for a minute, I think I can get the site clear for us'. The group looked a little confused, but did as they were asked. Kendy stood in front of the unconscious man and stared hard at him for a few seconds, then disappeared around the corner of the cabin. What re-appeared was an identical copy of the Site Supervisor- right down to the tea stains on his shirt. The village boys stood open-mouthed, and Nicky told them 'Don't worry- it's just a thing he does…'.

Kendy walked up the wooden steps of the cabin, paused, then kicked open the door. 'IS THIS WHAT I'M BLOODY WELL PAYIN' YOU FOR- KIPPIN' ON THE JOB? RIGHT- YOU'RE FIRED…NOW GET OFF MY DAMN SITE IMMEDIATELY!!!' he screamed. The Night Watchman leapt up in panic, grabbed his jacket, and without a word ran off toward his car at the top of the field. He turned on the engine and sped off into the night, forgetting to turn on his headlights, or close the driver's door. He would need to get the walkie-talkie aerial removed as soon as he could…

None of the OAPs seemed the least bit shocked at what they had just witnessed. Mr Leonard, with his Commando background, decided to take charge:

'Righto Squad…We are not going to get anywhere if we stand around like a lot of Wet Nellies (pardon my French, ladies). We need to get this site properly vandalised as quickly as possible. Now - Jenkinson…you find the keys to that digger. You can drop the bucket at the front and scoop the posts out in a fraction of the time that it will take us to do it by hand.'

'You'll have to wait until we have done the most important job first' said Mrs Sidney.

'And what might that be, Dear Lady?' he asked.

'Well – there's hot soup getting' cold in there, so once we've all had some of that I'm sure we'll all feel able to be better Vandals…'

There were murmurs of agreement all round, and the Seniors were soon inside the cabin, demolishing the soup ration which the

Watchman had kindly left for them. When they had finished, Mr Leonard urged them all to climb aboard the digger and hang on tight. Mr Jenkinson turned the ignition key, turned on the headlights, and with a roar, the digger set off across the field like a lumbering metallic dinosaur.

The digger made short work of uprooting the markers, and lurched across the trenches with no problem at all. Having completed the clearance of the far end of the field, Mr Jenkinson swung the vehicle around, lowered the bucket again, and prepared to attack the area in front of the trees.

'This is wonderful!' said Nicky 'They won't know what hit 'em!'

The digger set off slowly, cutting a broad swathe as it went. The boys followed a little way behind, being careful to dodge any flying posts as they surrendered to the metal jaw. It was Squiddy that noticed a sudden problem….'Oh God No!!!' he shouted, pulling at Calderman's sleeve. 'What's up?' called Nicky, who could now see the worried look on his friend's face.

'We've got trouble…' said Squiddy.

'What do you mean?'

'Look – Mr Jenkinson is asleep!!!'.

The digger had moved slightly off course. The "passengers" were looking anxious, and banging on the side of the cab - where Mr Jenkinson was sleeping soundly at the wheel.

'Quick- Jump!!' shouted Nicky.

'No chance - I'll break a leg…' called Mrs Sidney.

'I need the lavatory - urgent!!!' shouted Mr Snell.

There was a horrible inevitability about the new course that the digger was taking. The boys and the Pensioners could all see it, but could do absolutely nothing about it. Risking life, limb, and weak bladder, the OAPs decided to leap from the digger one by one. Most of them mercifully managed a soft landing. Mr Snell flew through the air, and by pure chance smashed through the door of the portable toilet which had been placed on site. His prayer in time of most urgent need had been answered - at least it would have been, had he landed the right way up…

Ignoring the Battle of Portaloo behind them, the boys ran toward the digger as it thundered onward. For some reason, human beings seem to be born with the idea that if they stand and flap their arms, then out-of-control machines will halt in their tracks. So that is what they did. It didn't help.

The metal toothed bucket of the digger hit the first of the elm trees at an approximate cruising height of four feet. The ancient boughs shuddered with the impact, and it looked for a moment as if the mighty trunk of the tree might withstand the onslaught. With an almost animal sound, the tree was wrenched from the soil, showering dirt and debris in all directions. There was a sound of rushing thunder as the branches made contact with the next tree in line, and then the elm fell sideways like a drunken man. With the tree gone, the digger once again picked up momentum, and tore out the next tree with consummate ease, spinning it aside like balsa. The third fared no better, but this time, the trunk spun up and over the cab of the digger caber-style. This impact was just enough to rouse Mr Jenkinson, who awoke in horror to find the cab in its own mobile forest. He immediately turned off the engine, and the monster ceased its predation…but now it was way too late.

Climbing down from the cab in tears, Mr Jenkinson tried to apologise to the boys and his friends for what he had done. There was no point in berating the poor man - it was after all, just a hideous accident. He was led away by the rest of the Pensioners, and the boys did their best to comfort him, and his friends…

As the boys watched the Pensioners fade into the distance, Kendy pointed to a bright light which was coming down the field toward them. The light turned out to be two lights. Headlights. Police car headlights. Out of the car leapt a Police Constable, who leapt out of the car measuring six foot one inch - and suddenly measured a height of four feet. The Policeman looked up at the boys from the depths of the trench which he had fallen into, and stated: 'Right then you boys – just what do you think you are up to here?'

Calderman (ever the swift thinker) answered 'Thank Goodness you arrived when you did Officer!' (the Constable looked completely thrown at this) 'We were walking across the fields from the town, when we saw lights, and heard someone start up the machinery over there. They started it up and drove it around, before trying to run us down. We tried to get them to stop by throwing some wooden markers at the digger, but they just drove on and smashed into the trees just there. We're sorry Officer - but we weren't able to stop them.'

(Mr Snell by this time, had emerged from the wreckage of the site toilet. He walked slowly up to the group, the smell arriving a full thirty seconds before he did).

“Sright Officers…’ he said, ‘Whoever they was what were tryin’ to steal the digger, drove straight at us - I would ‘ave been killed if these lads had not pushed me into the portable bog over there…’

Nicky clamped his hand over Kendy’s mouth to prevent the truth from making a break for it.

‘So did anyone get a good look at the thieves?’ asked the Policeman.

‘We couldn’t see Sir - the glass around the driver’s cab was too dirty’ said Mikey.

The second Police officer extended a hand, and tried to extract his colleague from the trench. As the first officer shot upwards, he shot downwards, and joined the mud and broken markers in the bottom of the trench. Their combined height was still nine feet eleven inches. Another figure suddenly joined the group. This person held out a voice recorder in the general direction of the boys. ‘And who the bloody hell might you be?’ asked the Police officer.

‘I might be Billy Johansson, famous formula one racing driver and celebrity fashion model’ said the man.

‘So - are you?’ asked the Constable (the one above ground level).

‘Nope…’ said the man ‘but I might be…’

‘You’ll be the bloke in handcuffs in a minute mate, if you keep up the smart act’ said the PC.

The man produced a grubby card ‘Pete Wiley – Granchester Herald...’ he stated proudly. He began taking photographs of the boys, in front of the wreckage of the digger and the flattened trees. ‘Now tell me what happened here?’ he asked. The PC was furious that his crime scene had been invaded. Whilst he took statements from the boys, Mr Snell led the reporter off to one side and gave him the full story about how six plucky schoolboys took on a desperate gang of digger thieves, acting in the public good. The newshound hoped that the odour which was emanating from Mr Snell would not affect his digital recorder. After he had double-checked the names of all involved, the reporter was gone as quickly as he had appeared.

Their Mothers were confused as to why all of the boys had come in so late that night. The Site Manager was confused as to what had happened to his mechanical digger, two hundred and fifty site marker posts, and why his Night Watchmen had left the site unattended - and now refused to take his telephone calls.

The village boys were a little confused at how their friend's schoolmate had turned into someone else.

Nicky and Calderman were confused as to how they had managed to get away with the whole thing - apart from the damage to the very things that they were attempting to save.

Mr Snell was confused when he was referred to in the Friday edition of the Granchester Herald as "Mr Smell…".

Chapter Twenty-Nine:

When the copies of the local "Rag" dropped through the letterboxes on Friday, there was some considerable confusion in certain households as to how their youngest offspring had made it onto the front pages (more of the thrilling story continued on page seven - and don't forget next week's Christmas Bingo Special...). 'Why didn't you tell us anything about this?' Nicky's Mum had asked, causing her son to take the morally correct course of action- and lie through his teeth. 'We just did what we thought was the right thing to do' he had explained. Mum smiled with pride, not least because none of her arch rival Mrs Hislop's kids had never managed to make it onto the front page of the local paper. Auntie took a more forensic view of the photograph... 'Why is that old man Snell standing there with his flies open?' she asked.

Kendy was not at all used to his new-found "celebrity", and had proudly taken a copy of the paper to school with him that morning. In fact, he had bought twenty-five copies, enough for all of his friends - with some left over for his family. And their neighbours. And the neighbours of his friends. He sat in class proudly holding the front-page article aloft, until Bannister had said in an exasperated voice 'Yes- we've all seen it...Now put it away Boy!!'. As his small slice of Media exposure was secreted in his desk, Kendy was already planning to have three dozen tee-shirts printed...

With the usual schoolboy-to-schoolboy and pupil-versus-Master banter flying back and forth (the less affluent banter was forced to travel by bus), the silent distress of one boy in the class seemed to have gone unnoticed. Nicky's group of friends were not what you would call "rowdy" in any sense, but when one particular voice was suddenly missing from the usual clamour - it pointed to something having gone awry. Merry was normally one of the more animated personalities within the group, but even the most casual observer would have noted that the boy was unusually silent and withdrawn. Things had come to a head in the Maths class, when he had been taunted by Lordsley to breaking point. He had gone from morose to maniac in a split second - and it had taken six people to pull him off his tormentor. Bannister the Mathematics Tutor was shocked at the boy's sudden frenzy - and when he had eventually calmed down, asked him to stay behind after the lesson and "have a little chat" with him.

The Master was more than a little worried about his pupil, as the sudden outburst was so out of character for the boy. When the rest of the class had left the room at the end of the lesson (glancing back over their shoulders, just in case their friend should decide to attack the Teacher with a slide rule - which would be a terrible miscalculation), Merry approached the front desk, with his head hung low. He was expecting a loud dressing-down for his behaviour in the class, but instead, Bannister instructed the boy to sit in his own chair at the front. The Master perched himself on the edge of the desk, and smiled at the crestfallen boy. 'Well young Merry - that was a bit of excitement, wasn't it? Is there anything that you feel that you want to tell me?' he asked. 'Not really Sir…only sorry for disrupting your lesson' said Merry. Bannister took off his jacket and threw it casually onto the front row desk.

'Now come come, my lad- that's not the behaviour which I expect from one of my brightest students. There must be something troubling you, to make you go mad like that?'

'Just Lordsley Sir - he's a pillock…'

'Yes, well… (Bannister had to stifle a laugh) I'm afraid that it's probably something in his DNA that he has inherited. If it's any consolation, I know his Father'.

'Is he a pillock too?' asked Merry.

'Yes - I mean no…I mean sort of, but - well let's just say that the Family has never been noted for their tact or ermm…' (at this point, Bannister seemed to glaze over, and when he spoke again, it was with the gentle, kindly voice of middle-aged Lady…)

'Now my Deary!! Don't you be worrying. Let's you and I have a nice chat, and we shall see what I can help you with…' Elsie Noakes had decided to intervene and save the day.

Merry stared at the face of Bannister for a few seconds, then burst into tears.

'It's my Mum…' he wailed.

Bannister (now under the control of Social Worker Noakes) put a friendly arm around the boy's shoulders. 'Now you just tell Auntie Elsie all about it' she insisted. Merry's response erupted in a flood of information which even Elsie struggled to take in all at once…

'Well Dad's been away on business for ages, and Mum said that he'd be back soon, but then we get a letter from him saying that he won't be coming back at all, and telling her that he will still pay the school fees and the car and the telly and the mortgage and that she will have to cancel her membership at the gym, and Mum went mad and rang him up and swore a lot at him, and said she didn't care if he never came back but I do and I miss him and he missed my Birthday and everything and now Mum's gone all weird and barmy…'

'Oh you poor boy!' sniffed Elsie, who was quite overcome, 'and how is your Mum now?'

'She went out and had the new car re-sprayed'.

'Well, that's alright isn't it?'

'Not when she has it sprayed Zebra-pattern it isn't!'

'But don't worry about that, it's only a car after all…'

'But it's not just the car, she painted the front of the house pink'.

'Well I like pink- pink's a nice colour'.

'And the dog…'

'Ah…well, that's certainly different'.

'Now she's sitting up all night watching Jeremy Kyle on the telly - and shouting and swearing at the screen when she sees men that have run off with other women. I have to do the cooking and cleaning, and she even shouted at me when I tried to cook bacon with the new iron…'

'It sounds as if your poor Mum might need to see a Doctor - do you think?'

'The Doctor refused to see her anymore, because she turned up for her appointment wearing my Dad's full Scuba-diving gear. And she nearly crashed the car trying to drive wearing flippers. Her snorkel got caught in the sunroof, and the airbag went off.'

'Might it help if I offered to take your Mum out shopping?' Elsie enquired.

'She can't go into our local Supermarket any more. The Manager has banned her. The first time, she came back with fifty-five packets of fish fingers, nine melons and a sweet potato. The second time, she said that it was one of her "Clothing Optional" days - and she decided to dash round with the trolley starkers. I have our food delivered online now, but I have to make sure that she doesn't get on the computer and order anything weird'.

'Like things that you don't eat?'

'No - like surface-to-air missiles from the MOD, and spares for oil drilling rigs…'

Elsie did her best to calm the poor lad down. She would have to do something urgently to help him- as the unfortunate lad was at his wits end, obviously with a Mother who was at the end of her wits. She would get Miles to take affirmative action. She would have a rally-round of all of her friends, and get the woman some help. She told the boy not to worry, and that she will get him as much help as he needed, adding that she would be looking out for him. Bannister suddenly found that he was "himself" again, and told Merry to hurry along to his next class - not really having much to add, after Elsie had done her work. He handed the boy a large bar of chocolate, and gave him a genuine smile.

'We will have to deal with this, it's terrible that a lovely young lad like that is tormented like that' said Elsie.

'I know just how he feels…' Bannister muttered.

'You know Miles…the more I come to think of it, the more that I think that Merry is absolutely right' she said.

'Right about what, exactly?' asked Bannister.

'That Lordsley IS a Pillock…'

New boy Jez Christo seemed to be settling in all right. He had been appointed "Mentors" amongst his form, who had shown him the ropes. If he was a really lucky boy, then perhaps later on, Matron too would show him the ropes, the chains, and of the more interesting leather straps (at least that was the Gospel according to Calderman…). He had been readily co-opted into the "let's go up town at dinner time and get a takeaway" club, and he seemed utterly fascinated that Davis could attend the first sitting of the school lunch, and yet miraculously appear with the rest of the lads when they tucked into a burger. 'Does he ever stop eating?' Christo had enquired: 'Of course - everyone has to sleep…' said Nicky. Yes, but Davis dreams quite often came with a side order of chips.

Finding himself quite flush with unfamiliar money, Christo had very generously offered to buy lunch for all of the gang. He ordered three large fried fish, and five long rolls. The boys were anxious as the food arrived over the counter. Bags of stuff kept emerging over the counter one after the other, and soon the lads were all burdened down by the sheer amount of food that they were given to carry.

'Bloody hell Christo!' said Calderman, 'What on earth did you order? You must have enough grub here to feed five thousand people!!'. Christo merely gave him a grin.

They made their way back to the Academy, handing out packets of food to bemused high street shoppers, and anyone who in their opinion looked hungry or a bit on the needy side. A homeless man who was sitting on the street corner with a sign which said "Hungry and Homeless" suddenly found himself in possession of several carrier bags of hot food, and two unexpected £20 notes - which had been tucked into the top of one of the bags. He had a wonderful lunch, shared it with his friends, fed his little terrier, and bought himself a nice strong cup of tea. Acting on sheer impulse, he decided to buy himself a lottery scratch card from the newsagent, and found that he had won £250,000.

Sometimes, little miracles happen right under your nose…

'I dinnae think that it's too difficult a concept for ye tae understand…' said Duggan.

He was taking his role as the new leader of the Syndicate very seriously, and had decided that were to be a few cataclysmic changes in the modus operandi of the Gang.

'I'm in charge the noo…' he declared, 'and I intend tae carry oot certain orders which hae bin' passed doon tae me by a Higher Office…' (actually, this was not true in any way, shape or form. Biddie Duggan only came up to just below her Son's shoulder on a good day). He looked at the faces of Figg, Swall and Fletcher. (Since it occupied the space on the front of Fletcher's head - one might be forced to deduce that it was, in fact, a face – but it was a damn close thing) The expressions of each of the men were blank. It was as if all facial movement had been stolen from them- what you might choose to refer to as a Blank Raid…

'So then Du - Boss…' began Figg, 'we don't do any more smash and grab jobs, we don't help ourselves to a nice 100% discount at Jewellers, and we don't keep any of the loot which we 'elp the young Toffs to dig up – is that right?'

'No… that isnae quite it' said the smiling Duggan 'We will still be pickin' up any unconsidered trifles what we may happen across, but we will be donatin' the profits tae Worthy Causes and those that is in need of it'. Still the men looked aghast, as though someone had just asked them to give their actual address, or urged them to fill in a tax return.

'I just don't get it…' said Swall.

'Aye - that's the idea Laddie…them as needs oor help is the ones that gets it'.

'But we'll get into trouble if we just go around givin' stuff away…' said Fletcher.

‘Och, I dinnae think so. I think that the Legal terminology for what I have in mind is “Charity”, and I cannae see the Polis takin’ too hard a line with that’. Duggan smiled.

‘Noo listen up…we will carry on with a few of our more “questionable” enterprises, and living expenses will of course be deducted. The profits will be used to help the poor, the needy, the destitute…’

‘Hang on a minute…’ said Fletcher, ‘that ain’t right. I ain’t happy givin’ my hard-earned cash to any of them that walks the street for a livin’…’

‘The word was “Destitute” Fletcher, and it means “having no money” said Duggan.

‘Well that’s us then - ‘cos we ain’t been paid’ said Fletcher, sulking.

‘Actually, this might be good fun, when you think about it’ stated Figg, who was probably thinking about how much he personally could divert away from the Good Causes pot.

‘Mr Figg…if you were thinking in the slightest way what I assume you to be thinking, then yes indeed, it will be good fun. It will be good fun for the Police to try and guess where the next one of your body parts will be found…’ said Duggan. ‘We shall begin with Mr and Mrs Whipple on Station Street. I hear that they were recently burgled, and are having great financial difficulties. We are sending them a Christmas card, and inside the envelope will be a gold bar. Mr Swall - you will be oor wee Postman for tonight!!!’.

Swall stood outside the tiny terraced house in Station Street. The paint was peeling badly on the front door and rotted windows, and he wondered just what the residents may have had, that any burglar would have considered worth stealing. He took out the envelope with its precious cargo inside, and just for the merest fraction of a second, felt a thrill of goodness run through his soul. Grinning like an MP on full expenses, he crept up to the door and carefully opened the letterbox - dropping the card and contents inside the house. He then sneaked back into the shadows opposite, to a point where he could see inside the room, but could not be seen by anyone peering out. He heard muffled voices from within, and then a kind of joyous scream. The front door opened quickly, but stuck half way, and a head poked out and scanned the street to try and spot the mystery benefactor. He turned and walked back toward Duggan’s flat with a warmer feeling than the time that they had pulled off the County Building Society job.

You know, a bloke could get to like this sort of thing. The Salvation Army Band were playing Christmas Carols on the town green. A smiling Captain shook a collection tin at him as he approached. He ignored him - but was in such a good mood, that he dropped a tenner into the shocked musician's euphonium.

Once the snowball of Good Deeds had been levered into movement, it's momentum was unstoppable. It was strange to see, but it was as if the gang of (almost) reformed criminals were trying to outdo each other in the generosity game. Fletcher had not quite got the hang of it all yet though - he had stolen a jacket from an expensive High Street outfitters, and then given the jacket straight to a Charity Shop- with a bar of gold in each of the pockets. Swall donated a bag of "odds and ends" of so-called "costume jewellery" to a shop that raised funds for the Elderly. The value of the very real jewels in the bag could have bought the shop many times over, and left enough change with which to buy the street - gift wrapping included.

Figg and Duggan visited the local Children's Home. They had a wonderful time handing out toys and gifts to the children and staff alike. Before they left, they made sure that the children all gathered around the Christmas tree and sang Carols. Duggan then gave Figg the nod - and he proceeded to tie little bags of golden coins onto the ends of the branches. He hoped that the children would not be too disappointed when the chocolate treat that they were expecting proved to be something else. Duggan wondered just how much chocolate it would be possible to buy with that number of solid gold coins…

Edgar the town Tramp was left speechless when he was approached in the street by a complete stranger and handed a mystery package. Inside the package was a magnum of vintage Champagne, a cut crystal glass, and a gold ingot. Edgar cried a tear of unsurpassed joy at the gift, although an hour later, he was still trying his best to open the bottle with the gold bar.

The Manager of the local Cats Home had heard the lorry backing up outside the front door. She heard it drive off again later, and hoped that it was not some cruel person who had left another cat and kittens on their doorstep. She opened the door, watched by several pairs of feline eyes. The pile of boxes of food was higher than her head, and stretched back all the way to the gates. Now she could make sure that all of the poor cats and kittens would be fed. Now she would not have to close the Sanctuary as she had feared.

There was a note on top of the nearest box, held in place by a rectangular paperweight. The note merely said "Merry Kitmas…" (of course-the paperweight turned out to be a gold bar).

'Tis the Season to be Jolly'…Mrs Finucane had decided to be very jolly indeed. For ages, she had been cleaning the Physics Laboratory, and from time to time peered in through the slit glass window into the ante-room at the back. She had often wondered just what the circle of bright blue light which regularly pulsated at the back of the room actually was. This was the one room in the Academy for which she did not have a key (access was strictly limited by the stern order of Professor Strangler himself). Today, she had found the door unlocked, and a student scribbling strange and (to her) meaningless equations at a desk. She recognised the boy as Ardley Senior (the smaller of the Ardley Brothers), and had clipped him around the ear for his cheek on more than one occasion. She went in. When the busy boy looked up from his calculations, she announced 'Now youse had better be tellin' me all about dat dere sparkly feckin' thing - or I might be forced to reveal who it was that done that unspeakable thing in the desk of Mr Rundell…' The boy turned a superb shade of sunset red, and began to give Mrs F a stuttering description of what the Vortex was, did, and could possibly be used for. Mrs Finucane laughed loudly, and said 'Well dere's a feckin' clever thing, and no mistakin''.

Sometime after this brief encounter with Science at the Cutting Edge, her natural sense of mischief had risen to the surface. As she had mopped and polished the corridor floors, she had begun to think of all the fun that she could have with the "Thing in the corner". When she had done her usual perfect job, she walked back to the Physics lab, whistling an Irish Rebel song to herself. All that she now needed was for that daft spotty lad to have left the door unlocked. He had…

Now our Mrs F had what could be termed an "adventurous" sense of fun, which had often left egg on the faces of persons who hadn't realised that they were even hungry. She paused again, as her impish sense of humour came up with a list of japery which could be performed with the assistance of a gizmo that allowed Time Travel. She took full advantage of the situation, like you would, like she did. There was little or no malicious intent in her actions: she merely wanted to see or at least imagine, the faces of the people who saw the results.

Archaeologists had been astounded when during a dig at Stonehenge, they had unearthed several previously-unseen graves. They were dumbfounded when one of the teams excavated a grinning Garden Gnome - complete with fishing rod.

A visitor to Victorian London would have been utterly appalled by the depravity to be found in some of the streets of the East End. They would certainly have raised a Dickensian eyebrow when they saw the Urchin strutting along the filthy street, listening to his I-Pod.

Most people with an interest will have heard of Otzi the "Ice Man", a Neolithic hunter from 3300 BC, whose mummified frozen body was found in the Italian Alps. No-one could explain however, how "Nanzi", a Neolithic woman, was found with a tin of Christmas Selection biscuits.

It may, or may not have been, a fun idea to present the famous seafarer Christopher Columbus with a Sat-Nav. Could have been a decent idea to have given him a charger for it though - just a passing thought.

Napoleon Bonaparte was having a bad enough time during the winter of 1812 outside Moscow, without some strange Irish lady appearing out of nowhere on top of a snow hill - and shouting 'Put yer Feckin' thermals on- Shortarse!!!'.

Naughty Girl!!

Chapter Thirty:

So it was true then…the St Onans Christmas Carol concert which would be held as usual in the massive Parish Church opposite the Academy was to filmed by the BBC as a Festive episode of their *Songs of Praise* series. Miss Piggott in her office, had taken a telephone call early in the morning from the Producers of the show to confirm this. She had 'Yes Sir'd and No Sir'd' her way through the conversation, before transferring the call through to Chambers in his - in the Head Master's study. She had turned an embarrassed shade of pink, and felt like she was a schoolgirl again, who has just been asked out on a first date by the most handsome boy in the Senior Year. With a quiff. And a scooter. This was despite the fact that the young man who had made the call had sounded more camp than three rows of tents.

Chambers took the call without showing any trace of undue excitement. He took it all in his stride - which was quite hard to do, as he was sitting down at the time. He stirred his cup of weak, tepid tea (why did the woman always bring him such awful tea? was it some sort of punishment?), and considered the immediate future. He thought of the Staff members, resplendent in their ceremonial robes, he thought of the Kitchen and Cleaning Staff in their Sunday Best: he formed a mental picture of the Academy Choir and the Orchestra as they brought forth music for the Congregation, and he thought of the whole school of boys who would all be on their very best behaviour.

So that's it then, he thought - we're buggered.

He "buzzed" through to Miss Piggott, and asked her politely if she would be so very kind as to gather the "Troops" in the Staff lounge as soon as possible. She had replied 'Yes - Head…' but he was sure that he had heard her add an extra word in the middle. There was a pause, and he held the phone as the ominous silence went on for a few seconds- broken by Miss P, who asked 'Did you forget something Dr Chambers?'. He thought for a moment, then replied cautiously, 'No…I don't think so'. He heard a sharp intake of breath from Miss Piggott, who declared in a slightly disapproving voice- 'To say "Thank you" for the tea perhaps?'. 'Oh…so that's what it was…' said Chambers. The line went dead.

The Acting Head always felt a sense of unaccountable dread when faced with a meeting of the Staff. They were all accomplished academics, and highly-respected in their own particular fields.

Singularly, they were in the main, intelligent, erudite, witty and loquacious. Put any two or more of them together, and spontaneous insanity would erupt. He often felt like a worker in a nitro-glycerine factory who was prone to sudden sneezing fits. Keeping any sense of order during gatherings of his colleagues demanded nerves of steel - and a Taser. He wondered if Deputy Heads across the country ever felt the same as he did, and if they were taking the same amount of medication in order to cope…

The Gaggle of the Learned Great walked, strode, ambled, tottered, stamped, stomped, and (in the case of Newhouse and Hyde-Jones), skipped their way into the room. Captain Brayfield stood scowling, and smelling strongly of spent matches. 'Look here Chambers…' he growled, 'What the winds of Watford is going on now? - we seem to be holding more meetings than Aintree…' Chambers did his best to smile pleasantly at the angry man. 'I have called you all in again to give you the news that we may all be immortalised on television. You may have heard the rumour that *Songs of Praise* want to film their Christmas show at our Carol Concert this year?'

'Well, is it true?' asked Madame Dreadfell.

'Yes – it's true' whispered Hyde-Jones.

'Are you sure?' she enquired.

'Yes – I'm sure that it is true that it's a rumour…' he replied.

Chambers ignored this exchange, and instead, tried to attract the attention of the Music Master, who was staring at a newspaper. 'May I please have your full attention, Mr Newhouse?...' he asked.

Newhouse folded his paper, and answered 'Sorry, Oh Great Deputy in the Head Department, but I was just reading this article in the entertainments section. I see that in the New Year's Honours List, some guy called "Wan Kenobi" has been awarded the OBE…'

'Is there nothing you can take for it...?' asked Hyde-Jones.

The Deputy Head ploughed on - knowing full well that it was like riding a pogo-stock in a minefield. 'Here are the facts. The BBC will be filming here. They are going to broadcast our Carol Concert. They will also be shooting some "cut-in" material in and around the Academy on the day before the concert. You will all try your very best to at least appear normal. Best Ceremonials will be worn for the concert. Our very careers may depend on how we are perceived on screen. PLEASE, I implore you, do not do anything which will embarrass either yourselves OR St Onans. If you are to be filmed - before you speak…THINK.'

('Or Sthwim…' came a voice from the back).

'I want no repetition of last year. Mr Rundell - I am sorry to inform you that you will not be required to give the Christmas address this year'.

'May I enquire as to why?'

'Because unless the Congregation is entirely composed of Citizens wearing togas and sandals, then the majority of attendees will not understand a reading given entirely in Latin…'

'More Fool They…Deputy Head'.

'Perhaps so - but it really will not do. And Dr Matthews… you turned up roaring drunk at last year's event!'.

'I was merely endeavouring to get into the Christmas Spirit!'.

'You had endeavoured to make your way into several establishments, where you purchased a vast quantity of spirits…'

'Sir…Drunk, I was certainly not. I made a special point of getting myself spruced up for the evening!'

'Yes, I remember it well – you had a wash and a shave in the font, if my memory serves me correctly…'

Matthews gave his usual happy shrug, and grinned.

'Mr Thwaite…what exactly are you wearing? – You did not manage to attend the Concert at all last year…'

'My Doctor advised against it – he said that I had "Chinese 'Flu" '

'Is that so...?'

'Well, he didn't actually use those *exact* words - but I'm sure that I must have picked up an inflection…'

Chambers glared at him, and carried on:

'I would ask each and every one of you to make sure, whatever else you may have to do, that at all costs - the boy Weatherill is FULLY DRESSED…That is all – thank you Lady and Gentlemen (Mr Thwaite gave the man a withering look, through heavy false eyelashes…)'.

One person who could not seem to raise the slightest morsel of enthusiasm for the upcoming concert and filming was Professor Darwin. It had not been a good term for him thus far. Apart from being constantly interrogated when strange species were observed strolling around the Academy, he had endured a host of other problems. The laboratory rats which were part of a "maze" experiment in the lab annexe had first formed their own union. He had become sick of having to pick up tiny placards from the floor of the lab. The rats were housed in small single units along one wall - but pretty soon they had knocked through each partition in order to form one long communal "hut". He had an inkling that something was afoot, as every time he entered the room, the rats would instantly stop whatever activity they were performing, and sit looking nonchalantly at him. One or two would even whistle… There had come one particular morning when he had entered the annexe and noticed no movement at all- there were no scrabblings, no protruding noses, and no twitching of whiskers to be seen. On closer inspection, he discovered that the rats at the front of the cages were all papier mache dummies, and the whole prison population of rodents had made a break for it during the night. Two weeks later, he had received a mystery postcard, which had merely stated "Home Run"- all the way from Mousehole in Cornwall.

He was also depressed because he was having to spend his Christmas alone. After one disastrous online dating experience (he arrived at the bar only to find that "Brigitte" was in fact a Plate Welder called Alec from Barnsley…), he had finally met a rather nice girl one Sunday in a country pub. He had been taken with her immediately, and very soon, Juliette had asked him to move in with her and her elderly Mother. Last year however, things had taken a sinister turn.

Mother was extremely deaf. Darwin would regularly have to shout loudly in order to find out if the dear lady would like a cup of tea. Sometimes, well most of the time, this could be quite a problem. There was one peculiar advantage, so to speak, that her condition did present.

'Brapps', 'Feeps', 'Squeakers', 'Flappers', 'Teargas Terrors', 'One-cheek Sneaks', 'Cushion Busters', and of course the dreaded 'Tear-Arse': were just some of the vast and varied array of farts that Darwin had been able to get away with, on a regular (and completely inaudible) basis.

He had arrived home from the Academy, and headed straight for the kitchen. He poured himself a large glass of wine, and made her Mother her usual cup of tea. He waved to the Mother as he gave her the tea, and walked over to the French windows to look out at the lawned gardens beyond. With great gusto and not inconsiderable ferocity, he committed at least four, if not more, of the above offences. He returned to the comfort of the sofa and sat down- noting that the

Mother was giving him a look of contempt. At that point, Juliette breezed in from work, and in a happy voice announced 'Hello Darling…how was your day? I just bet that Mother has been telling you all about the brilliant new digital hearing aid that she got today?...'

Hence, he would be pulling a cracker on his own this year…

Hyde- Jones and Newhouse were deep in conversation:

'I think that we'd better "play this one straight" Loopy...' said the English Tutor.

'Do you think that our jobs might be on the line then?'

'Could well be…' mused H-J.

'If you got the push from here, what other job would you fancy?' asked Newhouse.

'I dunno really – maybe a Transplant Surgeon?'

'Aaah! – a man after my own heart…' said Newhouse.

'What about your good self then, you mad rock and roll rebel?'

'Well that young band "Funderthuck" are doing quite well – getting a lot of attention, and they have asked me to think about becoming their Road Manager. I've already helped them to record their first single. They are still arguing about what the title should be though'.

'What is it called then?'

'Well, I suggested "Lost Love"- but they want their original title'.

'Which is…?'

'If you love something, then let it go. If it returns to you, then it is yours forever- if not, then buy a big rifle, hunt it down and kill it…'

'What's the B-Side?'

'A sweet little acoustic ditty called "*Don't scratch yerself when yer Nan's lookin*".

'How utterly charming…'

'And I've told the lads that I will get them to play at the Carol Concert, so that should get them noticed...'

'Pretty swiftly, I would imagine – and by all of the Authorities' said Hyde-Jones. 'I myself have been asked to nominate a promising student who in my opinion has shown great potential - to give the Christmas reading at the Concert. I will wager that I have the *ideal* boy in mind for the prestigious task…'

'You surely don't mean…'

'Oh Yes!…'

Rundell and Madame Dreadfell had a separate meeting of their own, over a cup of Earl Grey tea in the ostentatious comfort of Rundell's study. 'I know that I am addressing a kindred spirit when I say to you Madame: we must at all costs prevent the Peasants from turning this prestigious event into a mockery. I see it as up to you and I to rise above the low moral standards of the "Also-rans" with whom it is our combined misfortune to have to associate on a daily basis'.

'I also, agree 'wiz you on zees point…' said Madame, quite forgetting that she was originally born just outside Newark on Trent. Rundell gave her the look someone gives to someone when they want to give them a funny look (?).

'You will look magnificent on the screen…' he declared, as Madame preened herself in response. 'You and I shall be interviewed in front of my Vintage Jaguar, which I shall polish to perfection for the occasion'. He poured them both a fresh cup of tea: 'I am sure that any person of sane countenance would not think of dispensing with the services of two Tutors who embody everything that is noble, wholesome and elegant within this Academy…And let us remember, we are both Senior Masters…'

'I ain't that bloody "Senior", thank you very much!!' said Madame, having suddenly dug up her Gallic roots.

'I meant no offence Dear Lady…' he swiftly replied, shocked at just how quickly his colleague had crossed the Channel... 'I merely refer to the undeniable fact that you and I have a high degree of status within this Establishment, and a level of Social Grace which, I am sorry to say, our fellow Tutors are never likely to achieve…'

Mrs Finucane had heard their conversation. She had just happened to be passing Rundell's study, and had accidentally dropped a glass, which had accidentally fallen against the door. To stop it falling further, she had wisely put her ear against it. She was appalled at what she had accidentally heard, and saw another accident in her mind's eye - where she might be forced (purely by accident, you understand) to reveal the conversation word-for-word to the Commander-in-Chief of the ODD. He would certainly have a few good ideas as to how to deal with the likes of "Louis the Four Teeth, and Catherine of Arrogance..."

Since the incident with the trees, Nicky and the village lads had found themselves suddenly famous. Well, not exactly famous, if we're being honest here, it was probably a degree of notoriety which had temporarily settled upon their shoulders. But it was good news at some of the local shops, my word yes. There had been various "Freebies" handed out by the shopkeepers, the more "denture friendly" of which they had shared with their older accomplices. Nicky had even been asked for his autograph. Strictly speaking, it had been the Postman who had asked him to sign for a parcel which had come from his Cousins in New Zealand - but it still counted if you said it quick enough. He was quite disgusted that Jozza had not run down his front path waving a copy of the paper which bore his image on the front, and thrown herself at his feet, pledging undying love…

He was also quite disgusted that somehow, he had managed to get himself locked in the shed. Something, or someone, had pushed the door closed whilst he was in the shed checking Auntie's home brew wine as per instructions. The door had clicked shut, and to his horror, Nicky found that no amount of force seemed to be able to free him from his prison.

Dave the Chicken sat on the other side of the shed door. He preened his feathers as he listened to the boy calling for help. It had been a normal day in the pampered life of a domestic chicken, until he had overheard the family discussing what they should have for Christmas dinner. What he had overheard had made his plumage stand out in terror…It had been like listening to a group of assassins choosing which Cousin to kill. If they thought that they would get him anywhere near a packet of sage and onion - well, they could stick it straight up their jacksie. When he had seen the boy go into the shed…well, he had to take action, didn't he? Maybe a spell in solitary would encourage the boy to suggest the Vegetarian option this year. He laughed a chicken-type laugh.

'Dave – is that you?' called Nicky

'Oh, Clucking Hell – he heard me!!' thought Dave.

'Dave…I'm shut in – get me out of here!' said Nicky. He then thought to himself- 'just how sad has my life become - I've just asked a chicken to get me out of a shed…'

Dave put his chicken ear to the door, and pecked once or twice on the plywood panel.

'Dave - my little feathery Mate…this is a long shot…but I want you to go and get help. If you can understand me - peck twice on the door'.

Peck…Peck.

'Brilliant!! – now please go and let them know that I am stuck in the shed…'

Peck…Peck.

'Dave - don't mess about…go and fetch help!!'

Peck…Peck…Peck Peck Peck peck peck peck peck peck peck Peck…

(roughly translated as 'Who do you think I am - Cluckin' Lassie?).

Chapter Thirty-One:

It was a full two hours later when Nicky had finally been released from the wooden prison in which he had become incarcerated, which had been the result of a fowl deed. He had eventually been extracted by Uncle Joe, who had called round for a visit, and had felt the need to refresh himself with a draft or two of Auntie's lethal home brew. He opened the shed door with the level of care normally taken by a Bomb Disposal expert - in the full knowledge of the unpredictable nature of the fermenting products inside. Nicky was relieved to hear the latch on the door click open, then startled at the vision which stood before him. Uncle was taking no chances: he was wearing cricket pads, a crash helmet, several cushions strategically placed about his person, and heavy gardening gloves. A metal colander was tied around his waist by means of string- and it hung at groin level to protect Uncle's valuables. Nicky wondered if it might be Uncle's latest invention, to prevent groin strains…

'Oh, Hello Boy!!' said Uncle, as if finding boys in sheds was an everyday occurrence for him, 'How long have you bin' in 'ere then?'

'The same length as I usually am…' replied Nicky.

He ran back into the house, where he dumped himself down onto a kitchen chair, looking angry and flustered. 'Oh – we wondered where you had got to…' said Mum.

'Well I wish that you had wondered about that two hours ago - it was freezing in that shed' he replied.

'What were you doing for all of that time in the shed?'

'Trying to get *out* of the shed, Mum…that's what'. Nicky shivered, the cold having chilled him to the bone. He looked around the kitchen, to see if there was any sign of Dave the Chicken. 'I may need to use the telephone, if that would be okay?' he said.

'Anything urgent?' asked Auntie

'Not urgent as such - but I would like to give someone's neck a quick wring…'

Uncle had return from his expedition to the shed, and had removed most of the protective padding from about his person. He sat down on the chair opposite Nicky, and the colander, which was still in place, clanged against the edge of the seat. Joe poured himself a cautious measure of Auntie's finest, and studied his glass looking downcast.

‘So how’s the latest little venture in the world of International Commerce coming along then Joe?’ enquired Mum.

‘Not good- not good at all. The Yanks aren’t interested…’ he replied, sadly.

Since the launch of another rocket probe to the planet Venus, there had been a build-up of interest in all things to do with Space from the General Public. Because Joe kept a beady eye on the news, and his ear to the ground, he often got his head stepped on by passers-by as he was reading the newspaper. If and when Uncle detected the merest hint of a new Marketing opportunity, his Sales Radar would immediately switch on, scanning the airwaves for any chance to sell to the Public. His recent logic had followed this script:

Right then- what are the Public interested in at the moment? = Space.

What was the last really big event which sold the most merchandise? = Moon landing.

What is the most consumed product in the Country? = Tea.

So it was off to his attic, where he did his best thinking. After the floor had been liberally covered with screwed-up balls of paper, and nearly a whole box of new HB pencils used up- he had come up with a brilliant idea…He knew that his combination of an Herbal brew and Man’s greatest Space achievement would be a real money-spinner.

He had designed and produced a teabag in the shape of a half-moon, filled with Camomile tea. He had contacted the Americans - for permission to use their name, and to see what quantities they might like to order in advance. As it had turned out so far, it hadn’t cost him very much in overseas postage. It hadn’t cost anything at all, as he hadn’t had a single order for his new product.

‘What- not a single order?’ Mum had asked.

‘Not a sodding one…’ moaned Uncle.

‘Have you got any with you?’ asked Auntie.

Joe produced what was in fact a very well-made and nicely illustrated box. He placed it on the table. The box bore the image of an Astronaut on the surface of the Moon - with his feet up in a deck chair, drinking a steaming cup of tea.

“Give yourself some Space…!” the slogan on the box declared: “One small Sip for Man…Have yourself a relaxing cup of NASA Herbal Tea – the Tea of Tranquillity…”

Feeling sorry for Joe, they had tried his new product. They all sat at the table and sipped the hot, greenish-tinted fluid. No-one said a word for ages. Mum looked at Nicky, and he looked back at her. They both knew that what would follow was both unstoppable, and absolutely inevitable. Uncle looked hopeful…

Auntie drank the last of her beverage. She replaced her cup on its saucer with great reverence. Dabbing at the corners of her mouth with her handkerchief, she looked Joe directly in the eye, gave a smile, and declared:

'Well…that tastes like it has come from Uranus'.

Ignoring some of the more recent problems that seemed to have come his way, Nicky decided to try and get some advice from his Mum as to how he could help with the problem of his friend Merry. At the Academy were doing their very best to help their friend through his trying times- but when faced with the sort of problem that Merry was experiencing, Mum would know best… (unfortunately, not in the case of Merry's Mum at the moment, who had recently taken to dressing as Elizabeth I, rushing around the garden, and loudly declaring 'Drake is going around setting fire to people's beards - Off with his Bowls!!!').

Perhaps not before time, the decision had been made that what the poor woman required was some intense medical treatment, at a specialised medical unit which was used to dealing with such problems. Merry's Mum had been gently but forcefully placed in a large estate car, where she had sat in the back dispensing the Royal Wave and handfuls of small coins to her Loyal Subjects as they passed. Merry's younger Brother Danny and their Labrador dog Alfie, the country's largest producer of slobber, had been despatched off to stay with Merry's Aunt Virginia. This had solved one problem, but created another. It transpired that Merry could not stand his Mother's Sister, nor her Husband Brian. In fact, he would make any excuse, or on occasions feign an injury, so that he did not have to visit them. When they turned up at his house- he would immediately go missing until they were safely out of range – or preferably out of the County.

Nicky, Calderman and the boys had tentatively enquired as to what the problem with Merry's Aunt and Uncle might possibly be. The poor lad looked acutely embarrassed at the merest mention of their names, so it was obviously something major that was disturbing the boy. Eventually, and after much gentle questioning (and a little bribery with chocolate supplied by Davis), the awful truth finally emerged…

‘I’m not going to stay with them – I hate them!!’ Merry had moaned.

‘Why do you hate them, Merry?’ Nicky had asked.

‘Because I do - and they know why…’ came the terse reply.

‘But you must have a very good reason for not liking them?’ Calderman enquired.

‘I do…they’re just too weird’ answered Merry.

‘Well there are all sorts of “Weird” around - I mean, just take a look at our Masters for instance…’ suggested Jackson.

‘Yeah…but there’s “Weird”, and then there’s “Daft and Weird”…’ said Merry.

‘Same as here then...’ added Davis, munching away on something nutty…

‘NO!- you don’t understand…it’s what they wear…’ said Merry, quietly.

‘What do you mean? Do they go around in Nazi uniforms or something?’ asked Nicky.

‘It wouldn’t be so bad if they did…’ answered the boy.

Calderman adopted his “Doctor” stance, and tried to get to the bottom of the problem.

‘So, there is an issue with what they wear - is that what you are saying?’ he asked.

‘Yes…an’ that’s why I hate them, and that’s why I won’t go there, and that’s why I don’t want my Brother Danny anywhere near them…’ shouted Merry.

‘And what exactly is the problem with their clothes?’ said Nicky.

Merry looked around at the questioning faces of his friends. He thought that he might as well trust them to keep the secret - even if they were going to laugh at him…

‘The trouble is – They don’t wear any!!’ he said.

Ah, right then, so that would explain the boy’s reluctance to move in temporarily with his Aunt and Uncle. They were enthusiastic Naturists, who shunned clothing on a regular basis - whatever the weather, and whatever the occasion.

Merry’s younger brother Danny didn’t seem to be at all affected by their lifestyle choices, or if he was, then he did not show it. It was the fact that not only did they show it - but they made no attempt whatsoever to cover it, that Merry found so objectionable. He had awful memories of the school sports day at his younger Brother’s primary school, where they had turned up to give their Nephew some support and encouragement. There had been much talk, shock and horror from the other Parents. What had mentally scarred him the most, was when they both entered the Parents' sack race. Even though Aunt Virginia had romped home to win the event, the sight of that much oscillating flesh had greatly disturbed him. It was just an act of mercy that the Head teacher's camera had run out of film before the prize-giving photograph was taken.

'What - none at all?' Jackson had said in disbelief.

'Not a stitch…' Merry confirmed.

'What about in the Summer when - they had barbecues?' asked Calderman.

'Toasted buns all round!!...' added Davis.

'I bet no-one wanted a sausage either?' Jackson laughed.

Mum had made up her mind. She was unlikely to be moved from her position once she was settled on a plan. Nicky knew that he had inherited his stubborn streak from his Mother. Once he made his mind up, there was no shifting him.

He remembered the time that his own Primary School had held a Fancy- Dress contest. Nicky had absolutely insisted that Mum help him make a costume, so that he could enter dressed as a 1980's Pop Star. Mum had tried everything to talk her Son out of it, but to no avail – he was adamant…

Mum stood up and smiled.

'Right then…' she declared 'That settles it - Gerald will come and stay with us for as long as he needs to'.

It was now official – the Family would have a Merry Christmas…

Since each member of the Academy Staff had received the surprise news that they were to be featured on television, they had individually decided to make sure a) that they would be seen, and b) that they would be presenting the best image possible. Despite the fact that the visit of the BBC crew was only days away, Miss Piggott had already taken action. In the corner of her already somewhat cramped office now stood a treadmill. Every spare moment that she had was taken up by hurriedly changing into a bright pink leotard, donning a fluffy sweatband, and pounding along on the machine until she reached the point of near collapse. She had once attempted to answer the telephone whilst using the treadmill, but the caller had hung up on her, as he had mistaken her laboured and heavy breathing for a dirty phone call. To date, she had spent a total of £77.80 on various fitness DVDs, £106.40 on sports clothing, £367.99 on the treadmill, £75 on trainers…and lost a total of one pound four ounces in weight. Matthews had sighted the Lady in her leotard just the once- but that had been enough for him to declare 'All that she needs is an apple in her mouth…'

Professor Strangler had thinking too...and had come up with much the same idea to try and "turn back the clock a little" for the benefit of the cameras. He had recently become somewhat obsessed with the fact that his hair seemed to have gone wavy. His friend Darwin had stated that 'It's certainly waving bye-bye to your head!!'. So - the Strangler brain had gone into overdrive, and with a little help (and the odd thinly-veiled threat here and there) from his Students, he had invented and built the answer to his problem.

'I call it the TRU unit…' he announced to his fascinated colleague, Professor Darwin.

'The initials stand for "Temporal Reversal Unit". It is in effect, a smaller hand-held version of the "Vortex" in the back lab' he said proudly. 'I am quite pleased to say that it does exactly what it says on the label!'.

'And what exactly does it do, Richard?' asked Darwin.

Strangler gave his friend an excited look, and then fished half a dozen batteries out of a drawer. He then produced the unit - which resembled a thick pocket calculator with a small wire coat hanger stuck in the top of it.

'Wowee!!!' said his friend, 'And what is that?'

'It's basically a thick pocket calculator with a wire coat hanger stuck in the top of it…' he said. 'But thanks to a great feat of electronic engineering - the workings do something quite amazing!!'.

The Professor took the batteries, lining them up on the desk like copper-capped soldiers. He placed a battery tester onto each one in turn - clearly displaying the fact that each one of them was as flat as a pancake. He turned on the TRU unit, made a slight adjustment to the control dial in the middle, and made a slow pass over the line of spent batteries. When he had done this, he turned back to his colleague and asked:

'Well now…what did you think of that!!'

'Very nice…' said Darwin, 'It lights up a nice blue colour, and I like the humming sound that it makes'.

'Nonono!! -you're missing the point, Dear Boy!!' said Strangler.

He picked up the battery tester again and applied it to each battery on the desk. The reading on the tester now showed that each battery was fully charged. Darwin was impressed.

'So it's a device for charging batteries is it? Because I've already got one of those at home if you want to borrow it?'

Strangler gestured to one of the bench seats, saying 'I think you had better sit down before I tell you about the workings of the TRU unit. All I can say at this stage is that it may well change the course of Human History…'

'Okay - I'm sitting: Now tell me about it…' said Darwin.

Strangler placed the unit on the bench in front of him. He explained:

'You will be aware that our old friend "The Vortex" can shift time as a result of dimensional flux attractant principles? Well, I thought to myself, "What if the reversal of the Temporal Signature could be localised and contained in an altogether more compact setting, and its effects directed over a selected area in order to produce a flux reversal in one chosen site"?

'Well, we've all thought that now and again…' said Darwin, baffled. 'Tell me in simple terms Richard - what does the thing actually do?'

'It reverses the Temporal value over a given area to create a return to a previous dimensional state...'

'Could we, for the purpose of clarity (bear with me) imagine that I am in fact Mr Thicko von Thickleby from the village of Thickstone in the County of Thicklehampshire...?'

'Ah yes - if you wish…sorry! Well, it all began when a friend (who I am sure meant well) happened to mention that I seemed to be going "a bit thin on top". I began looking for a way to restore the thickness and consistency of the head of hair that I had in my youth. The batteries were a complete accident. I noticed that when I applied the TRU unit to them - they returned to the time when they were fully charged. I hope that the unit, when applied to my scalp, will return my head to the time when my hair was thick and luxurious. All we have to do is to turn back time slightly over a localised area - and Hey Presto!!'

'Or if you turn back time over your trousers… Sta-Presto!!' said Darwin.

'I don't think that you are taking this very seriously, are you?' asked Strangler.

It was some time later that Professor Strangler got the chance to fully test his life-changing invention for real. He had noticed that the remote locking key fob for his car was beginning to act rather strangely, and was locking the car again just after he had unlocked it, or had decided not to work at all. 'Ha Ha!!...it's the battery' he had thought to himself, 'Well now I have the very solution to the problem at my fingertips…'. He had pulled out the TRU device, attached the "Perimeter Activator Loop" and made a quick sweep over his car key fob. He pressed the key fob button confidently…nothing. It beeped, but there was no accompanying double flash from the car indicators to show that the vehicle had been unlocked. He tried again…nothing. Okay…he thought, perhaps the unit needs a little adjustment, as I may not have got the settings quite right. He decided to use the car key manually on this one occasion. The key did not fit the door lock. He stood and stared at the car key - and suddenly the realisation as to what had happened hit him right between the Temporal Lobes. The TRU unit had worked perfectly. It had reversed time. It had altered the car key back to the one which had previously hung from his old key fob - a car which he had sold four years ago…

He decided to take the bus home…

Word about the forthcoming television filming had spread through the Groundling Community like cheap supermarket margarine. Even the more self-disciplined and normally restrained members were already feeling the excitement:

'Shall we verily be seen all over the world?'

'Do I need to get the stains off my best jacket?'

'How come Thou hast more than one jacket?'

'Will we get to meet anyone famous?'

'Will I have time to get my hair done?'

'What's a television, exactly?'

Their twenty-strong choir was ready. It had been ready for weeks, in eager anticipation of the forthcoming Carol Concert. The Choristers knew their songs forward, backwards, and in the dark. They could sing them blindfold, and you would never know the difference - although some of the choir might be facing the wrong way. Jedekiah addressed them:

'My Children, Brothers and Sisters. You have all worked hard, and done well. Please remember that HoBi has given you your fine voices - and we give Him praise and humble thanks by using them'. A small hand was raised cautiously at one end of the row of singers…

'Elder…May I ask a question?' said the equally small owner of the small hand

'Why yes Child…what is it that you wish to know?'

'Are we going on "The X Factor", or is it "Britain's Got Talent" ...?'

Albert Brooks sat opposite Mrs Finucane (currently in the guise of Agent J- Cloth) at the rickety wooden table in his secret enclave up in the Groundsman's hut. They were both sipping from steaming mugs of tea - enlivened by huge drafts of finest "Irish Falling Over Water", as he referred to it. Very much enlivened, Mrs F was in full flow- recounting a story of how the late Mr Finucane (God rest him…) had come home late from the local pub drunk, after an evening out with his ex-workmates.

'So I says to Himself…what's dat dere sick all down the front of yer best jacket? And Himself says 'ooh - dat's where yer man Paddy O'Heaney was ill down me coat, the poor wee fella…' And he hands me the jacket. I'm after noticin' a ticket stickin' out of the top pocket, and sure, if isn't a ticket to one of dem "Lappy-Dancin" bars. Well I was about to start givin' out to Himself, when he says, 'I'm after findin' dat ticket on de floor of the Confessional when I went to Church last Sunday - 'tis nothin' to do with me at all…If ye look in the pocket, dere is a five-pound note which Paddy gave me to get me jacket cleaned, God Bless him'. So yer man takes off the rest of his suit, an' I ask him - 'So did ye all get roarin' drunk den?' Yer man says, 'No indeed, Oi am not drunk!!'. 'Good…says I - so you can walk down to Paddy's and get another fiver off'f him then'. 'Now why exactly would Oi be doin' that?' says he… and I says, 'Because it looks loike he's shit in your trousers too…'

The pair of them collapsed in fits of laughter, and Brooks filled their mugs again. They discussed their own very specific plans concerning the filming of the Carol Concert. Their attention to the smallest detail, and the timings of their planned actions, would have put the BBC to shame. Which may well turn out to be the case.

'Do you have a spare key for the old storage room where I stuck the cricket gear?' Brooks asked Mrs Finucane. 'Yes I have…' she replied, 'Do you have any more Booze?' 'Indeed I do, Agent J-

Cloth…' he answered. 'And do Oi take it that ye have a little something in mind for the Toffs at the Concert?' she enquired.

'Trust me…' said Albert – 'They'll be completely bowled over…'

Doctor Johnathan Darwin had been approached by Mr Duggan, who had made a very strange request, well- more of a suggestion really, but it was certainly something that Darwin had never in a million years expected. Now everyone knew that his lab assistant Bernie was in fact a Bigfoot, who had originally come over from the forests of North West America. He was loved and respected by all of the pupils at the Academy, not least for the fact that he was seven feet tall, and hairier than Lordsley's Sister on a bad day. It was in part due to the physical characteristics of the gentle giant, that Duggan had made his approach.

During the winter months, the forests of North West America can turn into a cold, harsh and unforgiving place. The snow settles in a cloying, thick blanket over the landscape, and little colour shows against the backdrop of purest white. The animals that make the forest their home change the colour of their coat in winter, to blend in with the snowy wilderness and escape the attention of predators on the hunt for food. Since Bernie belonged to one of the indigenous species of the forest, he too, at the onset of the frost and snow, had grown his own winter coat of white. Duggan had noticed this, and had approached Darwin with a view to asking Bernie if he might be willing to assist in a little "scheme" which he was cooking up. Bernie had sat patiently and listened, while the whole idea was explained to him, smiling benignly all the while. For a huge person of commanding size, Bernie had some unexpected "soft spots" for all animals.

Children, Kittens and Puppies especially brought out the gentler side of him, which was a pure delight to witness. When he heard that the plan would involve bringing joy to Children, he agreed to take part without question. The plan would involve a shave here, and a bit of extra padding there, but with Bernie's long white hair and beard, well - they were three quarters there already…

Madame had raced home after class finished. She had disappeared up into her elegant bedroom with the walk-in wardrobes and fitted mirrors. She had already been in there for two and a half hours. The room now resembled the horrific scenes often viewed on American television, where the television crew insist on shooting film of the town just after the tornado has passed through. The bed was piled high with Haute Couture, mixed with half-priced jeans from the sales, and the odd bit of retro clothing picked up for a song at car boot sales. It looked more like a scale model of the whale "Moby Dick", but built by a quilt maker. Dresses by Chanel lay arm-in-arm with long forgotten flared jeans and Afghan coats, and her old Pony Club jacket, which she just couldn't bear to throw out.

Somewhere in this heap of fashion crimes, shopaholic moments, and credit card frenzy - was something scintillating which would be just what she needed to be seen wearing as the cameras zoomed in for her close-up.

She took a sip from her glass of white wine (French of course, from that well-known purveyor of Gallic excellence- "Le Corner Shop").

Now to start on the shoes…

Chapter Thirty- Two:

It was never a good sign when a letter bearing the St Onans crest came through the letter box. The threatening envelopes were bound to contain either a) demands for funds pertaining to extra "activities" which you had never heard of, let alone would ever wish to take part in: or b) written confirmation of some hideous misdeed in which you - yes, you the Pupil had been involved in, or caused, or witnessed, or hoped would be forgotten about by now.

The ritual was always the same. The envelope would sit on the kitchen table, leaning upright against the toast rack (you know the one - the one that was Granny's, that Mum kept polished like the Crown Jewels). Breakfast would be eaten with each individual at the table not looking at, nor referring to, the alien object in front of them. When the regulation period of time had elapsed, Mother would casually reach over and pick up the letter saying, 'Well I suppose we had better find out what this is…' It's a letter Mum- we had already worked that one out. The letter was opened. The contents were read. Mum was not angry - so far, so good then.

'How nice!!' Mum said, 'Your Concert is going to be filmed for television…I'll have to wear my best c-…' She went very quiet as she read on. The letter was angrily folded, and thrust with considerable force back into the envelope. Nicky pulled out the letter, and studied the contents. So that was their game was it - bloody typical.

The letter spoke of what an honour it was to be filmed by the BBC. It told of the increasing numbers of Parents who regularly attended the Carol Concert. It made particular reference to the limited seating capacity of the Church. It also stated that only a very specific number of seats would be made available to Parents, due to the space required by local Businessman and Dignitaries, not to mention the Mayor and her retinue. The note also made reference to the fact that 'seating for Parents and guests will be made available by ticket application only, and please note that the allocated areas will be toward the rear of the Church, and may have a restricted view…'

So - not only would the local "Well-to-do" get seats automatically, but the "Peasants" were to be safely penned in at the back of the Church - safely out of the way of the cameras. The Church was always ranting on and on about how attendances were falling, and now just when people did want to put their bums onto the pews, they would have to fight for tickets!! Even then, they would have to peer around a pillar if they wanted to see anything.

'Well I shall not be going - and that's that' said Mum.

'But…I'm in the Orchestra, and don't you want to hear the Carols?' Nicky replied.

'I am not paying for the privilege of sitting at the back of a freezing Church, while they film the light shining off the Mayor's chain of office in the front row…' said Mum.

'So it's agreed then - we gatecrash the concert…' said Auntie.

'They won't let us in…' said Nicky.

'According to the Bible - everyone's name is on the Guest List!' replied Auntie.

You had to admit, she did have a point…

Professor Strangler was pacing up and down in the Physics lab ante-room. He had been hurriedly summoned by worried students, who had found an intruder on the premises. It would appear that a short gentleman wearing rather ragged clothing had appeared through the Vortex, and had wandered around the Physics lab - helping himself to all of their sandwiches in the process. When Strangler had arrived on the scene, the students had managed to subdue the unwanted visitor, and had restrained him by tying him to a chair. There he sat scowling, his large bare and very hairy feet taking up considerable space. The Professor had begun to question the little man as to who he was, how he got here, and what exactly he wanted. So far, the questioning had provided no answers. All that they had managed to get out of the intruder was that his name was "Yobbo", and that he wanted to have use of a telephone (well, actually - all he had gone on about was the fact that he "had to give somebody a ring" …). He was a very angry, tough, and unhelpful little chap…

As he walked around their "guest", Strangler noticed that a copy of *Lord of the Rings* had been casually left on the desk, where it had been hurriedly abandoned by a frightened student. Okay, that might explain a little of how the man had arrived - as the Vortex was apt to pick up stray vibration signatures from anything left too near to it, but he still needed to find out precisely what the aggressive little fellow was up to. Their repeated cajoling and questioning had produced nothing.

'My Goodness…' thought Strangler, 'He certainly is a hard Hobbit to break…'

Dr Chambers had already had a walk around the Academy and the Church in advance of the camera crew's arrival. Apart from the usual corridors which showed quite a few years' worth of apathetic neglect in their peeling and distressed paintwork, he had the feeling that even the Church needed some Festive "feature" in order to give a lift to the building. To this end, he met with Mr Bell-Enderby the Art Master, with a view to him producing some works of art on a theme of the Nativity. The Master was only too pleased to accept the "commission", and scurried off to begin preparatory sketches. There was always a slight niggling doubt at the back of his mind when dealing with Bell-Enderby, as he did tend to let his "fixation" get the better of him when he was painting - still, since his brief was on a Religious theme, things should be pretty safe for once. In his jacket pocket, Dr Chambers had his fingers very firmly crossed…

He barely had time to sit in the chair in his study, when a hysterical Miss Piggott burst in through the door, shouting something unintelligible, and spraying crumbs all over the room. Chambers leapt out of his chair and flattened himself against the mantelpiece, as the lycra-clad vision continued to shriek at him. He gathered his senses, and spoke to the demon in pink... 'What on earth are you saying Miss Piggott? - calm down, before you give yourself and me a heart attack…'

'It's Them!!!' she bawled…'It's Them!!!'

'For God's sake get a hold of yourself woman - and what are you spraying all over my study?' he shouted back at her.

'It's a Slimming Snack Bar Dr Chambers - and They're here!!!'

'Where are the Who, and who the hell are the who that are where…' he said, now completely flustered himself.

'It's the Camera Crew….' She bellowed - 'They've turned up early!!!'

From the plodding security of her office treadmill, Miss Piggott had observed a white van enter the quad. Out of the van had emerged a young woman and two men, one of whom was ambling around the quad and framing up "shots" with his hands. On the side of the van was the legend "BBC Outside Broadcast Unit". As Chambers brushed the shrapnel crumbs from Miss Piggott from his jacket, she raced back into her office in an attempt to make herself presentable for the cameras (she would deal with Chambers for referring to her as "Woman" later…by jingo yes).

Also ambling across the quad (in a variety of unsteady directions) was Dr Matthews. The young woman caught sight of him, and bounced happily over to introduce herself. She extended her hand, and announced:

'Hello there!! I'm Caroline from the BBC, it's lovely to meet you Sir…'

'I'm Gus Matthews from the History Department, and it's a delight to meet you too My Dear...'

'Would it be alright if Rupert and Lorenzo scout around a bit for some external shots?' she asked.

'They look rather old to be in the Scouts…' Matthews mused.

'I wonder if there is somewhere that we could sit down and chat about the history of the Academy?' she asked.

'Absolutely My Dear!!!' Matthews answered, 'I'm one of the oldest and most historical of the Relics around here. Now I know just the place for us to sit and talk, and I'll tell you all about why Barnes Wallis wanted to use the Academy as target practice prior to the "Dam Buster" raids during World War Two'.

'Did he really suggest that?' she enquired.

'No - but I would have done, if I were him…Now let me guide you to my favourite quiet corner, where we will be assured of a warm welcome' he told her.

'Is it nearby?' she asked.

'Not as near as I would like, but there you go. We can have a little drink while we chat'

'I don't really drink Mr Matthews…'

'Neither do I - it sounds like one of those expensive labels, I think I'll stick with Scotch…'

Matthews linked arms with the lady and propelled her out of the Academy gates, and over the road to the "Five Crowns". They sat down at a corner table, and Matthews delivered a more-or-less complete history of St Onans, whilst the young lady sat in rapt fascination. After twenty-five minutes in the company of Dr Matthews, she was so fascinated that she had trouble finding the door to the ladies' toilet.

Dr Chambers stood alone in the quad. He had drawn himself up to his full height, and approached the BBC van which was parked in front of the Boarding House. It was empty. (the van that is - not the Boarding House: well actually it was empty at the moment, but that is because the boys were all at their classes. Apart from Brindleham, who was in the infirmary with measles, and who had a cat's face drawn on him by some rotter while he slept…It might have been kinder if they had not used a permanent marker).

Well wasn't this just great…One minute there was a mass panic because the BBC had just turned up, and the next moment they had magically disappeared. As he was thinking, he was approached by two rather "arty" individuals.

'Why Hello there…' said one, 'Are you in charge here? How exciting!! Oh, where are my manners! I am Rupert, and this is my friend Lorenzo. We are just dying to start shooting around your quaint little school...'

Chambers was taken aback as the other man grabbed his chin and began twisting his head this way and that, examining his profile from all angles.

'Hmmmm, a bit on the "chiselled" side, but I suppose he might present well to camera with a bit of makeup' said the twister of face.

'Would you like to appear on film?' asked the man called Rupert.

'Well, I…I suppose if you think…I possibly could…' stuttered Chambers.

Rupert clapped his hands enthusiastically- 'Oh good!!' he said, 'Right then Dear…we will have a look at a few outdoor views, then some shots in the classrooms, and then I will see if Lorenzo can find an opening for you…'

Not on your life, Matey boy…thought Chambers.

Eventually, Matthews returned through the gate with his new (and rather unsteady) friend in tow. Caroline 'from the BCC…No-BCG, dammit!... GBH…BBC- that's right' introduced herself to Chambers at the fourth attempt, and he was glad that someone else had turned up who could divert the unwanted attentions of Lorenzo. The woman explained that they would like to film some quick shots of a class in progress, to give a "flavour" of the Academy to the viewers. Chambers agreed readily to this, as his priority at the moment was to put as much distance between himself and Lorenzo as possible. He suggested they might like to start up on the Old Block first floor. As the team collected their cameras and sound equipment from the van, Chambers sent a passing boy up to the chosen classroom to tip off the Master in charge that they were on their way. As it happened, this boy was Lordsley. As he sped off, Lorenzo gave Chambers a friendly wave from the back of the van.

The idea was to capture everyday education in action within the Academy. Nicky's Form were all lining up in the corridor, with the usual pushing and shoving taking place. As an out-of-breath Lordsley rounded the top of the stairs and headed for the classroom, the boys pounced on him.

'What's the rush then Lordsley?'

'The BBC are going to film in the class - and I am going to make a starring appearance. Do not even think of trying to stop me, or I shall inform Father - and then there will be consequences…'

The boys let Lordsley through. He returned shortly, wearing the smug smile of the self-important idiot.

'Make sure that you keep your mouth shut - and don't hog the limelight' Jackson told him.

'I shall do as I please, and I shall show that there are some pupils at this Academy who can display a higher than average IQ…'

'Give 'em my regards when you see them' said Merry.

Lordsley ignored him. He went to the locker outside the Form room, and took out his books. Turning away from the other boys, he pushed his way into the middle of the queue which was waiting to go into the class. 'And don't pretend that you know enough good French to give an oral report on "Where we went on last year's holiday"- you pompous little git…' called Calderman. Aha!! So they had given away the theme of the lesson had they…well he knew all about that subject, and he would show what a well-read and clever chap he was, and in front of the camera too!!

Lordsley couldn't wait to get into the classroom. He fought his way in, and sat down at the desk, pretending to ignore the cameraman and sound engineer at the back of the room. Madame had her back to the class, and was cleaning the blackboard. She carried on wiping the board as she asked the class 'Now- who will start us off by giving us all a short report?'

Henry Albert Lordsley stood up immediately, and delivered a verbal account in French of exactly what he and his family had done on last years' ski-ing holiday in the French Alps. His diction was clear (he checked) and his French accent good (he had practised). When he had finished, he stood and awaited the plaudits which he knew would surely follow.

When Madame turned around, he had rather a shock.

'That was a wonderful speech, with good detail and excellent accent Lordsley. I would point out though, that your French class is next door - this is Fourth Form Geography!!'

"Madame Dreadfell" was in fact Mr Thwaite in an auburn wig. There is no colour-chart equivalent for the shade of red that Lordsley appeared to turn. The Fourth-Form class all roared with laughter, as did the camera and sound team, who had caught the whole incident on film. The uproar could be heard from next door, where Nicky and Calderman punched the air with glee.

When Lordsley entered the class shame-faced, Madame gave him a detention for being late.

The BBC crew made their way around the Academy, and filmed various classes as lessons were taught. They were given lunch with the boys in the Dining Hall, and they were still laughing all the way through the meal due to the "Lordsley incident". Their travels after lunch took them up to the Old Library, with its mediaeval stonework, and its secretive signature on the window cills. On the way back down the path, Rupert pointed up to the iron guttering. Perched in a line were five ravens. The ravens were holding a sign under their claws which read *Keith's Mobile Mechanics- you'd be Raven mad not to try us*… The cameraman took out his equipment and caught the scene on film, then walked off shaking his head in disbelief.

'What was all that about then Keith?' asked one of the Ravens.

'I'll tell you what that was about, My Son…Advertising- Free Advertising…'

Eventually, the filming was concluded. The crew packed up their gear in the van, and with Lorenzo desperately craning his neck out of the back seat for a last glimpse of Dr Chambers, left the Academy. When they got back to the BBC, there were some intense discussions. Questions were asked. Difficult questions.

After heated talks had finished, the film team had to edit out a list of non-usable shots, these included:

A woman in a beret playing the accordion on the lawn.

Two tap-dancing Iron Age persons in animal skins.

A Sabre-tooth Tiger chasing a ball of wool.

A Middle-aged Lady in a pink leotard doing press-ups in the quad.

A singing Dinner Lady.

A Master in a biker's jacket who made an unbroadcastable gesture.

A boy who wandered past completely nude- apart from a flat cap.

A masked woman in lingerie who was clearly visible at the Boarding House window.

A Dodo which was wandering around carrying a packet of Custard Cream biscuits.

And there were others....

Chapter Thirty-Three:

The Reverend opened his eyes just enough to peer over at his alarm clock. Good Grief! only 3:25am. Something had woken him, and rendered him instantly alert. He listened for any strange sounds, but heard only the quiet concerto played by a house trying to sleep. His gaze fell onto the snow-globe which he had put on his bedside table, it had been a present from his Mother. He smiled sleepily as he watched the tiny flakes falling like…well, like snow. He turned his head back and gazed at the ceiling. The snowman inside the globe reminded him of when he was a b- hang on…he swept his head around and looked at the globe again, as he fumbled for the bedside light switch. He shielded his eyes as the light came on, then glanced over again at the table. The snow was still drifting down…. the Snowman was gone.

'A trick of the light…' he thought, and laughed to himself. There was a polite cough from the end of his bed. Felchingham shot up into a sitting position and stared. The Snowman at the foot of his bed was well over six feet tall, with pieces of coal for buttons, a battered trilby hat, and the obligatory carrot for a nose. It leaned over the end of the bed and peered at him with unblinking coal eyes. 'Get your slippers on Gerald Felchingham…' it said, 'I have something that you need to see…' Trancelike, the Rev did as he was instructed. The Snowman walked over and opened the door, gesturing for him to exit. 'Are we going to walk?' said the trembling voice of the Rev. 'Of course we are you little Prat - what did you think that we were going to do - fly?'.

They walked downstairs and out of the front door. It was snowing heavily. 'Bloody weather…' muttered the Snowman. There was a sudden swirl of white flakes, and the Rev found himself outside a dark house. He got a shove on the shoulder from the Snowman, and so he stepped forward and looked in through the window. There was no Christmas tree, no twinkling Fairy Lights, and no decorations to banish the dismal setting to the room. In front of a meagre open fire, a tall, thin man was measuring the size of the lumps of coal. He saw a young boy in short trousers sitting by the fire. He was attempting to look cheerful, and asked his Father 'What time will Father Christmas be coming Papa?' The man had scolded his son- telling him that Christmas was 'all about the birth of Christ, and not about material things'. He told the boy that his thoughts should be confined to Church, which they would attend all day tomorrow. The Rev then flashed back to his own boyhood, where his Father had been so severe, and he had sat for hours on his own playing draughts in the draught…His Father had insisted that he try to be so Holy that he had no fr - hey! Hang on a minute…that boy looks like me!! He turned away from the window, and the Snowman was walking off. The Rev ran to catch up with him.

He woke up with a jolt. That had been a scary dream. No more cheese before bedtime for him in future.

He awoke again with something wet slapping him across the face. It was a snow slap from the snow hand of the Snowman. 'Oy - Mush…' said the Snowman 'Follow me…'

They walked out of the house as before. Another gust of wind blew a blizzard into their faces. When the Rev had wiped his eyes clear of snow, he saw that they were in front of a familiar window. He stared in at the Staff Lounge at the Academy. There were tables groaning under the weight of buffet food, bright decorations, and bottles of all descriptions and sizes stood on a table at the end of the room. He seemed to float through the wall into the room. 'Bloody show-off…' said the Snowman, himself using the door. The Rev walked around the table set for the Staff Party. There was no place card with his name on it. Even his rams-skull coat peg was missing from its place on the wall. At the other end of the lounge, the Staff were all hugging each other, exchanging gifts, and even kissing under the mistletoe. He turned away. Without warning, he found himself on the Old Block corridor - outside his classroom. Only it wasn't his classroom: on the door was a sign which read "Yoga and Meditation Suite - please enter and be Enlightened". He heard distant voices saying, 'Oh yes…things really took a happier turn when they sacked the Divinity Teacher - there was always something a bit "dodgy" about him, if you ask me…'

He shot up in bed, now sweating in fear - what had he just dreamed? After calming his frayed nerves with a glass of water, he laid his head down again.

'OY…C'MON PILLOCK!!!' shouted the voice of the Snowman 'I'll have bloody well melted by the time you've got your act together…' This time, they only walked as far as his front door, where the Snowman spun him around to face back into his flat. Through the open door, the Rev could see a young couple being shown around the flat by an older woman - presumably an Estate Agent. The Snowman prodded him forward, and he walked nearer to the three people, and heard their conversation… 'Well yes indeed, it really is a spacious flat, but it would seem that no-one ever wants to live in it. I have had complaints that people can sense the presence of a great amount of evil here'. The young woman spoke: 'I see what you mean, I mean to say - the previous tenant must have been in an awful hurry to leave: and why did they take all of the fittings? All they left here was one solitary knob…' (The Rev thought that he heard another voice at this point, a sort of throaty chuckle…).

'Oh My God…do people really think I'm that Bad?' wailed the Rev.

'Dunno - probably…anyway, sod off back to bed. I'm off, it's freezin' standin' in this hallway' said the Snowman. 'Buy some double-glazing, you tight bastard.' With that he was gone.

Felchingham's eyes shot open. He scrambled for his alarm clock and hit the button to illuminate the dial - which was pointless, as it was already light…idiot. He ran to his front window, and called out to an old man who was passing 'I say!!...You there!!...yes you, old man…can you tell me what day it is?'

'Yers… It's Thursday – You Knob!!'.

Ahh…. sweet reality had returned.

Merry had arrived at, and been installed in, Nicky's house. There had been the usual amount of fuss from Mum. When an hour had passed, and Auntie had not got his friend in a headlock, he assumed that all was well. It would have been even better if Mum had not insisted in awarding pride of place to all things Merry. Nicky had been relegated to the "put up" bed in his room, while his friend got the comfy mattress. Mum had disappeared up to the village shops when Merry had told her that he was Vegetarian, and returned with a variety of products that might well have been invented by Uncle Joe (they weren't - just in case you were worrying...). Dave the Chicken had heard Merry's meat-free declaration, and had immediately hopped up onto his lap, where he now sat clucking happily, and preening his traitorous feathers.

The snow was still falling outside, and had moulded the landscape into gentle white curves. 'I hope that the roads will be clear enough for us to get to your Concert tomorrow' Mum had said, gazing out at the wasteland of white. Nicky went over to the desk and took out the music that he had been given to learn for "the show". He would be playing the snare drum and tympani in the Orchestra, but mercifully not at the same time. Mr Newhouse had pointed out that he wanted to see some real effort put into the performance, so Nicky made his way to his now shared bedroom, and practiced a few "moves" that would show his dedication.

Across the snow-covered fields and out toward the edge of the town, the children were squealing with delight at the sight of a seven-foot tall Santa, who had turned up at the Children's Home and was now liberally handing out gifts. One small girl who had leapt onto his knee had to be removed by the laughing Staff, as she had held the red-clothed figure in a vice-like grip for a full ten minutes. The grumpy eleven-year-old who "didn't believe in Father Christmas" suddenly had a change of heart when the beard that he tried to pull off proved to be very real indeed! Santa ended the visit with a bellowing cry of 'Now you be good Children, and a Merry Christmas!!!' His 'HO HO HO!!!' had very nearly broken the windows. Santa returned to the van which was waiting down the driveway. 'I like to be your Santa - he makes smiles…' boomed Bernie. The half-spectacles which Figg had provided had completed the transformation. 'Well done Santa!!' said Swall 'Now tonight we will call in on the Old Folk, and bring them all a little slice of magic too'.

Mrs Finucane and her Cleaning team stood at the door of the Physics lab ante-room and stared in disbelief. They could not see into the room through the narrow glass side panels. Even the oscillations of the Vortex were completely hidden from view.

Earlier in the day, the BBC cameraman had been standing rather close to the Vortex. His colleague had asked him what indoor "shots" he was looking to take. Unaware of the idiosyncrasies of the Portal, the man had answered 'Just a few quick ones - what I really need is a pee…'

The room was now packed up from floor to ceiling with small green vegetables.

Be careful what you wish for…

Chapter Thirty-Four:

As part of the extra-curricular activities which the boys undertook as part of a project to benefit the local community, was the scheme to visit the elderly residents of the nearby Care Home known as "The Glades". All of the boys who took part in these visits thoroughly enjoyed the company of the residents. It would be true to say that the building was packed to the rafters with more fun-loving eccentric Senior Citizens than you could possibly hope to shake a stick at. You might also want to hope that they did not shake their sticks in your particular direction. The Glades abounded with ex-Servicemen and Ladies, who had fought in battles around the world, and were now determined to fight against any suggestion that they be consigned to a life which consisted of television, luke-warm tea, and soggy biscuits. Some of the Masters from the Academy had joined the boys in their visits, with predictably unsettling results. Doctor Matthews for example, had been most insistent that what the ladies and gentlemen really needed to liven up their evenings at the Glades was a regular Cocktail Night. He had taken to turning up in his finest "Bartenders Kit", and dispensing vast quantities of dangerous-looking liquid medication to the residents, which was received and swallowed with much greater enthusiasm than any of the substances handed out by the Nurses. This had led to a great deal of high jinks, and equally low jinks for those suffering from back problems. Walking frames were thrust aside, several Ladies were severely surprised by the attentions of suddenly sprightly old men, and walking sticks were used as swords by laughing drunken "Musketeers". Things had finally come to a head when the Matron had firmly put a stop to the Wheelchair Jousting tournament which had taken place on the upper corridor. Mr Ellerby had spun off and out of the fire escape doors, and what had happened to Mr Bailey's rubber cap end could only be guessed at...

Mr Newhouse had taken great delight in helping the residents to form their own Heavy Metal band, and at the request of some of the more adventurous denizens of the Glades, had negotiated a hefty discount at the local tattoo parlour. Hyde-Jones had urged the people to look up the full meaning of the word "Adult" in the large-print dictionary. They did - and all agreed that it was not for them...

As an integral part of the "activity", each of the boys was allocated one of the Residents with which to form a friendship with. They all achieved this very quickly, and revelled in the company of the older people - who told them such interesting and sometimes quite gruesome stories. The boy who seemed to be most smitten with his newest friend was Jonef Kendy...

Kendy's allocated "Buddy" was a slightly-built Lady with a fierce bun of white hair. She had been introduced to the eager boy by one of the younger Carers, who wore a name tag with the "Y" in "Lucy" tip-exed out, and an "I" written in using a cheap felt pen.

"Ello now Dottie' she declared, 'I've brought a nice young man to come and talk to you - won't it be nice to have a good old chin-wag with someone for a change?' The Lady just sat and stared out of the dayroom window, out across the overgrown lawns, which like the residents, were showing all the signs of long-term neglect. The girl continued- 'Don't think that you have to stay and talk to 'er if you don't want to. She's 103 and she's deaf and almost blind too. She doesn't talk any more- 'asn't done for ages. She ain't got no family, and no-one visits 'er, but (she leaned over and raised her voice) SHE KEEPS SMILIN' AWAY, don't you Dottie.. .' The girl turned away and hurried out of the room, leaving the old Lady and Kendy quite alone. Kendy carefully walked around to face the woman, then bent down and gently took her hand in his. The hand was very thin, soft, and radiated loneliness from every pore. The boy stroked her hand whilst rummaging in his jacket pocket for his "crystal". He slowly withdrew the item, and after a check to ensure that they were still alone in the room, spoke to his new friend in hushed tones. 'Please do not be alarmed Madam - I assure you that I wish you no harm. I would very much like to talk to you if you will permit me - and I am sure that we will be friends'.

He made one or two rapid passes of his hand over the pebble-sized object, which he then placed in the open hand of the old Lady. Dimly at first, but with ever-increasing brightness, a beam of light issued forth from the crystal. It illuminated the face of the Lady, and she closed her eyes to shut out the intense light. When at last she opened her eyes again, she looked down at the crystal in her hand, and then into the face of Kendy. Her mouth opened in utter shock, and Kendy thought for a moment that she might be about to scream for help...Instead, her face lit up with a beaming smile, her eyes now cleared of the fog which had previously blighted her vision. She fixed the boy with a quizzical gaze...

'Are you...are you an Angel?' she hesitated.

'No Madam...My name is Jonef - and I'm a bit strange...' he answered.

The Lady put her finger to her lips as the girl re-entered the lounge bearing a cup of tea, which she placed on a table at the side of the Woman and boy - slopping a considerable amount of tea into the saucer in the process. "Ere's your tea Dottie - now you have a nice time with your visitor, won't you eh?' she said.

The Lady ignored the girl, and had returned to staring out of the window. 'It's such a shame, innit - poor old thing...' said the carer, before turning away and hurrying off again. There was silence for a few moments, and then the Lady whispered, 'Has that screeching moron gone now?' out of the corner of her mouth. Kendy confirmed that they were alone again.

When she spoke again, the Lady's voice was as gentle as a spring breeze through fallen leaves, but with a cut-glass aristocratic accent. 'Do come closer Young Sir...' she asked. She studied Kendy's face intently, as if fascinated by the sight of him. She took his chin in her hand, and turned it this way and that. 'You certainly do remind me of my Son George you know...' she told him. 'Does George come to visit you here?' asked Kendy. The woman looked sad and defeated for a moment - 'Oh no My Dear, Georgie passed away many years ago. He lived not far from here, but he and his family moved away, and it was such a very long way to come and visit me, but I quite understand... Yes, he moved away. I have had many, many friends here over the years, but they all seem to go away one by one. Now it's just me, and a load of young assistants who don't want to speak to us, or listen to us for that matter'.

'But you have surely made friends here?' asked Kendy.

'Well I hear voices, but I don't see too well - until now that is! They don't have much time for an old woman who cannot hear or see them, so I got used to not speaking, and sitting here enjoying my memories by myself' she answered.

'But the Staff do seem to be quite nice...' said the boy.

'Oh, they do seem to be jolly, but no-one takes the time to sit with me like you have today. I may be 103 years old, but that doesn't mean that I have stopped wanting human contact. Also, you may have noticed, the buggers insist on calling me "Our Dottie" She said.

'Is "Dottie" not an affectionate name?' asked Kendy.

'I'll tell you what it bloody well isn't - and that is my name!!' she scolded. 'My given name is Dorothea Harding'.

'You don't like "Dottie" then?' asked Kendy.

'My Dear...the very sound of that name gets right on my t-....nerves' declared the Lady.

Kendy held her hand, and they giggled together as Dorothea drank her weak tea with grace and elegance which would have shamed a Duchess.

'And whilst I may have impaired vision and hearing - there is absolutely nothing wrong with my sense of smell. I can tell you that one of those gels has only a passing interest in the matter of personal hygiene...' she declared. Kendy tried not to laugh.

'Why don't you tell me about yourself Madam...' asked Kendy.

'Young man - if you can perform miracles such as this, then you may certainly call me Dorothea...' she insisted. 'In a way, there is not much to tell, and in another way, there is far, far too much to remember. I often take my mind back to my childhood. Things seemed to be slower and much more gentle in those days. Nothing dashed past too quickly, at least, not so quickly that we didn't have time to look in wonder at things. Now it is *I* that have become slow, and time seems to race away from me. But oh yes! - I remember it all...'

'What were your Christmases like?' Kendy asked.

'Oh Bless you - Christmas was wonderful! When I was a girl, the whole house had the smell of Christmas puddings and pine needles, as well as Daddy and his Mulled wine. There was the huge tree in the living room, hung with baubles like jewels from the treasure of a foreign King, and we made brightly-coloured decorations out of strips of gummed paper. Daddy would turn off the lights, switch on the fairy lights in the tree, and lift me up high whilst I placed the star on the very top. There were chestnuts and crackers, and sugar mice and Carol Singers - and Snow!! Lots and lots of snow'.

Her voice once again became a mere whisper, and Kendy noticed a single tear on her cheek, as the wonderful images played out once more in her mind. He took out his clean handkerchief and wiped the tear away, as she turned to face him with the smile of a child.

'What would you like for Christmas, Dorothea?' he asked her, returning the smile.

'My Dear - there is nothing that I want or need, especially when you get to the age at which I find myself, unless of course you have some magical way of making me a young girl again?' she replied wistfully. There was more hope in her piercing blue eyes than Kendy felt able to cope with. Of course, there was something which he could do - but putting it into practice would lead to serious questions and consequences, and he knew with certainty that she would not be physically strong enough to withstand the rigours of a journey - however swift it might be. The crystal also told him that there was no point putting her through any such experience. He took what he thought was a cowards' way out, and asked:

'Well as your new Best Friend, Madam Dorothea, I really must get you a special Christmas gift. If you could have anything, anything at all, what special thing would it be?'

The Lady turned back to look out of the window. 'When I was a young girl...' she hesitated, 'Daddy gave me the most gorgeous Victorian doll for Christmas. She was dressed in satin and lace, and had the most beautiful face - made out of porcelain. I called her "Emily", and she and I would play all day up in the nursery, or out in the garden when it was fine. She was the very last gift that Daddy gave me before he went away to fight in the war. When he didn't come home after the fighting, Mummy cried a lot, so I told Emily that we both had to be big brave girls and help our Mummy to run the house. During the war I was evacuated out to the country. I don't know how, but I managed to lose Emily on the train somewhere. I cried for days. I didn't care about the bombs, I just wanted Emily back...'

'Well you never know...' said Kendy, 'Just occasionally, Santa likes to slip in a Christmas miracle for those boys and girls who have been very, very good'.

Dorothea patted his hand and told him 'I think that you might be my special Christmas gift yourself, Jonef. Talking to you today has shone a light into my soul again, and I feel wonderful. I shall miss you when you leave'.

'Well I shall soon be back...' said Kendy, 'and in the meantime, just you keep wishing, Young Lady...'

He kissed his new friend goodbye for now, and headed back to the Academy. All the time he was walking, his mind was formulating a plan to obtain a Christmas surprise for Dorothea. He made his way stealthily into the Physics laboratory, by-passing the expensive double security system by means of a plastic spoon, and tiptoed into the laboratory annexe. For what he needed to do, there was only one tool for the job. He hastily made some detailed calculations, and took out the Victorian silver hunter pocket watch from its display case on the wall. Professor Strangler would surely not mind if he "borrowed" the watch for a while? He had previously noted that Stig and his Iron-age companion seemed to have no difficulty in making regular return trips through the vortex. Since they invariably carried a small flint axe, the vortex presumably knew in which time period to deposit them, so he would use the watch as a "travel pass" to gain access to the precise period where he could obtain what he needed. That was the theory. He clutched the watch tightly. He gulped, apologised to his Father for committing an act of trespass, and stepped through the vortex...

Kendy stepped back through the actinic blue light circle which formed the portal of the vortex. He swiftly brushed the snow from his shoulders, and set his prize down on the nearest table. Opening the display cabinet on the wall, he carefully replaced the pocket watch and closed the case door, wiping it clean of any tell-tale fingerprints. He picked up his package and made his way silently to his locker in the corridor, where he leaned back on the closed door with a smile of satisfaction on his face. He was sorry that he had not been able to achieve his ultimate objective - but maybe, just maybe a small act would be enough...

He called his Parents from the ancient payphone outside the Staff lounge, and informed them that he would be a little late home. Replacing the receiver when the call had finished, Kendy picked up the package and walked out of the Academy: he knew that there was no need to rush. Arriving at The Glades, he let himself in via a side door, and made his way down the corridor to the immaculately-kept room where Dorothea lived, sat, and dreamed.

A short time later, he closed the door silently behind him.

After lessons had finished for the day, the boys were all eager to go back up to The Glades and visit their new friends again. The conversations between them were full of the stories which the Residents had told them - about ships, beach landings, lucky escapes and Spitfires over the Channel. They arrived at the main doors as an excited crowd of fans, all eager to see how the old folk liked the Christmas decorations which they had helped to put up. Kendy stood at the back of the noisy throng of boys, a strangely calm expression upon his face.

'Come in, come in!!' announced the Matron 'Our guests will be really pleased to see you all'. The boys hurried into the main lounge, where they were greeted warmly by the residents. Nicky noticed that Kendy had made no attempt to go down the corridor to visit his friend Dorothea. 'Don't you want to go and say hello to Dottie?' he asked.

'No, not today.' answered Kendy 'She isn't here today'. At that moment, the assistant known as "Luci" came up to Kendy, and hugged him, with tears in her over-mascara-ed eyes. 'Oh I'm so sorry...' she stuttered 'And especially on her birthday - she would have been 104 today too...' The room fell silent. The Matron hurried over and explained to the boys that poor Mrs Dorothea Harding had passed away during the night. She did not explain every detail however, as there was something which she was unable to explain, or understand.

Dorothea Harding was found in her bed by the assistant who brought in the early morning tea. She lay on her pillows looking as if the years had simply fallen away from her. She had the most angelic smile on her face, both peaceful and beautiful.

Clutched tightly in her arms was a Victorian doll dressed in satin and lace, with a face of smooth porcelain. The name tag attached to the doll said "Emily"...

Chapter Thirty-Five:

The Church was surrounded by vans in a variety of handy BBC sizes. Out of these vehicles trailed hundreds of bundles of cables, which slithered their serpentine paths up and into the great Parish Church, some through the side entrances, and some via the massive West door. Various Technicians and Cameramen were standing around in groups, smoking surreptitious cigarettes, or sipping steaming coffee from paper cups in the snow. One or two of the crew were filming last-minute images of the winter picture-postcard scene, with the Church and its surrounding trees covered in snowy splendour.

In the Assembly Hall, the boys of St Onans had sung the Academy Anthem to welcome in the day- or more accurately, to frighten it into hiding. Dr Chambers had now finished his sombre speech containing all of the "Do's" and "Don'ts" that today demanded. His commands may have been paid a little more respect, had some wag not affixed a "Gents Toilet" sign onto the front of the lectern. The boys were all looking forward to the filming, and "normal" lessons had been suspended for the day. Chambers looked up over his spectacles, and said 'And I hope that ALL boys will afford our guests every courtesy. I shall severely punish any boy who I find interfering with the Camera Crew (there were guffaws from the assembled Staff). If you don't know what it does - then keep your hands off it!!'

'Yes Mum…!' said a voice at the back.

'We have an excellent Orchestra, and a superb Choir: I see no reason why today should not be a day that we will all remember for a very long time…' he said.

As his last word faded, the large doors at the back flew open, and a figure strode into the Assembly Hall. Boys parted like the Red Sea as the man walked purposefully through the crowd and up onto the stage…'Good Morning Gentlemen…' he announced.

Dr Goodwill had returned…

Mr Newhouse the Music Tutor was more than ready…For some time, he had been rehearsing the Choir for such an event. He called the choristers to the stage and formed them up in an arc. 'I would like to welcome the Head back to the Academy with a little "acapella" number which we have been practicing - so this is especially for you, Dr Goodwill…'

The choir performed a brilliant version of *Rocket Man…*

Captain Brayfield was of a completely differing opinion on the subject of the influence of television upon young minds. 'Damned Television is solely responsible for the degeneration in morals and standards of the younger generation- and Society in general!!' he ranted. 'I will attend this debacle as instructed - but as a protest against the immorality which is broadcast by this ungodly Medium! As far as I am concerned, I have no interest in television. For me – the only way is Ethics!!!'

In the Physics laboratory, Mrs Finucane had come up with a brilliant idea for getting rid of the plague of peas…She had opened the door carefully, out had spilled the little green veg. She carefully picked her way through to the desk near the Vortex. Standing on the painted footmarks, she placed a Christmas card at the side of the Portal and waited. The Vortex had picked up what she had requested - just as she had hoped. In the ante-room, and spilling out into the rest of the laboratory, were a herd of rather confused Reindeer. The herd spied the vast amount of free food suddenly made available to them, and in true Reindeer style, got stuck in…

As Mr Posta was packing his "normal" clothes, and unpacking his Police uniform and Traffic waterproofs ready for use, there had come a knock at his door. At the door stood a severe-looking gentleman, with two other besuited colleagues just behind him. The man introduced himself - 'Good day Sir…Am I addressing Mr Posta?'. The Police officer confirmed that indeed, he was himself, and verified the fact with a flash of his card. 'Very nice Sir - Tesco Clubcard member, I see…' said the man. 'My name is Bessler: and myself and my fellow Trustees comprise the Board of Auditors and Administrators for St Onans Academy. We are in receipt of the information which you sent to us recently, and we would request that you join with us later today, when we will be taking up the matter of certain "discrepancies" in the General Accounts, with the current Head Master - Gerald Goodwill. It may be beneficial to us both for you to attend in your Official capacity, if you perceive my meaning…'

Posta nodded in mute agreement. Panic began to set in…'But I'm not…' he began:

'Oh yes you are Mr Posta - indeed you are. You will be collected…'

I just bet I will…thought Posta - just like Butterflies. These buggers are probably professional Ninja Accountants. I will end up poisoned, and pinned to the wall. And they probably claim back the money spent on the pins as "Business Expenses" ...

Dr Matthews had laid out his two best suits and ties for inspection. He stood tieless in his crisp white shirt, and scratched his chin as he tried to make up his mind.

'Now then...' he mused 'Black or Brown... Black or Brown - should I choose the Black one or the Brown one?' He came to a decision...Yes, of course, that was it!! 'I'll have the Stout to start with - and then move on to the Real Ale...' he said happily.

Accepting the gift of a "real" Christmas tree had, in hindsight, been a mistake. Mum and Auntie had thought that it might be nice for a change, to have the gentle scent of pine in the living room, to blend with the homely aromas of the Festive Season. The tree had been delivered as promised, on time, and with a minimum of fuss. As Mum and Auntie cowered in the corner of the living room with Dave the Chicken hiding under the sofa, they were forced to question if it had been a wise decision to get the tree from Uncle Joe. He had happily delivered and installed the beautiful tree without any mention of the little "extra" that had come with it. The very fluffy and very irate squirrel that had emerged from the luxuriant boughs, was now swinging from the light fitting, having already sped around the walls like a Wall of Death motorcyclist, and done something completely unnecessary and unsanitary over the mistletoe...

Mr Newhouse was admiring the shine on his newly-polished cowboy boots. He and his good friend Roy Hyde-Jones had agreed to go along with the request made by Dr Chambers - and attend the Carol Concert in best black tie and evening dress suits. The Music Tutor had been told that the biker's jacket that he had worn at last year's concert was 'Wholly unsuitable and not in keeping with the theme of the event'. The jacket had "Born to Ride" emblazoned on the back. Matron had stated that she could see absolutely nothing wrong with that...So! this year, Newhouse had a new slogan on the back of the jacket. This one was totally in keeping with the Christmas Message. It now read... "Born to a Virgin".

The afternoon had been taken up with endless "run-throughs" and "re-takes", whilst the BBC crew shot some of the more difficult angles inside the Church. Albert Brooks had been particularly helpful, and had assisted the crew to move in all sorts of technical equipment. He had secretly moved in some of his own "extra" machinery, just to be helpful.

Afternoon had decided to clock off exhausted, and had handed over to Evening. All over the town, and out in the villages, the boys and Parents were preparing to flock down to the Church for the Carol Concert. For some, the snow-covered roads would prove to be an obstacle - and there would be quite a few pairs of "Wellies" being worn under designer dresses tonight. The quad was already full of the cars of parents, and the surrounding roads were beginning to resemble a car auction in Norway.

Boys and Prefects had been posted at the West door to welcome the arriving Congregation. As for the "Preferential Ticket" scheme: well, Auntie was having none of it. She arrived with Nicky's Mum at the door, and was greeted by a smiling, yet nervous Prefect. When asked to show her tickets, she had miraculously produced a couple of BBC passes, which she waved at the boy. They were ushered into a middle-row seat with respect.

'How did you get us these seats?' asked Mum.

'BBC passes…' answered Auntie. Mum thought for a moment -

'Wait a minute - what are you doing with BBC passes?'

'I'm a member…'

'Oh no you are not - when have you worked for the BBC?'

'Retired member - says it there in black and white…' said Auntie.

Mum took a closer look at the "passes". She gave Auntie a look…

'I told you - "Retired Member BBC", plain as anything.

'Yes, very plain, it couldn't be clearer - "Bottesford Bowls Club".

'Alright, alright…now shut up and pass the popcorn, will you…'

The Church was now full to capacity, with the Academy boys at the front, and the Parents and Guests at the rear (apart from two...who had very good "middle" seats). The Vicar of the Parish Church led in his usual choir, and was puzzled when there seemed to be three times as many choristers as normal. The Groundlings smiled, and eased themselves in between the members of the Church singers.

With a bright spotlight shining down on £8.65 worth of hairspray, the Lady Presenter introduced the Carol Concert and welcomed the audience. As Mr Newhouse at the organ fired up the mighty instrument, the first Carol of the evening began - 'Hark the Herald Angels Sing'. As the Congregation sang, the cameras panned around, giving the people the chance to mime unconvincingly. Even experienced Dentists would have considered some of the extreme mouth opening on show as unnatural.

At the rear of the Church, Dr Chambers had pulled aside Bell-Enderby the Art Master, and was berating him about the Nativity scenes which he had painted - which were displayed inside the Church entrance. His main target for anger seemed to be the portrait of the "Madonna and Child" in the foyer. 'What on earth possessed you Man!!!' said Chambers 'All we required was a classic portrait of Mary and her Baby'.

'Exactly what I painted...' said Bell-Enderby, with pride.

'But for goodness sake look at it - are you trying to turn us into a laughing stock?' Chambers raved at the man. 'Do you not think that the Virgin Mary seems to be rather - shall we say...rather too generously endowed in the Infant feeding department?'

'It is perfectly normal for the bodies of pregnant ladies to make adequate physiological adjustments to accommodate the dietary requirements of their new-borns...' replied the Art master. Chambers raised his voice- 'But Good Grief Man!!..I mean, the way you have depicted the poor Girl, she could probably breastfeed Bethlehem!!!'

The camera continued its sweep down the nave of the church, and seemed to linger in disbelief at one individual who had dressed formally - very formally. Captain Hercules Brayfield had been ordered not only to attend, but to ensure that he wore his best suit. He had obliged, and stood proudly at the end of the aisle in a highly polished suit of armour.

The snow was now falling again, covering the vehicles of even the late-comers. There was a thick covering over the saucer of Kendy's parents, who had managed to squeeze their ship into the corner of the quad.

In the Church, the congregation were singing 'Once in Royal David's City' to the best of their ability. The aerial crane camera swooped and dived above their heads, and unfortunately caught the red, angry complexion of Professor Richard Strangler. Next to him, his friend and colleague Darwin asked him 'Did you use the TRU unit on your head then?' 'Yes, I damn well did...' said Strangler.

'Well, if you don't mind me enquiring - what went wrong?'.

Strangler explained that he had "treated" his head with the TRU unit, in order to take his hair back to its thick Teenage state. The unit had worked a little too well - and taken his face back to the time when he had suffered from acute Teenage Acne…

Dr Matthews meanwhile, had sauntered through the drifting snow into the van where the "live feed" and editing was taking place. He stepped into the van, marvelling at the dozens of little screens which were showing every filmed angle of the concert. Greeting the technicians warmly, he produced two bottles of fine vintage whisky, grabbed some paper cups, and after pouring the entire team generous measures, conducted some urgent negotiations….

The massive Groundling choir had just finished singing a Carol written by Elder Jedekiah especially for the occasion. Their voices had blended like magic, with the sound of the Trebles falling on the ears like purest silver. The audience burst into thunderous and extended applause. They were thanked by the Lady Presenter, who then announced that the next Carol 'In the Deep Midwinter' was to be sung by one of the Academy's own Tutors - the Mathematics Master, Miles Bannister. He confidently took his place at the front of the altar, looking every inch a star for the night. The boys and Staff all held their breath. He gently brushed a speck of dust from the sleeve of his dark blue velvet jacket, and began…

As the music began quietly, his rich Baritone floated out and over the entranced crowd, his voice the only sound in the vast enclosure of the church. So perfect was his projection, that he hardly needed the thin microphone angled towards him. He softly ended the first verse, and paused as he waited for the choir behind him to come in. Gesturing with his arm, he let the music swell around him, then sang again... 'OH MY LORD - I THINK I'VE LEFT MY FRONT DOOR UNLOCKED!!!' rang out the shrill voice of Elsie Noakes, 'SORRY LOVEY…I'LL HAVE TO GO AND CHECK - YOU NEVER KNOW WHO'S ABOUT, DO YOU!!' The microphone caught every word. Bannister carried on, as if he had been expecting to be interrupted. When the Carol ended, he gave a deep bow. He remained in this position, whilst the same female voice was heard to say 'Ohhh – has he finished? that's a shame - an' I was going to do the harmonies too!'. Bannister straightened up, grinned sheepishly, and whilst the audience applauded in a "what was all that about?" way, exited by a side door.

Mr Newhouse was going to enjoy this…It was now the turn of the Academy Rock Band 'Funderthuck' to play for the crowd. They had written a new song. It was called "The Messiah is Born – Time for a Lock-In!!". The Presenter had looked apprehensively at the towering Marshall speaker stacks at the side of the altar. Dry ice was flowing from behind the drum kit, off the drum riser, and down the aisle toward the congregation. The Lady had introduced the band: 'Will you please welcome….' She got the name wrong - oops.

Chambers had to admit that despite the Presenter just having said what she said, the tune that the band had played was pretty catchy.

Roy Hyde-Jones then read part of *A Christmas Carol* by Charles Dickens. He was superb, and held the audience spellbound. He removed his top hat with a flourish, and took his seat to generous and well-deserved applause.

As Dr Goodwill sat amongst the Invited Guests and local Dignitaries, basking in the reflected glory of his Academy's achievements, Dr Matthews was sitting at the Head Master's desk, in the Head Master's study, with a large glass of the Head Master's finest Cognac - fully lit by drunken technicians, and about to make a "Party Political Broadcast" of his own…. He took a sip of the glorious amber fluid:

'Good Evening Ladies, Gentlemen and Viewers everywhere. May I wish each and every one of you a very, very Merry Christmas. I do hope that you will indulge me by allowing me to address you in this season of Good Will. Indeed, it is concerning Goodwill that I feel I must address you…For many years (far too many for me to wish to recall), this Academy has been held in the very highest esteem by those who wish to see the highest standards of education taught. It was the wish of the Founder that all boys, whatever their circumstance - be they rich or poor, should be able to come to this enclave and receive teachings which would enrich their lives.

I feel that (hic) this has not been the case in (burp) recent times. We find ourselves as Staff, under the governance of one who has sought to exclude those of a poorer background from attending this estab(hic)lishment. We slef…we flind…we find ourselves lorded over by a man who chooses to divert Academy funding into his own already swollen coffers (burp). This man seeks to open up a commercial enterprise within the wine cellars of the Academy - (sacrilege - if you ask me…) and put the profits directly into his own capacious trousers!!

Here is the evidence…(he held up files and computer print-outs to the camera). He now seeks to miss…to demist…to dismiss Staff - including myself, so that he may make savings, and appease the Trustees, whilst the education of the boys suffers. This man may, as investigations take their course, be proven to be involved in receiving the proceeds of criminal activity. He has fleeced the richer parents, and denied opportunities to the less financially buoyant. Whilst the Academy falls down around our beers…sorry- ears, he is planning to flee to Parts Foreign with his stolen loot, and that misguided Clapperdudgeon from the office next door!!

I say you two…to you (hic) Gerald Goodwill - you Sir…are a Fake, a Phoney, and a Mountebank of the first order!! I for one care (burp) deeply about my Boys - and this (fart) Academy. I may be rather an old fart (fart), but in my many years, I have at least learned the difference between Right and Wrong. I have placed signed affidavits with the (hic) relevant Authorities, and (burp) I shall not rest until (hic, burp, fart) the honour and standards of this glorious Academy are restored. Thank you all…and…and, can I have a refill please, Benny?

...and perhaps one of those tasty things with the chicken, lettuce and tomato, that comes curled up in a sort of pancake?'

'Okay Dr Matthews…That's a Wrap…'

Chapter Thirty-Six:

'Silent Night…Holy Night' sang the younger members of the Groundling choir: and the calm, sweet voices of the children washed over the Congregation, bringing many a tear to the eye. As the second verse began, the song of the choir swelled into a wave of comfort and tranquillity, which washed over the listeners, and drowned the soul happily in its gentle melody….

At the same time, Bell-Enderby the Art Master was eyeing the seat of the "crane" cameraman. Ever the thrill-seeker, what he really, really wanted was a good old go on that camera lift. To this end, he had sent the technician at the foot of the crane (who was operating the lifting and directional controls) back to the editing van on a pretence of being urgently required by the Director. He rubbed his hands in glee, and gripped the direct controls. Under his command, the arm of the hydraulic unit swung up, up and out over the crowd. He halted the lift under the massive chandelier, which hung from its ancient chains in the middle of the aisle, with its dozens of candles. He gently began to raise the cradle arm...The cameraman began to panic as he suddenly found himself about to disappear upwards into a forest of lighted wax, not daring to look down, as the edges of the chandelier came ever closer. The cradle dropped beneath him without warning, and in terror he grabbed the chandelier with both hands. The man realised that he was a little closer to Heaven than he felt comfortable with. He had no fear of heights - but were he to lose his tenuous grip on the chandelier…well, that hard stone church floor would be a bit of a bugger... Now swinging precariously above the heads of the congregation like a Festive Trapeze artist, his communications headset fell from his head. Directly beneath him, Mrs Doreen Draper (local Businesswoman, Florist and occasional shoplifter) suddenly and unexpectedly found herself in direct contact with the Programme Director…

'Swing left, drop forward and zoom…' came the voice in her ear. Assuming that she was receiving Divine Instructions, she complied. The audience around her were suddenly startled by a well-dressed member of the local Institute of Trade and Commerce spinning around, plunging forward over the pews, and then running up the row - causing much needed work for Mr Wellerby the Chiropodist in the process. The now camera-less man above had now climbed up into the chandelier, marooned in his lofty, but tastefully lit swinging prison.

As the camera arm returned to ground level, Bell-Enderby dived into the seat, and directed the first person that he could grab to take charge of the motion controls. The nearest person just happened to be Albert Brooks, who had just finished positioning a little feature of his own. As he swung the Art Master up and over the heads of the people, the Director in the Control Room was baffled as to why he was suddenly getting zoom-in close ups of so many Ladies' chests. As the camera panned from one ample cleavage to the next, he bit clean through his pen…

As Good King Wenceslas looked out, he saw Mrs Draper wheeling around the Church in front of the bemused onlookers, who assumed that it was some sort of "Performance Art" in action. 'Left and pan out!! Left and pan out!! Screamed the Director, as yet more close-up female frontage came into view on the screen of his monitor. By this time, Mrs Draper had gone out of the door, and was currently describing wide confused circles in the snow. The poor woman lost a shoe, in the snow which you could describe as deep - crisp even.

Now every so often, if we are extremely fortunate, we may be present at an event that will stay in our mind for ever. It could be some dramatic action or event, or yet our presence in the audience at a speech that is made by a Great Man…We remember, and say with pride 'I was there'. Here he comes now, tucking in his shirt as he proudly struts to his place in front of the lectern. See how he climbs the wooden steps, and places his notes on the great polished brass eagle which sits atop…He smiles, and takes a breath…

'Ooaaroight Moi Luvvers!!!'

'An' it came to pass long ago - many years afore King Alfred burned down his Cake Shop, and the Lady of the Lactose sent King Arthur Penflaggon to a banquet where he got his sword stuck when he was stoned…That wonderful things were 'appenin'.

See - there was this family in Council accommodation in the Holly Land. Joseph, who was the Dad, had just received a letter tellin' 'im that Ee 'ad to get over to the Big City and see some bloke called David- and renew 'is Tax Credits. Now then: as it 'appens, 'eem 'ad a Wife, an' 'er name was Mary. One noight, She'm getting' a visit from this 'ere Angel- whose name was Peter Gabriel. Ee says to 'er - Don't be getting' yerself in a state, 'cos I bring Ee Great Tidy and Joy!!. Word is that moi Boss, 'eem sendin' you a bun for yourn oven…He'm set up to be the Son of God see: and she said "Jesus!", and Peter Gabriel told 'er - 'That'll do noicely!'.

Meanwhoiles, the old King Heron 'ad seen a star in the East End - an' he's sendin' out some of 'is wisest old Geezers out to foind out what's 'appenin'. Says Ee... 'Oim 'earin' that this star moight be signifyin' the birth of a Messiah - an' I need to get a Handel on it'. Eem sends the Three Wide Men - Cuspid, Meldrew, an' Bigbazaar off on their travels.

Mary and Joseph 'ave pitched up at an Inn by now, even though Mary 'as been sat on her Ass the whole journey. Well see now, there weren't no rooms available, 'cos they 'and't pre-booked, an' it's always busy at Christmas - unlike my Uncle Denzil, who would 'ave fitted them in at "The Fisherman's Waders" no problem. They ends up 'avin' to go round the back - and she 'as to 'ave her baby unstable. Roight…the three Stooges turn up - an' they've only gone and brought presents!! They gives the baby gold, French incense and more.

About the same toime - there's these Shepherds countin' sheep up in the hills, cos insomnia had just been invented. Your Fella Peter Gabriel appears with his Gang and tells 'em - "Oy- You Lot…leg it to Bethlehem. You'll find a baby wrapped in waddlin' clothes - lyin' near the mangle". So they'm leavin' their sheep, and goes over to the unstable place where the baby is. He is lyin' there with the ox and ass, and Oi would assume, perhaps the odd goat thrown in free gratis. They'm tellin' Mary, "We was goin' to bring presents, but we see that you 'ave already been given a load of livestock - very sensible gifts, if you ask us".

The baby is sleepin' in Heavenly peace, until that is - some little kid with a drum turns up and wakes him up.

Oi just 'opes that the Shepherds didn't come back to an empty field, with one very fat wolf in the middle of it…

Then a Host appears, and introduces Peter Gabriel again, and he and all of his Angel mates sing "Glory be to God: Hose Hannah - she's the Highest: Peace on earth and Good Will to all men whoile you're at it!!" ….

Aall Roight M'Dears - thank yew and Goodnoight!!'.

When the congregation had finished listening open-mouthed, the applause was deafening. Hyde-Jones leaned over to the Lady Mayor, nudged her in the ribs, and said 'That's my Boy!!!'. In future Debating competitions, other Schools may have their own archers of insight, and snipers of irony, but no-one could prepare themselves for the New Clear Weaponry of Master William Trevill.

As the assembled throng were busy trying to catch a glimpse of three ships which had apparently come sailing in (no further details from the local Coastguard or Harbourmaster were available), Mrs Finucane was preparing…Albert Brooks was good to go.

The Director was now sitting back in his leather swivel armchair, and grinning the grin of one who has given up on trying to keep any control over events. Matthews had supplied him with a very large drink, which he had hurled down his throat - closely followed by some of its close family. His wonderful Festive programme seemed to be largely composed of figures in suits of armour, singers with split personalities, and endless zoomed-in views of ladies' bosoms. He had desperately switched cameras in an attempt to avoid the unwanted boob-fest. The shot panned across the row of upstanding citizens of the town. At the end of the row was a smiling boy who was wearing a Santa hat…only a Santa hat, at that.

Now there seemed to be something very wrong with his Presenter…

Due to the cold weather that prevailed, the Lady Presenter had with her a small cylinder of oxygen - which she was using at regular intervals to help with her asthma. Unseen by either the camera or the BBC security staff, some well-meaning individual had swapped her oxygen for another identical cylinder. Identical that is, except in one respect. The "replacement" cylinder contained Helium…

'And now Ladies and Gentlemen- let us raise our voices…' she began, in a high-pitched Chipmunk squeak that Walt Disney would have been proud of. She clamped her hand over her mouth, as if to prevent any further cartoonesque voice-overs from escaping. In the control van- the Director shrieked 'If she raises her bloody voice any higher - we'll get hate mail from Bats and Dolphins!!!'. Since her oxygen had been secreted near the end of the organ, the Presenter rounded angrily on Mr Newhouse, accusing him of switching cylinders. 'Just what do you think you have done to me?' she piped in fury. 'Don't you dare speak to me in that tone of voice Madam…' said Newhouse, as the choir behind him collapsed in fits of uncontrolled mirth.

Dr Goodwill had seen enough, he carefully levered himself up and out of his (well padded) seat in the front row of Dignitaries.

Walking as quickly as his old injury would allow, he made his way down the aisle. He never made it to the front. His progress was curtailed by Bell-Enderby, who was swung down on the crane arm by Albert Brooks, and whose feet caught under his armpits- as he was then lifted up swiftly toward the heavens. Down at floor level, Brooks handed over the controls to Dr Matthews, who just happened to be passing with glass in hand. He looked at the control panel, looked at the laughing man in the crane seat- with the other helpless fellow dangling over the congregation, and decided to do the decent thing. The decent thing in this case was to slam the crane cradle into "full right" position, and lock the motor drive. The camera crane arm now began to pick up speed as it rotated - Dr Goodwill being flung out sideways as centrifugal forces kicked in.

By now, the audience of boys were in hysterics, apart from Davis, who was passing out mince pies to all and sundry at 50p a go, and himself munching on a chicken leg.

The Cameraman held prisoner in the chandelier was seriously considering his chances of being able to accurately time a leap from his current perch onto the camera crane arm as it passed beneath him. As the crane spun on yet another pass, one of Goodwill's expensive brogues had come off and struck Madame full in the face. The band, choir and orchestra now got themselves into position for the carols which would be the "finale" of the concert. Above their heads, the cameraman, his hands now covered in a liberal helping of candle wax, slipped and caught his ding-dong merrily on high...

As the massed voices and instruments fired up, there was not much chance of even God being able to give the Merry Gentlemen any rest. The herd of Reindeer that had previously dined so very well and unreservedly on the mountain of peas, had been led and directed by Mrs Finucane (now Agent J-Cloth in full "attack" mode) up to, and now into the Church. They trotted up the aisle in pairs, bellowing occasionally and getting the odd antler entwined in some of the more expensive fur coats.

At the front, one Reindeer had turned to his friend and remarked - 'Hey, Rudy...Your nose looks very sore Mate - is it okay?'.

Now the combination of fresh vegetable material in quantity, plus the unpredictable digestive routines of a Reindeer, are not what we might call easy partners. It would certainly not be at all easy to clean that Church carpet after nature had taken its course. The more liquid of Reindeer deposits was currently taking its course back down the aisle, where the feet of the congregation were performing a frantic tap-dance in order to avoid it. Albert Brooks turned on the large wind machine at the back, whilst tipping thousands of pieces of shredded paper into the front of the fan from a cardboard box. The effect was stunning - Goodwill, still orbiting on the end of the crane arm like a captive satellite, had been blinded by a sudden flurry of "snow", and lost his grip on the feet of Bell-Enderby. He had flown in a graceful arc over the Lady Mayor, landing on Gideon Rundell the Latin Tutor and stunning him. No comfort or joy for he, I feel.

The Director had long since given up. He now sat back on the long leather sofa in the van, with a large drink in one hand, and his other hand full of Angie the Work Experience Trainee, who was sitting on his knee and gaining experience that would probably never be featured on any future CV.

The whole Church went into a rousing version of 'O Come All Ye Faithful'. This was the highlight of the Carol Concert as far as Nicky was concerned, as he and two of his friends were at the front of the Orchestra- playing the snare drums. He stood and played proudly, hoping beyond hope that Mum and Auntie could both see him. When he was between beats or rolls, he twirled his drumsticks high above his head: pure "showing off" he knew - but he didn't care, and he got a nod and a wink of encouragement from Mr Newhouse the Conductor. They came to the last verse 'Sing Choirs of Angels…', and to Nicky's ears, it sounded as if they had indeed joined in. The mighty crescendo thundered around the vaulted space of the Church, and all of the boys suddenly felt twelve feet tall…

It was at this point that Albert Brooks let loose with the automatic bowling machine which he had sneaked in, all the way down from the sports pavilion. Whilst he aimed, Agent J-Cloth fed the machine with snowballs which they had prepared earlier. He had lined it up so that he would get a good range of bombardment onto both the Staff and the snottier members of the Business Community. As the last chorus with its beautiful descant began, Brooks let the machine do its worst. Snowballs began to rain down on the selected members of the crowd, with wet and deadly accuracy. Matthews kept up the seasonal effect with a constant blizzard of fake snow.

High on the crane, Mr Bell-Enderby had stopped his cries of 'Wheeeeee!!' as the arm rotated. He had found the "remote" box, and had stopped the crane so that he could focus in on what looked like a very promising pair of 44 Double-D's in row twelve. Matron had joined the choir in front of the altar, wearing what Mr Newhouse would have described as 'The skimpiest Santa outfit that I have ever encountered' (what he actually said was later reported as 'Hnuurrr…Fnnarrr…Yaarrghhh!!'). As she raised her arms in celebration of the last chord…several boys came over all unnecessary, a loud 'Bonngg!' was heard from the lower armour of Captain Brayfield, and the snow on the head of Mr Chisholm the Butcher completely melted in a small cloud of steam…

Mr Newhouse raised his arms, giving a windmill twirl before signalling the last note. The last of the snowballs had fallen. Nicky hurled his drum sticks into the crowd. The fake snow fell gently as the Reindeer nibbled the edge of several Sunday Best jackets, and the boys cheered loudly.

Hyde-Jones snatched up the Presenter's microphone and declared…. 'And so from all of the Boys and Staff here at St Onans Academy - may I thank you for joining us here on this very special occasion, and I wish each and every one of you a Very Merry Christmas…'.

'And Cut!!' slurred the Director, before collapsing over the arm of the sofa.

Chapter Thirty-Seven:

Whilst there was a rumour across the Media that the viewing figures for the Christmas edition of 'Songs of Praise' had never been higher, the mass adulation for the concert from St Onans Academy was not shared by everyone. It had only been the merest scintilla of elapsed time before the letters of complaint had flooded in. These had been swiftly followed by texts and e-mails, and telephone calls. And a message sent by pigeon. Which was never seen again, sadly. It would also appear that there had been a surprising number of requests for signed photographs of, and contact details for, the Matron.

There is a point where the Venn diagrammatic circles of incandescent rage, anger, fury, incomprehension, and the sudden deflation of an inflatable medical cushion all intersect. Dr Goodwill stood within this small domain.

The Christmas Carol Concert traditionally denoted the "winding down" of the Academy for the Festive holiday. Goodwill was so wound up, that he was actually humming quietly…He knew that there was in actual fact very little that he could do. The event had now passed into history. The fact that the whole debacle had occurred on his watch was the bit that was causing him to grind his teeth. This had happened at the very point where he had hoped to put his secret plans into action- and he had hoped to do so without drawing attention to himself or the Academy until he was a very, very long way away. He would enact the usual farce of venting his anger on the Staff, blunting the metaphorical HB pencil of his ire on them: in short, it would end up being utterly pointless. These were a bunch of Social Maladjusts who thought that the Bayeux Tapestry was probably an attempt by the French to recreate Spanish bar food…

Like the Sewage worker who toiled beneath the busy streets, searching for that lost diamond ring…he supposed that he had no alternative but to go through the motions.

Into the Staffroom they came. It was the usual parade of Freak Show Academia as far as Goodwill was concerned. They had been of some limited use to him from time to time, as he had attempted to raise the profile of the Academy within educational circles (and more to the point - raise the level of his clandestine bank accounts from the extra fees charged), but now they were more akin to crop circles, diverting to look at for a while, but altogether mysterious - and probably created by some weirdo. He could not wait to let go of the reins, and for all he cared, the wildly meandering stagecoach that was St Onans could drive straight over the cliff edge…

He stared with barely-hidden contempt at the assembled Staff. Mr Thwaite (or whatever the strange man was calling himself this week) stood balancing on a pair of impossibly high stiletto heels. Madame Dreadfell and Gideon Rundell both had the ridiculous haughty look of someone who thought themselves to be above reproach. Mr Newhouse the Music Tutor looked hung over, and seemed to have slept under something strange. Matron was as usual, quite improperly dressed, and looked as if she had slept on something comfortable - quite possibly a Music Tutor. That old dipsomaniac Matthews was missing, but no doubt would be propping up the bar of the "Five Crowns" enjoying his liquid breakfast. The usual faces, the usual excuses, and the same old game of shifting the blame onto the nearest colleague. Well not today - today would be very, very different. Oh yes indeed.

'I am glad to see that almost all of you have made it through the snow to be here today' he began. 'I am sure that you are all eager to get away for the Christmas Holiday, as I can assure you am I – therefore I shall get straight to the heart of the matter. Leaving aside the farce of last night's Carol Concert, let us move on to the subject of the rationalization of the Staff salary budget as pertains to this Academy. I have undertaken a lengthy and in-depth study of all expenditure. Following my investigations, I can announce that there will be a significant truncation in Staff salary costs. Cuts will be made in the following departments…' (the Masters held their breath, here we go…) 'In no particular order…Art- all extra classes will cease. There will be no more "out of school" trips to visit galleries and museums. Biology - the post of Laboratory Assistant will be cut: there will be further cuts in equipment and research material…'

'What about dissection - will that be cut?' asked Darwin.

Goodwill chose to ignore him. 'Chemistry - lab material stocks will be assessed and sold off as required. No new materials are to be ordered. English - there will be no more drama sessions out of hours, and all theatre trips and visits will cease. Music - the ridiculous funding of a "Rock Band" will end with immediate effect. Valuable instruments will be auctioned off, and private tuition will only take place if accompanied by the appropriate hourly fee. Physics - the massive and costly drain on our limited electricity resources called the "Portex", or

"Vortal", or whatever the damned thing is, will be dismantled immediately. There will be no further funds for "special projects" either. French - the Summer trips to our "twin" Academy in the South of France will cease. The student exchange programme will be closed down. History - the post of Assistant Tutor will be cut. There will also be no "Special Working Clothing" allowance paid in future. It is my plan to rent out our Sports Grounds to neighbouring schools, and the post of Grounds Keeper will be terminated. ('He'll be back…') said a voice at the rear. 'Meals and Catering will be put out to tender, which will release the entire current Kitchen Staff. Cleaning too, will be subject to outside bidding - and I am dispensing with our present Cleaning team. The present History Tutor Dr Matthews will be retired, and the rest of the remaining Staff will undertake "Career Reviews" on a bi-annual basis. Anyone not deemed to be performing adequately in their role will be subject to dismissal. There will also be other significant changes…'

'Yes - Indeed there will!!' said the voice of Mr Bessler from the Venerable Board of Trustees, who had entered the room unnoticed as Goodwill had spoken.

The immaculately-dressed man edged his way through the throng of shocked Masters, causing Mr Thwaite to plummet from his heels and land unceremoniously in a chair.

'My sincere apologies for the interruption, Ladies and Gentlemen. I am here today under the direct instruction of the Board of Trustees. I am sad to say that We have recently been privy to certain information, passed to us by an obviously concerned individual, that has brought to light certain "anomalies" of a delicate financial nature. I am here to clarify the matters, and to make certain changes myself.'

'The Staff should leave, I think, Mr Bessler…' said Goodwill.

'No - I think not Sir. Having heard the speech which you just delivered, I think that it is vital that all members of the Faculty hear what I have to say, especially in the light of what I have to say myself.' He smiled at the assembled Staff. 'Do please take a seat one and all…' he purred. He crossed to the expensive leather armchair of Gideon Rundell, and smiled at him until he vacated the seat. He sat down, saying 'You are most kind...' The overall impression was that this man was a smiling tiger. Who hadn't had breakfast yet.

He placed a smart briefcase on his lap, and flicked open the latches - causing Goodwill and several of the Masters to jump. Mr Bessler took out several serious-looking sheets of paper from the case, as well as some computer discs. There was an odd tap at the door, but luckily, all that it needed was a new washer.

'If I may begin, Dr Goodwill…could you please be so good as to explain the link between the Academy and "Goodwill Offshore Holdings Ltd" - a concern which is registered in, let me see…ah yes – the Isle of Jersey'.

'That is merely my private company, which I set up to hold my personal Pension funds for my retirement…' stated Goodwill, with a dismissive wave of his hands.

'Ah yes, I see…personal and private…' said Bessler. 'Could you explain then, why significant amounts of funds from the Academy would appear to have been diverted into this "personal and private" account of Yours?'

The Staff all turned to stare at Goodwill.

'Where monies have been paid to the Academy, I have often found it much quicker to have the funds cleared through my personal account, and then sent on to the Academy bank' Goodwill quickly stated. There was a pause, and the Staff sensed that an entertaining reply from Mr Bessler was on its way…

'Quicker to clear…I see.' He said. Goodwill smiled at him.

'So it is just the matter of the funds not actually finding their way back to the Academy- and of course you keeping any interest which may have accrued, that we have to consider here – is that correct?' Goodwill's smile vanished.

'And may I possibly ask you to explain as to why a similar Holding Company would appear to exist located in the Cayman Islands- by the title of "Amity Securities Ltd?"

'I own a villa there…' said Goodwill.

'The Amity Villa Horror…' said Mr Newhouse, in a loud whisper.

Goodwill reddened, and continued… 'Well...erm, I do have to have an account there to pay for the running costs of the villa and other sundries, you see…'

'Oh indeed, I do see…' said Bessler, 'It must be such a worry for you to have to maintain the upkeep of the property. There must be rather a lot of "sundries" to be paid for - as I notice that that you have over $2,000,000 American in the account…'.

The Staff all turned back to look at Goodwill. This was fun! And it was cheaper than a seat at Wimbledon (which Goodwill could have afforded by the sound of it). The Head Master's face was now as white as a Tennis-player's best shirt.

'I also note that regular payments are received by you from a rather mysterious account named "FSF" or some such' said Bessler.

'I have absolutely no idea who that might be!!' stated Goodwill, now panicking.

'How wonderful then, to be the beneficiary of the generosity of complete Strangers…' replied the unruffled Trustee. His unflappable calm was now beginning to disturb Goodwill, who was mentally calculating his chances of a clean getaway via one of the large windows.

'My attention is also drawn to this document here…' said Bessler, proffering another sheet of paper. 'This is a document by dint of contract between the Academy and Granchester Public Museum. The details therein pertain to the promise that over the Academic Year, any artefacts or antiquities recovered by the Archaeological Society will be offered over to the Museum for public display. Could you tell me the exact number of items - particularly gold, that have been donated to them?' Goodwill mumbled something incoherent.

'Sorry - didn't catch that Dr Goodwill…well, not to worry, as I have the exact numbers here. The total items given over for display over the past two Academic Years has been…let me see…got it right here…ah yes, four. I assume that you have a perfectly logical explanation for this?'

'It's not really a contract, it's more of a "wish list"…' said Goodwill.

'In strictly Legal and Contractual Terms Headmaster - I expect that you're wishing that you hadn't signed it clearly at the bottom then…' declared Bessler.

'I have done nothing wrong!!' squeaked Goodwill, 'My conscience is clear!!'.

'So is water Dr Goodwill, and yet so many unfortunate people seem to drown themselves in it…' said Bessler.

'I am making cuts and savings that will ensure the financial future of the Academy!!' declared Goodwill, rising from his seat.

'Which leads me conveniently on to my next point, Headmaster - do please resume your seat' said Bessler impassively. 'Following these disclosures, we the Board of Trustees have been regrettably forced to re-evaluate the actions and financial activity of the current Head of this Academy. We find that not only is there acute financial mismanagement, but that there have been determined attempts by yourself to prevent exposure of the facts. We are well aware of the draconian cuts which you plan to make, and find them both unacceptable and a threat to the efficiency of St Onans. We are forced to conclude that had these matters not come to light, then there would only have been one significant beneficiary of all of the monies saved, would you care to hazard a guess as to whom?' asked the Trustee.

Goodwill sat in silence, not daring to look left or right. His face was now a glowing red - having been heated by the fires of all the bridges which he had burned...

Matthews entered the room... 'He means that if we hadn't cottoned on to your crooked schemes - you would have trousered the lot, you thieving, bent old bastard!!!'

(It might be worth mentioning at this point, that before the meeting had started, Agent J-Cloth had turned on her radio transmitter. Brooks had ensured that every spoken word was being transmitted throughout the Academy via the classroom speaker system. Boys stood transfixed in classrooms and corridors as the drama played out over the airways. A large and angry group of them were now congregated outside the Staff room).

Goodwill knew that he was backed into a corner, and therefore, decided that the only course of action was to tell the absolute truth...

'It was Piggott!!! It was all her idea to stick the money away. She said that she thought that I was not paid enough - and that the Academy owed me...She did all of the computing, and the banking, so it's not my fault...I didn't know what she was doing!!' he shouted out.

Goodwill now risked a look around the room at the Staff. It was clearly apparent by the looks on their faces that those that didn't want to kill him, wanted to do something extremely unpleasant to him with a variety of kitchen utensils. He had every reason to be worried - as Betty Bradley had brought some with her...

Matthews approached the Headmaster, and leaned over so that they were almost nose-to-nose. 'I realise that you are a little busy at the moment Head, but I wish to introduce you to a very good friend of mine...'

'What do you mean, you drunken old fool?' sneered Goodwill.

'Allow me to introduce myself...' said a man who appeared from behind Dr Matthews.

‘I am Detective Sergeant Michael Posta of the Granchester and County Police…’.

Chapter Thirty- Eight:

Mike Posta stepped forward and flashed his Warrant Card at the astounded Dr Goodwill. Behind the Officer, Goodwill could see two more strangers who also had a "Policey" sort of look to them. As he stared at them, he knew that the Serves You Right Fairy had waved her magic wand and turned his cosy little world into poo. The other officer, in an expensive coat, but with cheap teeth, spoke to Posta as if they were alone in the room:

'So what the hell is all this about Posta? Why have you dragged me all the way back here again? I had expected to see some melted gold laying around the place as you promised - and now you tell me that all you have is an old Geezer fiddling the books?'

Matthews placed a hand on the man's shoulder, and a glass of scotch in his other hand.

'What I think you are failing to realise, is that this Officer, acting at all times under deep cover, and with the utmost professionalism and skill, has single-handedly taken it upon himself to expose the foul deeds being perpetrated by our so-called Head Master. Not only do these crimes - for that is what they clearly are, owe their resolution to the hard work and diligence of this man: but he has without aid gathered evidence, spoken to witnesses, and provided records to prove the case. I hear that you are soon to promote him to the role of Traffic Control. If so - then I for one say well done Sir!!!, you have proven beyond reasonable doubt that you are a first class arse. I shall look forward to reading the facts concerning your decisions when I see the story in the Local and National Press…'

DCI Parker had a sudden brainwave… 'Look - I for one never doubted the lad, he's one of my best Officers, and although he doesn't realise it - he has just got himself a promotion – well done Posta...' he said. At the back of the room, Mr Newhouse turned to Hyde-Jones and offered him a crisp from his packet, saying 'Well I still think that it was Mrs Thrasher, in the Library, with the stuffed ferret wot done it…'

Goodwill stiffened, and stood up. He placed his hands in his trouser pockets and calmly stated… 'Well if you are expecting some damn stupid kind of apology from me, then to hell with the lot of you. Yes - I have been taking money out of this crumbling Asylum for years. I have put up with you lot of fools for more years than I can stand. Your abysmal behaviour cheapens both the Academy and Teaching in general. As for money - yes, what they pay me for overseeing this shambles is by any standard piss-poor. I have merely taken the money out of the hands of fools, and put it to better use. You have no proof that I had no intention of paying the money back, and what is more - I have the funds with which to defend myself in Court by means of the best Barrister that money can buy. Let us see what he or she has to say about your so-called "evidence" and your petty suppositions…'

The room fell silent as Goodwill and Posta stared at each other.

'Well…What have you to say now?' declared Goodwill.

'Gerald Allenby Phinges Goodwill: I am arresting you on the charges of theft and embezzlement of funds from St Onans Academy, also for the offences of Tax Evasion, defrauding Her Majesty's Customs and Excise of due revenue, money laundering, being in receipt of stolen goods and the unlawful disposal thereof, unlawfully possessing recovered Archaeological artefacts, planning to open a drinking establishment without due licence or application, obtaining monies by deception, - and being a complete twat…

You have the right to remain silent. You do not have to say anything, but it may harm your defence if you do not mention when questioned, something which you later rely on in court. Anything you do say may be given in evidence.'

Miss Piggott was in tears… 'But Headmaster!!' she wailed: 'What about all of our plans to fly off to our own perfect little desert island? I have sold my cottage and cashed in all of my Life Insurance policies! What about our dreams…together under the stars, hand in hand, strolling across the sand. Long, cool drinks with umbrellas in them, and hammocks slung between the curving trunks of languorous palm trees?'

'Dear Miss Piggott. What I had in mind was a peaceful and hedonistic retirement, somewhere where the climate was beneficial, and the inhabitants companiable. I was seeking peace, tranquillity and luxury in which to gather my thoughts and absorb the beauty of the scenery. What on earth ever possessed you to think that I would involve you in my little dream, I simply cannot begin to imagine…'

'But Gerald…I thought…'

'Madam, you thought wrong…'

Miss Piggott retreated to the end of the room in floods of tears, to be comforted by the Female Police Officer. Hyde-Jones, Darwin, Bannister, Newhouse and the rest of the Male Staff, all shuddered as the vision of Miss P in a sarong danced across their mind.

'You are a Cad and a first-class Bounder…' said Matthews.

'How dare you - I am the Head Master!!' Goodwill answered angrily.

'Which would seem to lead me quite nicely onto another of my main points' said Bessler. 'We of the Board of Trustees feel that we cannot tolerate a person whose conduct has rendered them unfit for office, to be left in charge of the Academy. To this end, Ladies and Gentlemen, I am instructed to announce that with immediate effect – the Post of Headmaster of St Onans is to be revoked in respect of its current incumbent. We have appointed a new Head. The Gentleman in question has paid us a great complement by joining us from his previous school, St Jude's, in the East End of London. His name is Reverend Vernon Farmer, and he will take up the post of Headmaster at the start of the next term. In the interim, Dr Chambers will continue to run the Academy with, I am sure, his usual level of excellence.'

The Staff heard the groan from the boys outside, who had heard the declaration word for word.

'May I ask a question?' said Dr Matthews, 'Why of course…' answered Bessler.

'If Goodwill is out of the equation, then what will happen about all of the cuts that he was planning - I mean, are all of our jobs secure?'

'The Trustees will not honour any suggestions or plans laid by the former Head. Savings must be made of course, but these will be looked at over time, and at the appropriate juncture. I see no reason to reduce Staff numbers'.

'I'll drink to that!!' said Matthews.

As the cheers died down, both inside the room, and from the boys outside, Goodwill was handcuffed by the Police Officers. He allowed himself to be guided to the door by Posta (now promoted to full Detective Sergeant). The Female Officer opened the door, but just before they led the ex-Headmaster out, Miss Piggott called out:

'I do apologise, but I still have a little gift for Gerald before you take him away…would it be alright if I give it to him?' The Policemen shrugged, then nodded agreement.

Miss Piggott approached Goodwill and stood before him. She turned slightly, as if to retrieve something from a pocket. She then spun and brought her knee up into his groin with tremendous force…As the man bent double in agony, the Male members of Staff all winced.

'Thank you, Officers…' she said.

The boys lined up to form a walk of shame for their disgraced former Head. They made not one sound as he was led up the corridor of pupils with a crouching gait. The disgust at their betrayal was evident in their accusing stares. Goodwill paused just before he was put into the back seat of the Chief Inspector's car, and took one last long look around the quad. His eyes opened wide…

Facing the car was a giant hand fully six feet tall, constructed of snow. The index and middle fingers were extended to form an unmistakeably English gesture of contempt. Written in front of the sculpture in the snow were the words 'Up Yours – Merry Christmas from the ODD'. The Police Officer bundled him into the car. The door slammed shut, as did the door on the career of Dr Goodwill.

No-one watched as the car drove away…

Chapter Thirty- Nine:

Now we who are fortunate enough to live in the Northern Hemisphere have a curious but unbreakable habit of looking forward to, if not secretly wishing for snow - especially during the Festive season. There are of course peoples in the farther Northern Regions, who have snow for most of the year, and know just how to carry on their daily lives in spite of a thick blanket of the white stuff. Sven Jorgenstannensson does not have any kind of breakdown if he finds a large snowdrift blocking his door in the morning. He may even have to tunnel out of his driveway in order to get to his car (which he then has to dig out), but it is all taken in his well-insulated stride. In short, Countries like Sweden, Denmark and Iceland just pull on an extra pair of thick woollen socks and get on with it. Their roads are clear, and the transport system still functions. Children may ski to school, but basically, what the heck! - folks just get on with stuff…

Our own attitudes toward snow can be neatly summarised as a matter of quantity. There is a very great difference between helping Daddy to build Frosty the Snowman on the back lawn, and helping to find Daddy after the unexpected avalanche.

Imagine the plight of someone who has never come across the magical substance which we call snow…

As the Parents, visitors and general "well at least it gets us out of the house"-ers had trooped into the Church last night, they had all admired the snow sculpture of a "UFO" in the corner of the quad. They had praised the boys for their creative abilities. The object was still in situ, now covered with a fresh layer of snow which had softened any sharp edges. If a passer-by had scraped off the thick layer of white, and placed their ear against the hull of the ship, they might possibly have caught some of the heated discussion which was taking place within:

'Yes Dear, I know Dear…Yes, I am aware of that Dear, but we always use the Time-Nav setting on "Auto" when we take a trip through the wormhole. No Dear, I'm not a complete Shwattza Dear - there must have been some interference with the travel unit on the way in.'

'All I am saying is that anyone but an utter *KerDic* would have at least got us here on time- now we can't pick Jonef up until all of the "Terras" have gone, or it will be Proxima 7 all over again…We missed Jonef's Concert as it is…'

‘But Dear, I can’t use the scan unit - the ship is covered in a weird white substance…’

‘Look…even I can read the scanner. It clearly shows that the covering is composed of nothing more than frozen Hydrogen Dioxide’.

‘Exactly - what can I do Dear?’

‘You could whack on the external heaters and melt it off, you *P:yellka…*’

‘There’s no need for that language Dear…’

‘I told you - you should have let me drive…’

‘But you know that you have “difficulties” parking’.

‘I parked the ship perfectly when we went to your Parents’ for your Birthing Day…’

‘Yes, you did Dear…right on top of my Mother’.

It was business as usual with the Parents of Jonef Kendy. They had arrived to collect their Son to take him home for the Christmas break. What they could not have planned for was the way in which the Vortex field had interfered with their ship’s navigation, landing them automatically in the correct location, but then locking the doors on them. There was nothing to do but sit it out and eat their P’chargurra sandwiches, and of course, argue.

Mrs Betty Bradley, her Staff, and the Groundlings had laid on a celebration buffet in the Assembly Hall. Mr Thwaite had insisted that he be allowed to create, cook, and bring in some buffet delights of his own. The Staff and boys were mingling, and chatting in groups in a very relaxed manner- now that all of the excitement was over. Even the hyper-rigid Dr Chambers had relaxed, to the extent that he had come today in brown suede shoes. Mr Newhouse had made a point of stepping on them, just to keep the musical tradition alive.

Darwin was drinking coffee and talking to his colleague Dr Strangler…

‘So then: who would have thought it! a brand new Head!!’

‘Well technically, that might not be possible quite yet, I mean even with the major advances in transplant technology, we are still some way- ‘

‘A new Head*master*, I meant…’

‘Yes, and I must say that I was more than a little worried when I heard who it was that was taking up the position…’

‘How so?’

'Well now, I have come across this Vernon Farmer a few years ago. I took an Assistant post at his school, well I say school, it was more like a prison unit with books. The man is a hard-line disciplinarian. He makes the boys and Staff iron their shoe laces to get them flat. He once had a boy handcuffed to a radiator for not writing on both sides of the paper'.

'Doesn't sound too bad…?'

'Ah, but the radiator was on a scrap metal dump at the time'.

'I hear that he once expelled someone for attending school with dyed hair?'

'Yes - it was his Wife…'

'News is starting to get around. The Staff are worried. I have already heard rumours that he will bring in Corporal punishment in the form of floggings!'

'Well I tell you, if he tries that sort of thing here - there will be a backlash…'

One of the more inspiring and amazing sights to be witnessed at the gathering was that of Albert Brooks, who had worn a suit for the occasion. He and Mrs Finucane were laughing and chatting over a nibble or two, with no sign of planned menace…just yet.

Dr Matthews had viewed with disdain the lack of liquid refreshment on offer. He grabbed a boy who happened to be passing, who just happened to be the new boy Jez Christo.

'Do me a favour lad' he said, 'just nip along to the tables down at the end and see if you can grab me something to drink will you?'

'I'm sorry Sir…' said Christo, 'Dr Chambers has banned alcohol from the event. The best that I can do is fetch you some mineral water from the top table'.

'Is it that French stuff "Eau Dear" or whatever?' enquired the Master

'No Sir - Captain Brayfield tipped all of that down the lavatory, and replaced it with English spring water…'

'I see…very well, that will have to suffice then - be so good as to bring me a couple of bottles over please Dear Boy'.

Jez Christo edged past Dr Chambers and selected two bottles of water. 'For Dr Matthews Sir...' he said, as the Deputy Head gave him a quizzical look. 'My word!!!' said Chambers, 'Well tell him to keep it up - and well done from me'.

Christo smiled as he carried the bottles back to Dr Matthews, who was doing his best to explain to Madame Dreadfell that "Sutton Hoo" was not in fact a question. He took the dark green bottles from the smiling boy, and poured them both a large measure into a paper cup. His eyes, and those of Madame, widened as they found that they were drinking a very passable Chardonnay…

Christo had moved off, possibly in a mysterious way.

There was more than a little uproar at the middle table. Mr Thwaite was thoroughly enjoying himself acting as Waitress, as he sashayed between the assembled Staff with trays of his canapes. His gliding progress had been halted by Captain Brayfield, who had called him over and made a loud complaint about the quality of his vol-au-vent:

'Thwaite…what the damnation is the filling in these pastries?' he demanded.

Thwaite looked at the small pastry delight and answered 'Captain, those are the ones that I made specially - they are Crab Paste…'

'It tastes bloody awful Man…is it fresh?' asked the Captain.

'I got it fresh yesterday, Captain' answered Thwaite, now rather hurt.

'Well the taste is disgusting - where did you get the Crab Paste from?'

'From the local Pharmacy…'

The gathering continued to be friendly and jolly. Betty Bradley had even gone to the trouble of hanging a large sprig of mistletoe above the top table. Reverend Felchingham had not noticed it as he stood beneath it munching his "devils on horseback". The Matron had. She made a bee-line for the unsuspecting man (she always liked a man who could wear black with style) and dived on him. He unexpectedly found himself to be overcome with the Christmas Spirit, and completely overcome by the amount of fresh Matron that was thrust upon him. There was barely a second's delay, as Mr Newhouse elbowed the Rev out of the way, and substituted the attentions of the Clergyman for his own.

Hyde-Jones was making idle chat with Miles Bannister. 'Shame about the small "surprise" that I organised for the Concert' he said.

'How do you mean Roy? I thought that it all went rather well'.

'Yeah, but I had a word with my mate Phil, who was supposed to make a special appearance dressed as Santa - but the silly bugger didn't show up!!'

This was indeed completely factually inaccurate in every respect: Phil Partridge was a good friend of the English Tutor, and a regular and highly-trained skydiver. Hyde-Jones had asked Phil to provide a great surprise and spectacle for the kids at the Carol Concert by parachuting into the quad as Santa before the service started. Phil had indeed leapt from a light aircraft, despite the snowy conditions, with a large sack of gifts for the children. We can only assume that he did not pay enough attention to the low-level winds around the Academy. He had overshot the quad by a distance of several yards, enough to drop him into the trees of the Head Master's gardens. His landing had not yet been noticed, and he swung in the branches of the tree in his red outfit, having spent a freezing night out in the cold. It would be a very long time before Phil Partridge would do another favour for Roy Hyde-Jones...

(Oh yes...it should be noted that against all odds, he had landed in a Pear Tree...)

Nicky and his friends were excitedly discussing what they were planning to get up to during the Christmas break, and how come Davis seemed to have been able to clear six plates of sausage rolls on his own. They were now all getting into the Festive mood - and there was much talk of what presents they were going to buy for their respective Parents. Merry had been very quiet at this point, but cheered up when promised a trip to the town via Nicky's Uncle Joe's vintage car (the word "sedative" was not mentioned at this point, Nicky would have a discreet word with his friend later).

Calderman had them all in fits of laughter as he described how his house would become a kind of "ground zero" for mad Uncles and Dotty Aunts of all descriptions. His description of playing *Trivial Pursuit* with them all last Boxing Day - where the prize was a chance to win their own dentures, went down particularly well. All of the lads agreed that whoever could just turn up at their respective houses whenever and however they wished. The only member of the gang who received strict dress instructions was R Weatherill esquire. It would have been nice to have invited their friend DeVere over for Christmas, but again, he had vanished. It would not be until the BBC vans returned to the Shepherds Bush Centre, that they would discover that they had picked up a small and rather unkempt extra piece of equipment.

There had been the great celebratory Christmas lunch served in the dining hall. The boys were served by the Staff, and there were crackers, even for those who were deemed to be already deserving of that label. Matron had worn her tiny Santa outfit again, and it was uncanny how so many of the boys seemed to be so clumsy as to drop their cutlery onto the floor, requiring her to bend over and pick the items up. The Groundling choir had given an impromptu performance of Carols in the hall, and tables had been soundly pounded in recognition of their superb efforts. Jedekiah was even persuaded to don a paper hat.

Kendy had been wished well by the Staff and boys, and released early from the Academy, due to the great distance which he had to travel to get home (he hadn't given precise details of course, just a hint that it was "abroad" and far away). He had approached the saucer sitting in the quad, pressed a hand-held device, and when no-one was looking, slipped inside to join his waiting (and still arguing) Parents. In his pocket, the mysterious crystal was pulsing steadily with a gentle light from within its heart.

'Hello Son!!' his Father said, hugging the boy.

'Hello Dear!!' said his Mother, still attempting to strangle his Father.

When he managed to wrestle himself free of her grip, Father rubbed his hands together and said, 'Right then Son…will you do the honours on the Transfer Scanning for us?'

Kendy smiled, and spoke aloud for the computer to record who was on board, and what transfer adjustments would need to be made for their journey through the Wormhole and back to their home world.

'Three Status One Occupants…Two Adult and One Juvenile to transit - plus one Subject to transit in Energy Stasis Capture…' he declared.

The Computer began to make the necessary preparations, and lights began to flash on the numerous panels around the cockpit, accompanied by a comforting humming. The computer was either running pre-flight checks, or perhaps it had forgotten the words again…

Nicky was doing his best to reassure Merry that he would be fine up at his house for the holidays. 'Look- I know that you'll be missing your Mum, but don't worry Mate - I will lend you mine for a bit. She's the proper "Mum Shape", and I'll throw in a free helping of Auntie too. You will like my Mum, she's just the same as your Mum, I assure you'.

'No, she's not...' said Merry 'Your Mum doesn't dress as a Giraffe and tell everyone that her name is "Rodney" does she?'

Nicky had to admit that well no, it hadn't actually happened yet.

Duggan the ex-Crime Syndicate Boss, now full-time benefactor and Metalwork Tutor could not have been happier. They had just paid for a brand new 10-seater van which they had donated to a local group of Deaf Pensioners. The van could now be seen driving around the town full of happy, warm and dry Senior Citizens. On the side of the van was stencilled the legend "The Eh? Team" ...

They had also been happy to help Darwin with the small matter of what to get for Bernie as a Christmas gift. It had been decided that the ideal present would be a return flight ticket to North West America, where our Bigfooted friend could spend some quality time back in his native forest - and visit the resting place of his dear late Wife Saskalia. Bernie was overcome with emotion when presented with the gift, and hugged them all. Fletcher in particular, would be nursing those bruises for quite a few weeks to come...

Matthews was quite beside himself. As recognition for his assistance in bringing to book the evil Dr Goodwill, and for securing him a swift promotion, Posta had presented him with a magnum of champagne. The History Tutor was gushing in his thanks- and immediately insisted that Posta join him and his Wife for Christmas dinner. The plan was to cook the turkey in juices augmented by whisky, brandy, gin and best Navy rum. The meat would be basted in the sauce until moist and tender. The bird would then be put aside until later - and they would all drink the gravy.

Mr Newhouse had accepted the offer of coming to stay with Roy Hyde-Jones. The conditions were, that he was on no account to trick HJ into going on an unscheduled "Festive Bender", and that he was (if at all possible) to ensure that he remained fully-dressed. Newhouse stated that he was under prior Contractual Obligations, and thus could give no concrete assurances ...

The Sports Masters Burke and Hair (Carter) had already exchanged gifts. Carter had given Burke a brand new track suit, and had sent his old one to a Charity Shop. They in turn passed it straight on to a firm of Solicitors. Burke had presented Carter with a small but beautifully-wrapped box. Carter shook the box in anticipation, but the sound it made gave no clue. 'I warn you…' said Carter, 'If what's in this box turns out to be more glue for my toupee - I know where you live…' His hairpiece sniggered.

Chapter Forty:

Above the rusty gutters of the Old Library, but just under the old weathered slates which shifted around like a bored audience at a bad amateur dramatic play, the Ravens nudged each other. 'No, go on- you give it to him…' said a raven called Gary. Another bird known as "Wallace" passed over a rather badly-wrapped parcel to the "head" Raven Keith. 'Open it now!! Open it now!!' insisted the rest of the birds. Keith tore off the paper, and revealed a small pair of red overalls, with the name *Keith's Bike Repairs* written on the back. Keith wiped a tear from his eye with his wing and said 'Aaaw…Lads- you really shouldn't have...' 'Well it's just a little token gift' said Wallace, 'we didn't know what to get you, and we gave you roadkill last year, so we thought that we'd do something a bit special this time…' Keith admired his new working uniform. 'I'm touched Lads - very touched…' he said.

There was a large natural Christmas tree in the corner of the Old Library. A spectral figure in Elizabethan dress was hiding a wrapped present underneath the green boughs. Even through the elegant wrapping paper, it was possible to make out that the gift inside was Horse's head shaped…

Stig of the Damp and his Iron-Age companion had exchanged Seasons Greetings - and then hit each other over the head with rocks. But in a Festive and rather Jolly way…

The Reverend Felchingham himself was unable to resist the inexorable influence of the Christmas Spirit. His recent "revelation" seemed to have mellowed him a little. He had suddenly felt the urge to run up to his classroom, and scrub the chalk pentagram from the floor. He had got about half way round, when there was a sudden smell of sulphur, and a charred envelope appeared in the centre of the circle. The Rev looked around the room in terror, but the letter did not seem to be posing a threat, so he cautiously reached out and picked it up. It was still warm…He opened the letter, half expecting some awful explosion, but none was forthcoming. To his utter amazement, the envelope contained an invitation to a Festive party. It read "The Dark Lord Satan invites you to his annual Winter barbecue and party…Dress optional…please bring a bottle and a Bird – RSVP"

'What on earth is this?' thought the Rev

'IT'S FROM DER BOSS…' thundered the voice of Abolochyn the Demon, who had appeared in the centre circle without warning. The Rev fell backwards in shock…

'Ho Yurs…Ee wants to know if Yer fancies comin' to 'is annual Bash down there at his gaff…Ee said it woz the least he could do…Ee says "Der Bloke is a little Tit - but he does try hard, I'll give 'im that…" and Ee sent me 'ere to RSVP' said the Demon.

'What is the RSVP bit?' asked Felchingham.

'I fink dat it's "Rip Souls from Varius Peoples" said the huge being.

'Gosh, I'm sorry - would you mind telling him thanks from me, but I already have plans…' said the Rev in a shaky voice.

'Don't suppose The Boss will mind, it ain't a formal 'do'- it's only a barbecue' said the Demon. Felchingham's curiosity had got the better of him at this point…

'Excuse me asking, but what does He normally cook at these barbecues?'

'It's Atheists mostly, if Ee can get 'old of 'em…' he answered.

The Rev quickly changed the subject - 'What is that smell?' he asked.

'Dat's me!! It's called "Whiff of Hades - for Men". Der Boss gave it to me'.

'Look, now this is just a pure shot in the dark you understand, and please do feel free to say no if you wish - I really won't be offended…but how do you fancy joining me for Christmas dinner? it would be nice to have a guest, and you have made the effort and put on your dinner suit, so what do you say?'

'You want me to come to your place for dinner?'

'Certainly, I do…'

'Will we be able to watch "The Sound of Music" on telly?'

'I'm afraid not…'

'Thank F*** for that!!- Count me in Mate!!!'

High above the snow clouds and approaching the Arctic Circle, Biddie Duggan was sitting in the front seat of her private jet with a cheeky little girl on her knee. She was now happily 'retired' from her dubious hobby of crime, and had decided to take parties of 'Puir Wee Kiddies' to see Santa in Lapland. The pure joy and excitement on the faces of each of the little mites was worth every penny. Whilst she bounced the child on her knees, she unwrapped the Christmas present that her Son had given her before she had set off. Inside the box was a single Christmas cracker. She pulled the cracker with the help of the little girl, and out of it came a plastic ring with a glass diamond set in it. There was a note too...It read 'You told me that money talks- so I am making it say Hello to a lot of people. Merry Christmas Ma - from your loving Son, Gregor'.

Biddie put on the ring -

It was the most precious piece of jewellery that she had ever owned...

The weather was beginning to close in. Actually, when you think about it; that is rather a ridiculous phrase to use. The Weather is doing exactly the same thing over a very wide area, apart from one or two places where they can't afford weather. At the moment, the wind and snow had decided to form a blizzard tribute act: hence, it was snowing sideways across the Academy. Dr Chambers had looked out of the window, and decided that it might just be a wise idea to call a quick assembly, and then let the boys go home. It could only be a matter of hours before some of the roads out of the town became impassable. He broadcast the call to muster via the Academy public address system, interrupting *White Christmas* by Bing Crosby - which Mr Newhouse had insisted be played throughout the school.

The boys trudged into the hall, brushing the worst of the snow from their shoulders. The Staff filed in somewhat raggedly, and sat in their chairs on the stage. Some thoughtful wag had already nailed a Christmas stocking onto the front of the lectern. Chambers had noticed it, but did not feel inclined to investigate whatever it had been filled with - just in case...

He called the room to attention, and did his best to ignore a certain young man who stood in the middle of the boys wearing a bobble hat and ski goggles.

'Thank you, Boys and Staff,...' he began, 'I shall not keep you too long, as I am eager to release you early due to the bad weather. I simply wish to thank you for all of your hard work this term, and say a special thanks to everyone who has helped out at our various events. I would also like to thank the Staff for lending me their support ('ta - now let me 'ave it back...!!called a voice at the rear). I can also tell you that as from the start of the next term, we will have a new Headmaster in place. I am sure that you have all heard rumours about the person who is coming to take up the post, so I can confirm that his name - '

'Is Reverend Vernon Farmer…' said the man as he strode in through the rear doors…

A gap swiftly opened up in the crowd of boys, and Farmer swept down the middle like a Roman Emperor. He looked left and right at the students of the Academy as he passed, giving them a look similar to that which one might give something which one had passed earlier, so to speak. Striding onto the stage, he marched directly up to Dr Chambers, waiting for him to vacate the centre-stage position. He gripped the lectern, and went to move it to a central position. It had been glued again…The titters of the boys enraged the man -

'ENOUGH!!!' he bellowed…and the hall fell silent.

'In my time as a Headmaster, I have seen that a little Education can cover a multitude of Sins…And as I look around myself at the pupils and Staff of this Academy - all I can see at first glance is nothing more than a Sinful Multitude…' he stated.

'If he's the Comedian, I can't wait for the Main Act…' whispered Hyde-Jones.

The new Head subjected the English Master to a death-ray stare. Newhouse gave him a little wave, and he turned away.

'I have heard of the reputation of this Academy. Trust me Gentlemen - that reputation will be built upon and enhanced on a daily basis. You seem to me to have become complacent. I have already witnessed disrespect and indolence. This will not do. I intend to reinforce discipline and standards within St Onans, and I can tell you all that here, as in my last school, my word will be Absolute Law…'

'That's two words…' called a voice. The lighthouse glare swept the hall…

'There will be changes - very big changes for some of you. I shall inspect every aspect of Academy life on a daily basis. I shall not tolerate slackers. I shall return to the time when we could all live our lives as the Academy Motto tells us: "Membris Nostris Stare Superbum" – Our Members Stand Proudly!!'.

The boys stood silently in their rows. Rundell actually saluted the man in Gladiatorial style. Dr Matthews unscrewed the cap of his silver hip flask and took a large gulp of whisky - 'Right then Boyo…' he mused, 'let's see just how long you last then…'.

Reverend Vernon Farmer gave a final glance of distaste to the assembled boys as he swept down from the stage, and out of the hall. As the doors banged shut behind him, no-one in the hall dared to move for a minute or so. It was Mr Newhouse who broke the silence…

'So, hey Kids!!! You have yourselves a Very Merry Christmas - do you hear?!!!'

Even Dr Chambers allowed himself to laugh this time.

The Staff lined up at the exit, and shook the hand of every boy on their way out (all except Davis, who seemed to be coated in sugar and jam...). They had all seen the future, and boy oh boy…it didn't look pretty. Outside, the boys said their "Cheerio's" to their friends. Perhaps as a reaction to their recent "baptism of fire" with the new Head, none of them seemed to want to be the first to leave, as if they felt that they needed the safety of the herd for protection. It was Calderman that eventually said 'Okay Fellow Inmates - let's escape for the Holidays before we get frostbite...Everyone remember to keep in touch'. It would have been a nice touch if the Academy bell had rung at this point: instead, it only managed a "clunk"- due to the fact that some scamp had put a large Santa hat over it, and hung a white beard underneath…

As the boys fought their individual ways home through the blizzard, Dr Darwin was in the Physics lab with his friend Professor Strangler. Since he was the unofficial "keeper and curator" for the Vortex in the ante-room, Strangler had the responsibility of shutting the experiment down for the holidays. He dared not leave it running - because he was not at all certain what might emerge through the Portal in his absence. Darwin had joined his friend in the lab and found him pondering over some sheets of paper and a table cloth - all of which had various complex notes and equations scribbled on them.

'Surely you're not still working Dick?' asked Darwin.

'Oh no…just putting an idea to bed' said Strangler.

Darwin looked over his colleague's shoulder at the complicated mathematical scribblings…'Care to let me in on the secret?' he asked.

'Well…if you insist' said Strangler. Darwin made himself comfortable, with the Physics Master at the wheel, it often proved to be a longer journey than you had expected…

'I had been working on the electronic stimulation of Quartz crystals and conglomerates with a view to recording their precise pulsation timings. I set up the TRU unit to act as a sort of "mini" hand-held version of the Vortex for the purpose of scanning the rocks. I can only assume that I must have somehow managed to connect the link in reverse, because I seem to have sent out amplified pulses from the TRU unit through the main Vortex loop. Assuming that I sent a pulse out at one hell of a ratio, then the Vortex has sent the stimulus out across the nearest thing to it…'

'Which was?'

'Well, the wall actually'.

'So why do you look so worried, so an amplified signal hit a wall - so what?'

'You don't understand - neither did I until I worked it out…These walls are the same composition as all of the walls of the Old School. They are mainly quartzite rock, with a smattering of Mica, Feldspar and trace mineral - plus a lot of what we Physicists technically refer to as "crap". The TRU unit is basically a loop. The Vortex Portal Transmission Field is another loop. If you look here at these plans of the Academy (he unrolled an old architectural drawing which was very faded) you will clearly see that the shape of the Old Block is, well, another loop. Now as you will know, if we stimulate a Quartz crystal with electricity, it produces a very regular pulse. The walls of the Old Block are crammed with Quartz! So for a bit of a joke, I hooked up the ole' computer. I typed in a simple message, wound up the current, and pressed "send" to see what would happen'.

'What was the message, just out of curiosity?'

'The message I sent was "Hello"..'

'Okay, fine. So, what was the result of this little prank?'

'Something odd…'

'Such as?'...

'Erm…I got a reply…!!'

Darwin stared at his friend. He definitely had "that look" in his eye again. (You know the one: the look that Orville and Wilbur Wright would have had if someone had just walked up to them and handed them the keys to a Typhoon Eurofighter. Yep - that's it).

'So if, and I'm only speculating here…if I am hearing you correctly, then I am at this moment having a pre-Christmas drink with a man who talks to walls?' said Darwin.

'Exciting...isn't it!!' said Strangler. 'I've only just begun to figure out how I'm going to carry out more experiments with "communication", but preliminary results would clearly seem to indicate that the outer walls - if not the entire Old Block of the Academy may well be able to behave as a thinking entity. This demands further study!! I need to put a team on this - this could be the big one!!'

'As in "cock-ups that I have ever made" do you mean?' asked Darwin.

Strangler gave his friend a mildly disapproving look. 'Right…' he said, 'Let me show you something…'

He crossed the room and typed like a man possessed on the keyboard of the computer. He then looked back at Darwin, grinned, and plugged in a strange looking cable. At the end of the lead was a very old and clumsy-looking switch, with "ON" and "OF" written on it in thick marker pen. Strangler motioned to his friend to look out of the window. There was nothing to be seen - the blizzard had created a complete "white-out" beyond the glass. Strangler said 'Just watch…' and pressed the switch to the "ON" position.

Darwin blinked as there was a sudden flash and a change in the light entering the room via the long windows. The blizzard had stopped. It was no longer snowing. It was no longer snowing, because what Darwin was now looking at was dry, sandy desert, with rolling dunes that faded into the far horizon….

'I think perhaps that the Old Block walls are acting like another Vortex - and shifting the Academy in time, or at least within some compatible lateral dimension. It's quite interesting though, what do you think Johnathan?'

'I think I've shit myself….' Murmured Darwin.

Strangler turned back the switch, and back came the snow as if a page had been turned. He shut down the system, taking care to avoid getting too close to the Vortex before it "powered down". Darwin had left in rather a hurry - he would catch up with him later. He couldn't wait to get back next term and have a good old play with his new toy. Turning off the light in the ante-room and drawing the blinds, he simply could not resist running back over to the computer and sending one last message to the Old Block before the power shut down. He typed "Merry Christmas" and pressed the "send" key. He closed down and locked the lab doors.

A while after he had gone, a pair of small red and green lights flashed on and off briefly.

The computer clicked.

A message appeared on the screen.

It read... '**And the same to you**…'

Chapter Forty- One:

See amid the Winter snow…Nicky had decided to give up on trying to walk in anything approaching a normal manner - and fell over. Merry laughed, and recued his friend from the drift into which he had plunged, keeping a watchful eye out for tell-tale signs of yellow snow, because this was after all, a rural community.

Once inside the house, coats were abandoned to drip in the hall, and shoes left to form tiny lakes around themselves. Mum had hot drinks ready for the boys, and Auntie was busy wrapping some weirdly-shaped gift at the kitchen table. 'Hello Lads!!' she said in greeting 'I bet you're glad to see the back of School for a few days eh?' 'Like you wouldn't believe!!' answered Nicky. 'Have you got anything planned this evening?' Mum asked, 'No Mum - we're going to eat too much, then sit in front of the telly and watch *Raiders of the Lost Ark* or whatever's on' said Nicky. Merry was curious as to what Auntie was wrapping. 'That looks a funny shape!' he declared. 'Yes, it's a bugger to wrap Gerry - and it's all the fault of Joe's Wife'. Nicky enquired what the problem was, and why Uncle's Wife Marjory was in any way implicated.

Mum drew in a breath, and began: 'Well we had ploughed our way through all of the snow in town to buy Joe's Wife a really nice item of knitwear for a Christmas present. You know how hard she is to buy gifts for - with her shape and everything, so we thought that the jumper was a great idea. Joe then comes in and announces that the present is no good at all - due to the medical problem which she has'.

'What's the matter with her?' asked Merry.

'Joe says that she has been diagnosed with "Angoratriskaidekaphobia", and it's a chronic condition apparently' said Mum.

'What on earth is that? It sounds serious' said Nicky.

'Joe says that she has an acute fear of owning more than Thirteen sweaters…' said Mum.

Merry looked shocked, but Nicky just shrugged. Once you got to know Uncle Joe in any regular capacity, this was just another day…

When the adults were safely ensconced in the kitchen enjoying a sneaky sherry or five, Nicky introduced Merry to the cornucopia of confusion that was "The Desk". 'It will answer questions if you put a note in the small drawer' Nicky told his friend. This seemed to trouble

Merry, so Nicky thought that the best thing to do was to get him to try it.

The boy wrote on a scrap of paper 'What will make my Mum better?'. He put the note into the drawer, and closed it. They waited a while before looking inside. The reply was written on blue paper, it read 'Time…'. Merry didn't seem to really understand this, and scribbled another hasty message- 'what do I do, if I visit Mum, and she doesn't remember me?'.

The reply came back swiftly. This time, the small square of writing paper smelled faintly of roses…'Then you must remember Her…' it simply stated.

So, there was snow, there was Family, there was Dave the Chicken. They had a tree, lights and decorations. The boys, Mum and Auntie all sat in front of the fire in the living room and enjoyed each other's company. Soon, the long-awaited fat person with the beard would be arriving - luckily, not Cousin Sheila this time.

Without saying any words, both Merry and Nicky instinctively knew what the other one was thinking. They had survived some bizarre incidents this term, and had some serious fun. What worried them most of all was the coming of the new Headmaster. They both knew that things were going to be frighteningly different next term.

The atmosphere of the Academy had suddenly frozen along with the weather, in one single afternoon. Would the "nicer" Masters stay at St Onans - or would the new Dictator drive them out? They both worried as to exactly what sort of place it would be, that they would be coming back to next term. Nicky felt a panic begin to rise...and he hoped that it wouldn't be a return to his first days at the Academy, which had been full of fear and anxiety. He had the horrible feeling that the comfy suede loafer of his school had just had its toe heavily stamped on by the jackboot of Change. Was his Christmas goose about to be well and truly cooked?

Only time would tell….

As Master William Trevill had observed - 'Gawd 'elp us Ev'ry One!!...'

****

Nicky is now Fifteen...

His Academy friends and his Village Mates are fifteen too. Apart from the ones who aren't…

There have been Cataclysmic changes at St Onans.

The Academy is trembling at the hands of a supremely strict disciplinarian (no- not Matron for once).

It is the strange and terrifying point in a boy's life when he is too young to be taken altogether seriously as almost Adult, and too old to get away with the stuff that he did as a Child. Nicky is trapped in a dreadful 'Limbo', which he will have to bend over backwards to escape…

Throw in a few raging Hormones, some Rock and Roll, light the touch paper - and stand well back…

Coming Soon!...

Spring Term: (or- The Sap Rises!)

The latest chapter in the Saga of St Onans Academy… (oh, and Dave the Chicken too)

34360735R00186

Printed in Great Britain
by Amazon